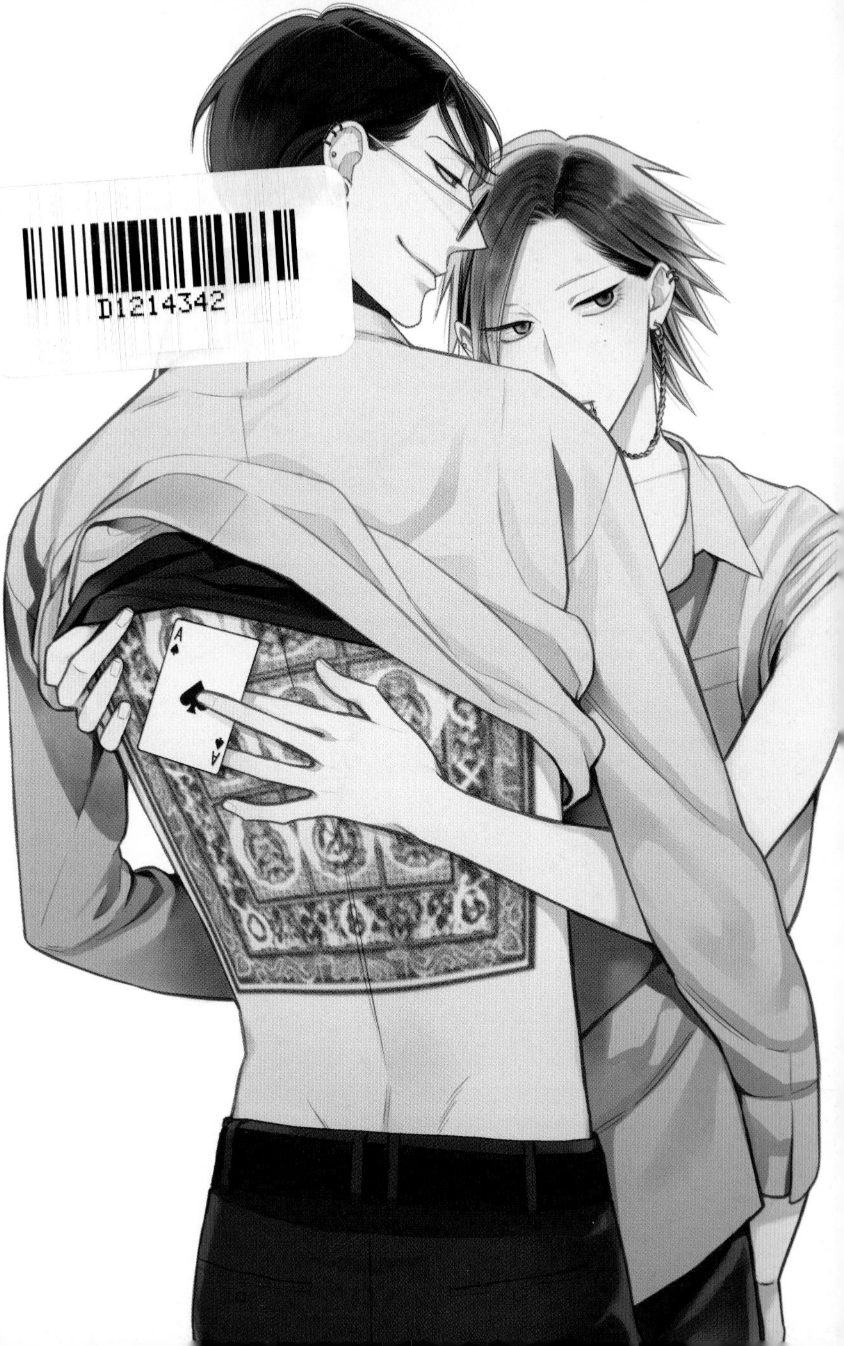

CONTENTS

Caste Heaven

3

CHISE
OGAWA

CASTE GAME

RULES

◆ CASTES ARE DETERMINED BY PLAYING CARDS.

THE GAME BEGINS WHEN AN EMPTY BOX OF CARDS IS PLACED ON THE TEACHER'S PODIUM. THAT'S THE SIGNAL TO THAT PARTICULAR CLASS THAT THE CASTE GAME WILL BE PLAYED THAT AFTERNOON AFTER CLASS. STUDENTS MUST FIND ONE OF THE PLAYING CARDS HIDDEN THROUGHOUT THE SCHOOL AND BRING IT BACK. THAT CARD DETERMINES THEIR CASTE.

◆ THOSE IN A LOWER CASTE MUST OBEY THOSE IN A HIGHER ONE.

CASTES ARE ABSOLUTE. ALL STUDENTS ARE REQUIRED TO SUBMIT TO THE RULES OF THEIR CASTE UNTIL THE NEXT TIME THE GAME IS PLAYED.

◆ THOSE WHO CHOOSE NOT TO PARTICIPATE IN THE GAME OR SEEK TO DISRUPT IT WILL BE ASSIGNED THE CASTE OF TARGET BY DEFAULT.

HIERARCHY

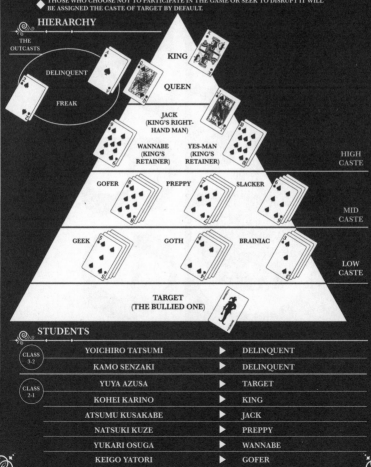

THE OUTCASTS

DELINQUENT

FREAK

KING

QUEEN

JACK (KING'S RIGHT-HAND MAN)

WANNABE (KING'S RETAINER)   YES-MAN (KING'S RETAINER)

HIGH CASTE

GOFER   PREPPY   SLACKER

MID CASTE

GEEK   GOTH   BRAINIAC

LOW CASTE

TARGET (THE BULLIED ONE)

STUDENTS

CLASS 3-2	YOICHIRO TATSUMI	▶	DELINQUENT
	KAMO SENZAKI	▶	DELINQUENT
CLASS 2-1	YUYA AZUSA	▶	TARGET
	KOHEI KARINO	▶	KING
	ATSUMU KUSAKABE	▶	JACK
	NATSUKI KUZE	▶	PREPPY
	YUKARI OSUGA	▶	WANNABE
	KEIGO YATORI	▶	GOFER

CASTE HEAVEN
EPISODE 12

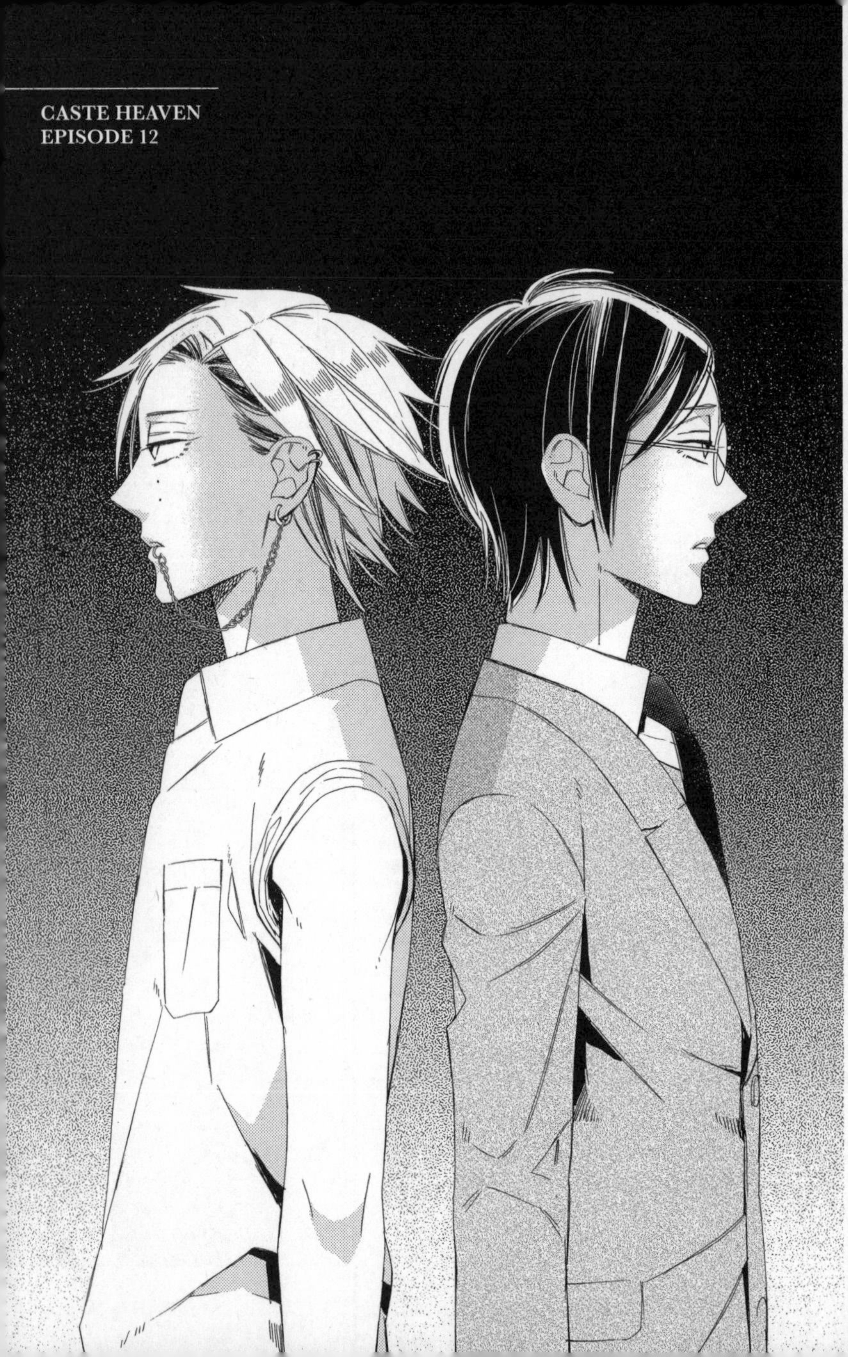

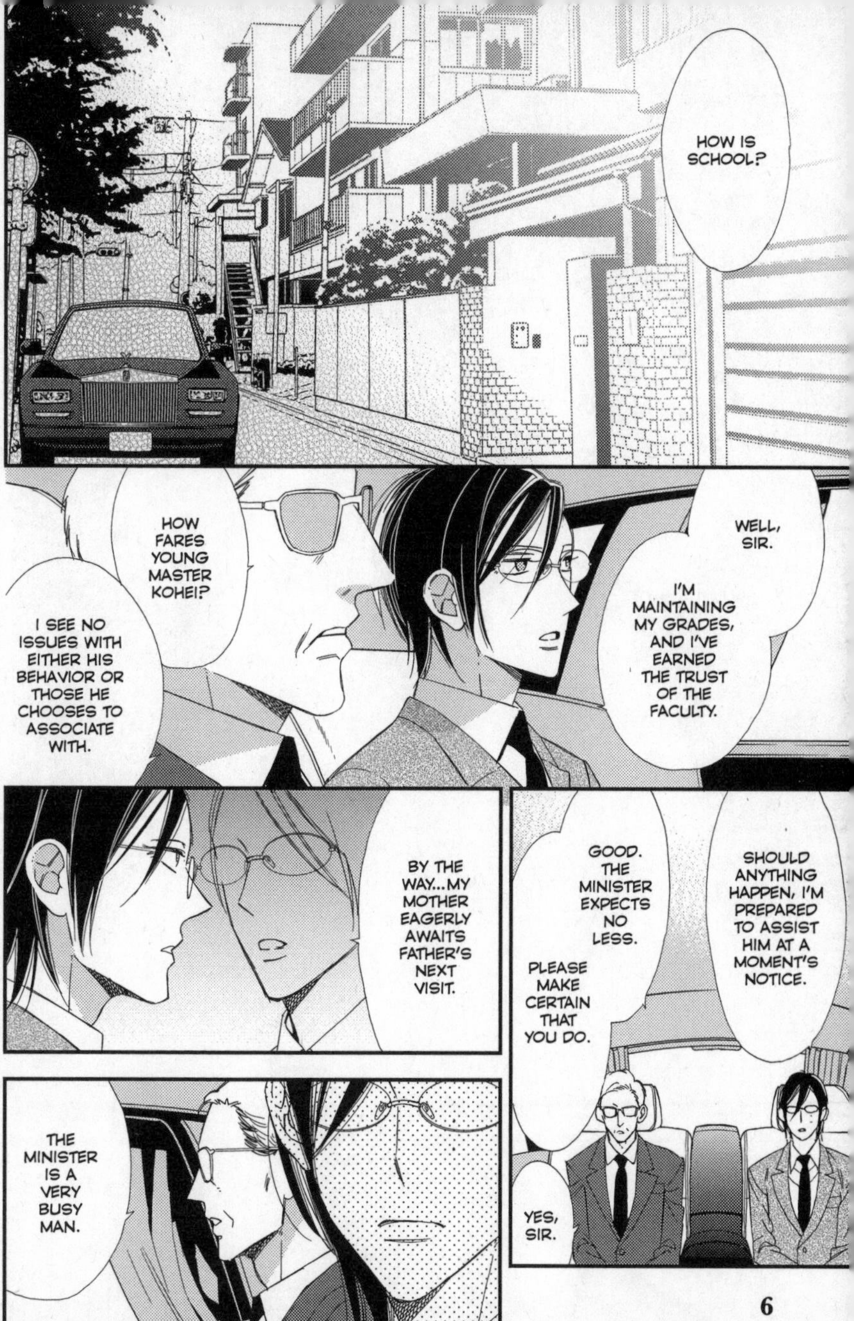
HOW IS SCHOOL?
WELL, SIR.
I'M MAINTAINING MY GRADES, AND I'VE EARNED THE TRUST OF THE FACULTY.
HOW FARES YOUNG MASTER KOHEI?
I SEE NO ISSUES WITH EITHER HIS BEHAVIOR OR THOSE HE CHOOSES TO ASSOCIATE WITH.
SHOULD ANYTHING HAPPEN, I'M PREPARED TO ASSIST HIM AT A MOMENT'S NOTICE.
GOOD. THE MINISTER EXPECTS NO LESS.
PLEASE MAKE CERTAIN THAT YOU DO.
YES, SIR.
BY THE WAY...MY MOTHER EAGERLY AWAITS FATHER'S NEXT VISIT.
THE MINISTER IS A VERY BUSY MAN.

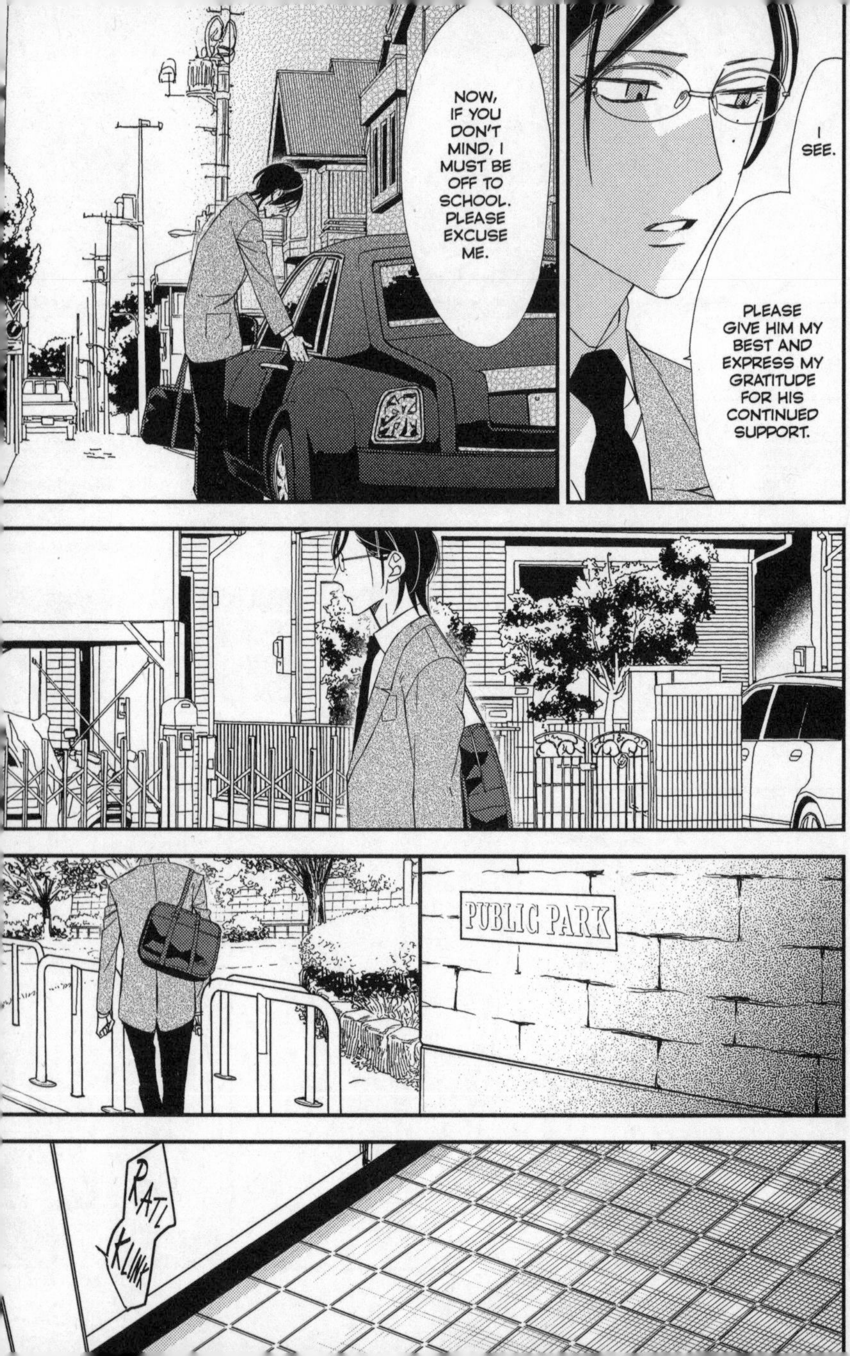
I SEE.
PLEASE GIVE HIM MY BEST AND EXPRESS MY GRATITUDE FOR HIS CONTINUED SUPPORT.
NOW, IF YOU DON'T MIND, I MUST BE OFF TO SCHOOL. PLEASE EXCUSE ME.
PUBLIC PARK
RATL
KLINK

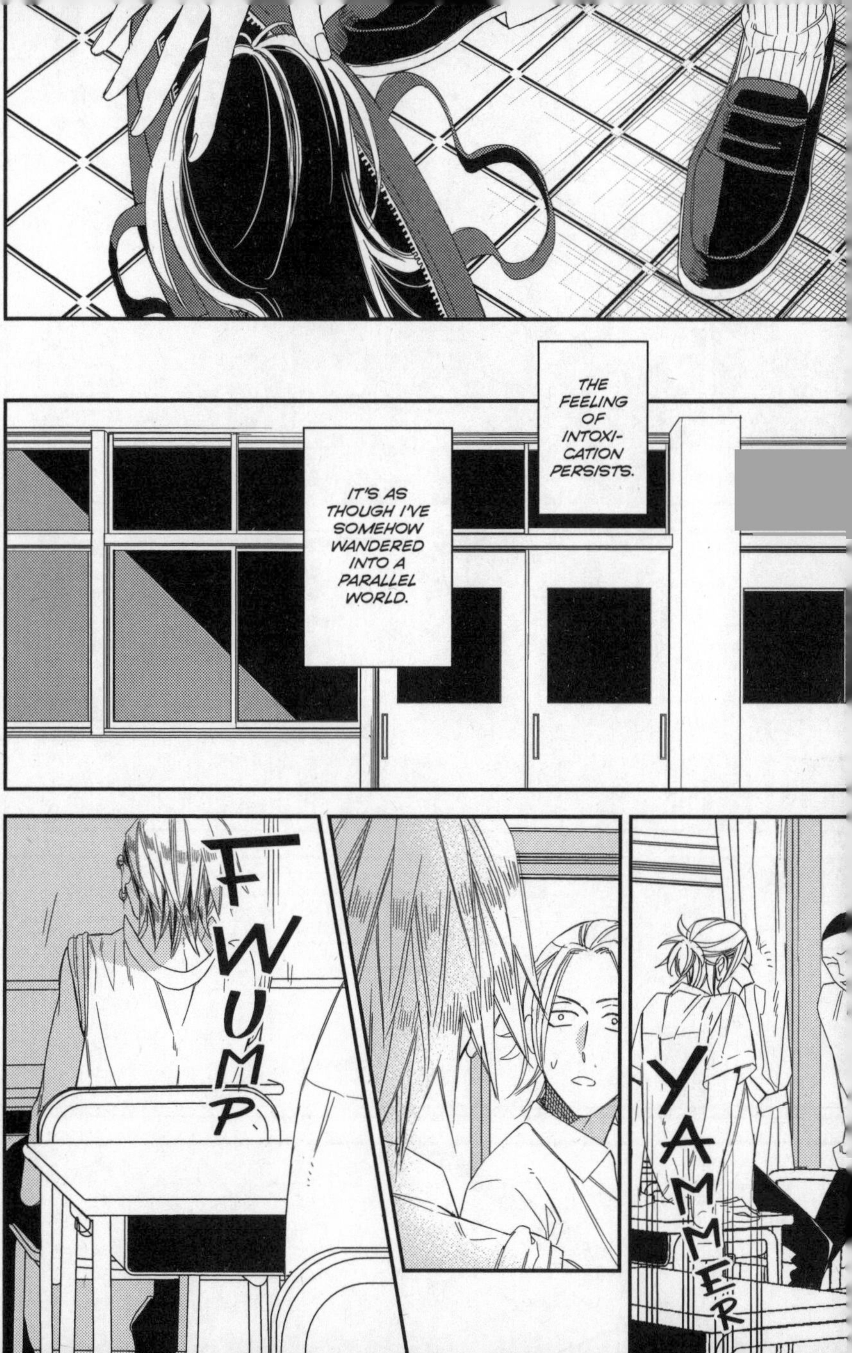
THE FEELING OF INTOXICATION PERSISTS.
IT'S AS THOUGH I'VE SOMEHOW WANDERED INTO A PARALLEL WORLD.
YAMMER
FWUMP

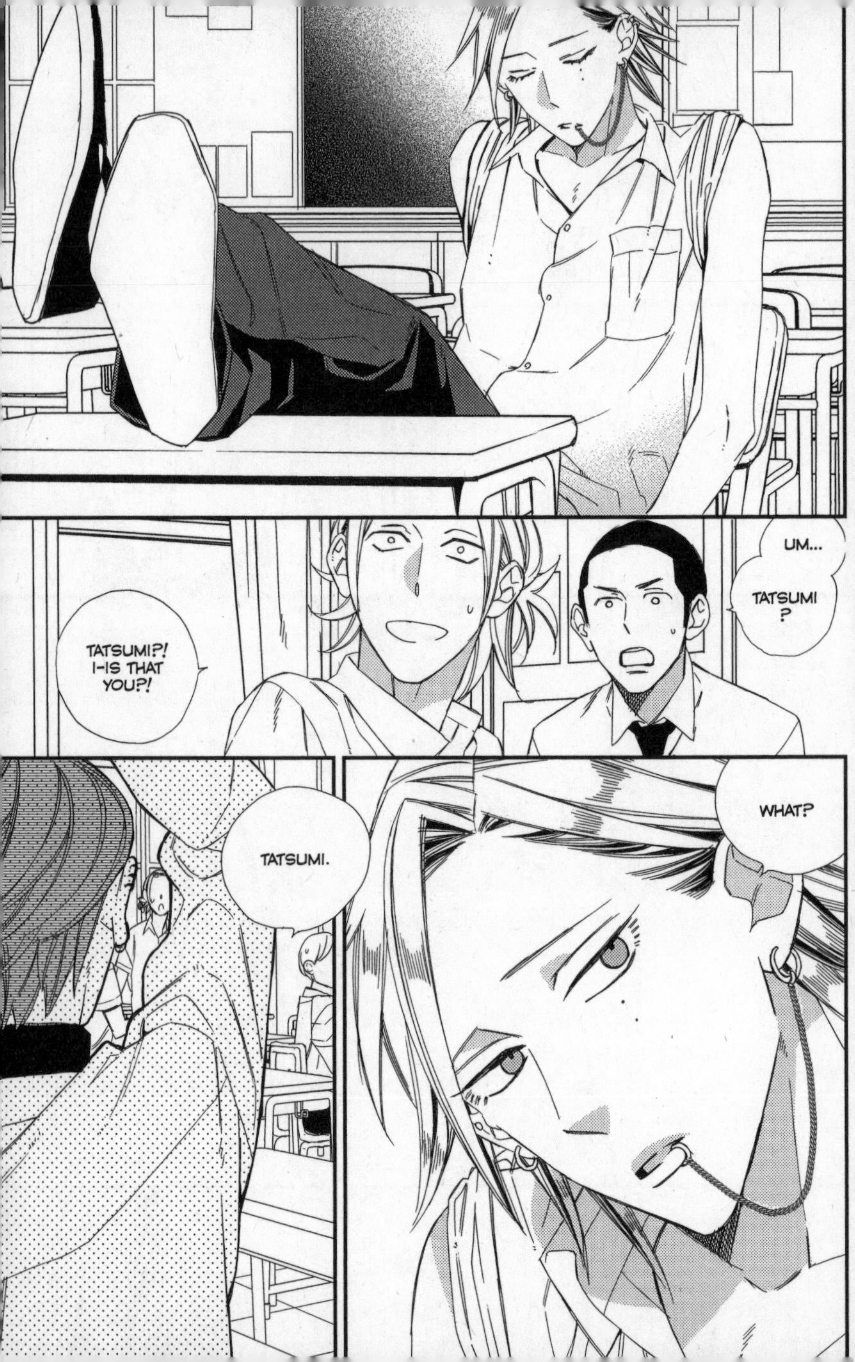
UM... TATSUMI?
TATSUMI?! I-IS THAT YOU?!
WHAT?
TATSUMI.

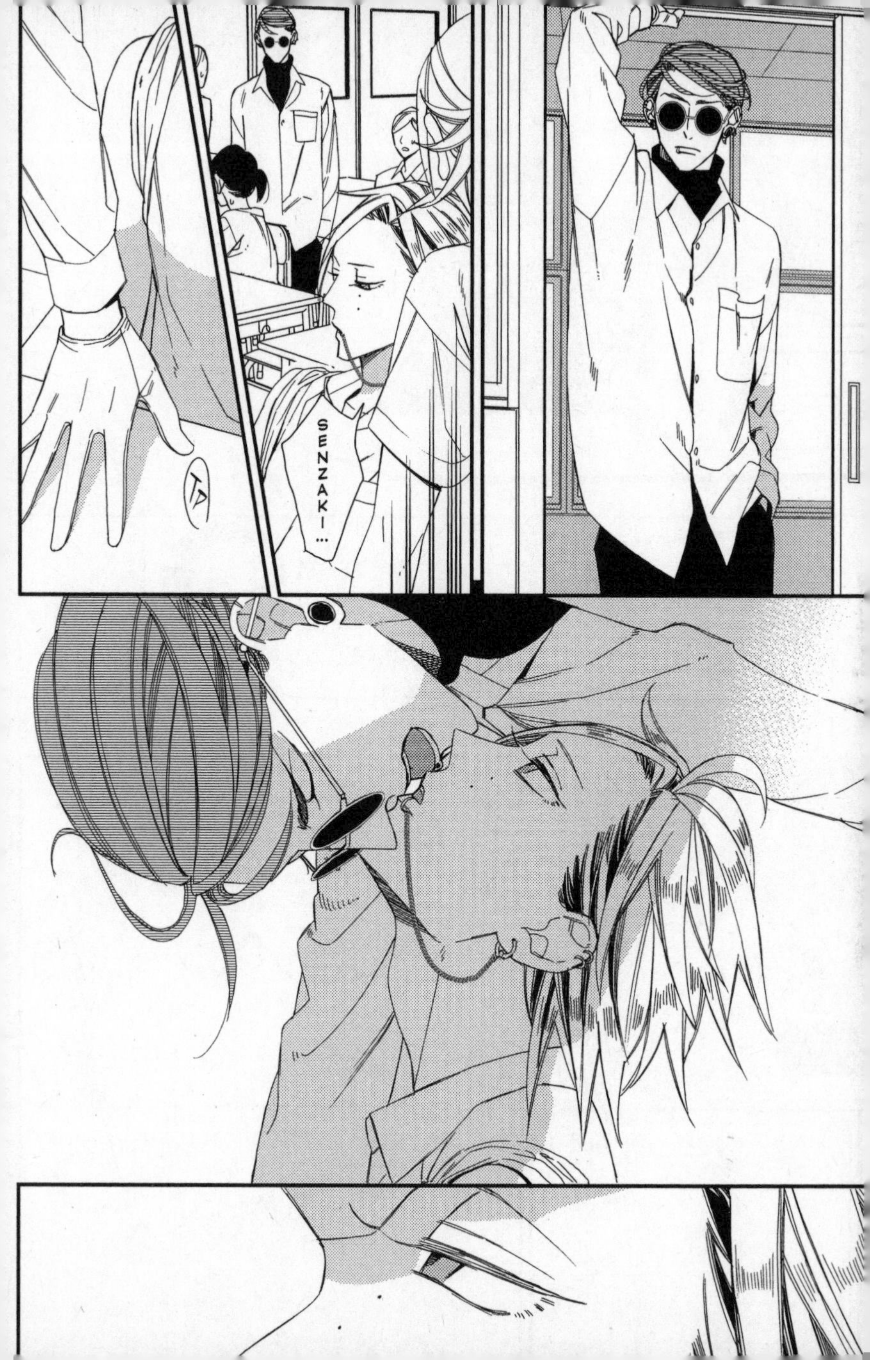
SENZAKI...
TP

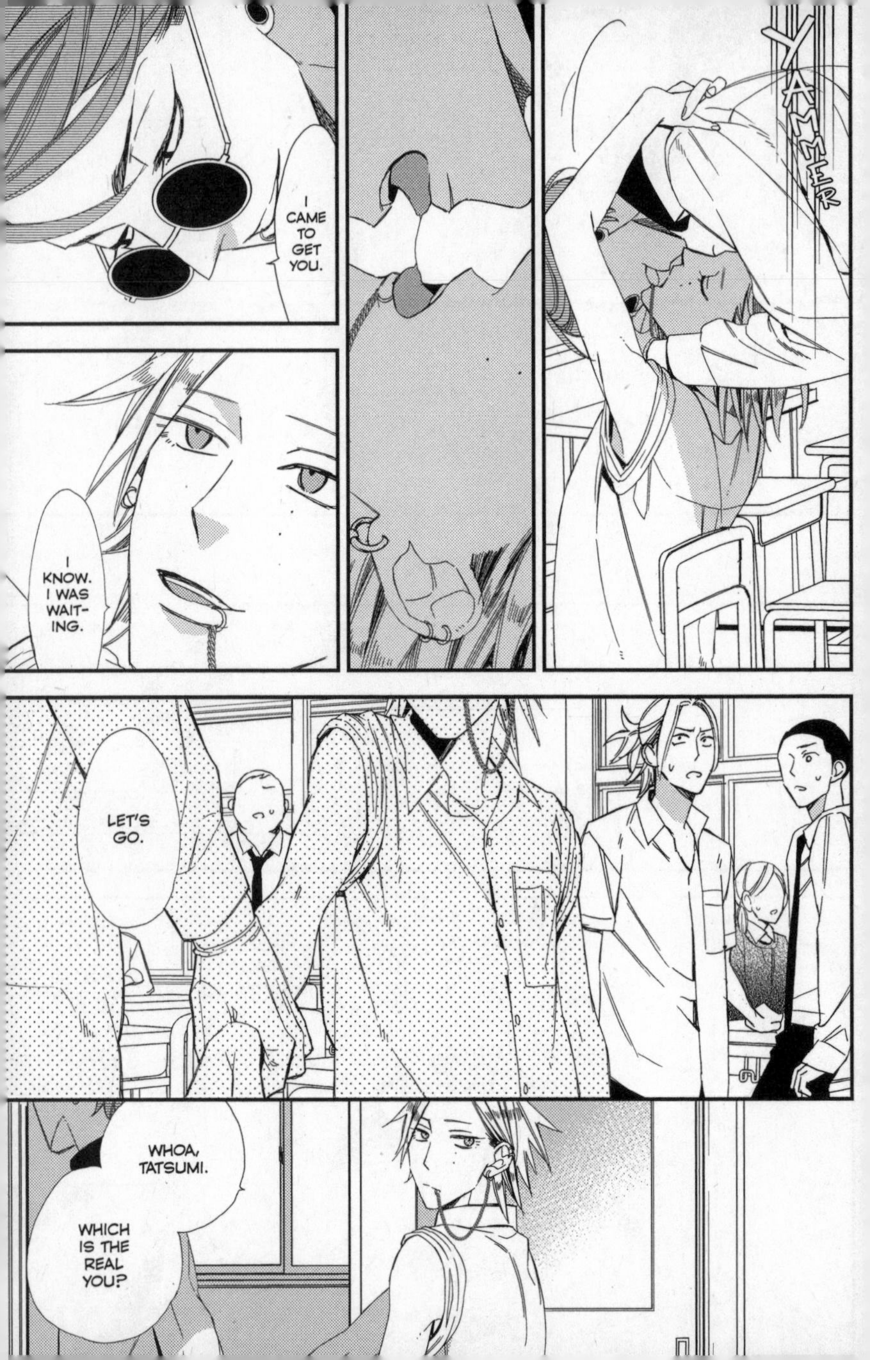
YAMMER
I CAME TO GET YOU.
I KNOW. I WAS WAITING.
LET'S GO.
WHOA, TATSUMI.
WHICH IS THE REAL YOU?

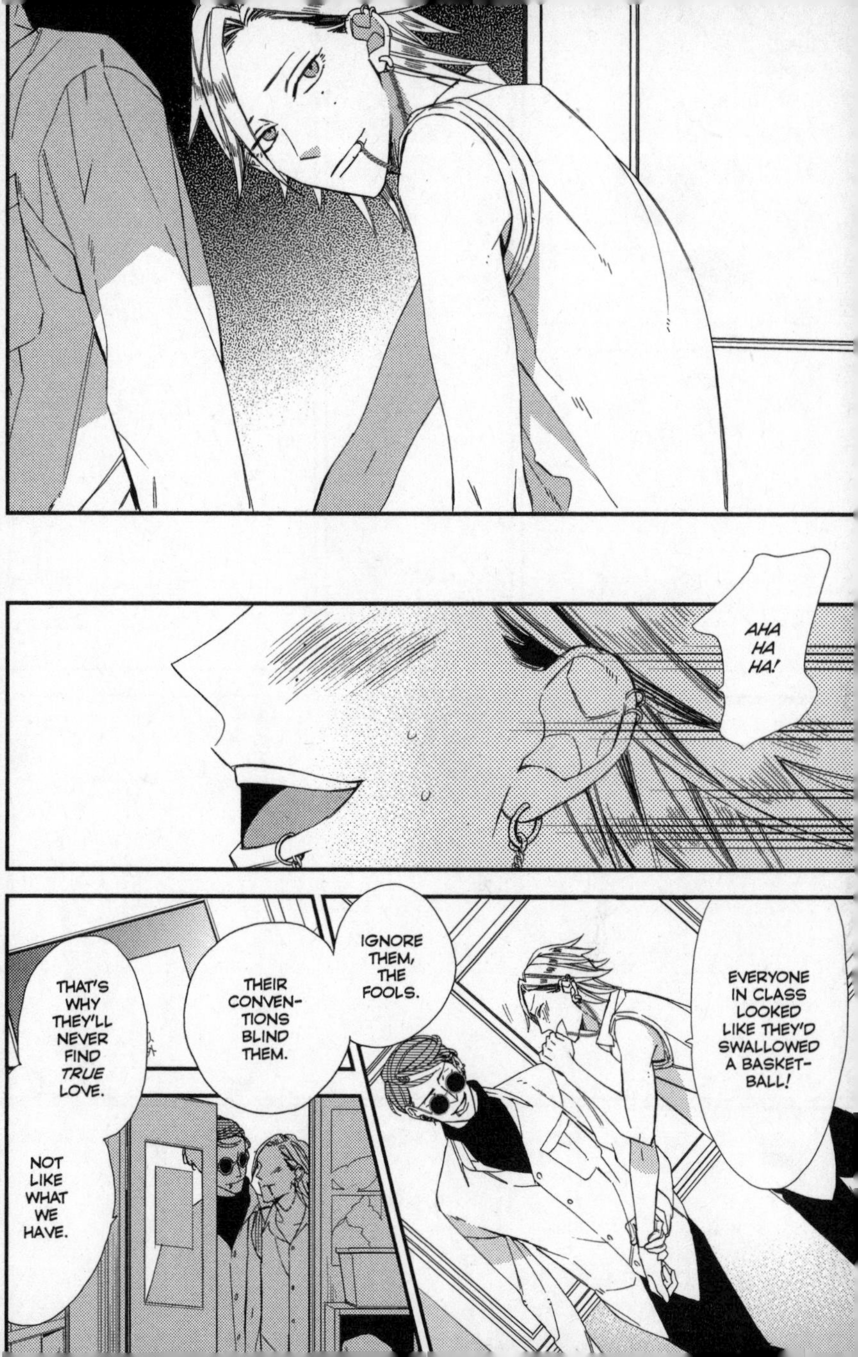
AHA HA HA!
EVERYONE IN CLASS LOOKED LIKE THEY'D SWALLOWED A BASKET-BALL!
IGNORE THEM, THE FOOLS.
THEIR CONVEN-TIONS BLIND THEM.
THAT'S WHY THEY'LL NEVER FIND *TRUE* LOVE.
NOT LIKE WHAT WE HAVE.

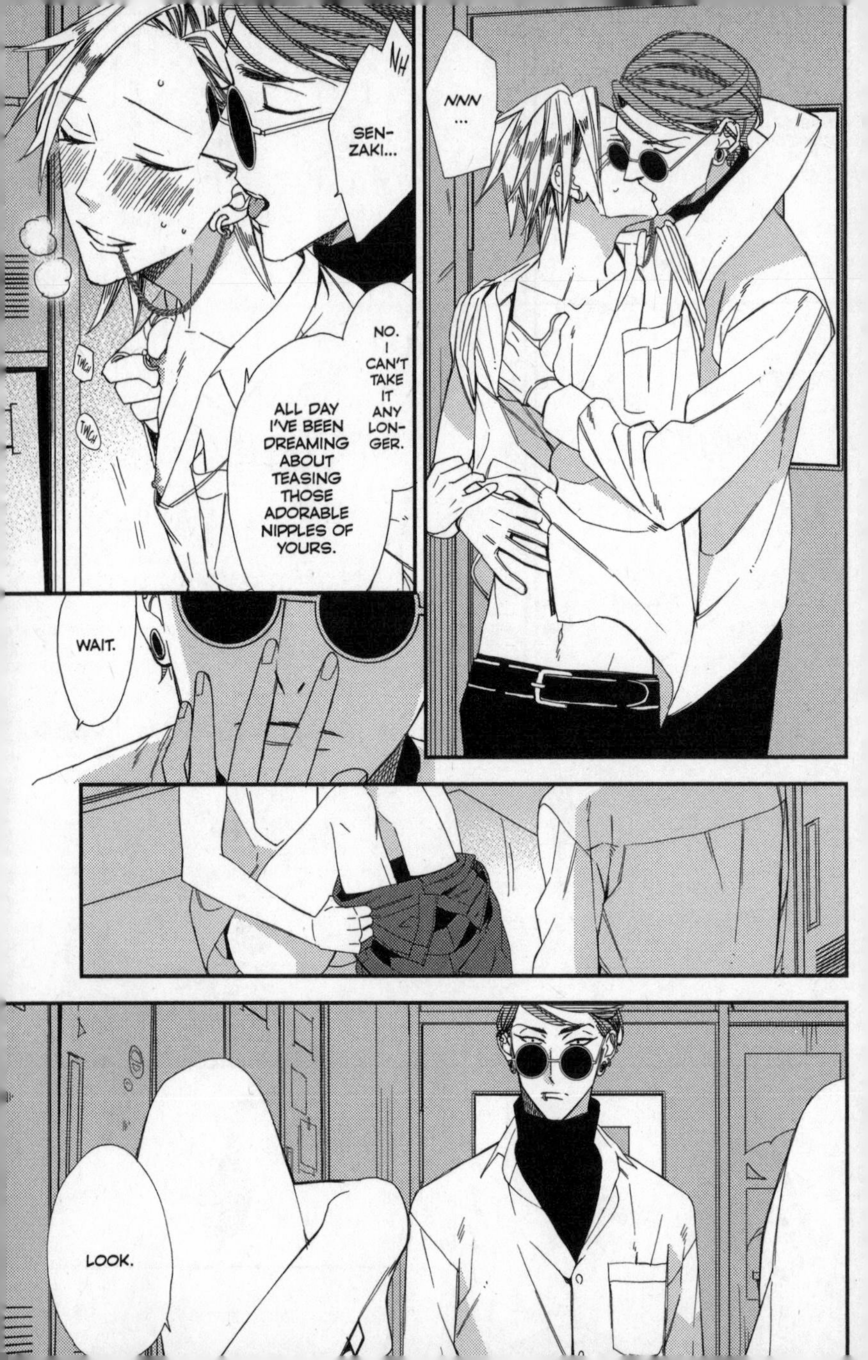
NNN ...
NH
SEN-ZAKI...
NO. I CAN'T TAKE IT ANY LONGER.
ALL DAY I'VE BEEN DREAMING ABOUT TEASING THOSE ADORABLE NIPPLES OF YOURS.
TWCH
TWCH
WAIT.
LOOK.

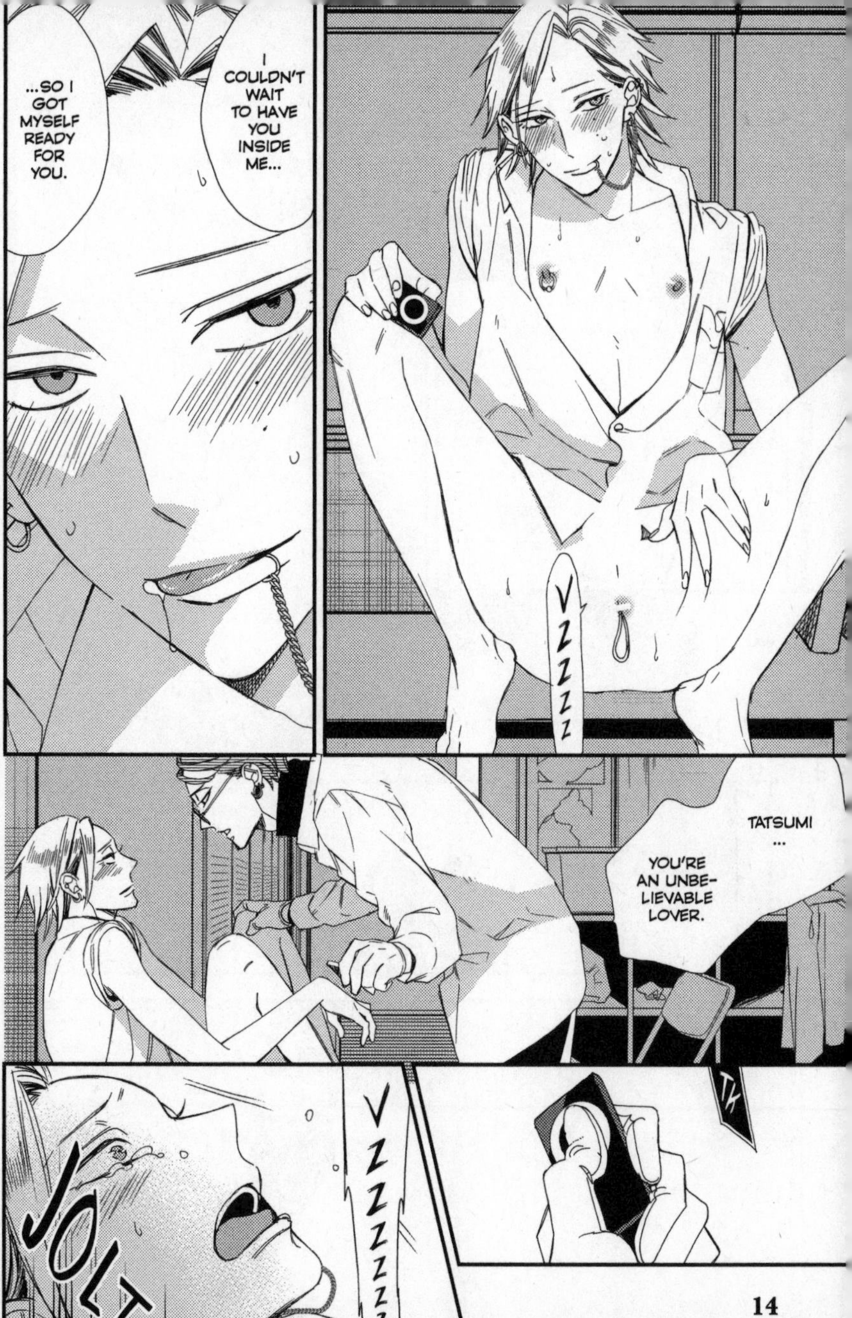
VZZZZ
I COULDN'T WAIT TO HAVE YOU INSIDE ME...
...SO I GOT MYSELF READY FOR YOU.
TATSUMI ...
YOU'RE AN UNBE-LIEVABLE LOVER.
TK
VZZZZZZZ
JOLT

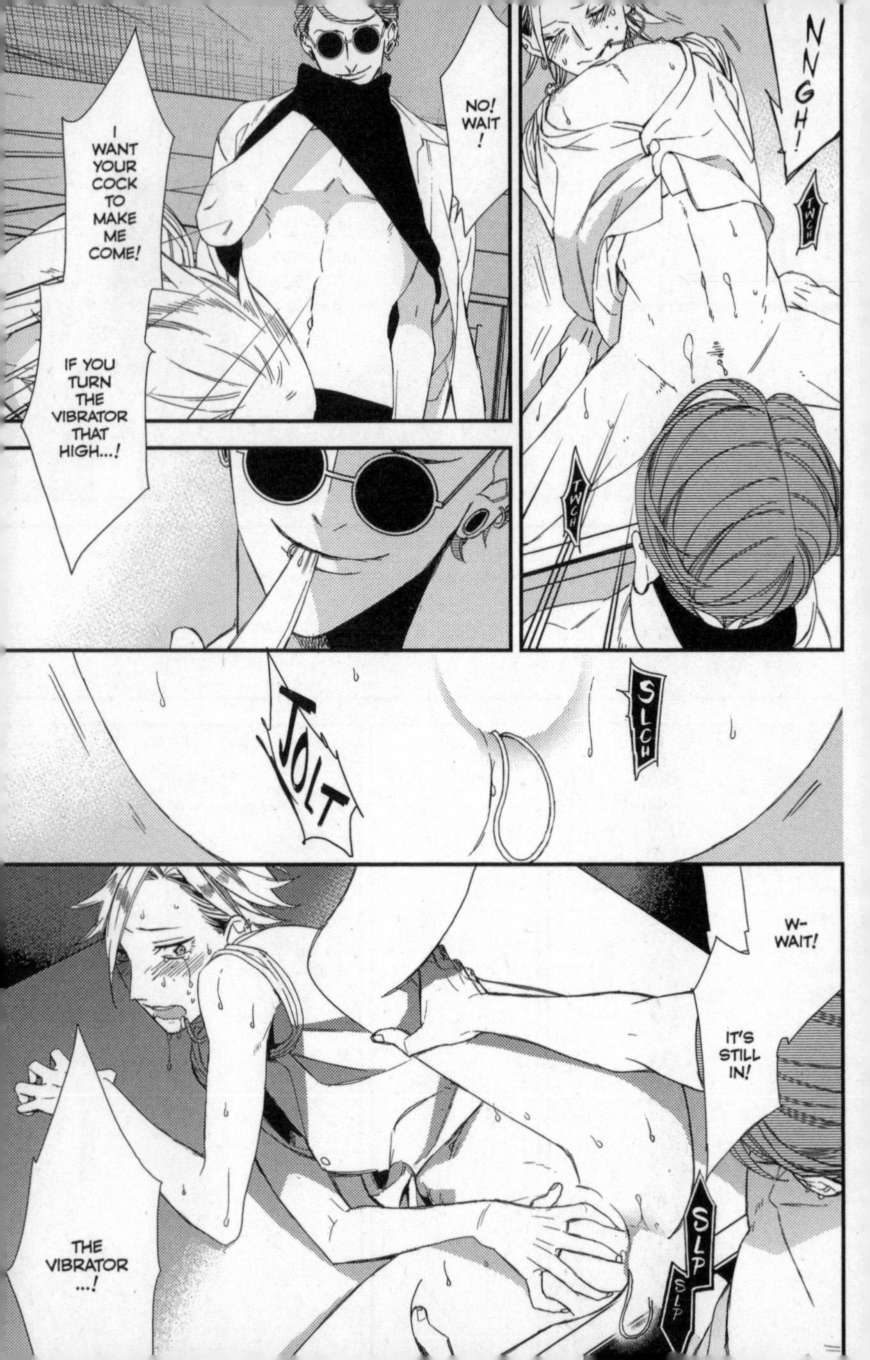
NNGH!
TWCH
TWCH
NO! WAIT!
I WANT YOUR COCK TO MAKE ME COME!
IF YOU TURN THE VIBRATOR THAT HIGH...!
SLCH
JOLT
W-WAIT!
IT'S STILL IN!
SLP
SLP
THE VIBRATOR...!

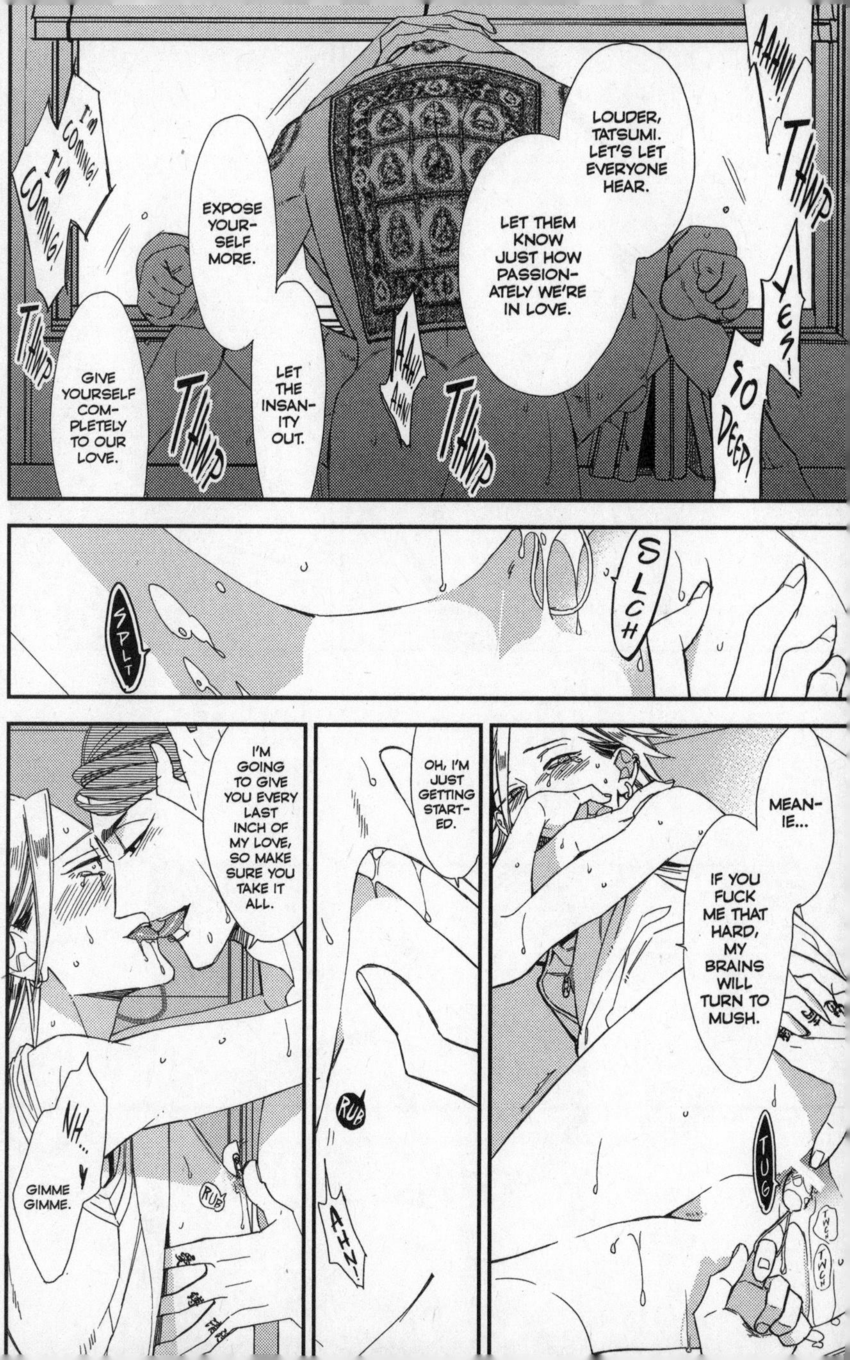
AAHN!
THWP
YES!
SO DEEP!
LOUDER, TATSUMI. LET'S LET EVERYONE HEAR.
LET THEM KNOW JUST HOW PASSIONATELY WE'RE IN LOVE.
THWP
AAH! AAH!
EXPOSE YOURSELF MORE.
LET THE INSANITY OUT.
I'M COMING! I'M COMING!
THWP
THWP
GIVE YOURSELF COMPLETELY TO OUR LOVE.
SLCH
SPLT
MEANIE...
IF YOU FUCK ME THAT HARD, MY BRAINS WILL TURN TO MUSH.
TUG
TWCH
TWCH
OH, I'M JUST GETTING STARTED.
RUB
AHN!
I'M GOING TO GIVE YOU EVERY LAST INCH OF MY LOVE, SO MAKE SURE YOU TAKE IT ALL.
NH... ♥
GIMME GIMME.
RUB

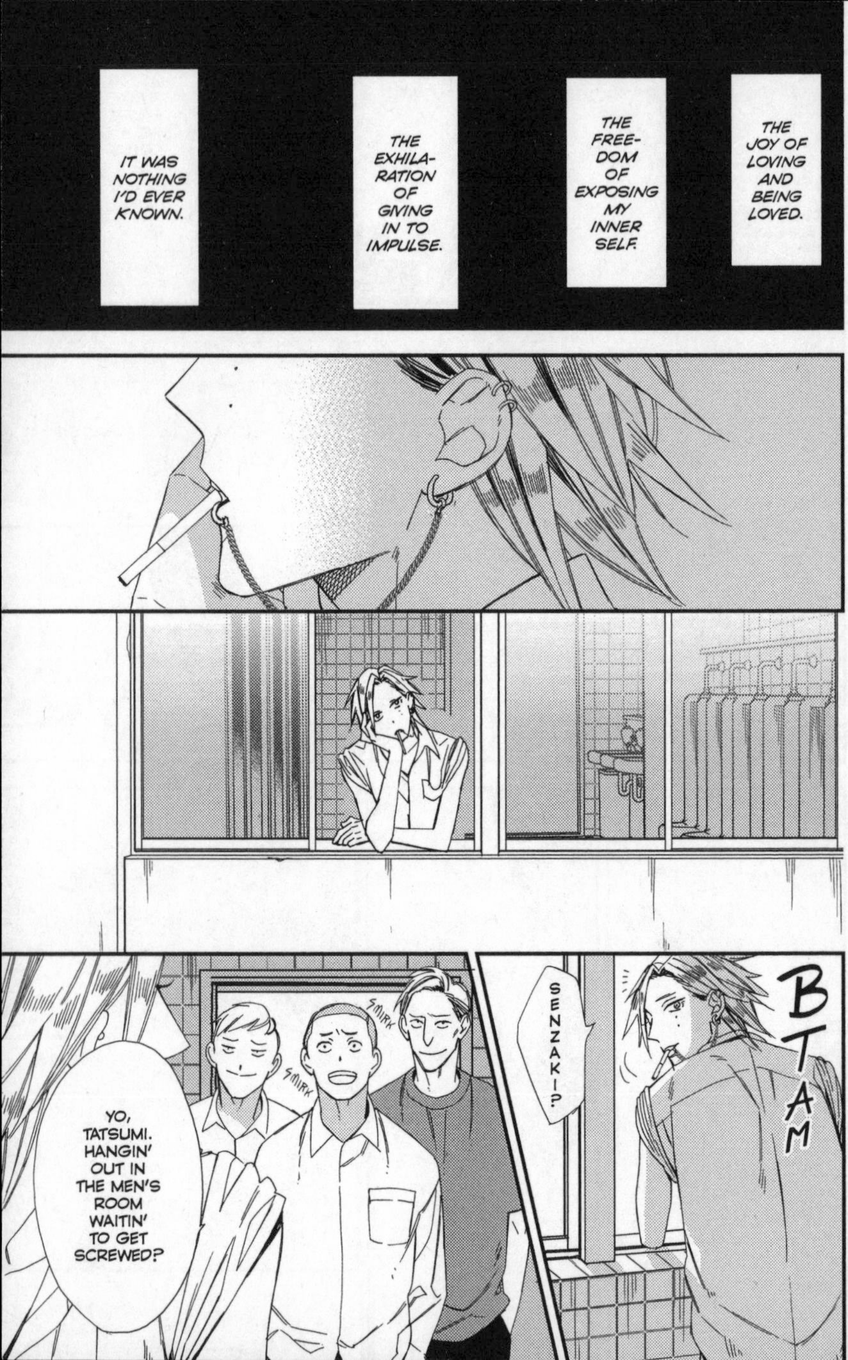
THE JOY OF LOVING AND BEING LOVED.
THE FREEDOM OF EXPOSING MY INNER SELF.
THE EXHILARATION OF GIVING IN TO IMPULSE.
IT WAS NOTHING I'D EVER KNOWN.
BTAM
SENZAKI...?
SMIRK
SMIRK
YO, TATSUMI. HANGIN' OUT IN THE MEN'S ROOM WAITIN' TO GET SCREWED?

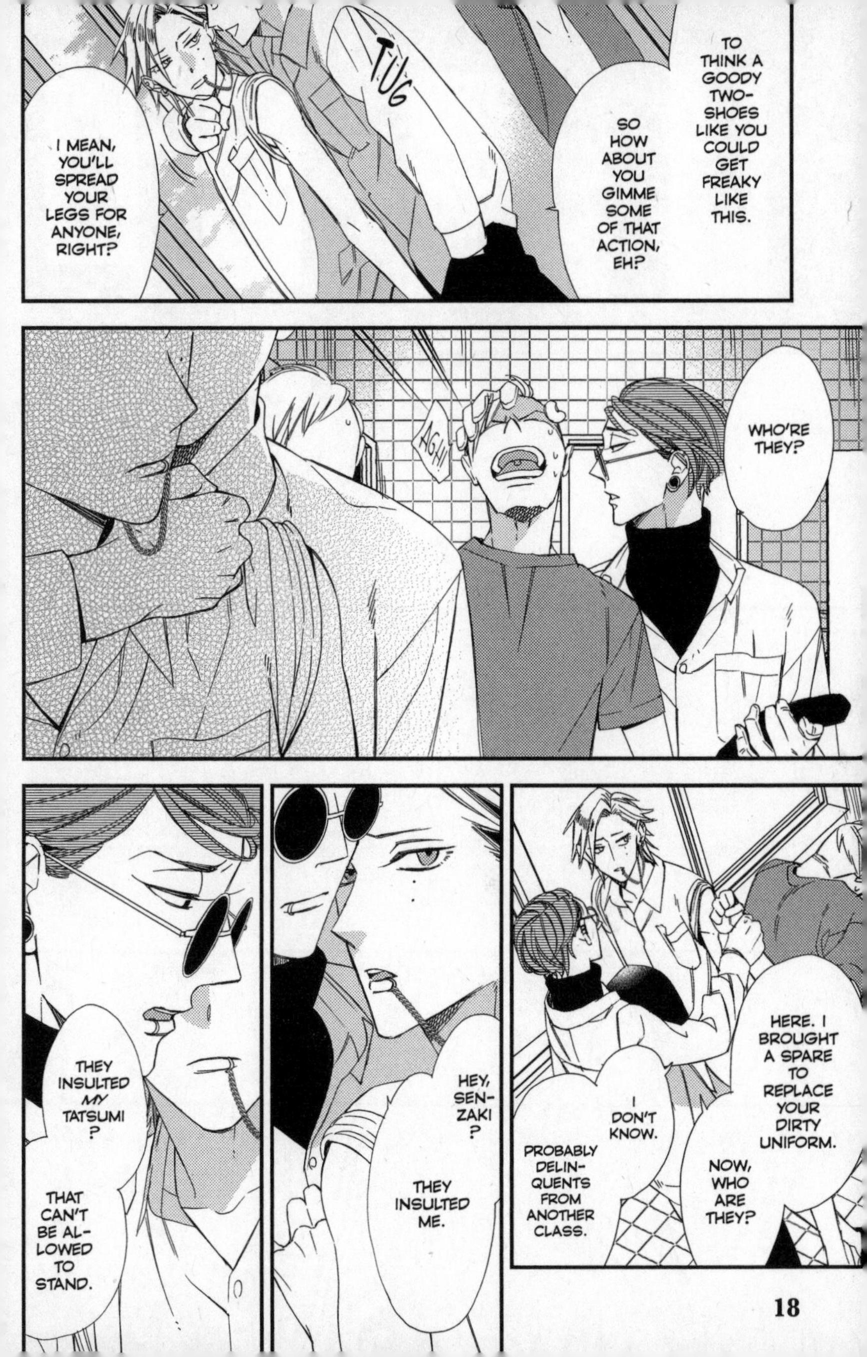
TO THINK A GOODY TWO-SHOES LIKE YOU COULD GET FREAKY LIKE THIS.
SO HOW ABOUT YOU GIMME SOME OF THAT ACTION, EH?
TUG
I MEAN, YOU'LL SPREAD YOUR LEGS FOR ANYONE, RIGHT?
WHO'RE THEY?
AGH!
HERE. I BROUGHT A SPARE TO REPLACE YOUR DIRTY UNIFORM.
NOW, WHO ARE THEY?
I DON'T KNOW.
PROBABLY DELINQUENTS FROM ANOTHER CLASS.
HEY, SENZAKI?
THEY INSULTED ME.
THEY INSULTED *MY* TATSUMI?
THAT CAN'T BE ALLOWED TO STAND.

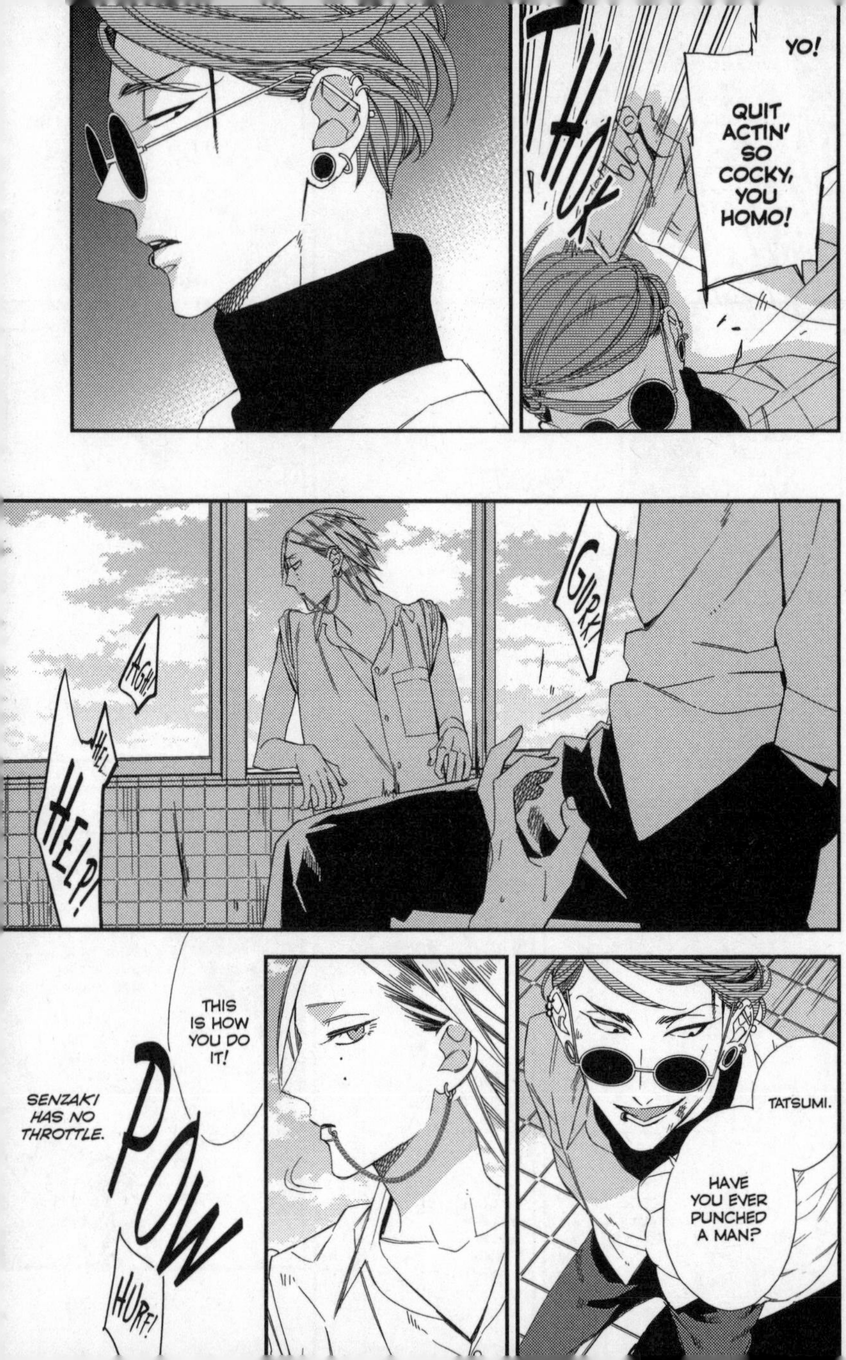

THOK
YO!
QUIT ACTIN' SO COCKY, YOU HOMO!
GURK!
AGH!
HEL
HELP!
TATSUMI.
HAVE YOU EVER PUNCHED A MAN?
THIS IS HOW YOU DO IT!
POW
HURF!
SENZAKI HAS NO THROTTLE.

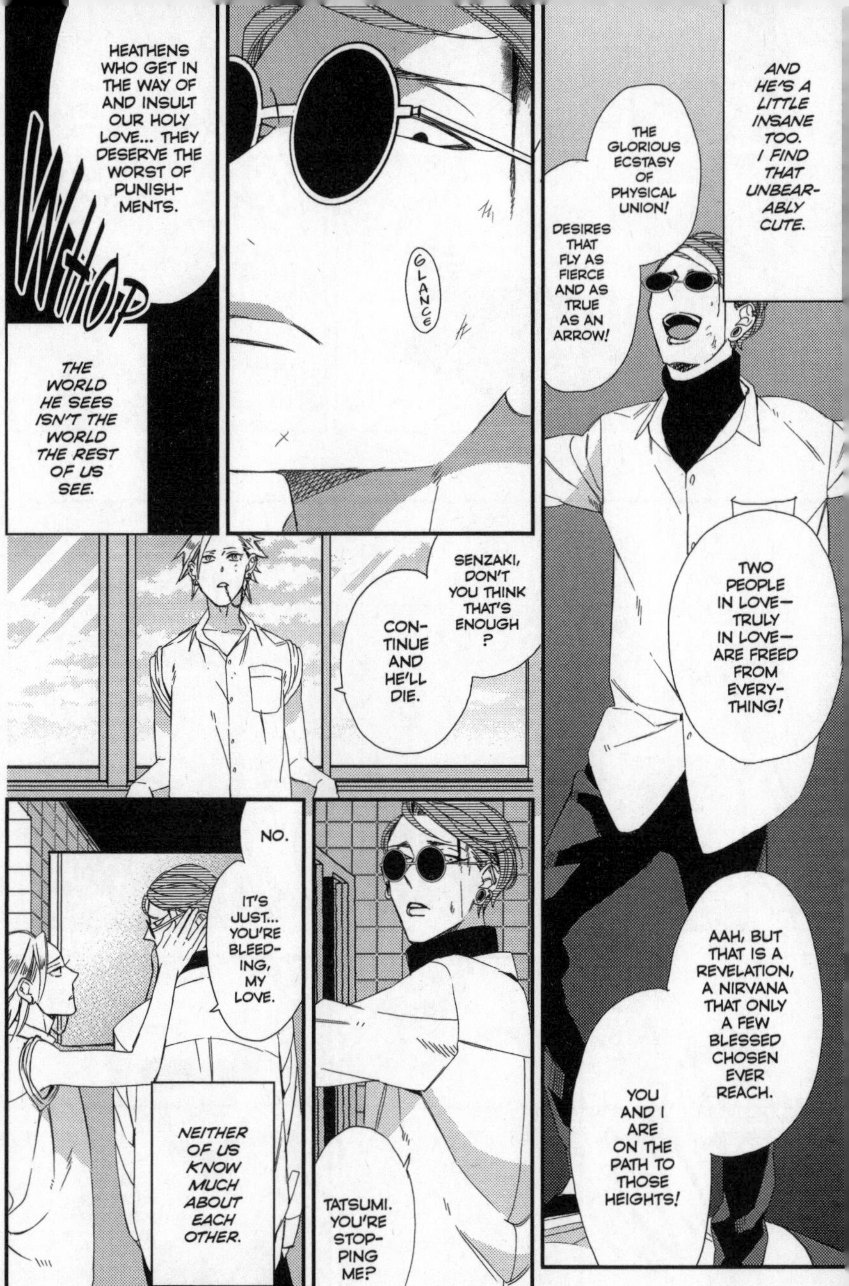
AND HE'S A LITTLE INSANE TOO. I FIND THAT UNBEARABLY CUTE.
THE GLORIOUS ECSTASY OF PHYSICAL UNION!
DESIRES THAT FLY AS FIERCE AND AS TRUE AS AN ARROW!
TWO PEOPLE IN LOVE—TRULY IN LOVE—ARE FREED FROM EVERYTHING!
AAH, BUT THAT IS A REVELATION, A NIRVANA THAT ONLY A FEW BLESSED CHOSEN EVER REACH.
YOU AND I ARE ON THE PATH TO THOSE HEIGHTS!
GLANCE
HEATHENS WHO GET IN THE WAY OF AND INSULT OUR HOLY LOVE... THEY DESERVE THE WORST OF PUNISHMENTS.
WHOP
THE WORLD HE SEES ISN'T THE WORLD THE REST OF US SEE.
SENZAKI, DON'T YOU THINK THAT'S ENOUGH?
CONTINUE AND HE'LL DIE.
TATSUMI. YOU'RE STOPPING ME?
NO.
IT'S JUST... YOU'RE BLEEDING, MY LOVE.
NEITHER OF US KNOW MUCH ABOUT EACH OTHER.

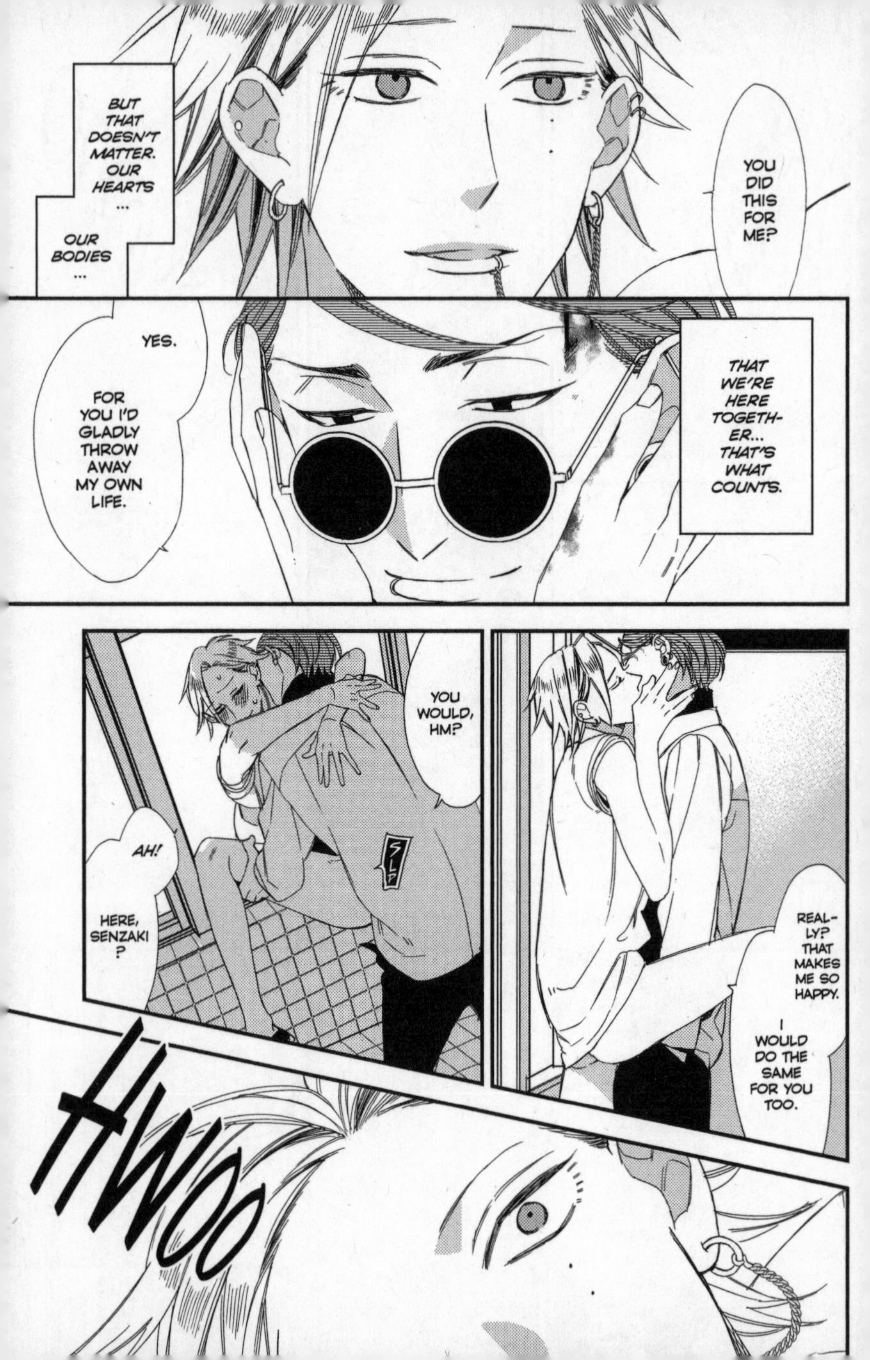
YOU DID THIS FOR ME?
BUT THAT DOESN'T MATTER. OUR HEARTS ... OUR BODIES ...
THAT WE'RE HERE TOGETHER... THAT'S WHAT COUNTS.
YES. FOR YOU I'D GLADLY THROW AWAY MY OWN LIFE.
REALLY? THAT MAKES ME SO HAPPY.
I WOULD DO THE SAME FOR YOU TOO.
YOU WOULD, HM?
AH!
HERE, SENZAKI?
HWOO

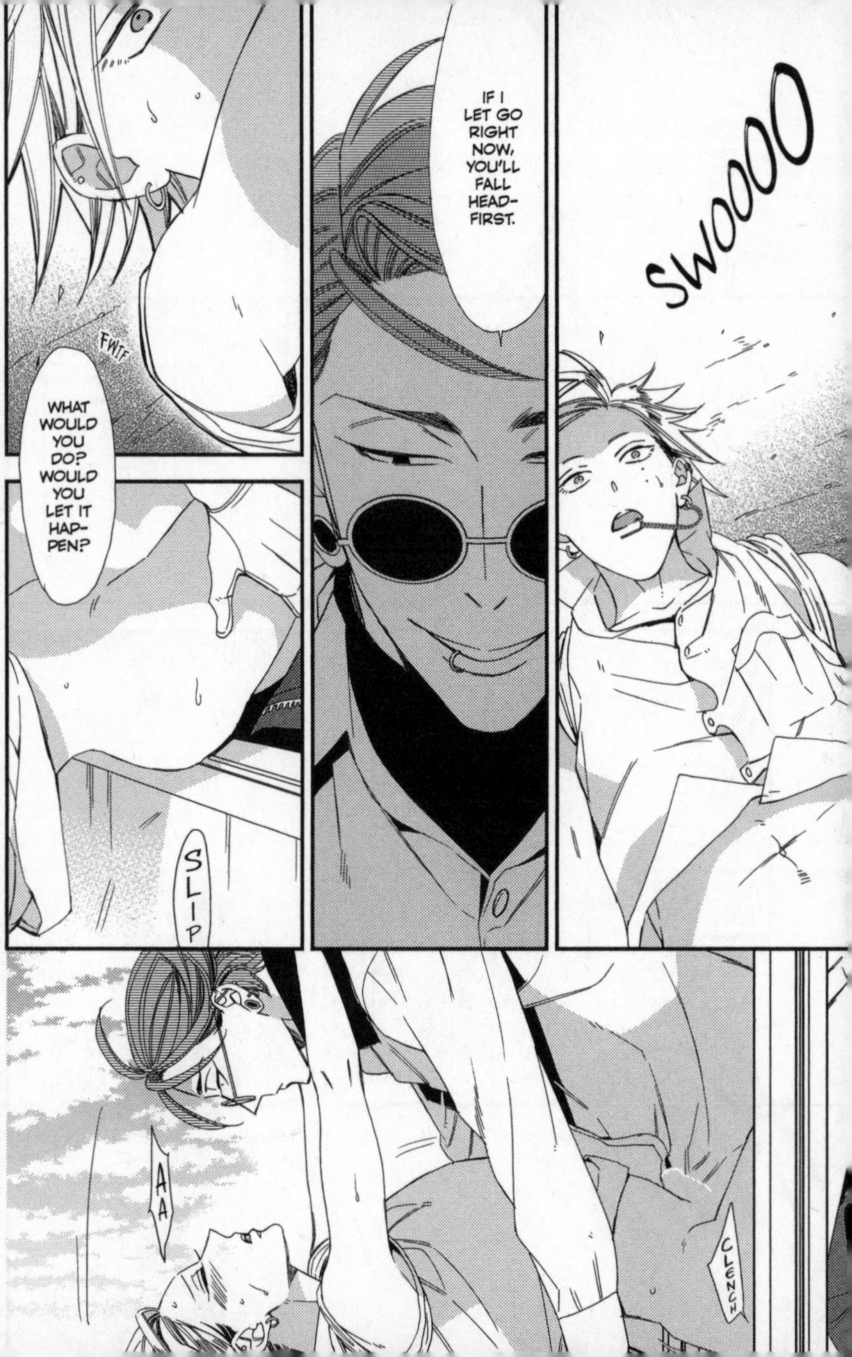
SWOOOO
IF I LET GO RIGHT NOW, YOU'LL FALL HEAD-FIRST.
FWIF
WHAT WOULD YOU DO? WOULD YOU LET IT HAP-PEN?
SLIP
CLENCH
AA

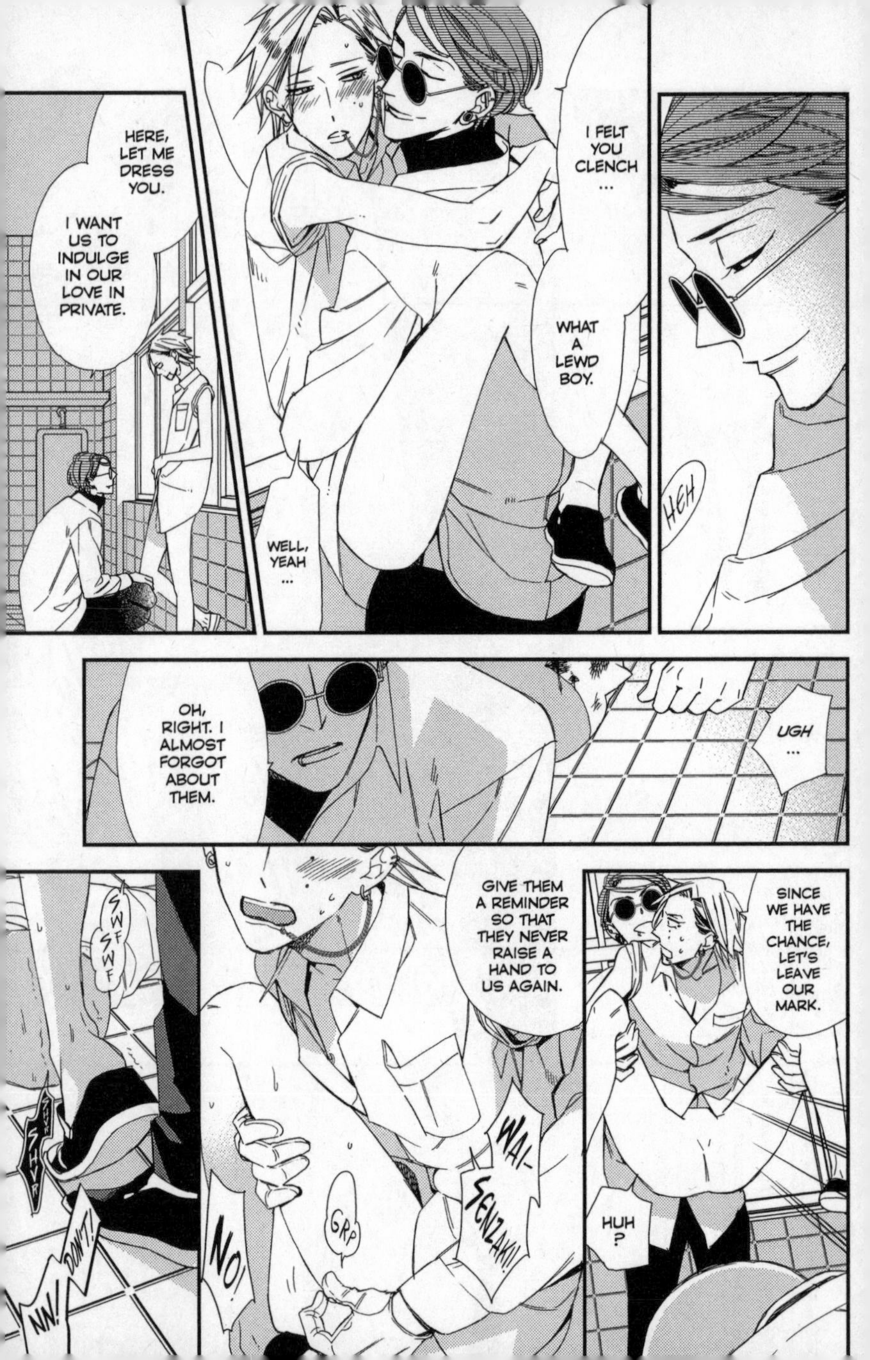
HEH
I FELT YOU CLENCH ...
WHAT A LEWD BOY.
WELL, YEAH ...
HERE, LET ME DRESS YOU.
I WANT US TO INDULGE IN OUR LOVE IN PRIVATE.
UGH ...
OH, RIGHT. I ALMOST FORGOT ABOUT THEM.
SINCE WE HAVE THE CHANCE, LET'S LEAVE OUR MARK.
HUH ?
GIVE THEM A REMINDER SO THAT THEY NEVER RAISE A HAND TO US AGAIN.
WAI- SENZAKI!
GRP
NO!
SWF SWF
SHVR
DON'T!
NN!

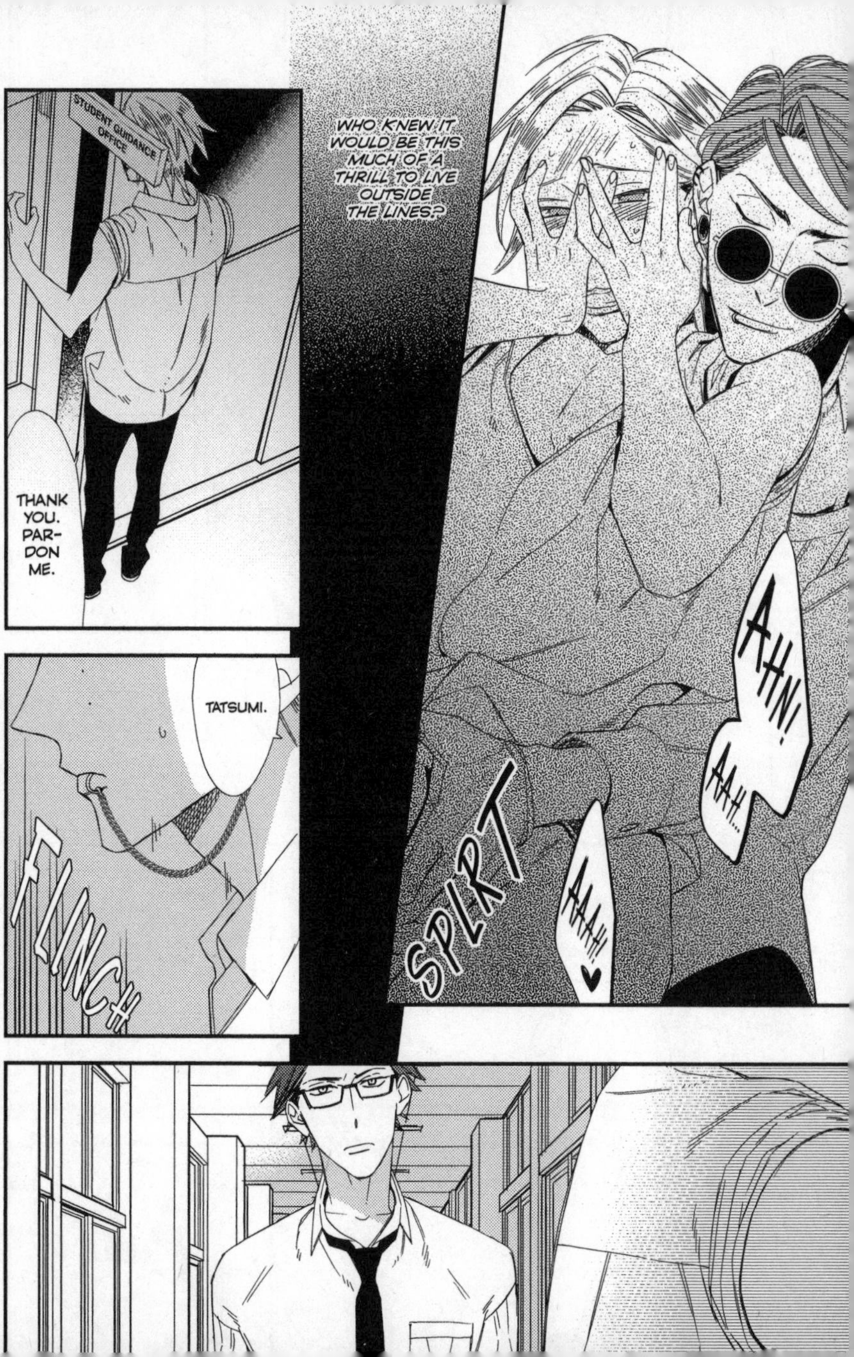
AHN!
AAH...
AAAH!!! ♥
SPLRT
WHO KNEW IT WOULD BE THIS MUCH OF A THRILL TO LIVE OUTSIDE THE LINES?
STUDENT GUIDANCE OFFICE
THANK YOU. PARDON ME.
TATSUMI.
FLINCH

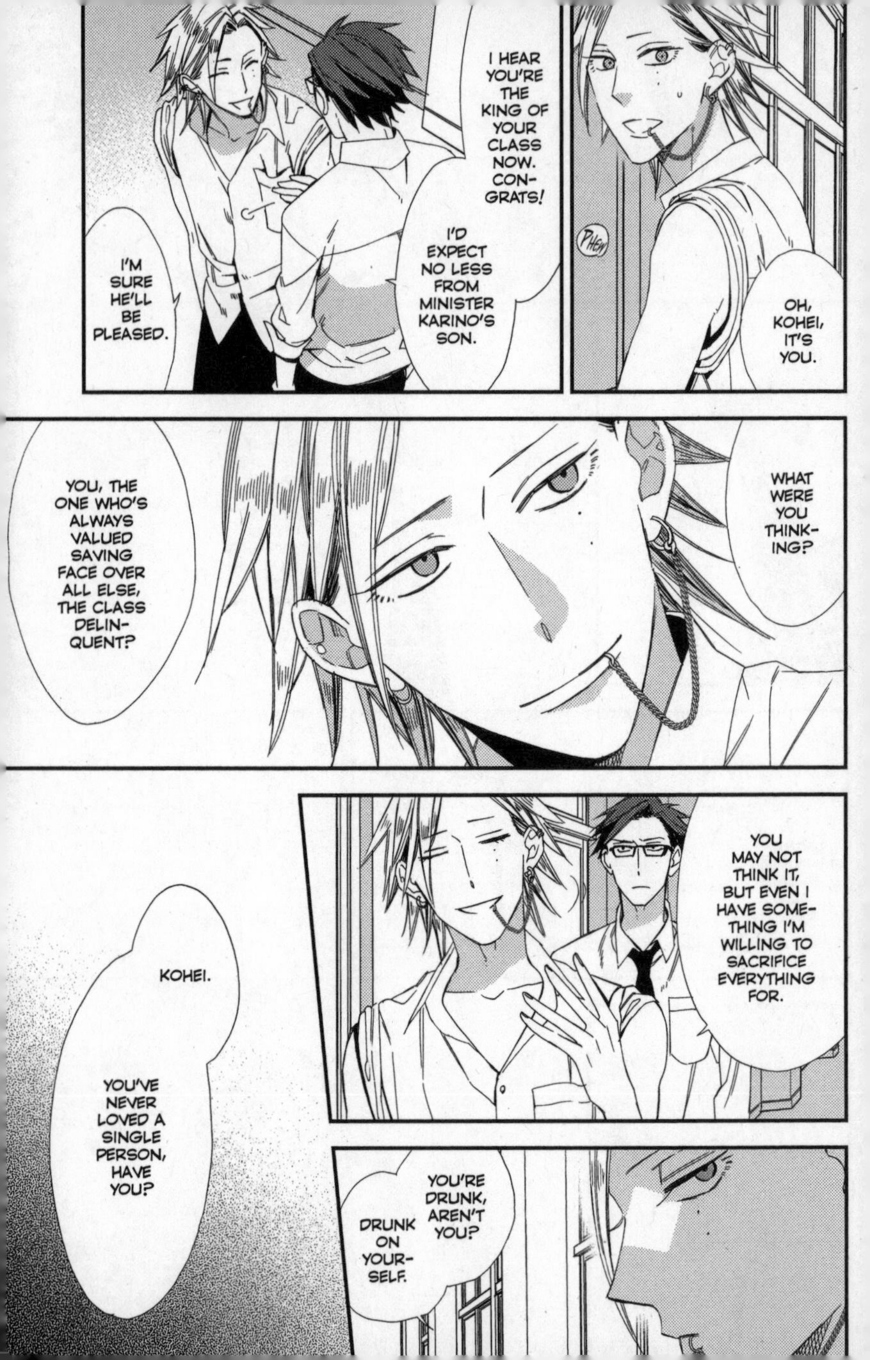
PHEW
OH, KOHEI, IT'S YOU.
I HEAR YOU'RE THE KING OF YOUR CLASS NOW. CON-GRATS!
I'D EXPECT NO LESS FROM MINISTER KARINO'S SON.
I'M SURE HE'LL BE PLEASED.
WHAT WERE YOU THINK-ING?
YOU, THE ONE WHO'S ALWAYS VALUED SAVING FACE OVER ALL ELSE, THE CLASS DELIN-QUENT?
YOU MAY NOT THINK IT, BUT EVEN I HAVE SOME-THING I'M WILLING TO SACRIFICE EVERYTHING FOR.
YOU'RE DRUNK, AREN'T YOU?
DRUNK ON YOUR-SELF.
KOHEI.
YOU'VE NEVER LOVED A SINGLE PERSON, HAVE YOU?

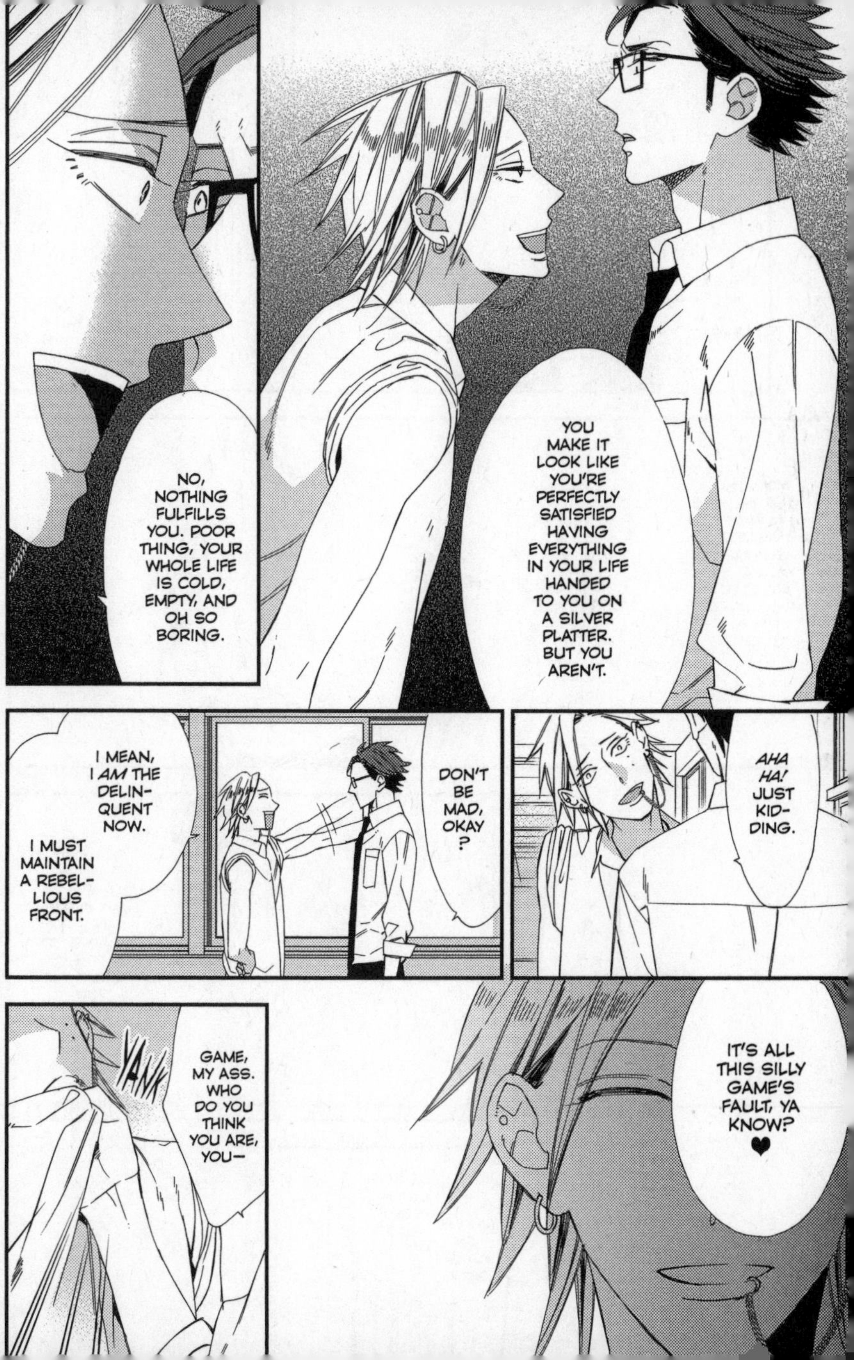
YOU MAKE IT LOOK LIKE YOU'RE PERFECTLY SATISFIED HAVING EVERYTHING IN YOUR LIFE HANDED TO YOU ON A SILVER PLATTER. BUT YOU AREN'T.
NO, NOTHING FULFILLS YOU. POOR THING, YOUR WHOLE LIFE IS COLD, EMPTY, AND OH SO BORING.
AHA HA! JUST KIDDING.
DON'T BE MAD, OKAY?
I MEAN, I *AM* THE DELINQUENT NOW.
I MUST MAINTAIN A REBELLIOUS FRONT.
IT'S ALL THIS SILLY GAME'S FAULT, YA KNOW? ♥
GAME, MY ASS. WHO DO YOU THINK YOU ARE, YOU—
YANK

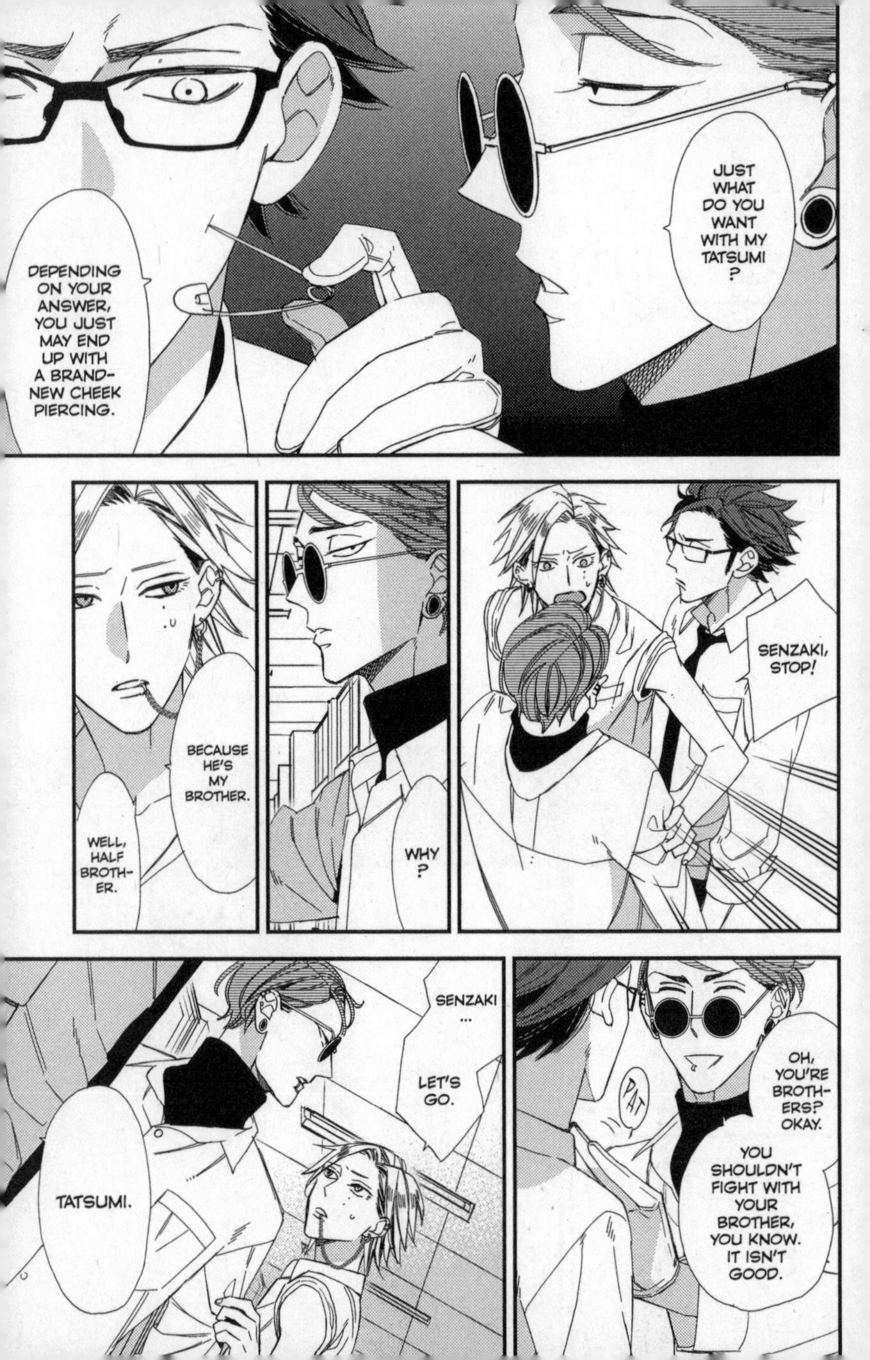
JUST WHAT DO YOU WANT WITH MY TATSUMI?
DEPENDING ON YOUR ANSWER, YOU JUST MAY END UP WITH A BRAND-NEW CHEEK PIERCING.
SENZAKI, STOP!
WHY?
BECAUSE HE'S MY BROTHER.
WELL, HALF BROTHER.
OH, YOU'RE BROTHERS? OKAY.
PAT
YOU SHOULDN'T FIGHT WITH YOUR BROTHER, YOU KNOW. IT ISN'T GOOD.
SENZAKI...
LET'S GO.
TATSUMI.

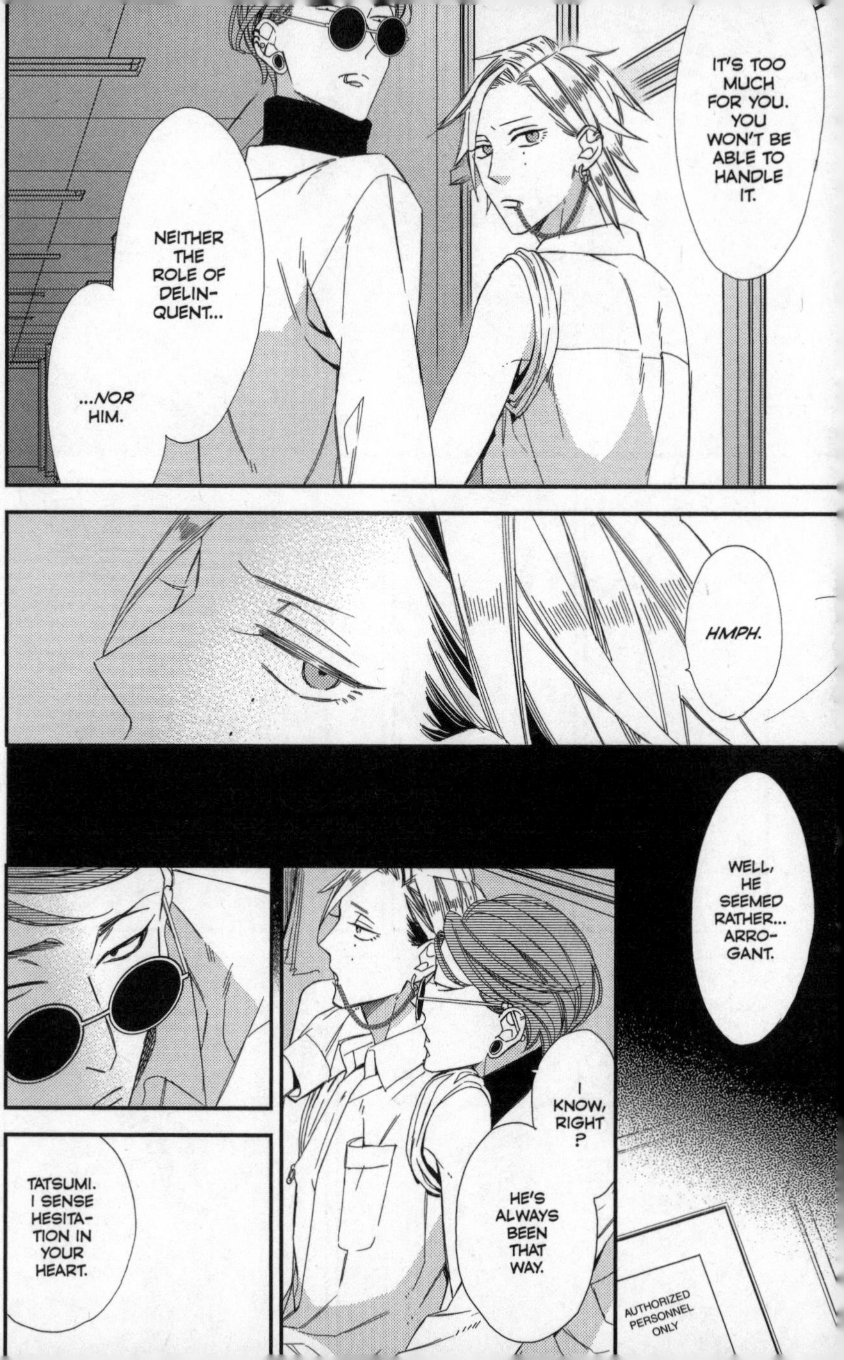
IT'S TOO MUCH FOR YOU. YOU WON'T BE ABLE TO HANDLE IT.
NEITHER THE ROLE OF DELIN-QUENT...
...*NOR* HIM.
HMPH.
WELL, HE SEEMED RATHER... ARRO-GANT.
I KNOW, RIGHT?
HE'S ALWAYS BEEN THAT WAY.
AUTHORIZED PERSONNEL ONLY
TATSUMI. I SENSE HESITA-TION IN YOUR HEART.

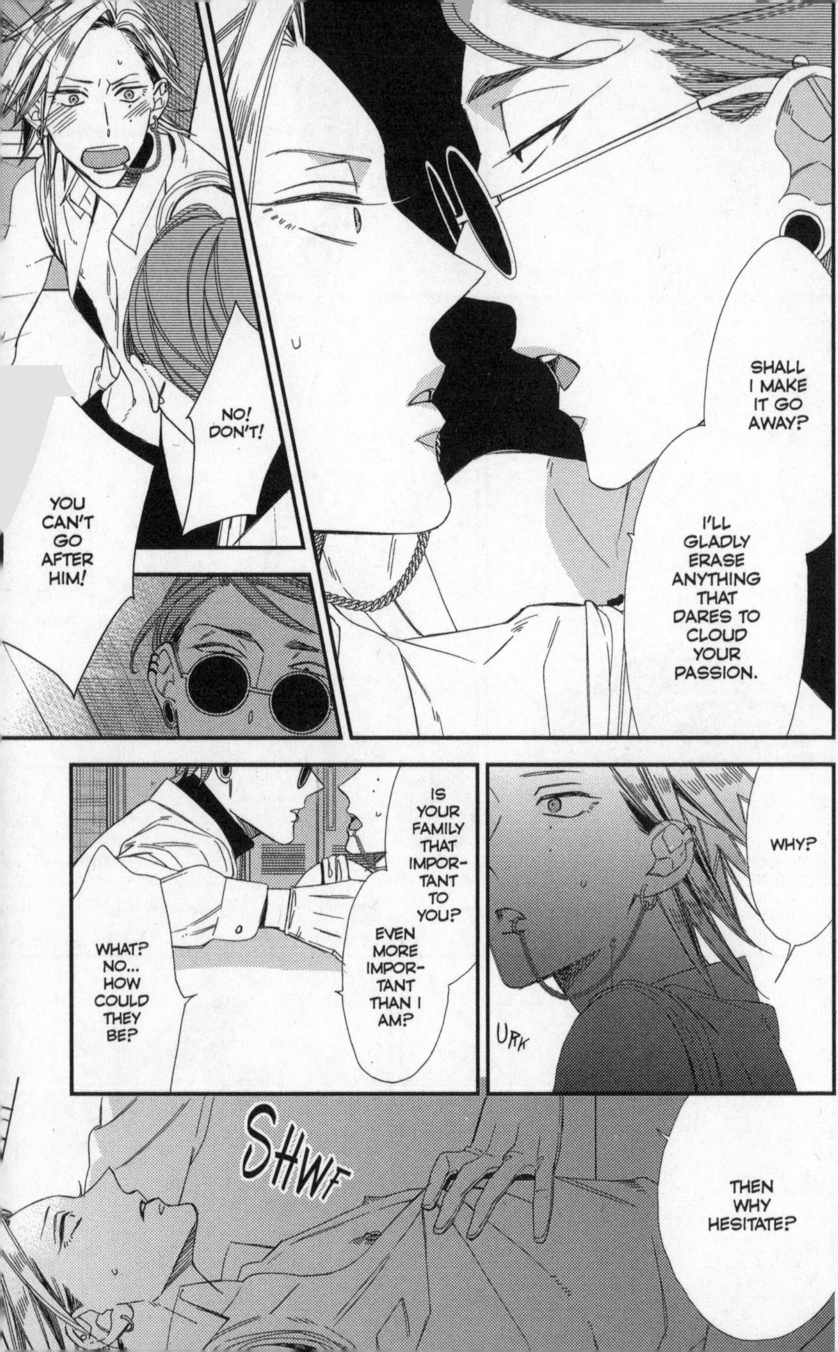
SHALL I MAKE IT GO AWAY?
I'LL GLADLY ERASE ANYTHING THAT DARES TO CLOUD YOUR PASSION.
NO! DON'T!
YOU CAN'T GO AFTER HIM!
WHY?
URK
IS YOUR FAMILY THAT IMPOR-TANT TO YOU?
EVEN MORE IMPOR-TANT THAN I AM?
WHAT? NO... HOW COULD THEY BE?
THEN WHY HESITATE?
SHWF

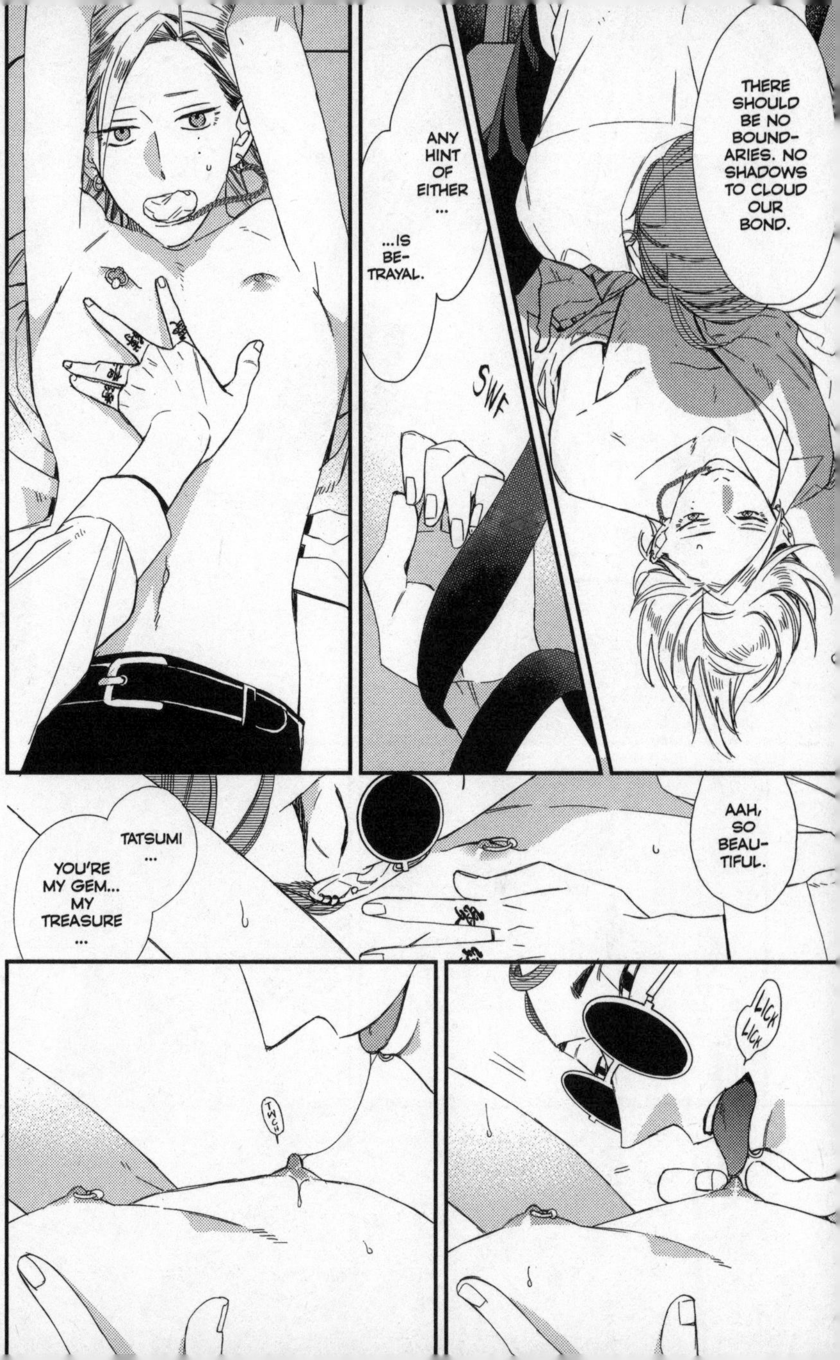
THERE SHOULD BE NO BOUNDARIES. NO SHADOWS TO CLOUD OUR BOND.
ANY HINT OF EITHER...
...IS BETRAYAL.
SWF
AAH, SO BEAUTIFUL.
TATSUMI...
YOU'RE MY GEM... MY TREASURE...
LICK LICK
TWCH

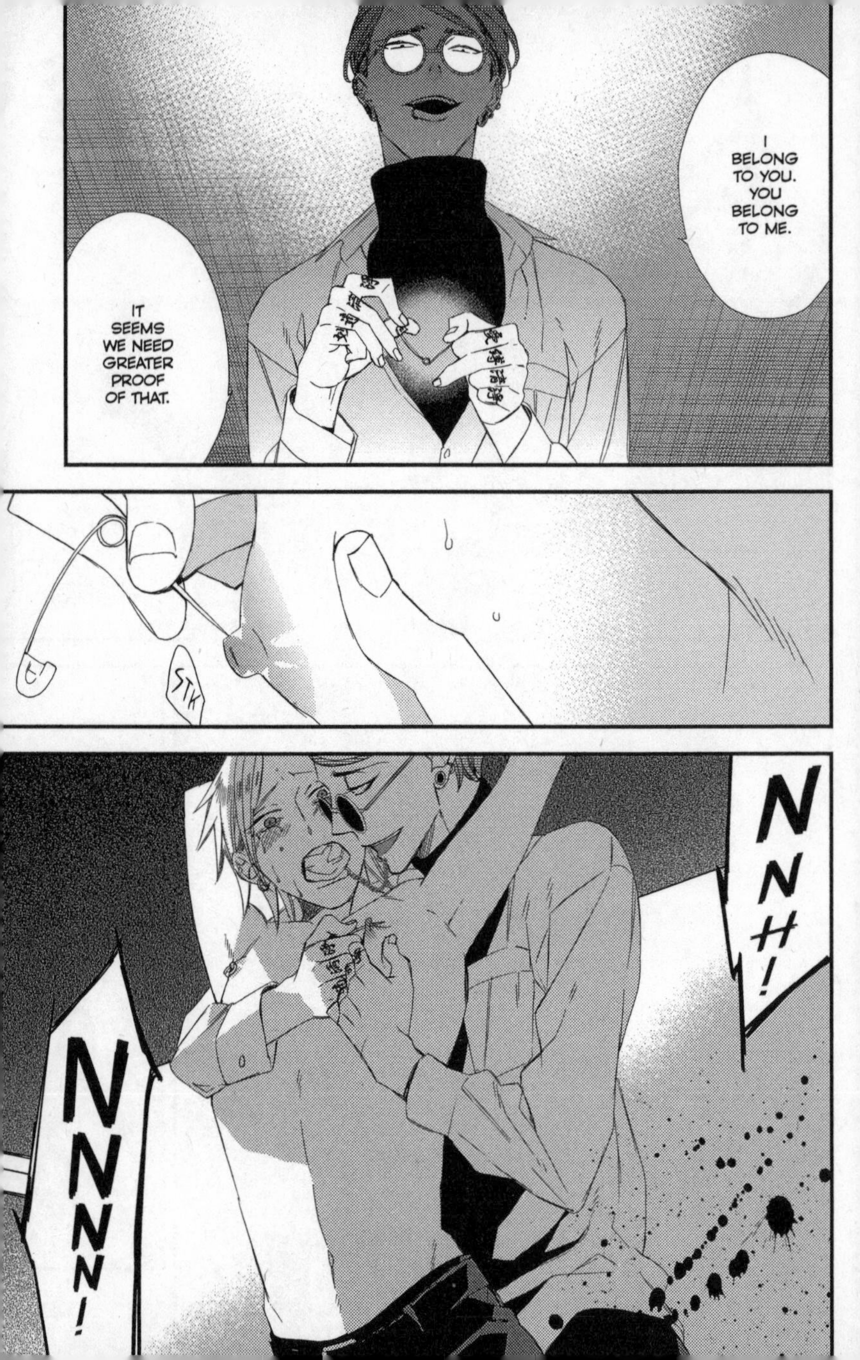
I BELONG TO YOU. YOU BELONG TO ME.
IT SEEMS WE NEED GREATER PROOF OF THAT.
STK
NNH!
NNNN!

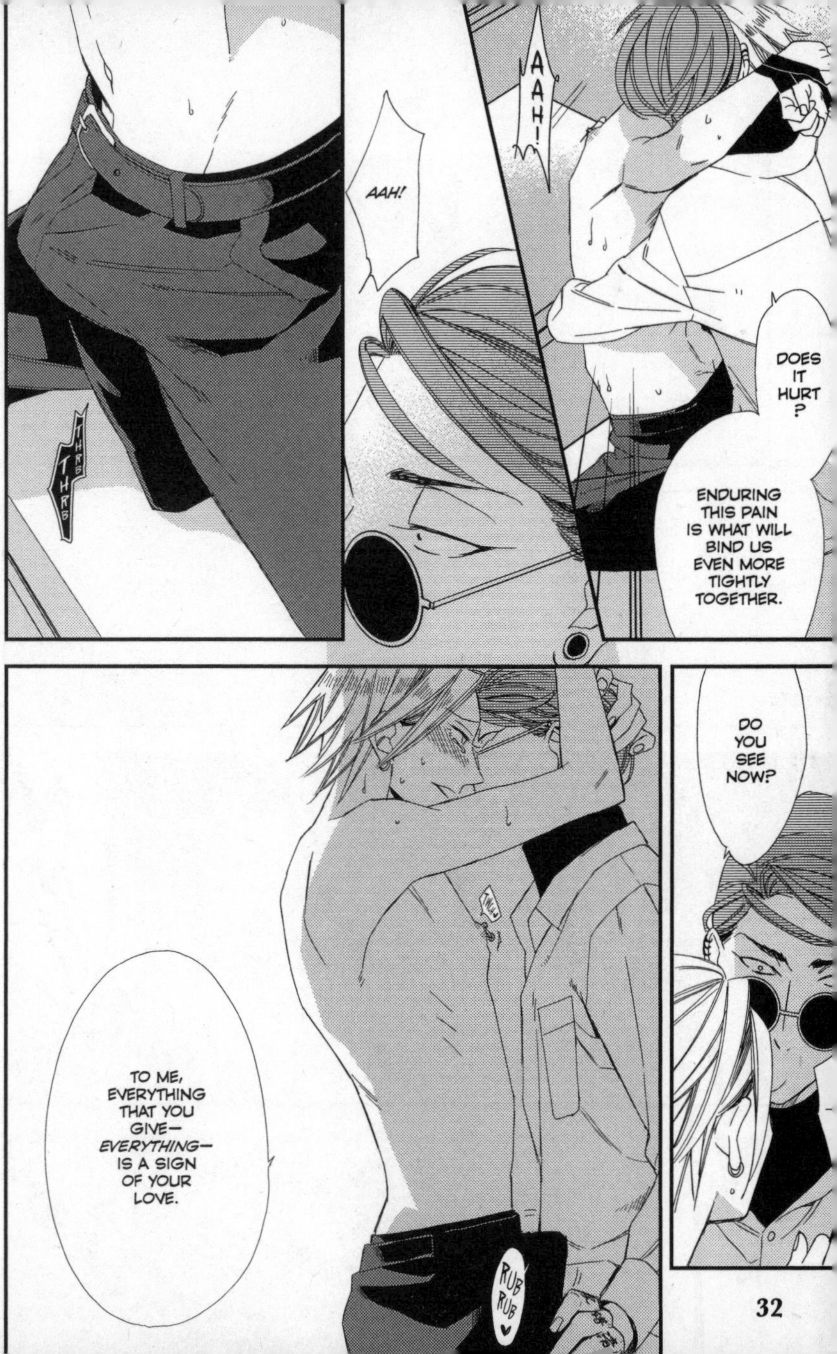
AAH!
DOES IT HURT?
ENDURING THIS PAIN IS WHAT WILL BIND US EVEN MORE TIGHTLY TOGETHER.
AAH!
THRB THRB
DO YOU SEE NOW?
TO ME, EVERYTHING THAT YOU GIVE— *EVERYTHING*— IS A SIGN OF YOUR LOVE.
RUB RUB

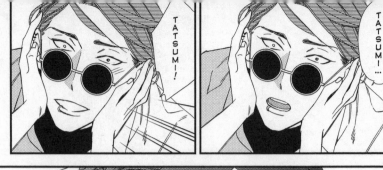

TATSUMI!

TATSUMI...

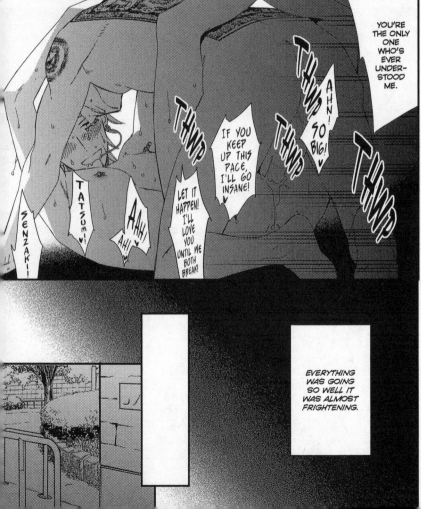

YOU'RE THE ONLY ONE WHO'S EVER UNDERSTOOD ME.

THWP

AHN! SO BIG!

THWP

IF YOU KEEP UP THIS PACE, I'LL GO INSANE!

THWP

THWP

LET IT HAPPEN! I'LL LOVE YOU UNTIL WE BOTH BREAK!

TATSUMI!

AAH! AH!

SENZAKI!

EVERYTHING WAS GOING SO WELL IT WAS ALMOST FRIGHTENING.

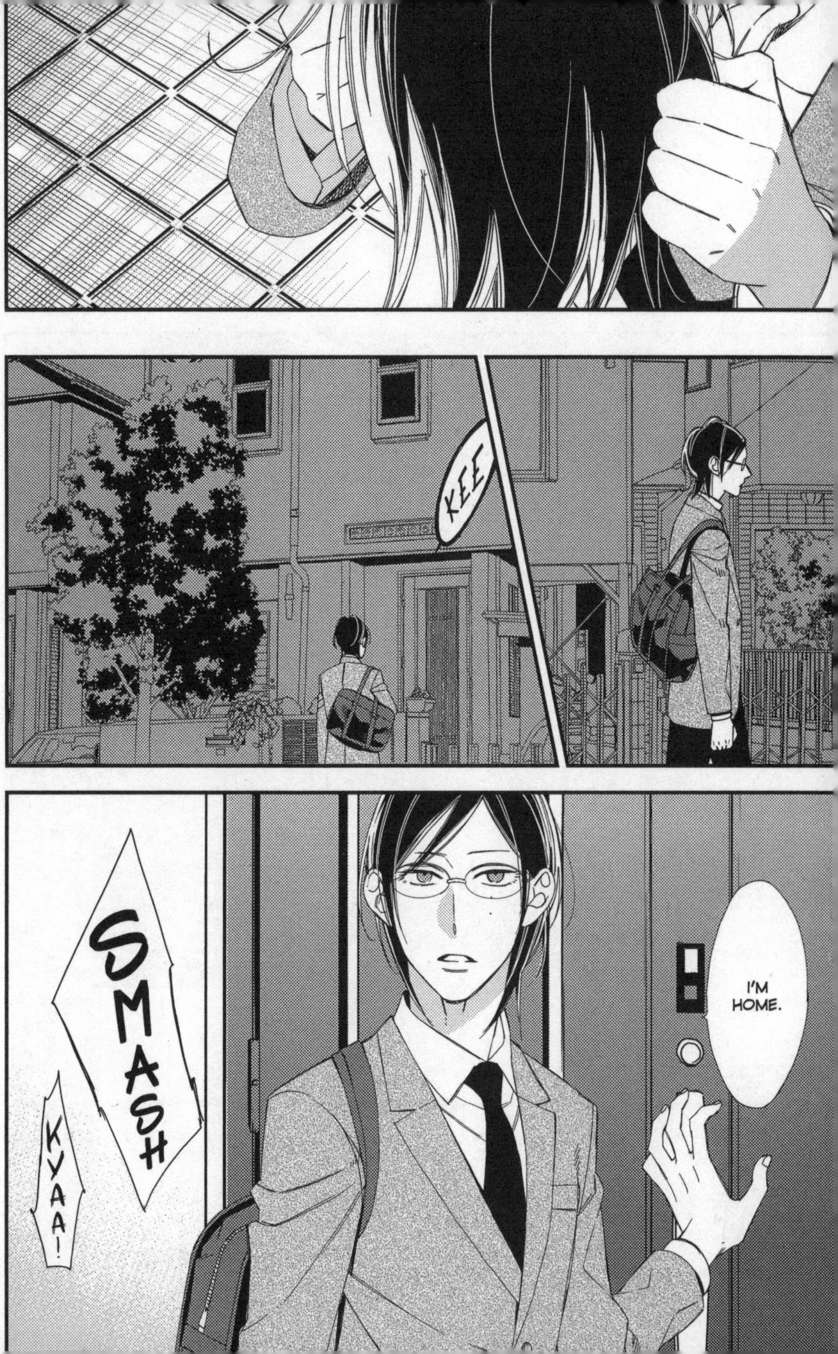
KEE
I'M HOME.
SMASH
KYAAA!

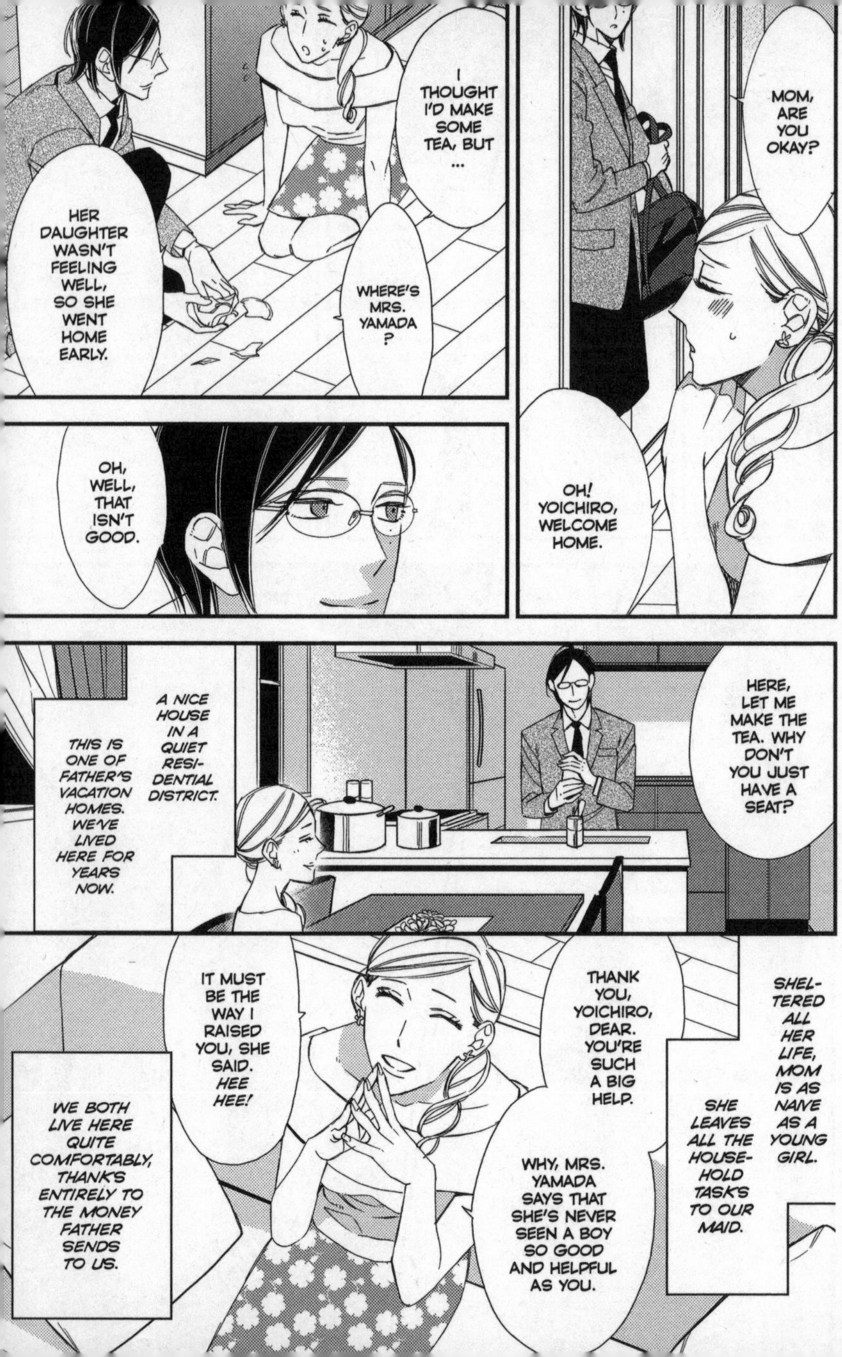
MOM, ARE YOU OKAY?
OH! YOICHIRO, WELCOME HOME.
I THOUGHT I'D MAKE SOME TEA, BUT ...
WHERE'S MRS. YAMADA?
HER DAUGHTER WASN'T FEELING WELL, SO SHE WENT HOME EARLY.
OH, WELL, THAT ISN'T GOOD.
HERE, LET ME MAKE THE TEA. WHY DON'T YOU JUST HAVE A SEAT?
A NICE HOUSE IN A QUIET RESIDENTIAL DISTRICT.
THIS IS ONE OF FATHER'S VACATION HOMES. WE'VE LIVED HERE FOR YEARS NOW.
SHELTERED ALL HER LIFE, MOM IS AS NAIVE AS A YOUNG GIRL.
SHE LEAVES ALL THE HOUSEHOLD TASKS TO OUR MAID.
THANK YOU, YOICHIRO, DEAR. YOU'RE SUCH A BIG HELP.
WHY, MRS. YAMADA SAYS THAT SHE'S NEVER SEEN A BOY SO GOOD AND HELPFUL AS YOU.
IT MUST BE THE WAY I RAISED YOU, SHE SAID. HEE HEE!
WE BOTH LIVE HERE QUITE COMFORTABLY, THANKS ENTIRELY TO THE MONEY FATHER SENDS TO US.

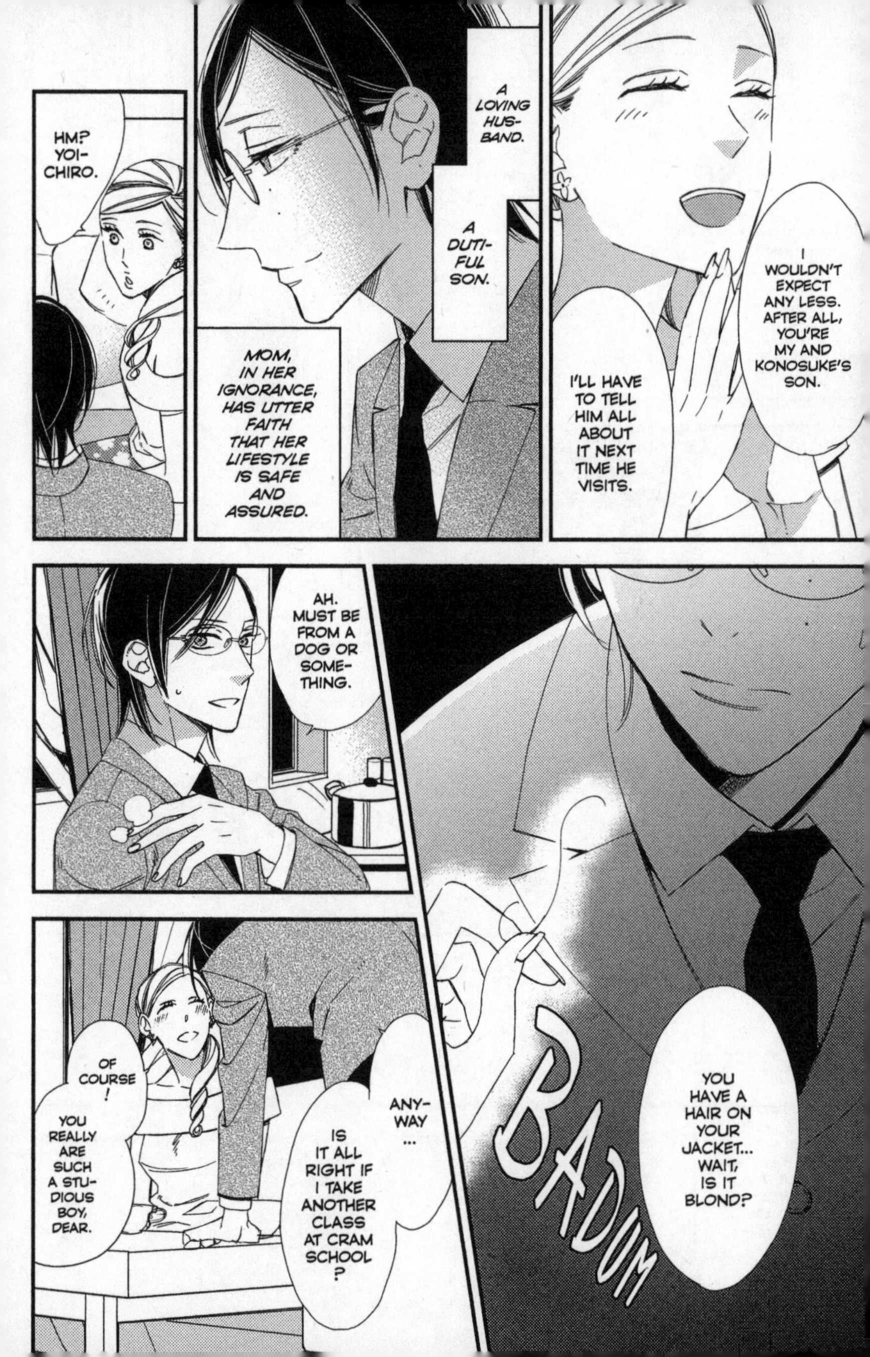
I WOULDN'T EXPECT ANY LESS. AFTER ALL, YOU'RE MY AND KONOSUKE'S SON.
I'LL HAVE TO TELL HIM ALL ABOUT IT NEXT TIME HE VISITS.
A LOVING HUSBAND.
A DUTIFUL SON.
MOM, IN HER IGNORANCE, HAS UTTER FAITH THAT HER LIFESTYLE IS SAFE AND ASSURED.
HM? YOICHIRO.
BADUM
YOU HAVE A HAIR ON YOUR JACKET... WAIT, IS IT BLOND?
AH. MUST BE FROM A DOG OR SOMETHING.
ANYWAY...
IS IT ALL RIGHT IF I TAKE ANOTHER CLASS AT CRAM SCHOOL?
OF COURSE!
YOU REALLY ARE SUCH A STUDIOUS BOY, DEAR.

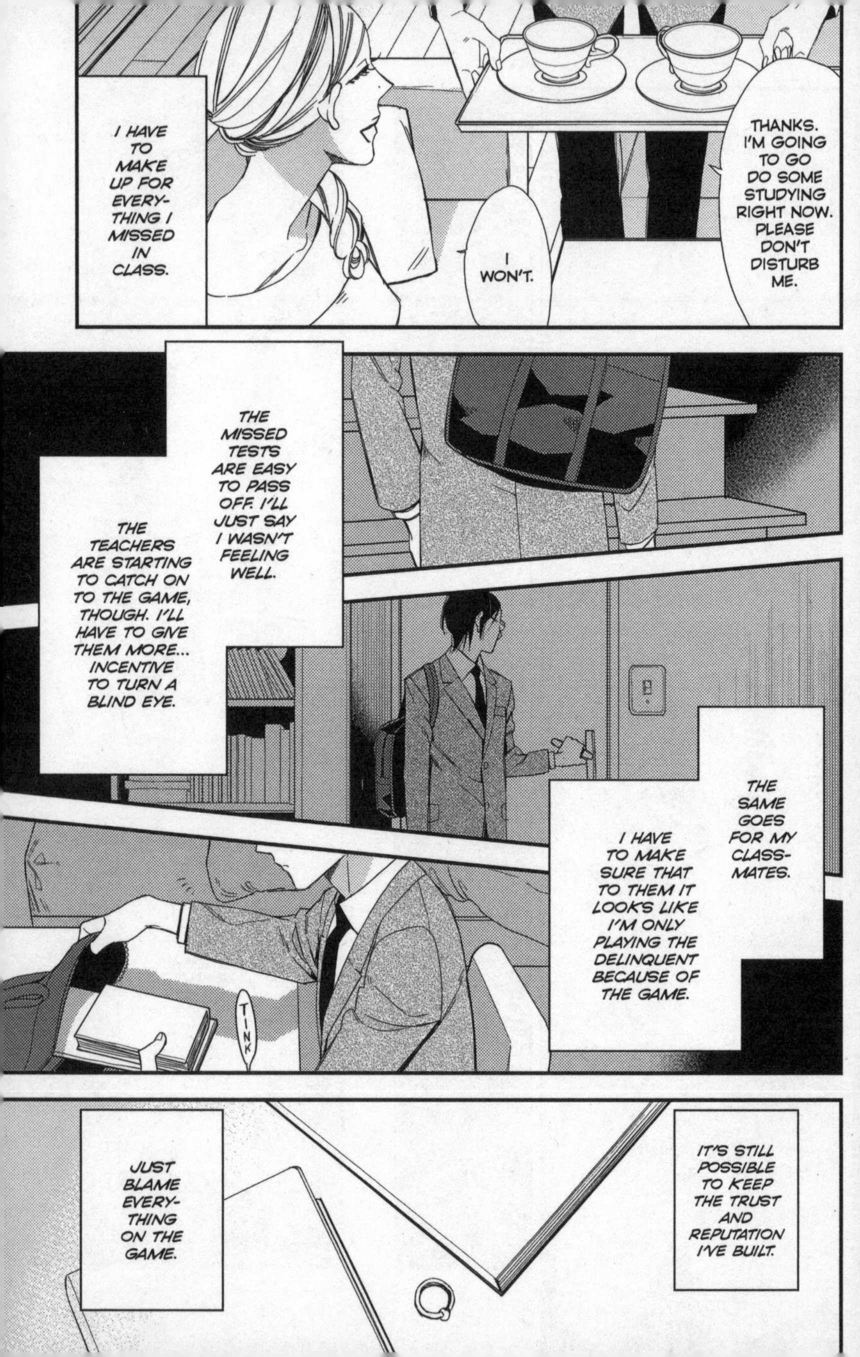
THANKS. I'M GOING TO GO DO SOME STUDYING RIGHT NOW. PLEASE DON'T DISTURB ME.
I WON'T.
I HAVE TO MAKE UP FOR EVERYTHING I MISSED IN CLASS.
THE MISSED TESTS ARE EASY TO PASS OFF. I'LL JUST SAY I WASN'T FEELING WELL.
THE TEACHERS ARE STARTING TO CATCH ON TO THE GAME, THOUGH. I'LL HAVE TO GIVE THEM MORE... INCENTIVE TO TURN A BLIND EYE.
THE SAME GOES FOR MY CLASSMATES.
I HAVE TO MAKE SURE THAT TO THEM IT LOOKS LIKE I'M ONLY PLAYING THE DELINQUENT BECAUSE OF THE GAME.
TINK
IT'S STILL POSSIBLE TO KEEP THE TRUST AND REPUTATION I'VE BUILT.
JUST BLAME EVERYTHING ON THE GAME.

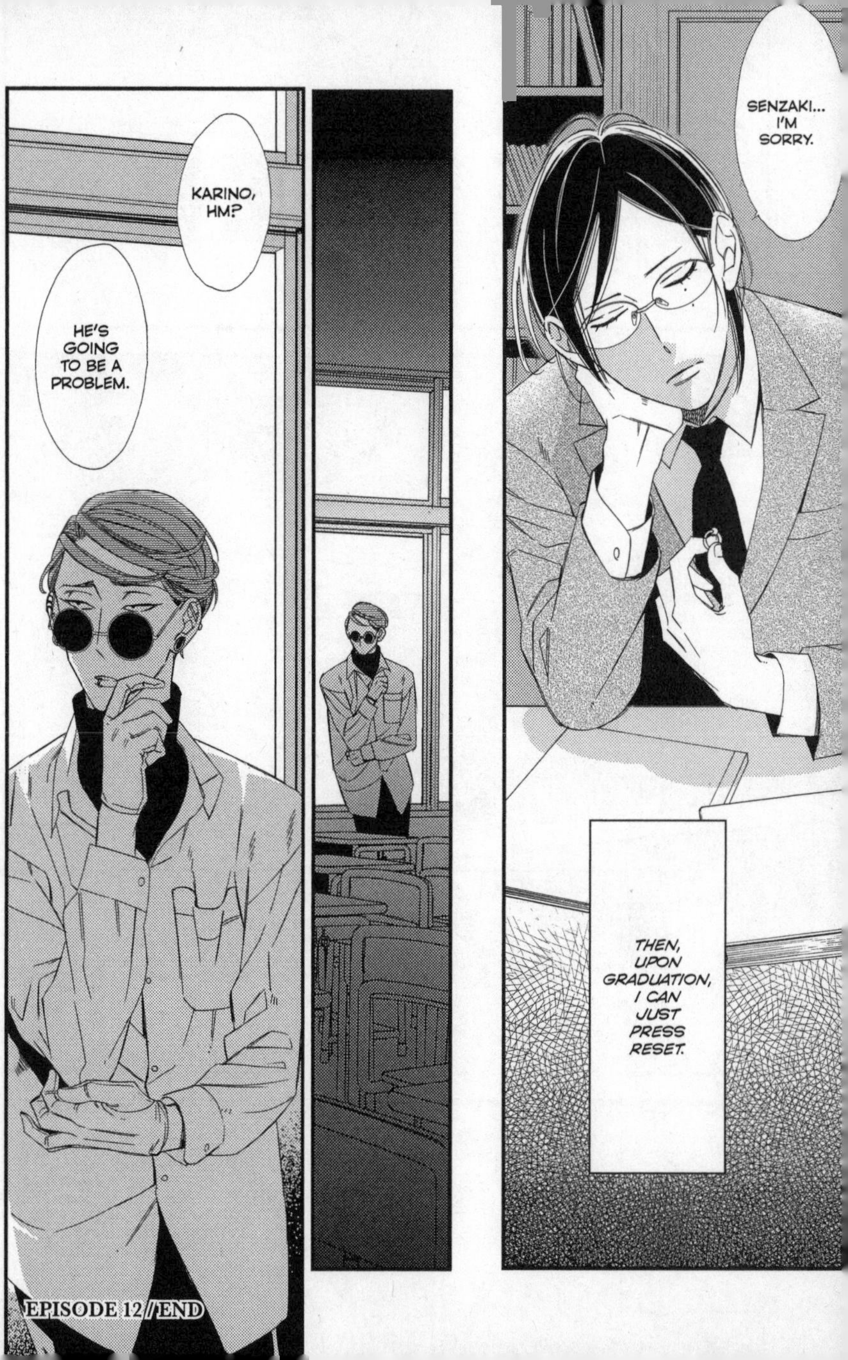
SENZAKI... I'M SORRY.
THEN, UPON GRADUATION, I CAN JUST PRESS RESET.
KARINO, HM?
HE'S GOING TO BE A PROBLEM.
EPISODE 12 // END

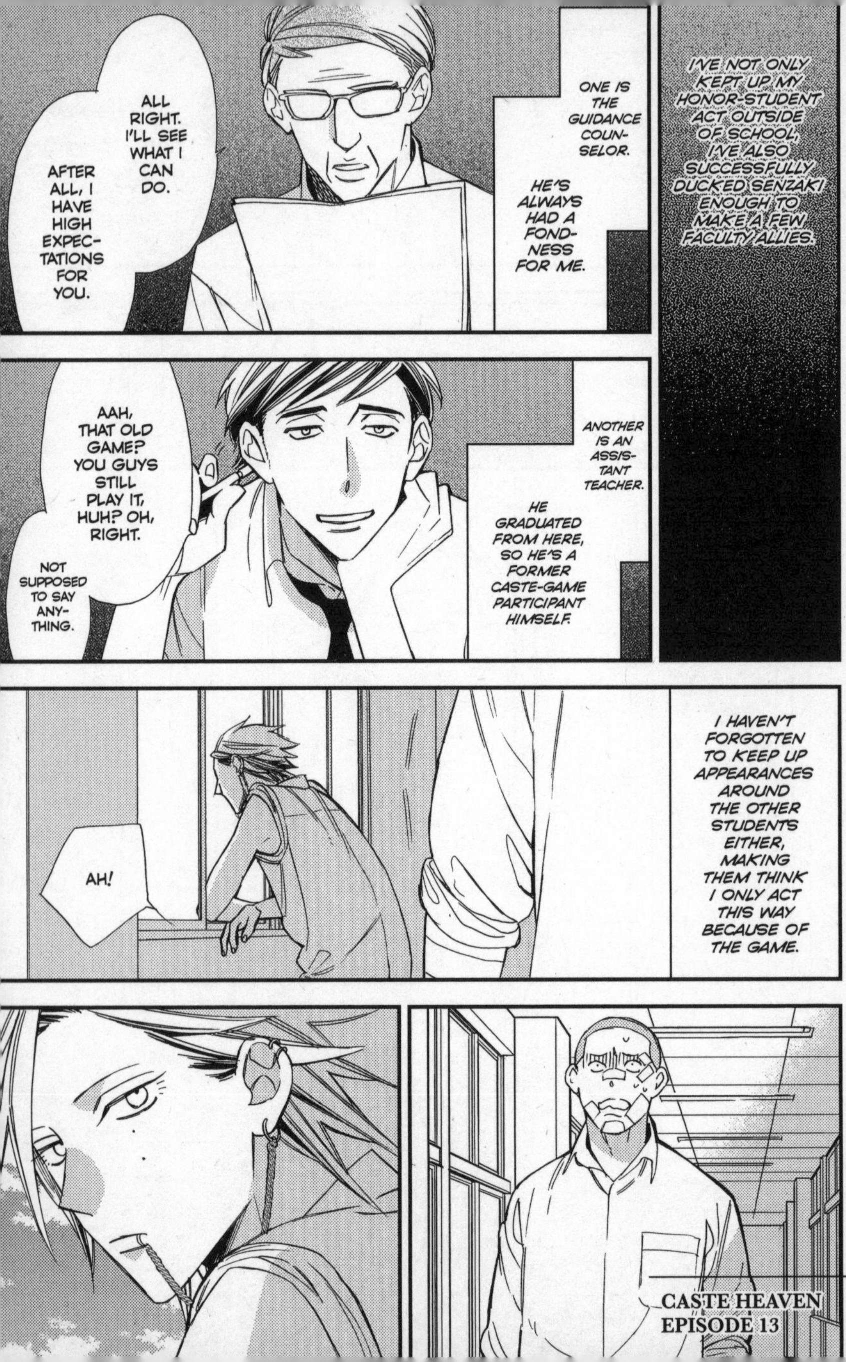
I'VE NOT ONLY KEPT UP MY HONOR-STUDENT ACT OUTSIDE OF SCHOOL, I'VE ALSO SUCCESSFULLY DUCKED SENZAKI ENOUGH TO MAKE A FEW FACULTY ALLIES.
ONE IS THE GUIDANCE COUNSELOR.
HE'S ALWAYS HAD A FONDNESS FOR ME.
ALL RIGHT. I'LL SEE WHAT I CAN DO.
AFTER ALL, I HAVE HIGH EXPECTATIONS FOR YOU.
ANOTHER IS AN ASSISTANT TEACHER.
HE GRADUATED FROM HERE, SO HE'S A FORMER CASTE-GAME PARTICIPANT HIMSELF.
AAH, THAT OLD GAME? YOU GUYS STILL PLAY IT, HUH? OH, RIGHT.
NOT SUPPOSED TO SAY ANYTHING.
I HAVEN'T FORGOTTEN TO KEEP UP APPEARANCES AROUND THE OTHER STUDENTS EITHER, MAKING THEM THINK I ONLY ACT THIS WAY BECAUSE OF THE GAME.
AH!

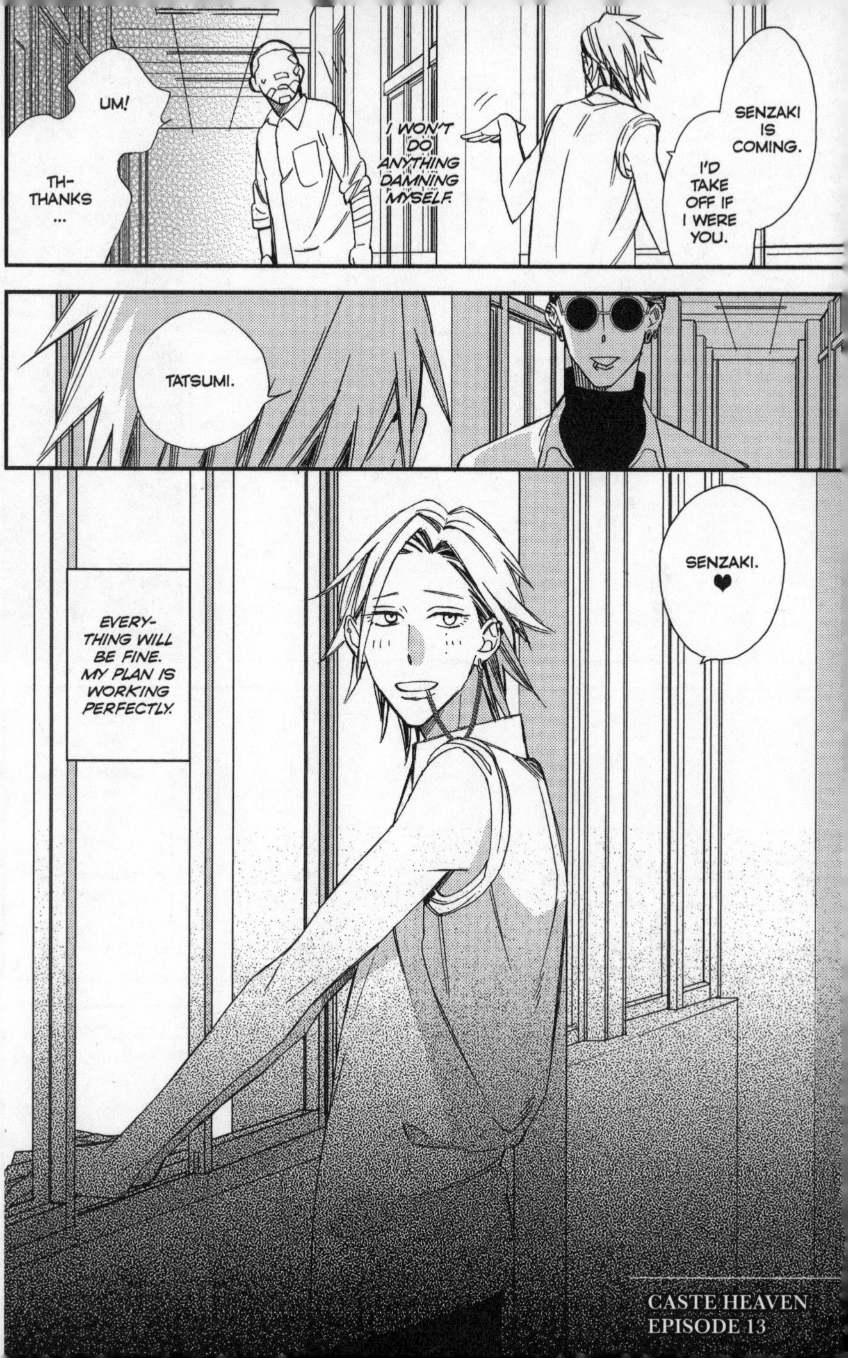
SENZAKI IS COMING.
I'D TAKE OFF IF I WERE YOU.
I WON'T DO ANYTHING DAMNING MYSELF.
UM!
TH-THANKS...
TATSUMI.
SENZAKI. ❤
EVERYTHING WILL BE FINE. MY PLAN IS WORKING PERFECTLY.
CASTE HEAVEN EPISODE 13

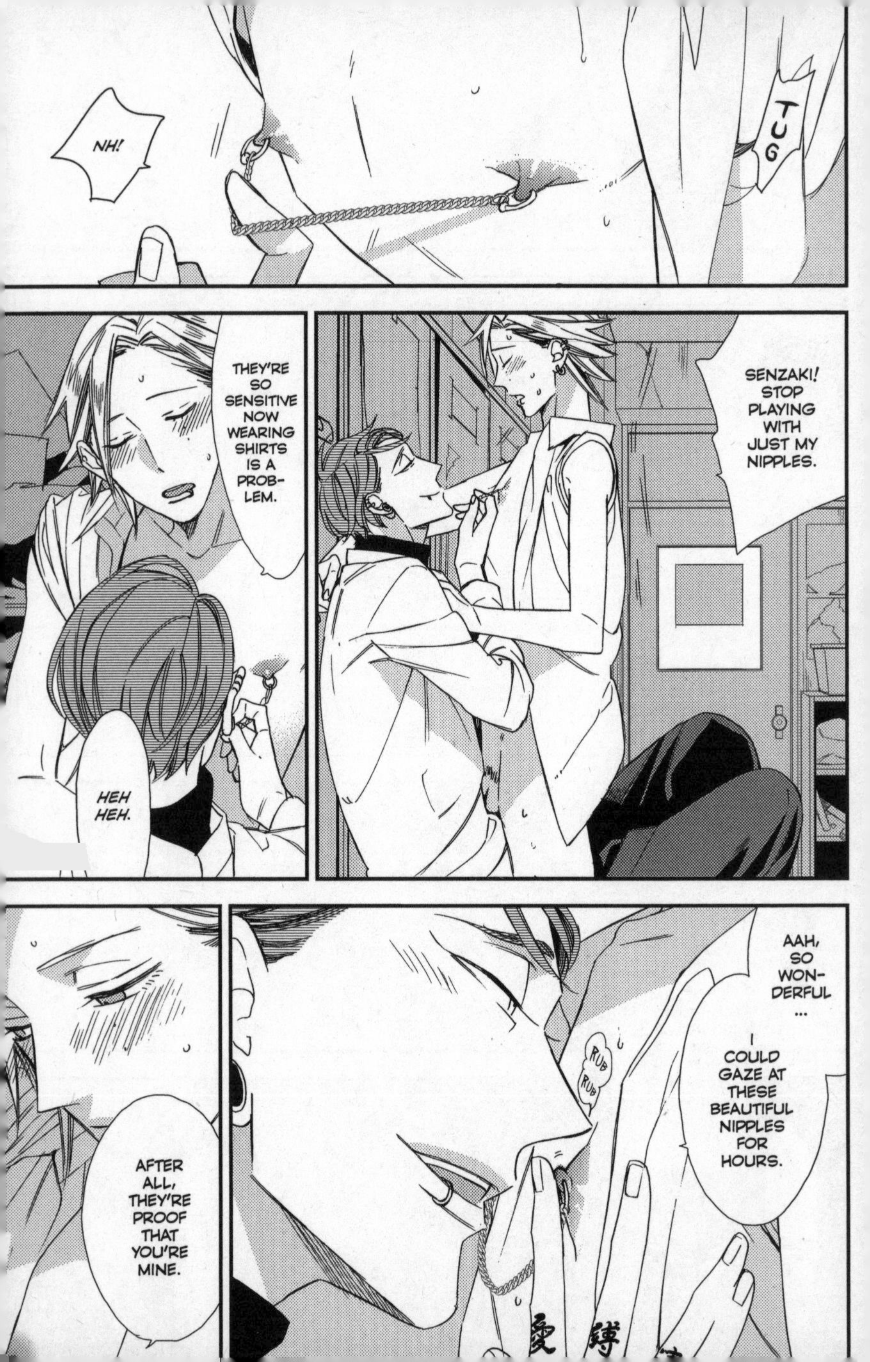
TUG
NH!
SENZAKI! STOP PLAYING WITH JUST MY NIPPLES.
THEY'RE SO SENSITIVE NOW WEARING SHIRTS IS A PROB-LEM.
HEH HEH.
AAH, SO WON-DERFUL ...
I COULD GAZE AT THESE BEAUTIFUL NIPPLES FOR HOURS.
RUB RUB
AFTER ALL, THEY'RE PROOF THAT YOU'RE MINE.

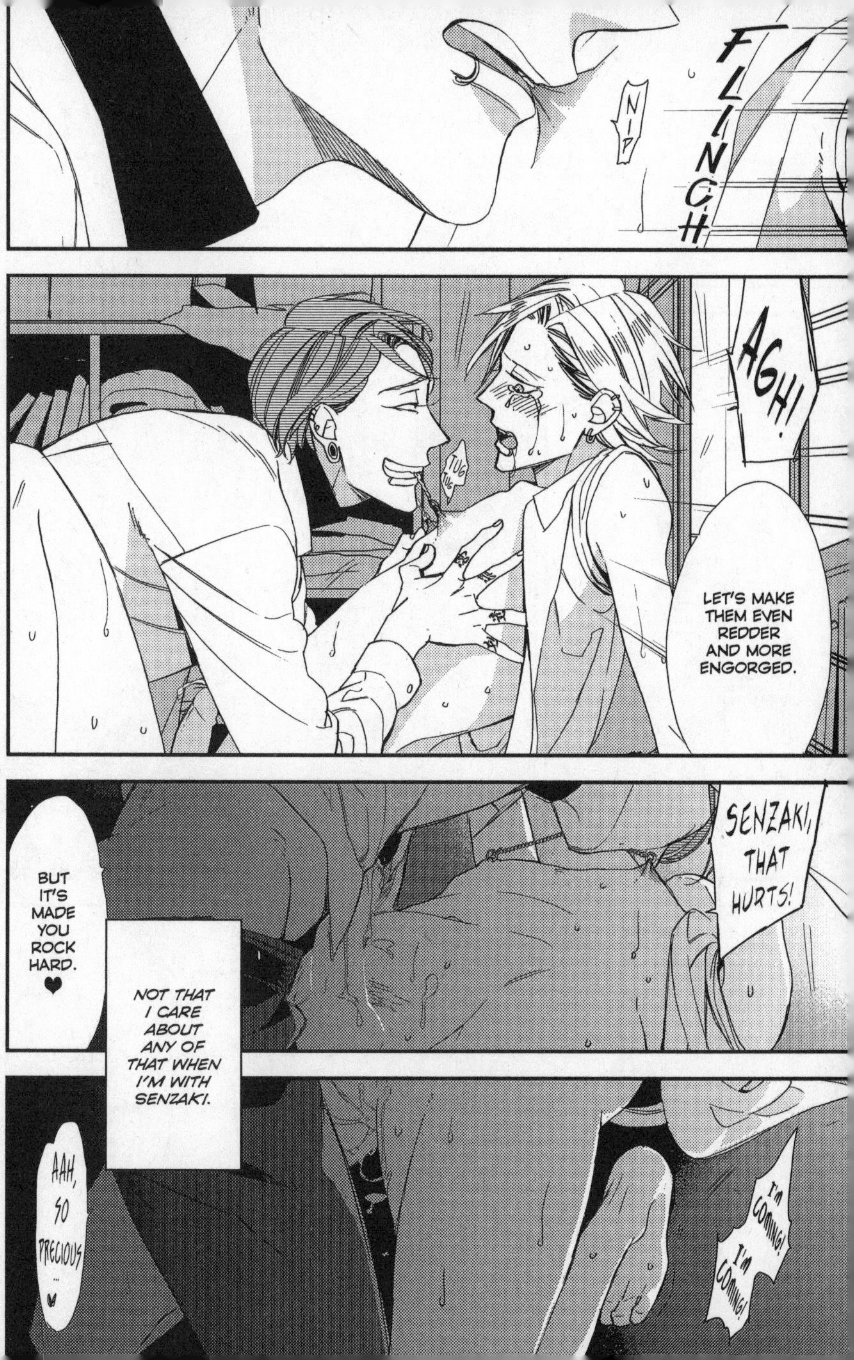
FLINCH
NIP
AGH!
LET'S MAKE THEM EVEN REDDER AND MORE ENGORGED.
TUG TUG
SENZAKI, THAT HURTS!
BUT IT'S MADE YOU ROCK HARD. ♥
NOT THAT I CARE ABOUT ANY OF THAT WHEN I'M WITH SENZAKI.
I'm COMING! I'm COMING!
AAH, SO PRECIOUS... ♥

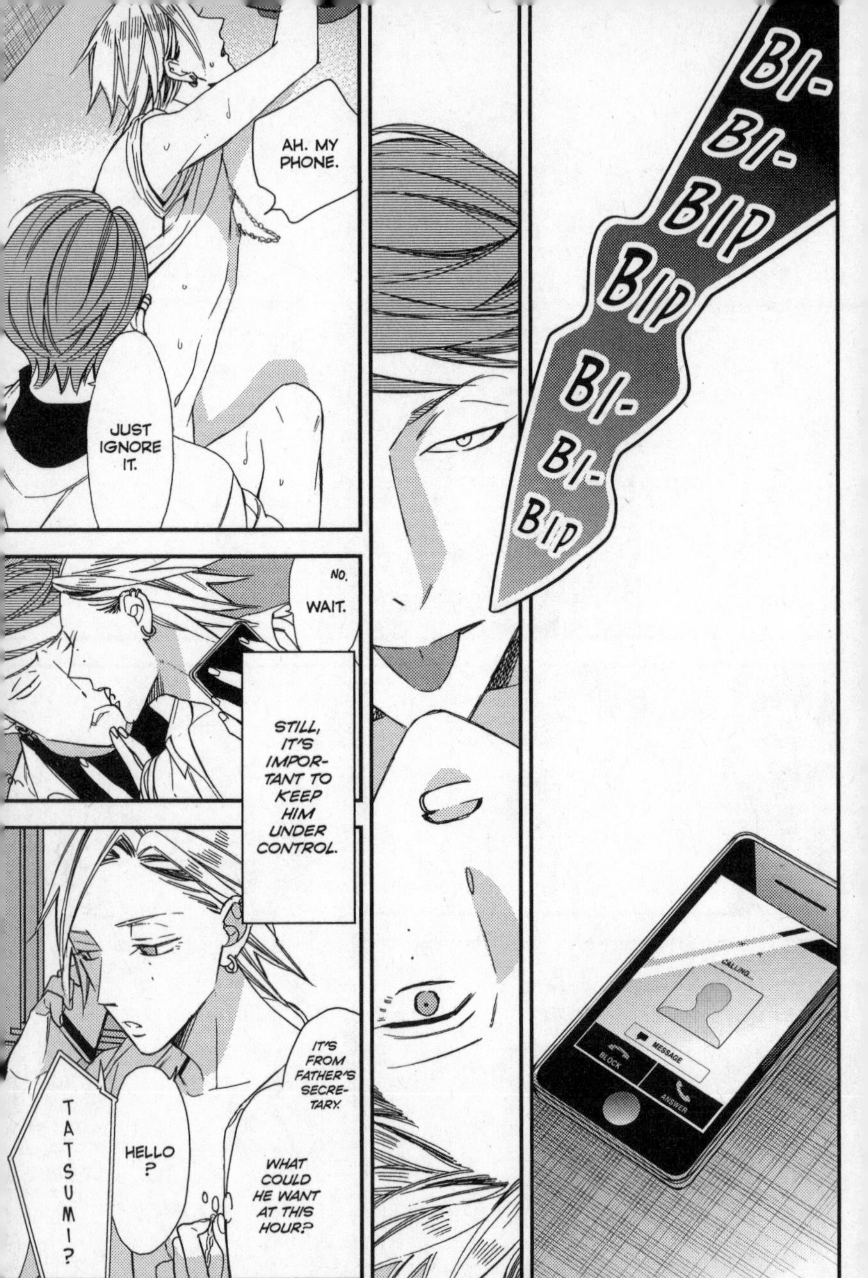
BI-BI-BIP
BIP
BI-BI-BIP
CALLING...
MESSAGE
BLOCK
ANSWER
AH. MY PHONE.
JUST IGNORE IT.
NO.
WAIT.
STILL, IT'S IMPORTANT TO KEEP HIM UNDER CONTROL.
IT'S FROM FATHER'S SECRETARY.
WHAT COULD HE WANT AT THIS HOUR?
HELLO?
TATSUMI?

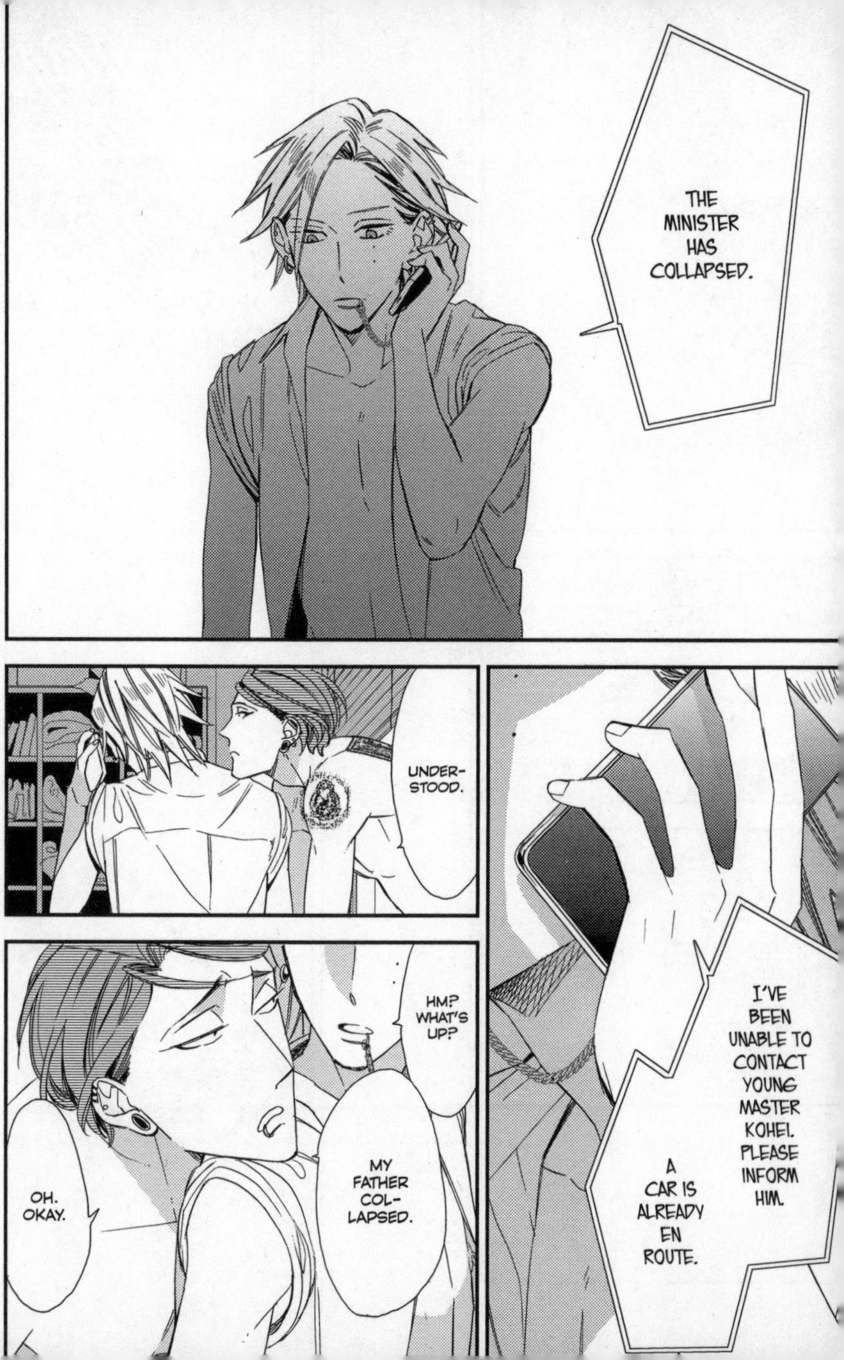
THE MINISTER HAS COLLAPSED.
I'VE BEEN UNABLE TO CONTACT YOUNG MASTER KOHEI. PLEASE INFORM HIM.
A CAR IS ALREADY EN ROUTE.
UNDER-STOOD.
HM? WHAT'S UP?
MY FATHER COL-LAPSED.
OH. OKAY.

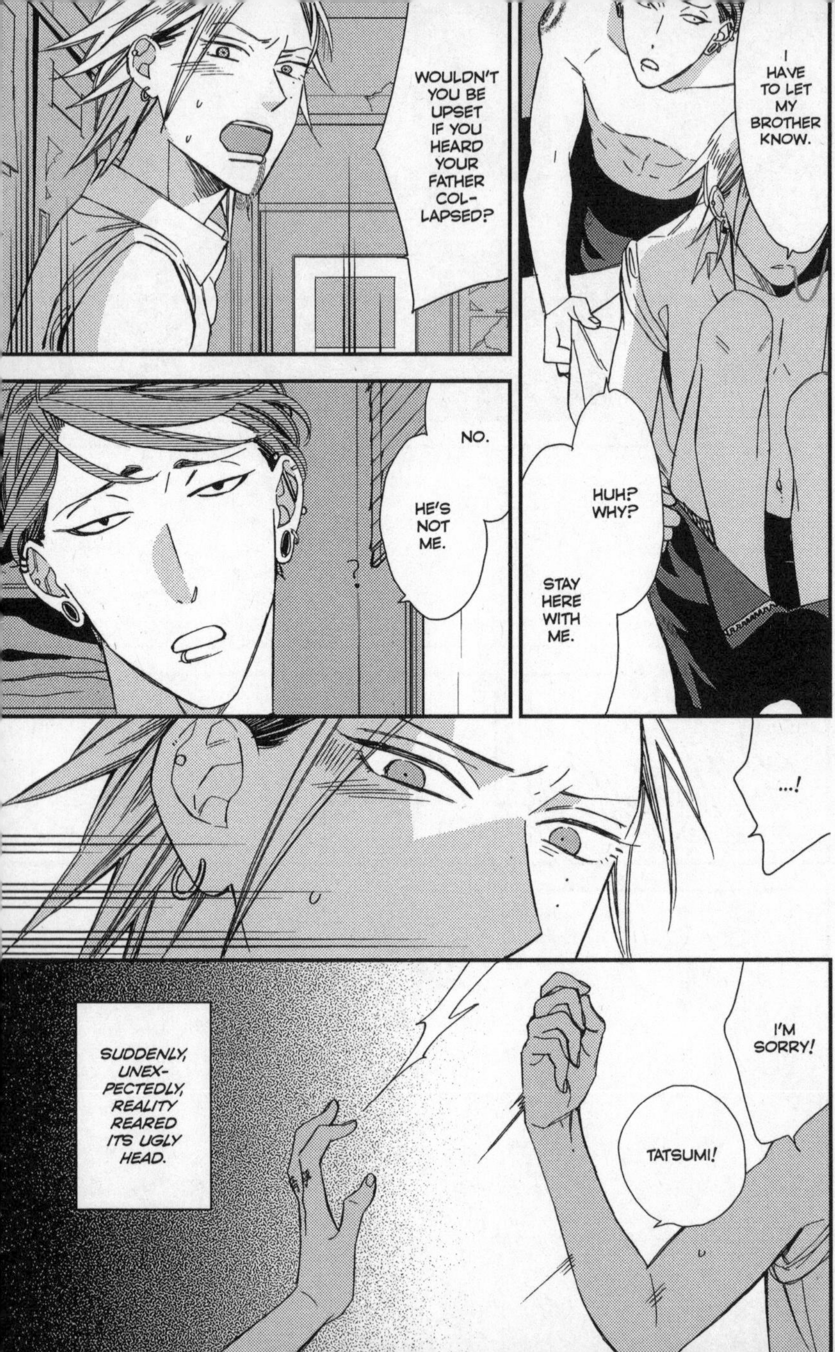
I HAVE TO LET MY BROTHER KNOW.
HUH? WHY?
STAY HERE WITH ME.
WOULDN'T YOU BE UPSET IF YOU HEARD YOUR FATHER COL-LAPSED?
NO.
HE'S NOT ME.
...!
I'M SORRY!
TATSUMI!
SUDDENLY, UNEX-PECTEDLY, REALITY REARED ITS UGLY HEAD.

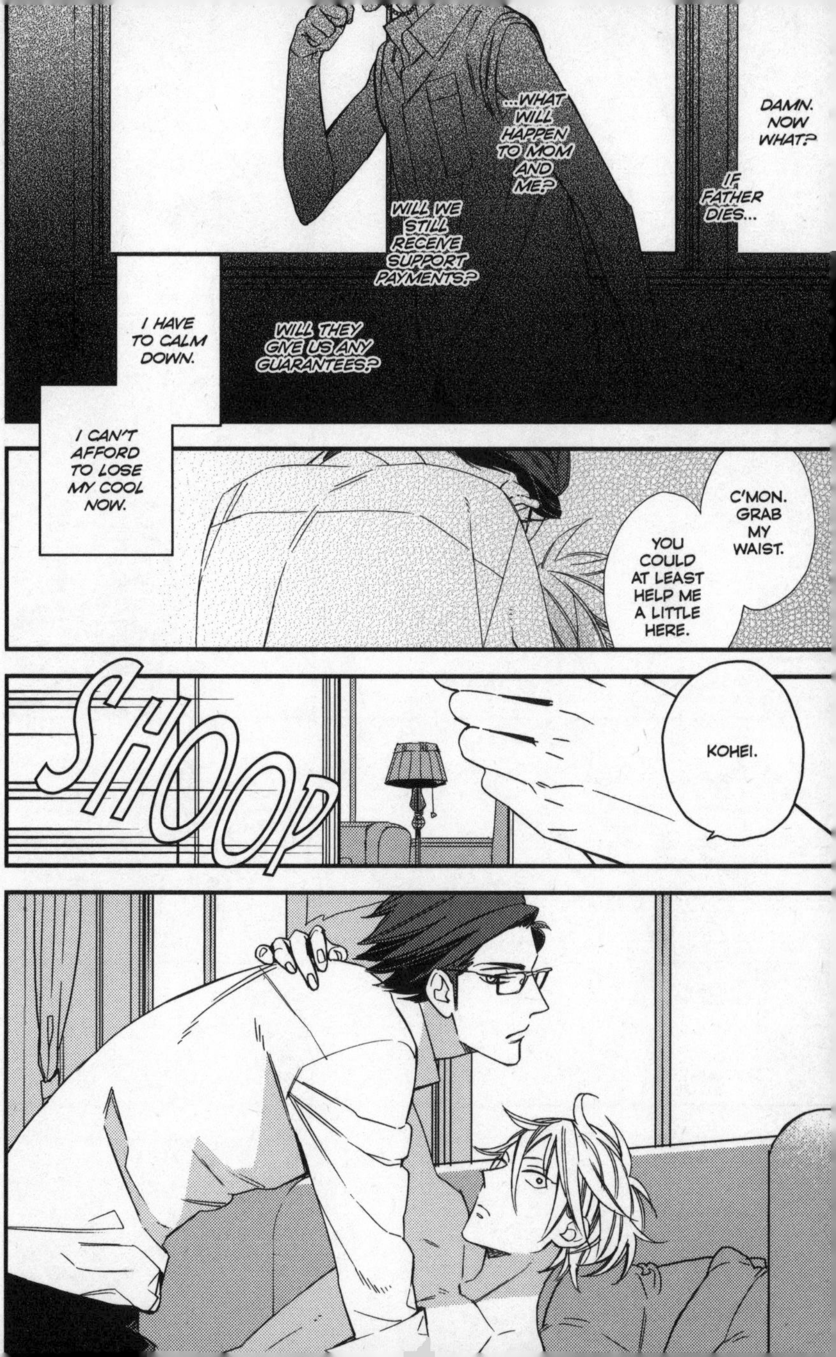
DAMN. NOW WHAT?
IF FATHER DIES...
...WHAT WILL HAPPEN TO MOM AND ME?
WILL WE STILL RECEIVE SUPPORT PAYMENTS?
WILL THEY GIVE US ANY GUARANTEES?
I HAVE TO CALM DOWN.
I CAN'T AFFORD TO LOSE MY COOL NOW.
C'MON. GRAB MY WAIST.
YOU COULD AT LEAST HELP ME A LITTLE HERE.
KOHEI.
SHOOP

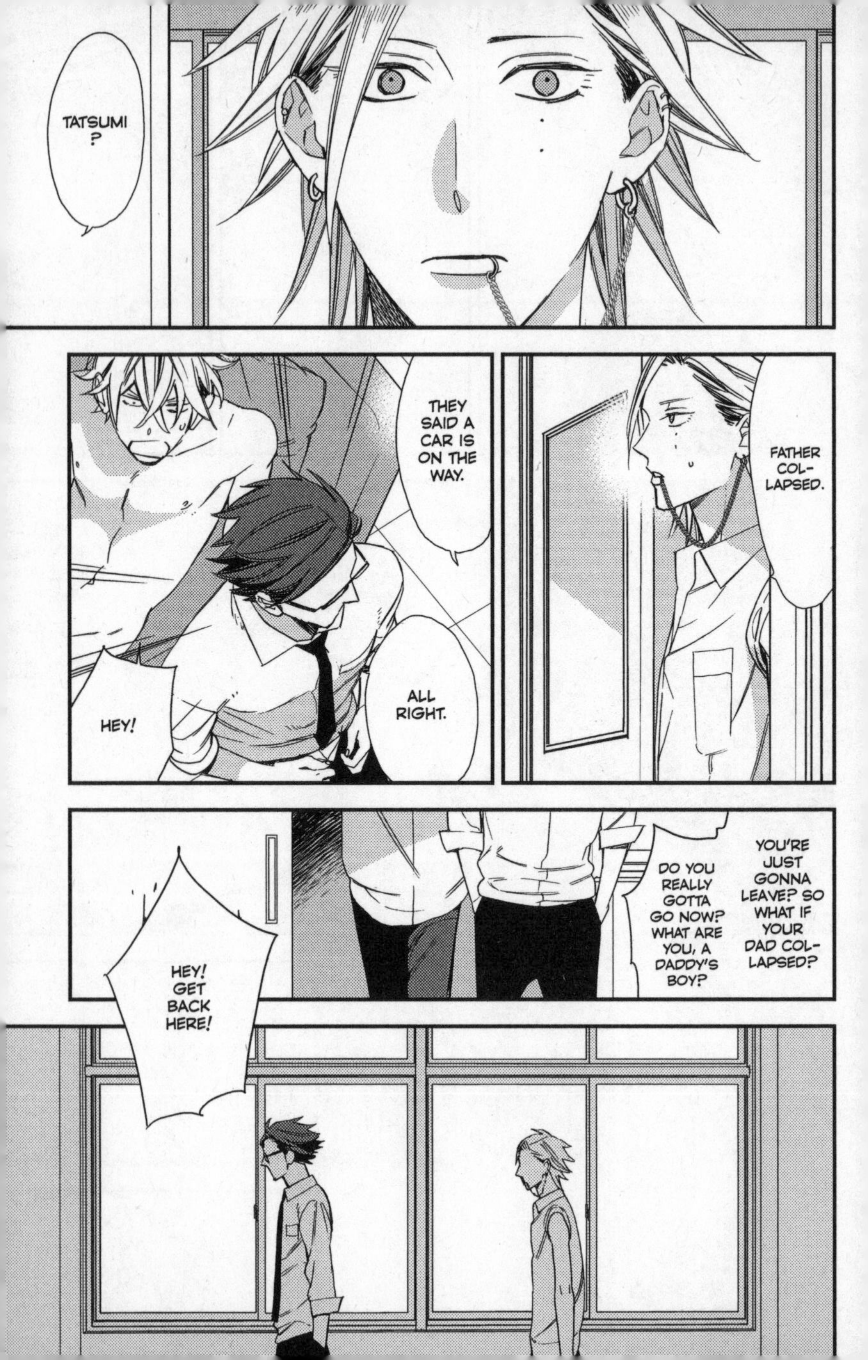
TATSUMI?
FATHER COL-LAPSED.
THEY SAID A CAR IS ON THE WAY.
ALL RIGHT.
HEY!
YOU'RE JUST GONNA LEAVE? SO WHAT IF YOUR DAD COL-LAPSED?
DO YOU REALLY GOTTA GO NOW? WHAT ARE YOU, A DADDY'S BOY?
HEY! GET BACK HERE!

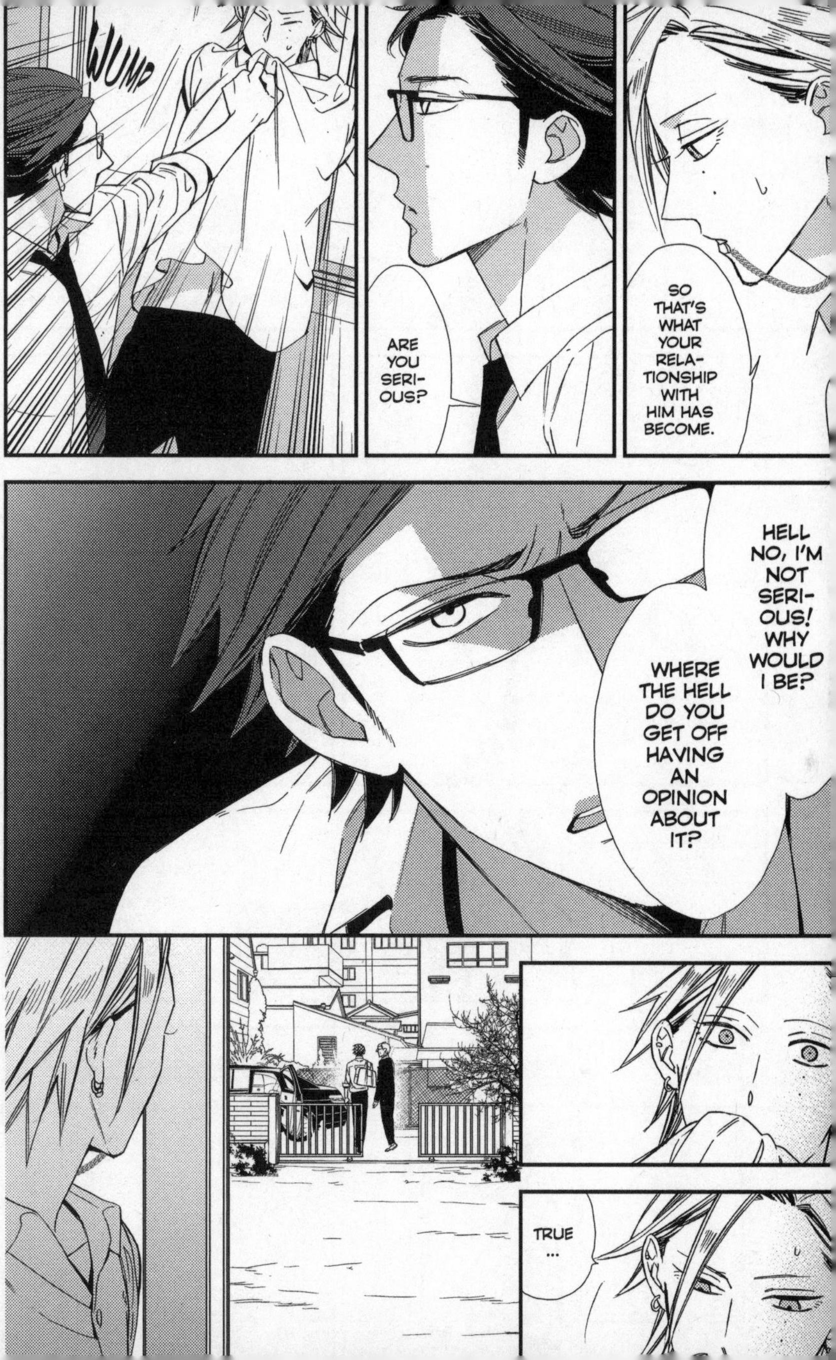
SO THAT'S WHAT YOUR RELA-TIONSHIP WITH HIM HAS BECOME.
ARE YOU SERI-OUS?
WUMP
HELL NO, I'M NOT SERI-OUS! WHY WOULD I BE?
WHERE THE HELL DO YOU GET OFF HAVING AN OPINION ABOUT IT?
TRUE ...

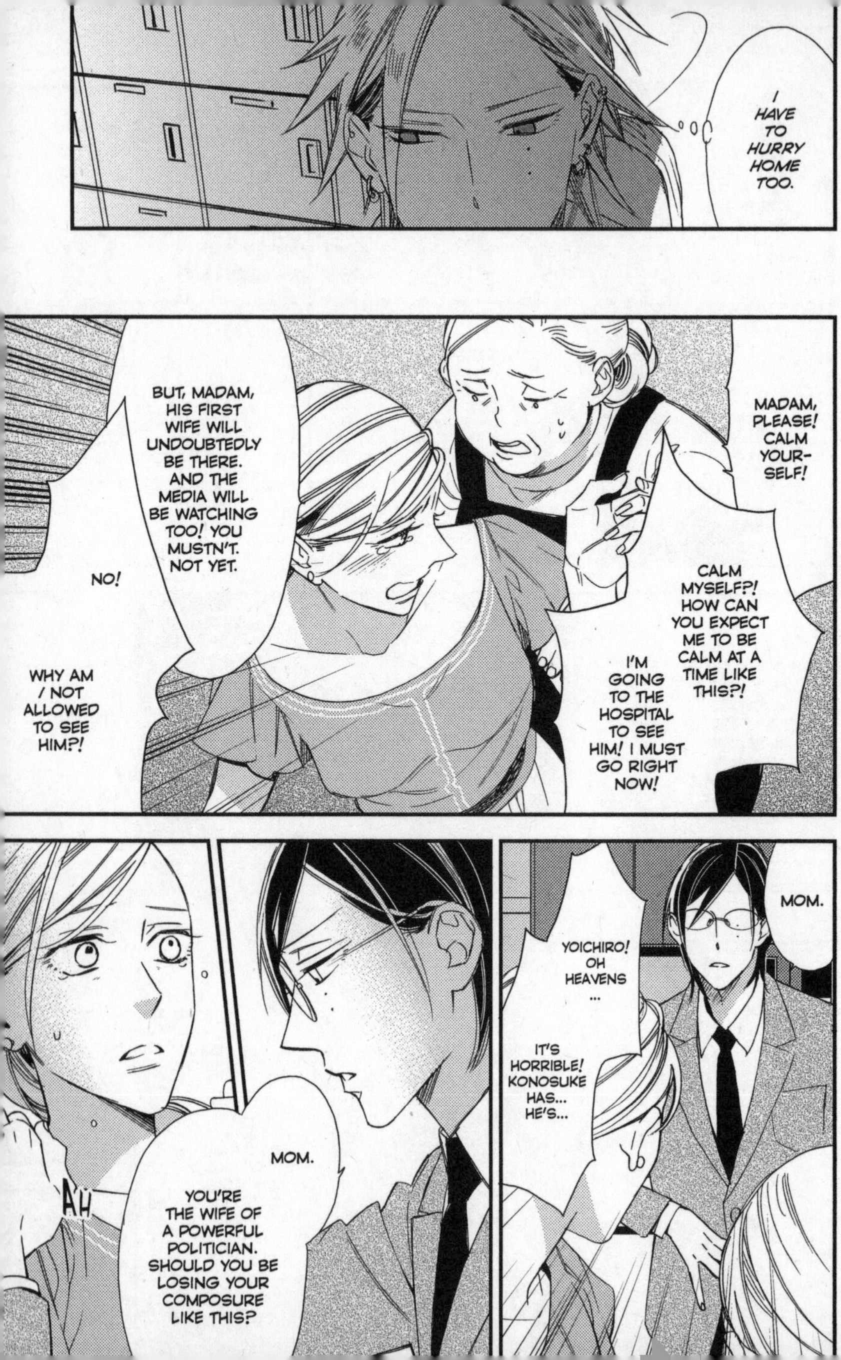
I HAVE TO HURRY HOME TOO.
MADAM, PLEASE! CALM YOUR-SELF!
CALM MYSELF?! HOW CAN YOU EXPECT ME TO BE CALM AT A TIME LIKE THIS?!
I'M GOING TO THE HOSPITAL TO SEE HIM! I MUST GO RIGHT NOW!
BUT, MADAM, HIS FIRST WIFE WILL UNDOUBTEDLY BE THERE. AND THE MEDIA WILL BE WATCHING TOO! YOU MUSTN'T. NOT YET.
NO!
WHY AM I NOT ALLOWED TO SEE HIM?!
MOM.
YOICHIRO! OH HEAVENS ...
IT'S HORRIBLE! KONOSUKE HAS... HE'S...
MOM.
YOU'RE THE WIFE OF A POWERFUL POLITICIAN. SHOULD YOU BE LOSING YOUR COMPOSURE LIKE THIS?
AH

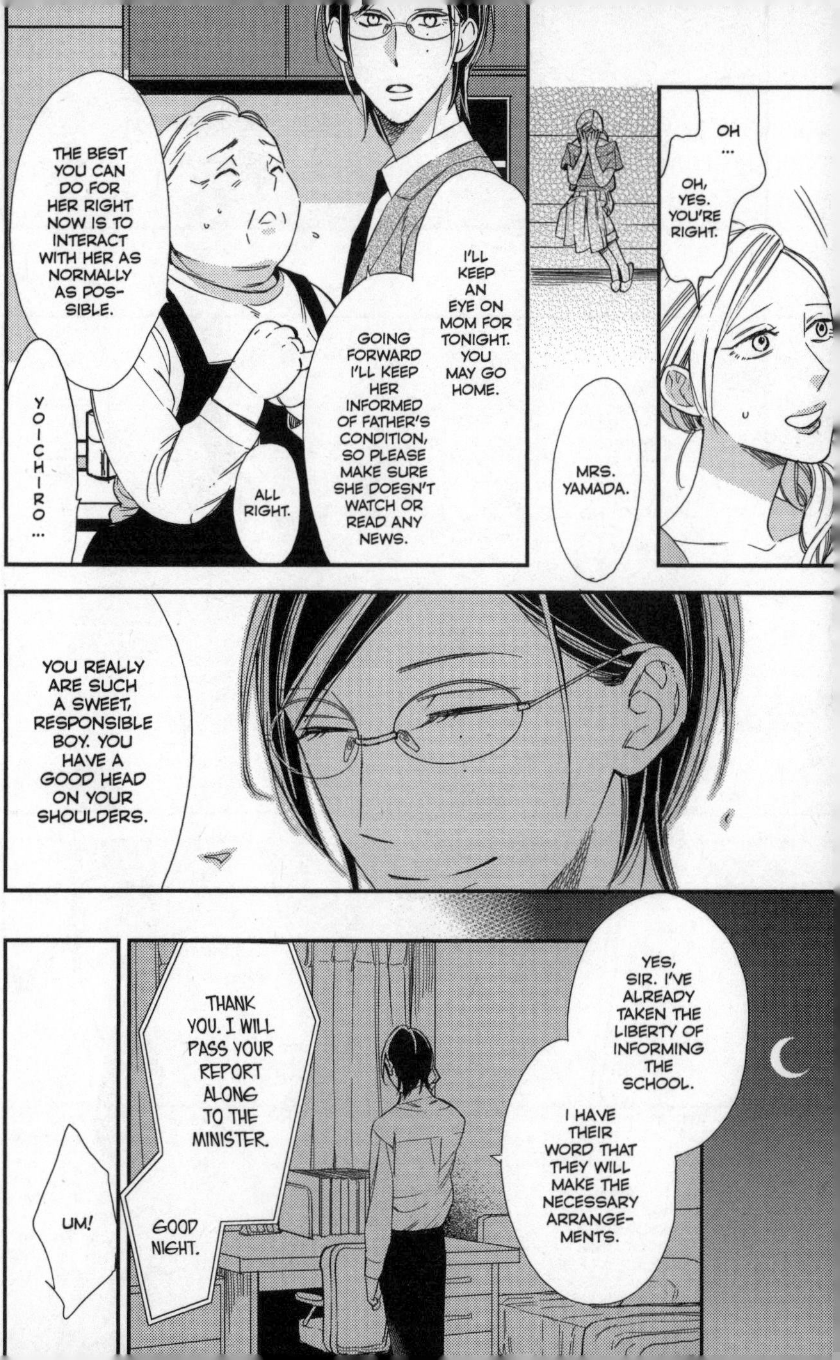
OH ...
OH, YES. YOU'RE RIGHT.
MRS. YAMADA.
I'LL KEEP AN EYE ON MOM FOR TONIGHT. YOU MAY GO HOME.
GOING FORWARD I'LL KEEP HER INFORMED OF FATHER'S CONDITION, SO PLEASE MAKE SURE SHE DOESN'T WATCH OR READ ANY NEWS.
ALL RIGHT.
THE BEST YOU CAN DO FOR HER RIGHT NOW IS TO INTERACT WITH HER AS NORMALLY AS POS-SIBLE.
YOICHIRO ...
YOU REALLY ARE SUCH A SWEET, RESPONSIBLE BOY. YOU HAVE A GOOD HEAD ON YOUR SHOULDERS.
YES, SIR. I'VE ALREADY TAKEN THE LIBERTY OF INFORMING THE SCHOOL.
I HAVE THEIR WORD THAT THEY WILL MAKE THE NECESSARY ARRANGE-MENTS.
THANK YOU. I WILL PASS YOUR REPORT ALONG TO THE MINISTER.
GOOD NIGHT.
UM!

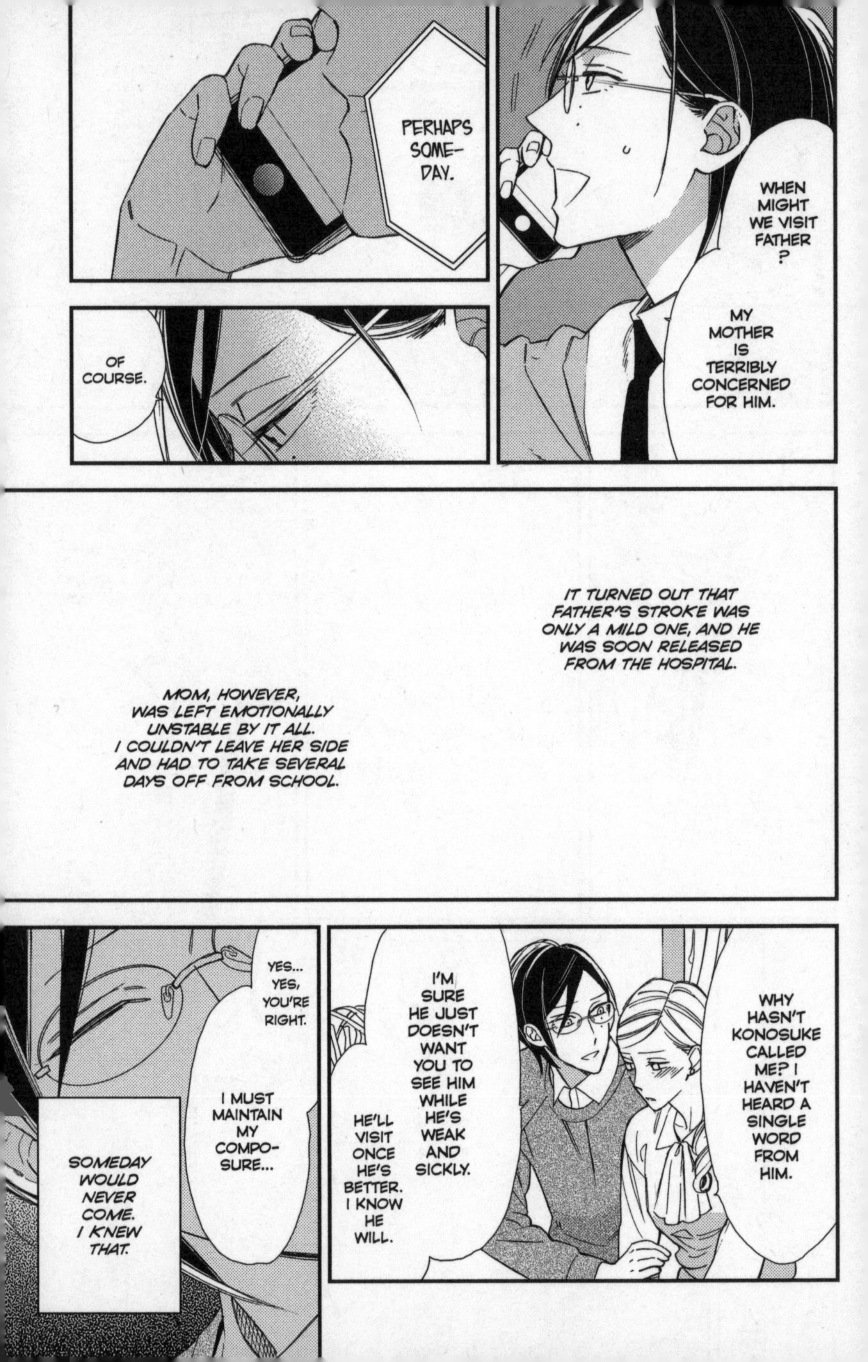
WHEN MIGHT WE VISIT FATHER?
MY MOTHER IS TERRIBLY CONCERNED FOR HIM.
PERHAPS SOME-DAY.
OF COURSE.
IT TURNED OUT THAT FATHER'S STROKE WAS ONLY A MILD ONE, AND HE WAS SOON RELEASED FROM THE HOSPITAL.
MOM, HOWEVER, WAS LEFT EMOTIONALLY UNSTABLE BY IT ALL. I COULDN'T LEAVE HER SIDE AND HAD TO TAKE SEVERAL DAYS OFF FROM SCHOOL.
WHY HASN'T KONOSUKE CALLED ME? I HAVEN'T HEARD A SINGLE WORD FROM HIM.
I'M SURE HE JUST DOESN'T WANT YOU TO SEE HIM WHILE HE'S WEAK AND SICKLY.
HE'LL VISIT ONCE HE'S BETTER. I KNOW HE WILL.
YES... YES, YOU'RE RIGHT.
I MUST MAINTAIN MY COMPO-SURE...
SOMEDAY WOULD NEVER COME. I KNEW THAT.

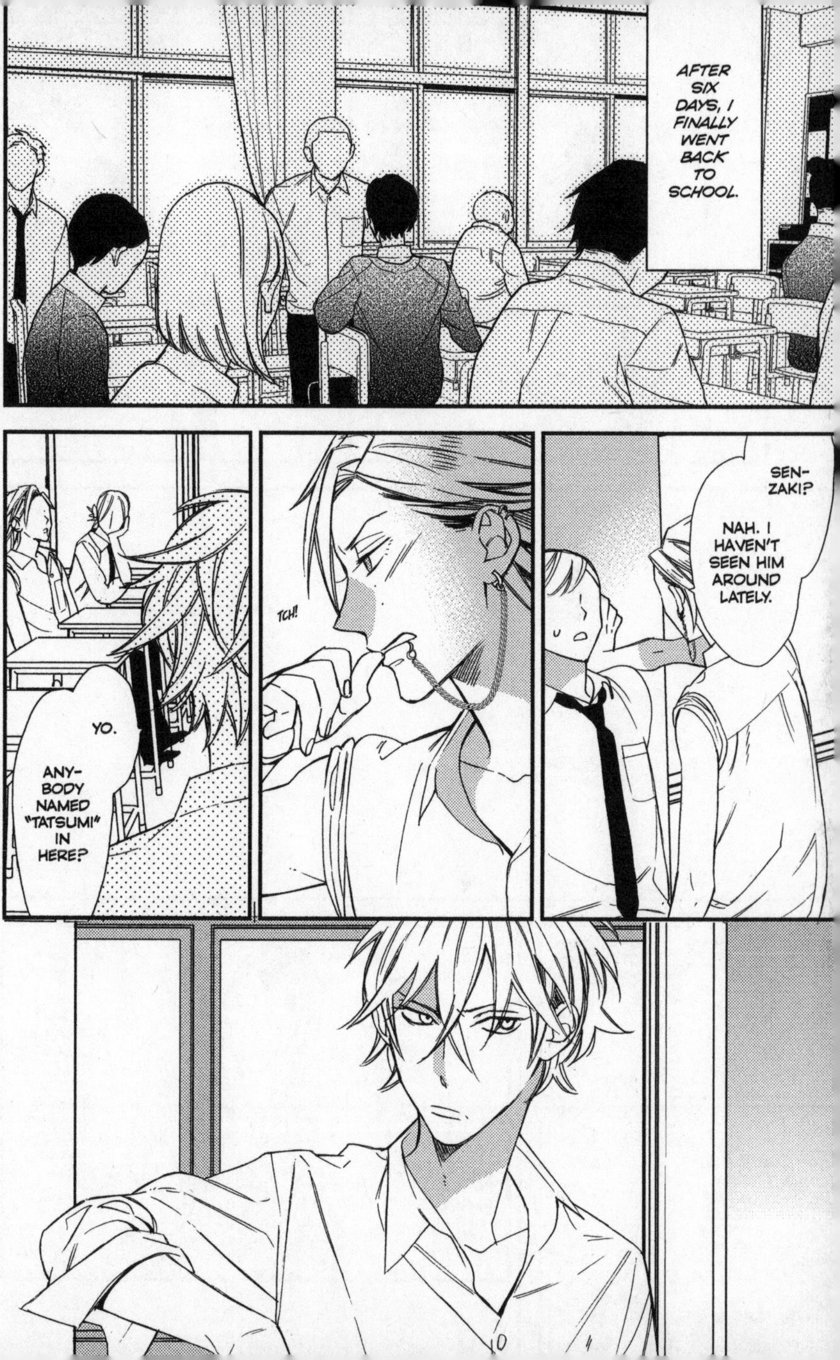
AFTER SIX DAYS, I FINALLY WENT BACK TO SCHOOL.
SEN-ZAKI?
NAH. I HAVEN'T SEEN HIM AROUND LATELY.
TCH!
YO.
ANY-BODY NAMED "TATSUMI" IN HERE?

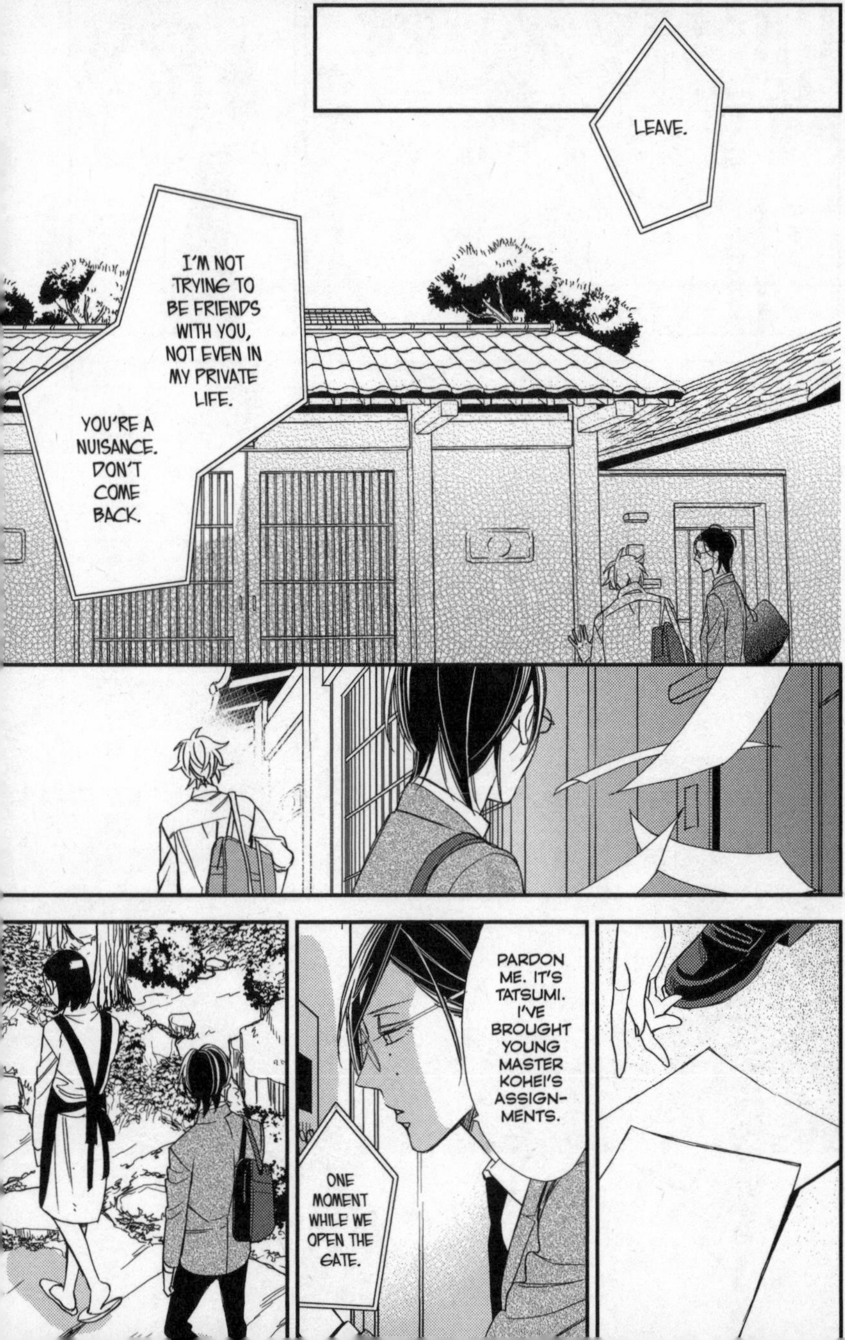
LEAVE.
I'M NOT TRYING TO BE FRIENDS WITH YOU, NOT EVEN IN MY PRIVATE LIFE.
YOU'RE A NUISANCE. DON'T COME BACK.
PARDON ME. IT'S TATSUMI. I'VE BROUGHT YOUNG MASTER KOHEI'S ASSIGNMENTS.
ONE MOMENT WHILE WE OPEN THE GATE.

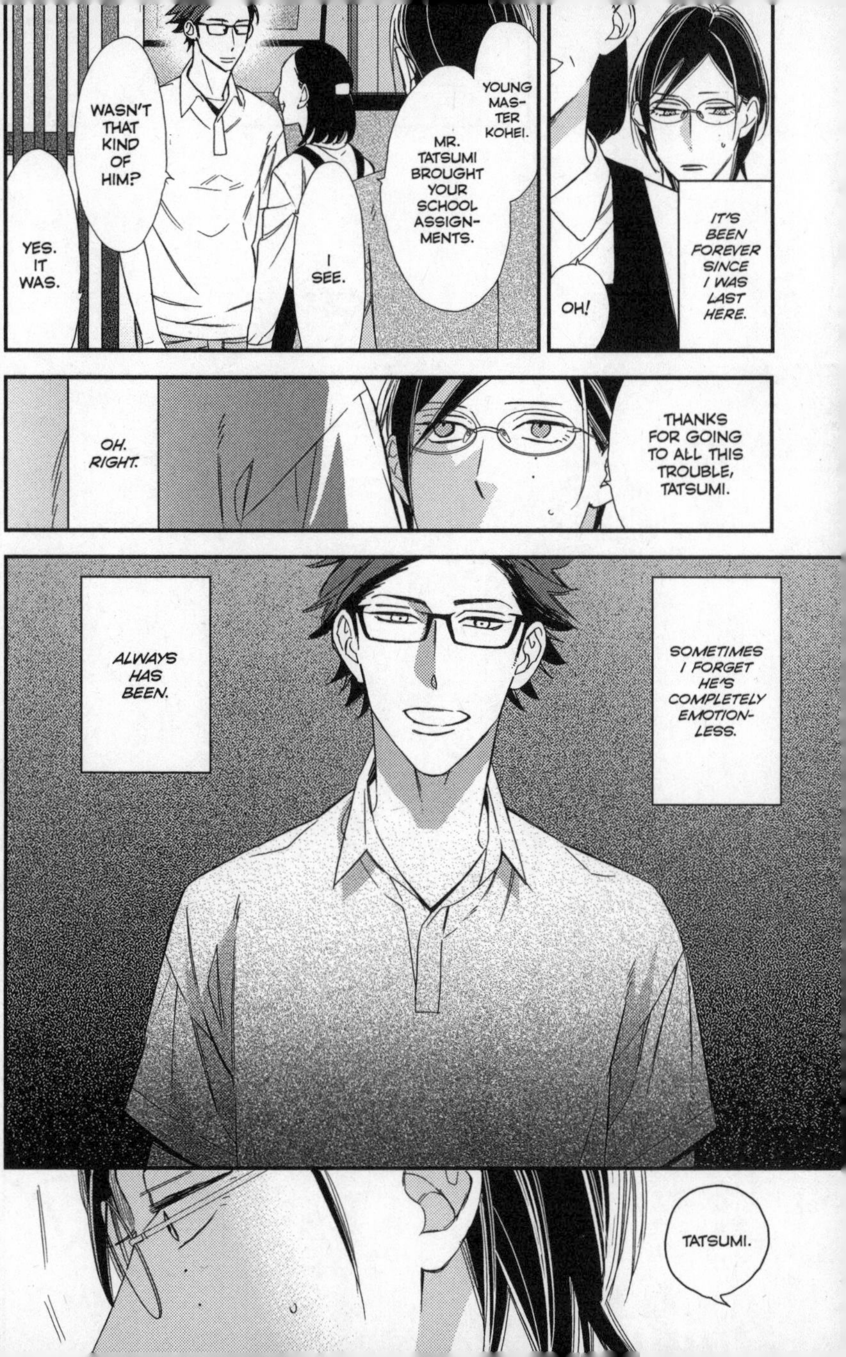
IT'S BEEN FOREVER SINCE I WAS LAST HERE.
OH!
YOUNG MASTER KOHEI.
MR. TATSUMI BROUGHT YOUR SCHOOL ASSIGNMENTS.
I SEE.
WASN'T THAT KIND OF HIM?
YES. IT WAS.
THANKS FOR GOING TO ALL THIS TROUBLE, TATSUMI.
OH. RIGHT.
SOMETIMES I FORGET HE'S COMPLETELY EMOTIONLESS.
ALWAYS HAS BEEN.
TATSUMI.

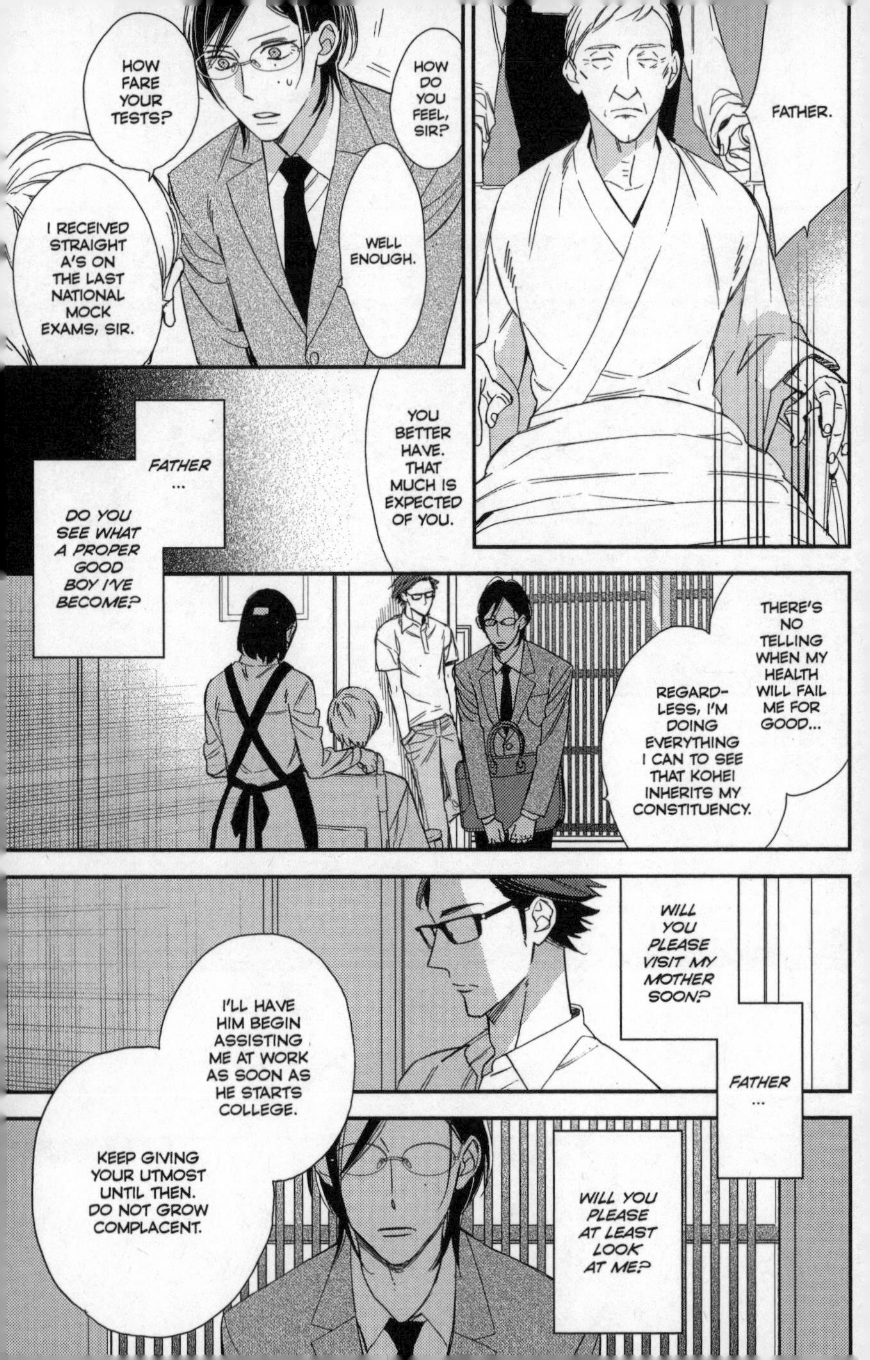
FATHER.
HOW DO YOU FEEL, SIR?
WELL ENOUGH.
HOW FARE YOUR TESTS?
I RECEIVED STRAIGHT A'S ON THE LAST NATIONAL MOCK EXAMS, SIR.
YOU BETTER HAVE. THAT MUCH IS EXPECTED OF YOU.
FATHER ...
DO YOU SEE WHAT A PROPER GOOD BOY I'VE BECOME?
THERE'S NO TELLING WHEN MY HEALTH WILL FAIL ME FOR GOOD...
REGARD-LESS, I'M DOING EVERYTHING I CAN TO SEE THAT KOHEI INHERITS MY CONSTITUENCY.
WILL YOU PLEASE VISIT MY MOTHER SOON?
FATHER ...
I'LL HAVE HIM BEGIN ASSISTING ME AT WORK AS SOON AS HE STARTS COLLEGE.
WILL YOU PLEASE AT LEAST LOOK AT ME?
KEEP GIVING YOUR UTMOST UNTIL THEN. DO NOT GROW COMPLACENT.

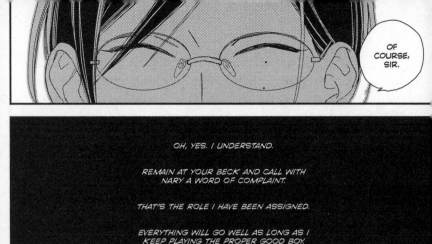

OF COURSE, SIR.

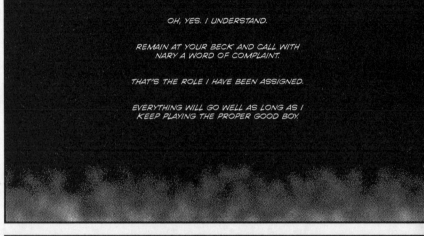

OH, YES. I UNDERSTAND.

REMAIN AT YOUR BECK AND CALL WITH NARY A WORD OF COMPLAINT.

THAT'S THE ROLE I HAVE BEEN ASSIGNED.

EVERYTHING WILL GO WELL AS LONG AS I KEEP PLAYING THE PROPER GOOD BOY.

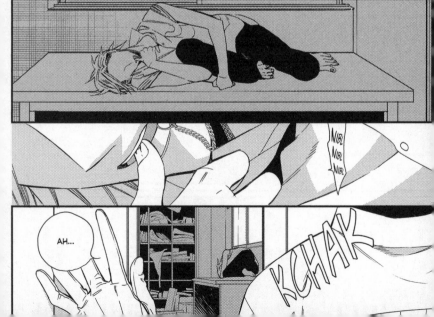

NIBL
NIBL
NIBL

AH...

KCHAK

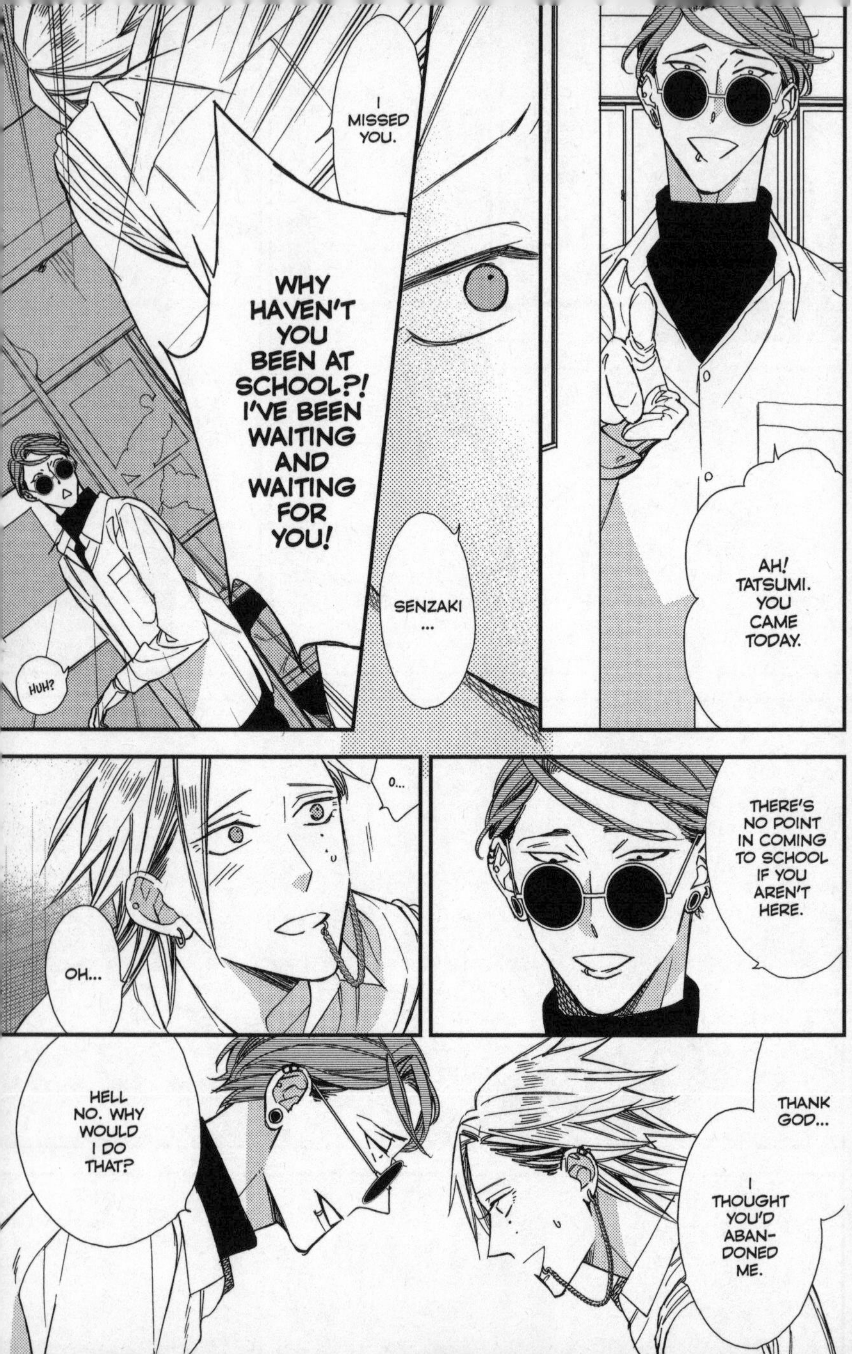
AH! TATSUMI. YOU CAME TODAY.
SENZAKI...
WHY HAVEN'T YOU BEEN AT SCHOOL?! I'VE BEEN WAITING AND WAITING FOR YOU!
HUH?
I MISSED YOU.
THERE'S NO POINT IN COMING TO SCHOOL IF YOU AREN'T HERE.
O...
OH...
THANK GOD...
I THOUGHT YOU'D ABAN-DONED ME.
HELL NO. WHY WOULD I DO THAT?

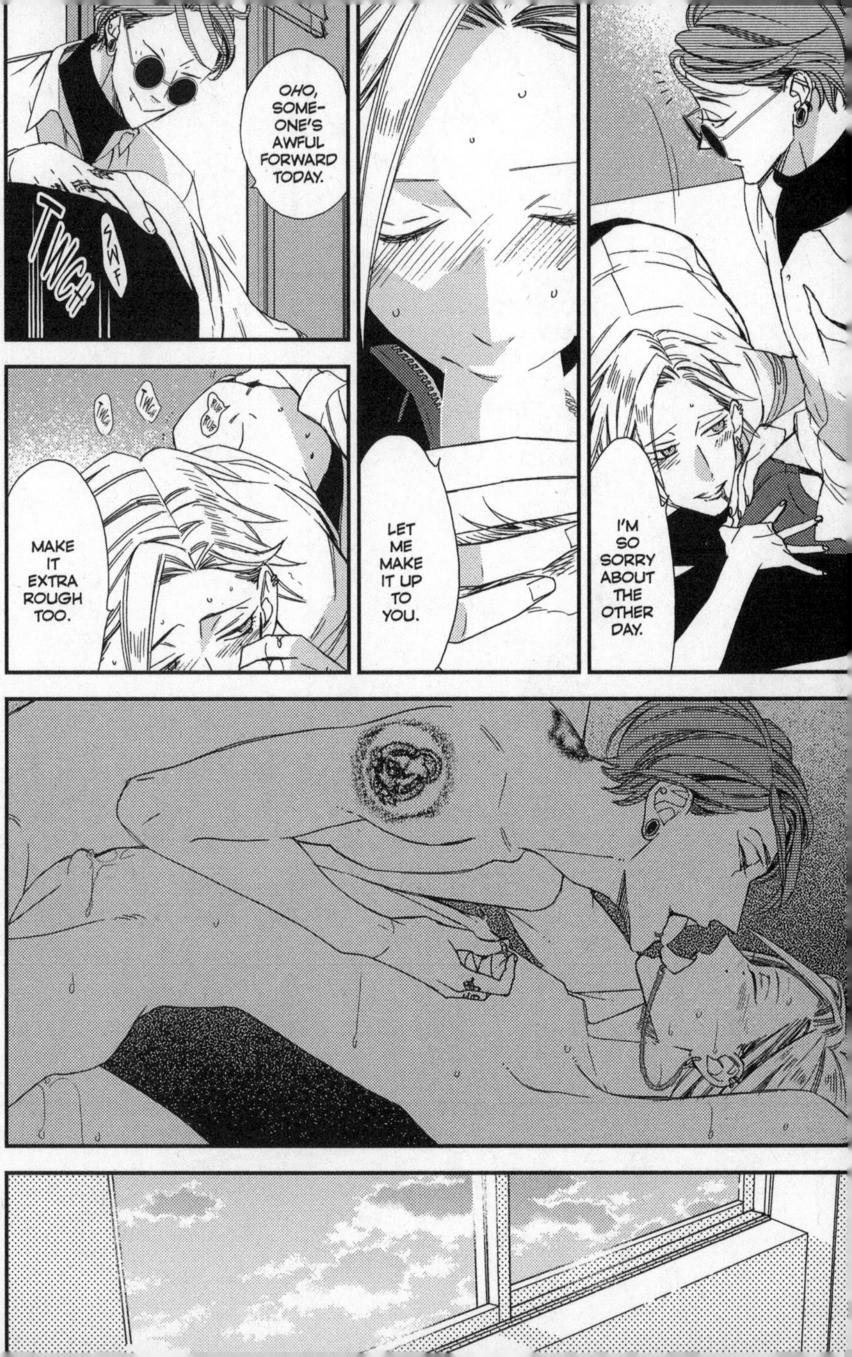
I'M SO SORRY ABOUT THE OTHER DAY.
LET ME MAKE IT UP TO YOU.
OHO, SOMEONE'S AWFUL FORWARD TODAY.
SWF
TWGH
TWGH
TWGH
MAKE IT EXTRA ROUGH TOO.

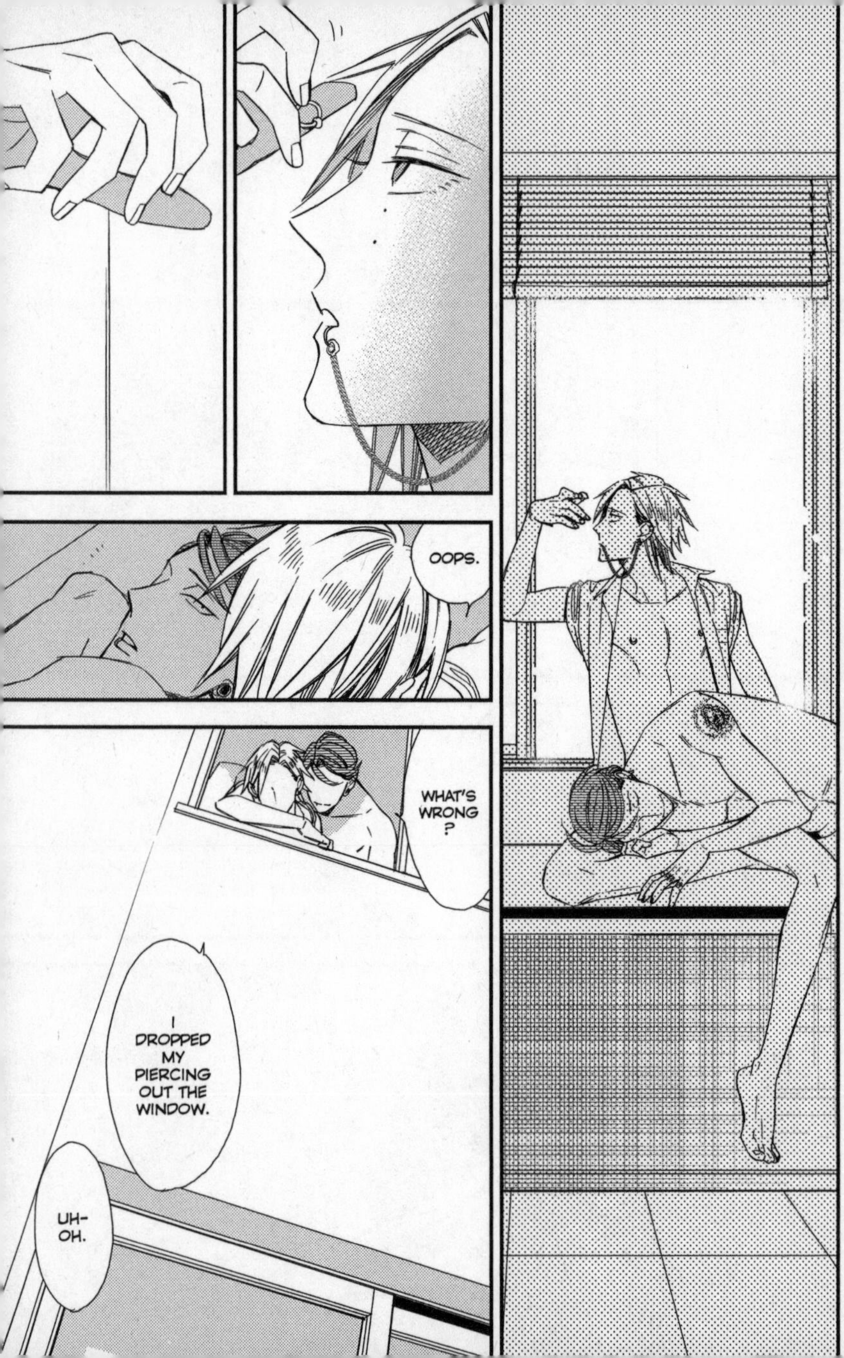
OOPS.
WHAT'S WRONG?
I DROPPED MY PIERCING OUT THE WINDOW.
UH-OH.

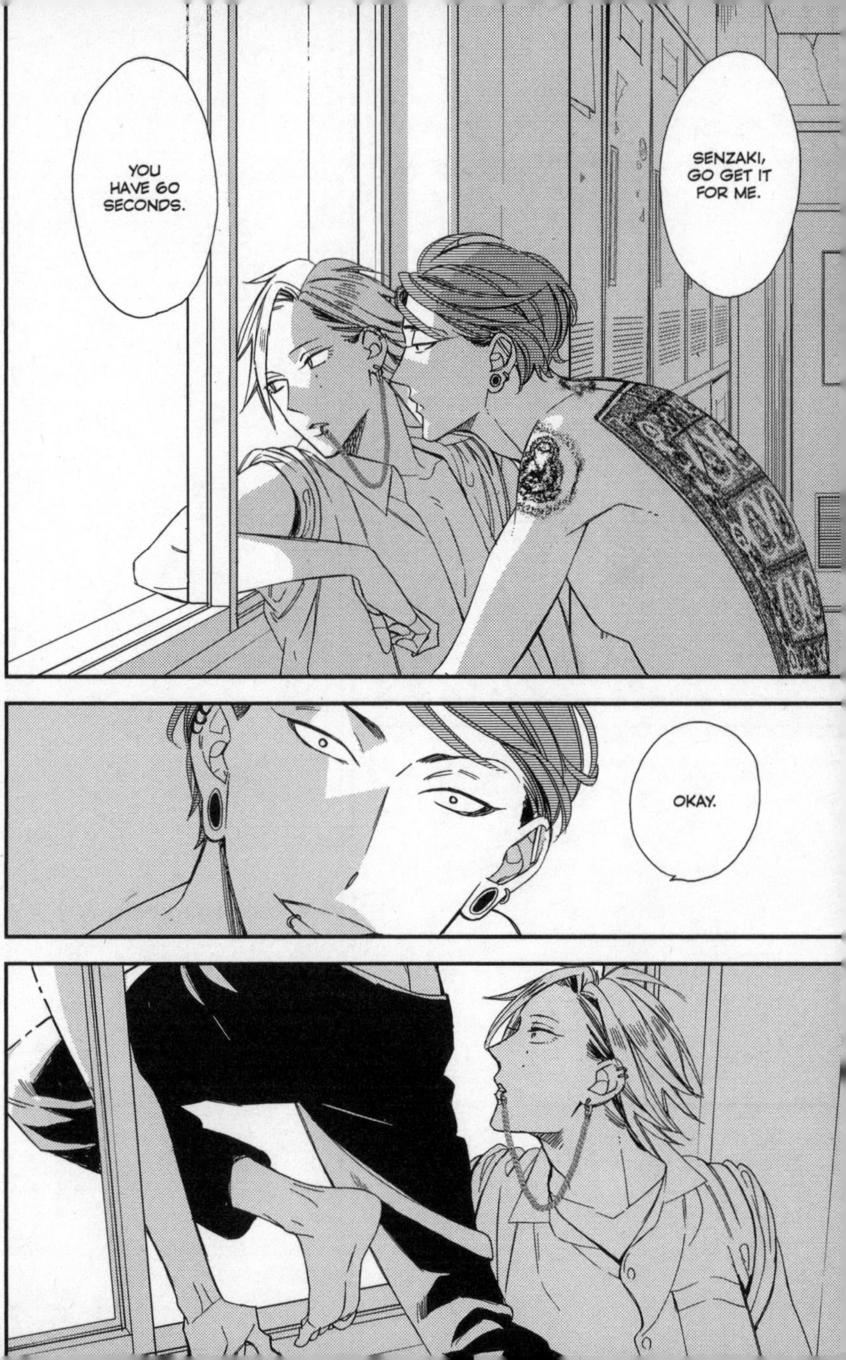
SENZAKI, GO GET IT FOR ME.
YOU HAVE 60 SECONDS.
OKAY.

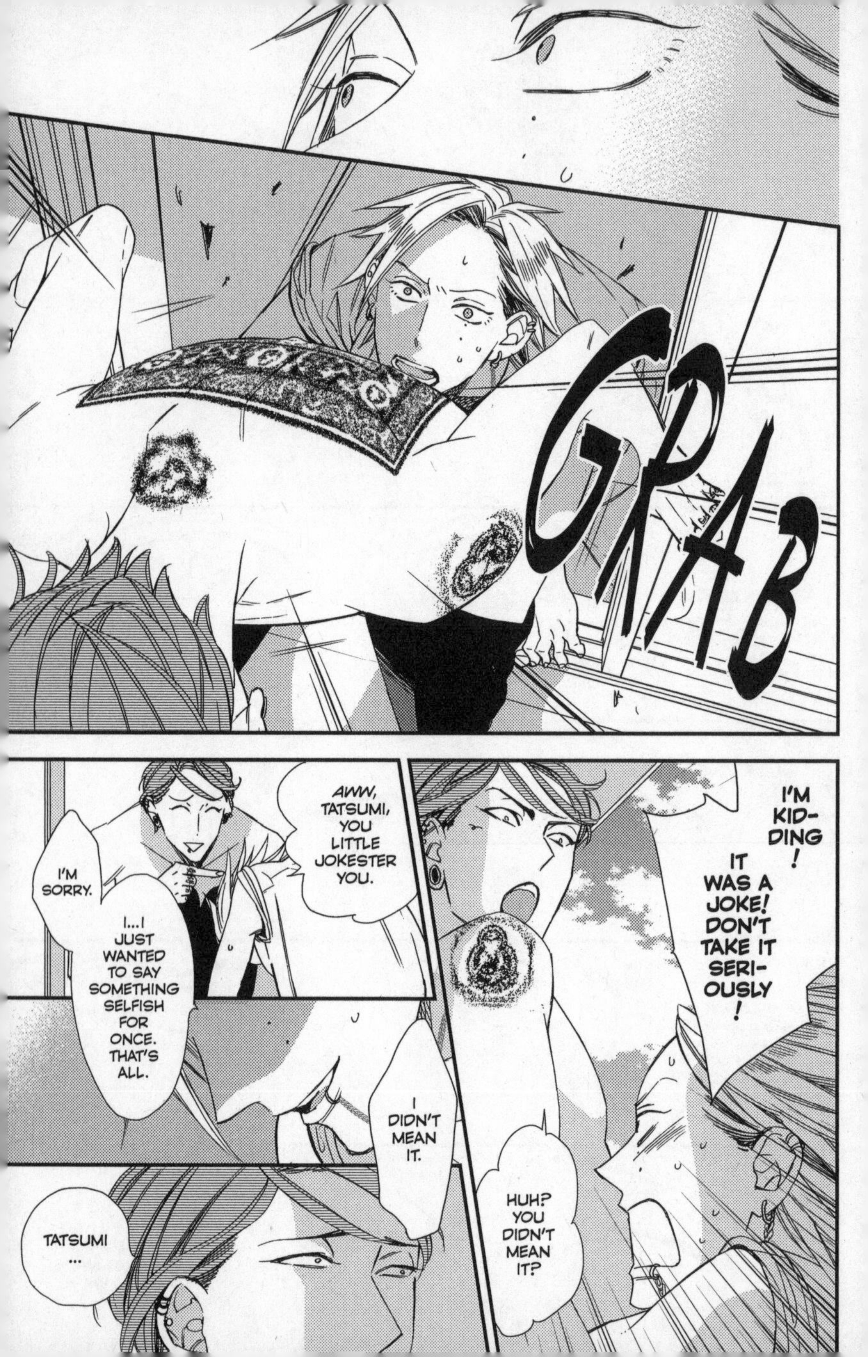
GRAB
I'M KIDDING!
IT WAS A JOKE! DON'T TAKE IT SERIOUSLY!
AWW, TATSUMI, YOU LITTLE JOKESTER YOU.
I'M SORRY.
I...I JUST WANTED TO SAY SOMETHING SELFISH FOR ONCE. THAT'S ALL.
I DIDN'T MEAN IT.
HUH? YOU DIDN'T MEAN IT?
TATSUMI ...

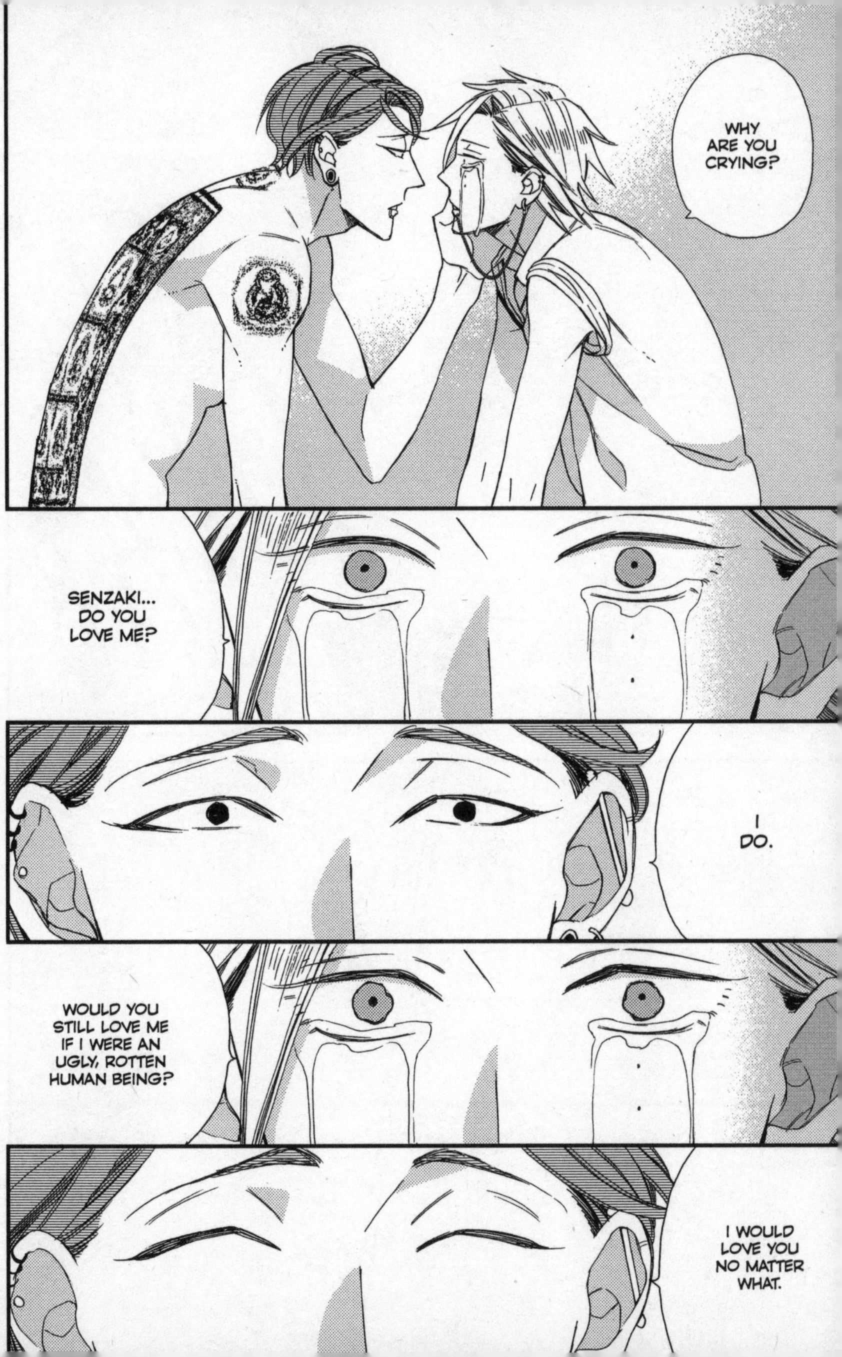
WHY ARE YOU CRYING?
SENZAKI... DO YOU LOVE ME?
I DO.
WOULD YOU STILL LOVE ME IF I WERE AN UGLY, ROTTEN HUMAN BEING?
I WOULD LOVE YOU NO MATTER WHAT.

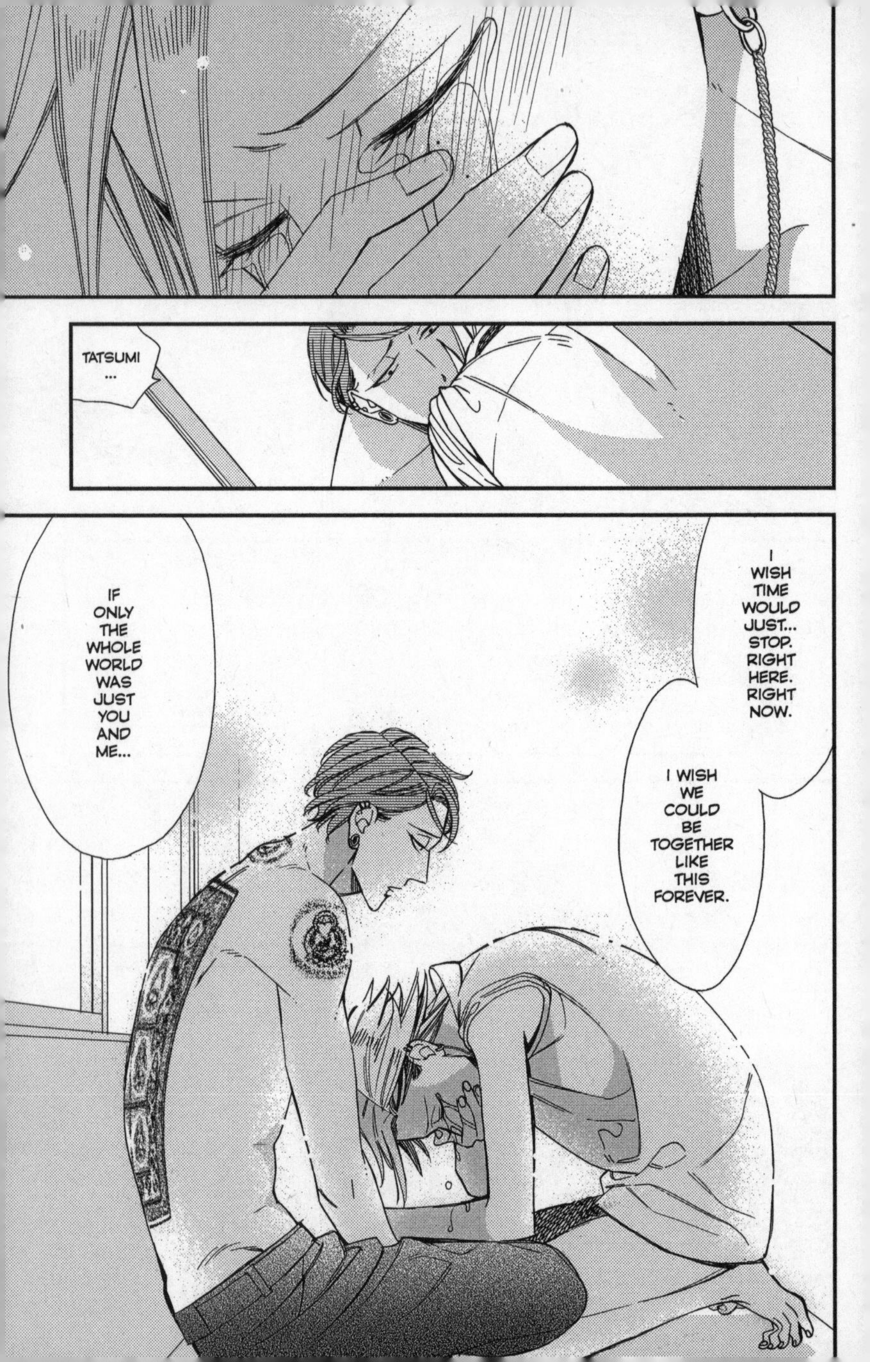
TATSUMI...
I WISH TIME WOULD JUST... STOP. RIGHT HERE. RIGHT NOW.
I WISH WE COULD BE TOGETHER LIKE THIS FOREVER.
IF ONLY THE WHOLE WORLD WAS JUST YOU AND ME...

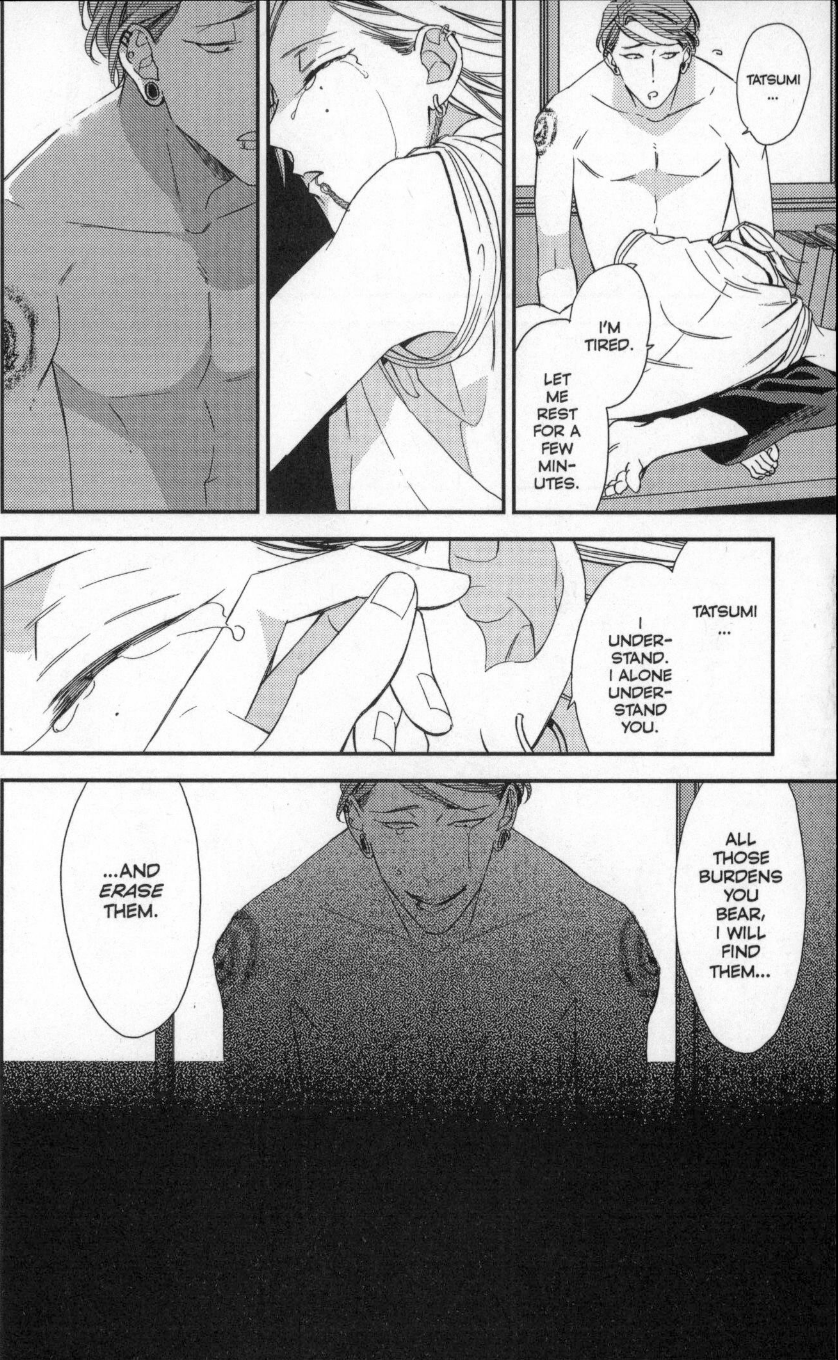
TATSUMI ...
I'M TIRED.
LET ME REST FOR A FEW MIN-UTES.
TATSUMI ...
I UNDER-STAND. I ALONE UNDER-STAND YOU.
ALL THOSE BURDENS YOU BEAR, I WILL FIND THEM...
...AND *ERASE* THEM.

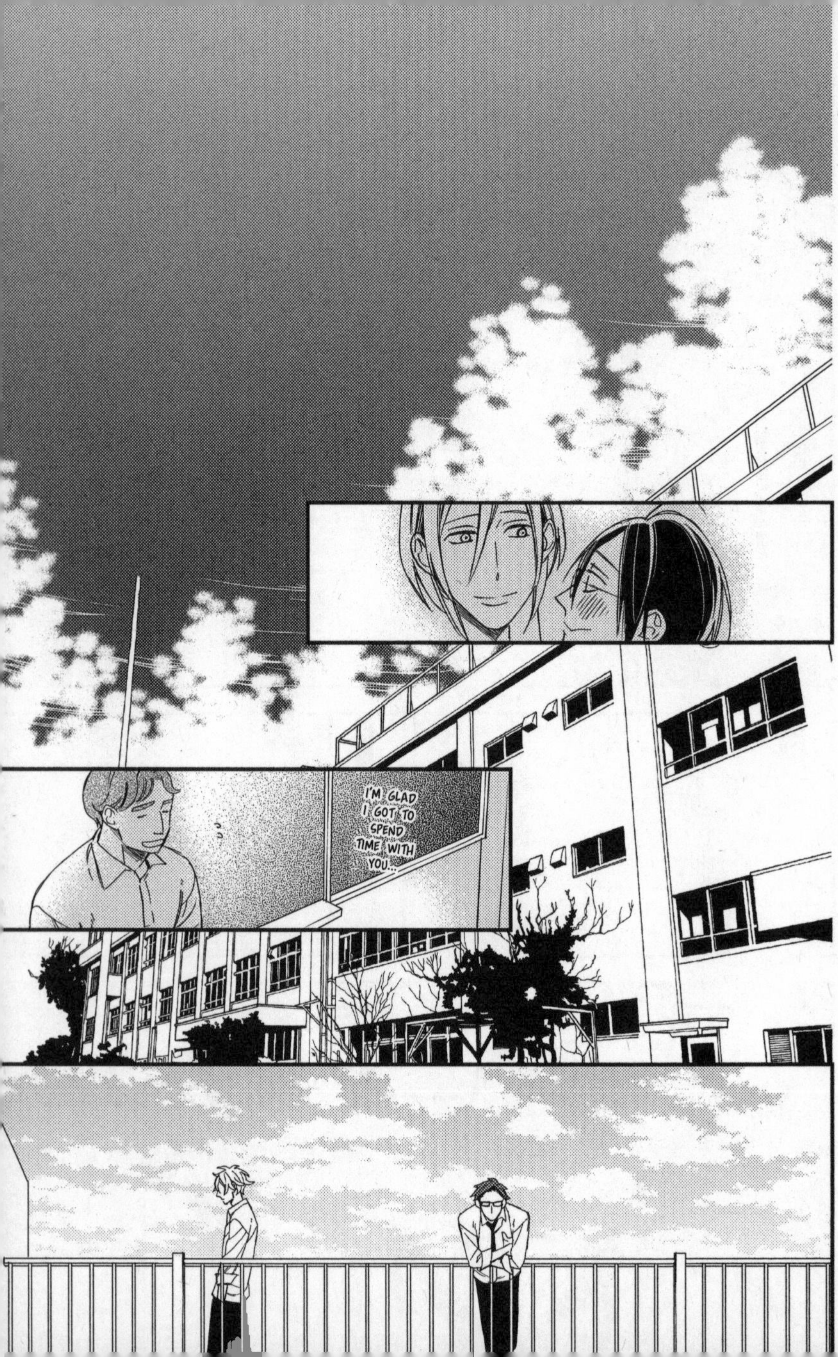
I'M GLAD I GOT TO SPEND TIME WITH YOU...

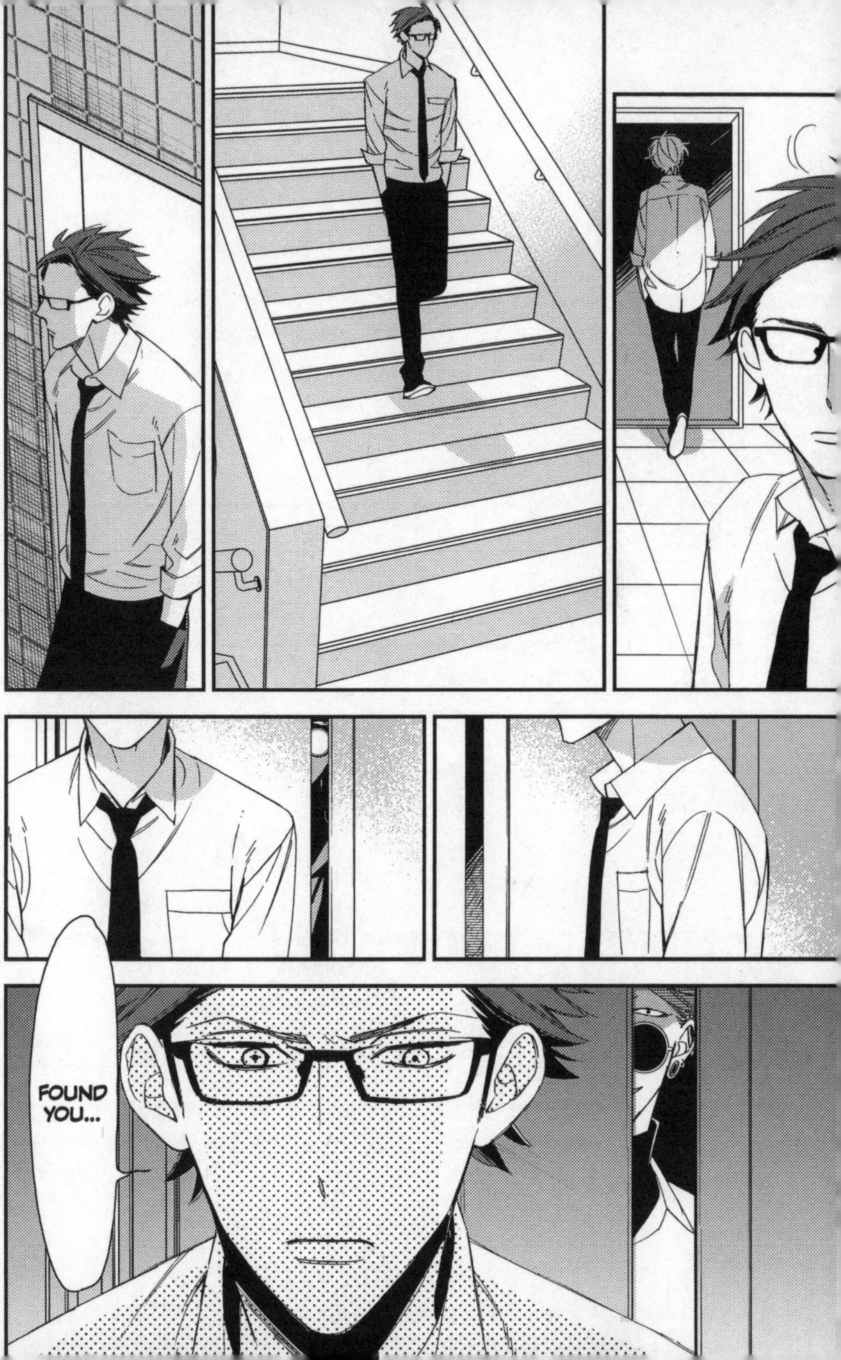
FOUND YOU...

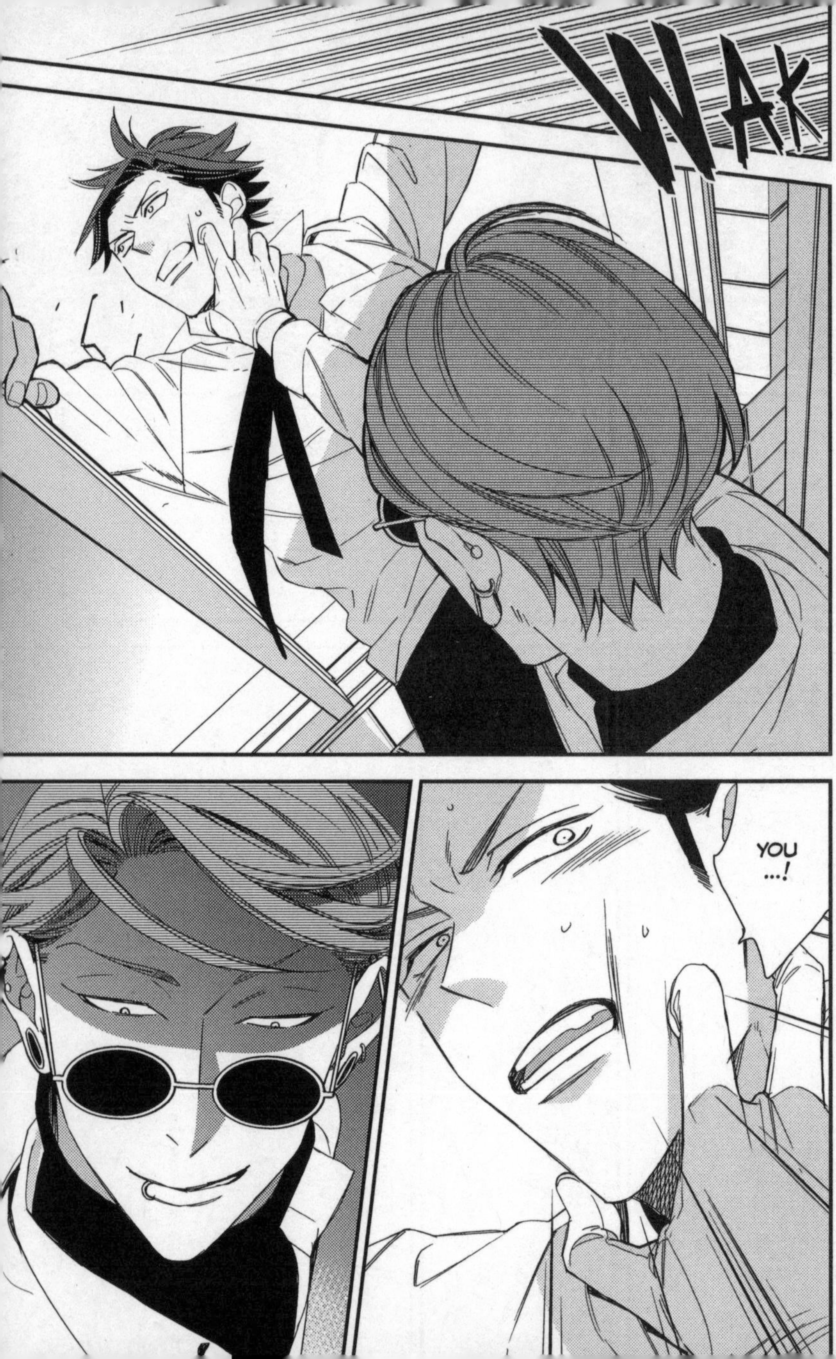
WAK
YOU ...!

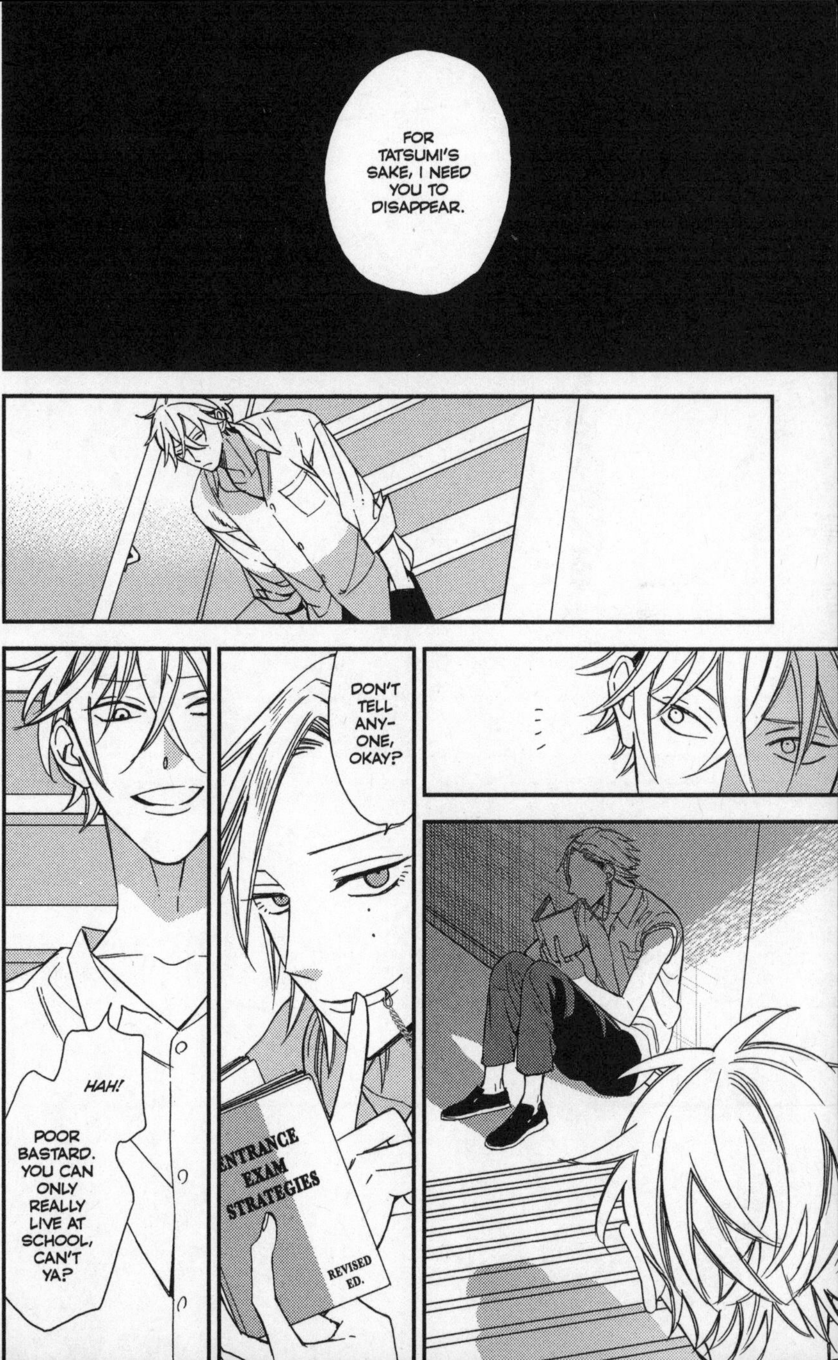
FOR TATSUMI'S SAKE, I NEED YOU TO DISAPPEAR.
DON'T TELL ANY-ONE, OKAY?
ENTRANCE EXAM STRATEGIES
REVISED ED.
HAH!
POOR BASTARD. YOU CAN ONLY REALLY LIVE AT SCHOOL, CAN'T YA?

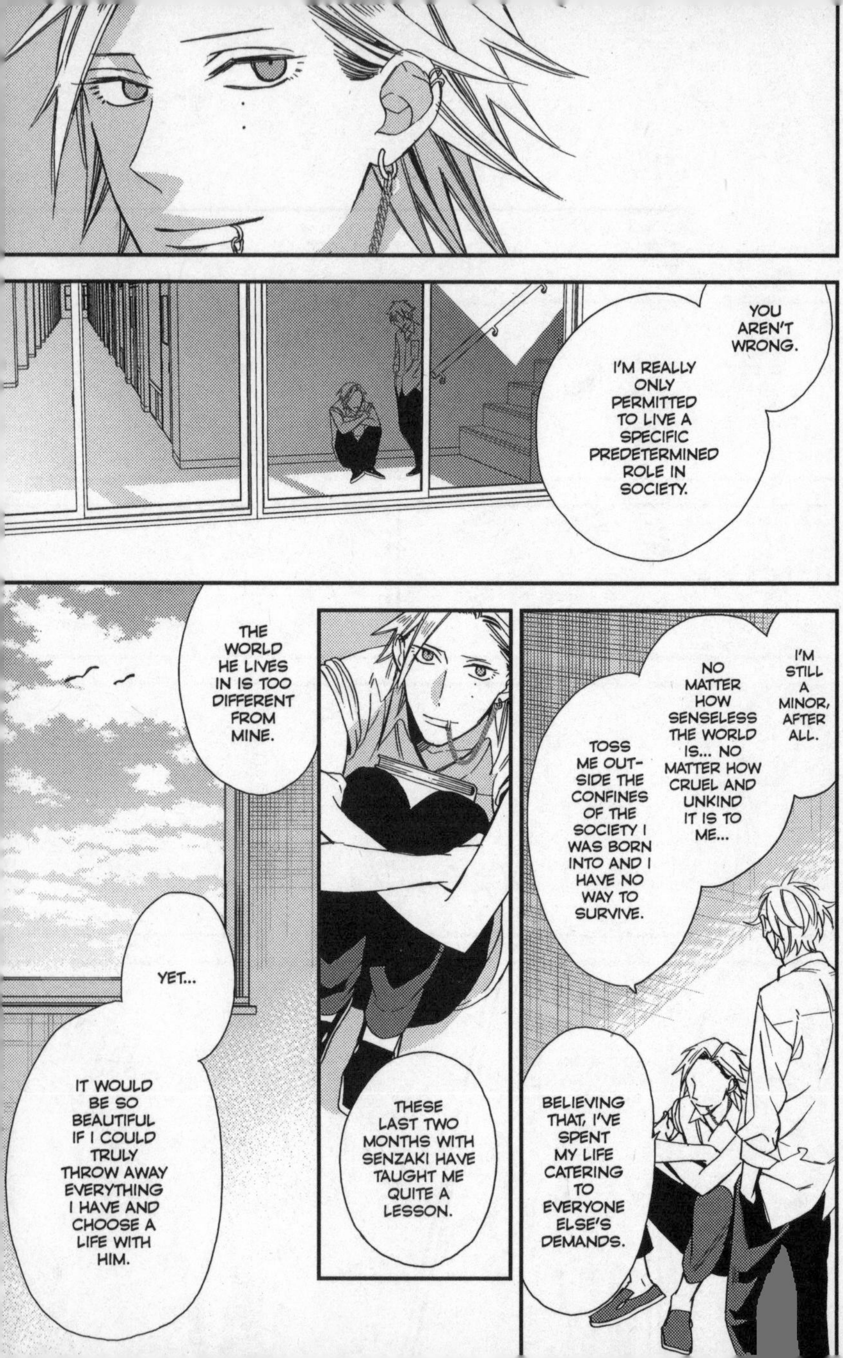
YOU AREN'T WRONG.
I'M REALLY ONLY PERMITTED TO LIVE A SPECIFIC PREDETERMINED ROLE IN SOCIETY.
I'M STILL A MINOR, AFTER ALL.
NO MATTER HOW SENSELESS THE WORLD IS... NO MATTER HOW CRUEL AND UNKIND IT IS TO ME...
TOSS ME OUTSIDE THE CONFINES OF THE SOCIETY I WAS BORN INTO AND I HAVE NO WAY TO SURVIVE.
BELIEVING THAT, I'VE SPENT MY LIFE CATERING TO EVERYONE ELSE'S DEMANDS.
THESE LAST TWO MONTHS WITH SENZAKI HAVE TAUGHT ME QUITE A LESSON.
THE WORLD HE LIVES IN IS TOO DIFFERENT FROM MINE.
YET...
IT WOULD BE SO BEAUTIFUL IF I COULD TRULY THROW AWAY EVERYTHING I HAVE AND CHOOSE A LIFE WITH HIM.

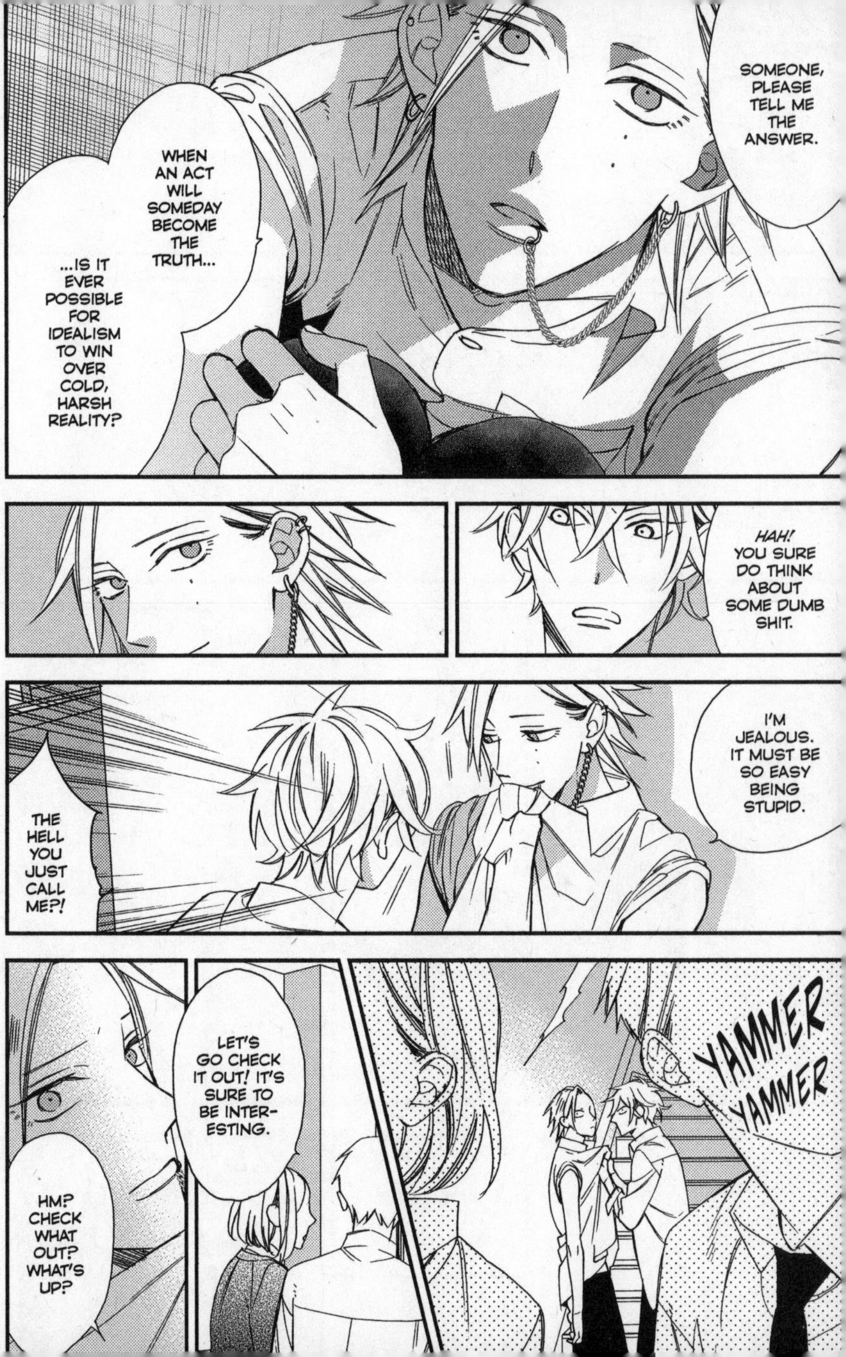
SOMEONE, PLEASE TELL ME THE ANSWER.
WHEN AN ACT WILL SOMEDAY BECOME THE TRUTH...
...IS IT EVER POSSIBLE FOR IDEALISM TO WIN OVER COLD, HARSH REALITY?
HAH! YOU SURE DO THINK ABOUT SOME DUMB SHIT.
I'M JEALOUS. IT MUST BE SO EASY BEING STUPID.
THE HELL YOU JUST CALL ME?!
YAMMER YAMMER
LET'S GO CHECK IT OUT! IT'S SURE TO BE INTER-ESTING.
HM? CHECK WHAT OUT? WHAT'S UP?

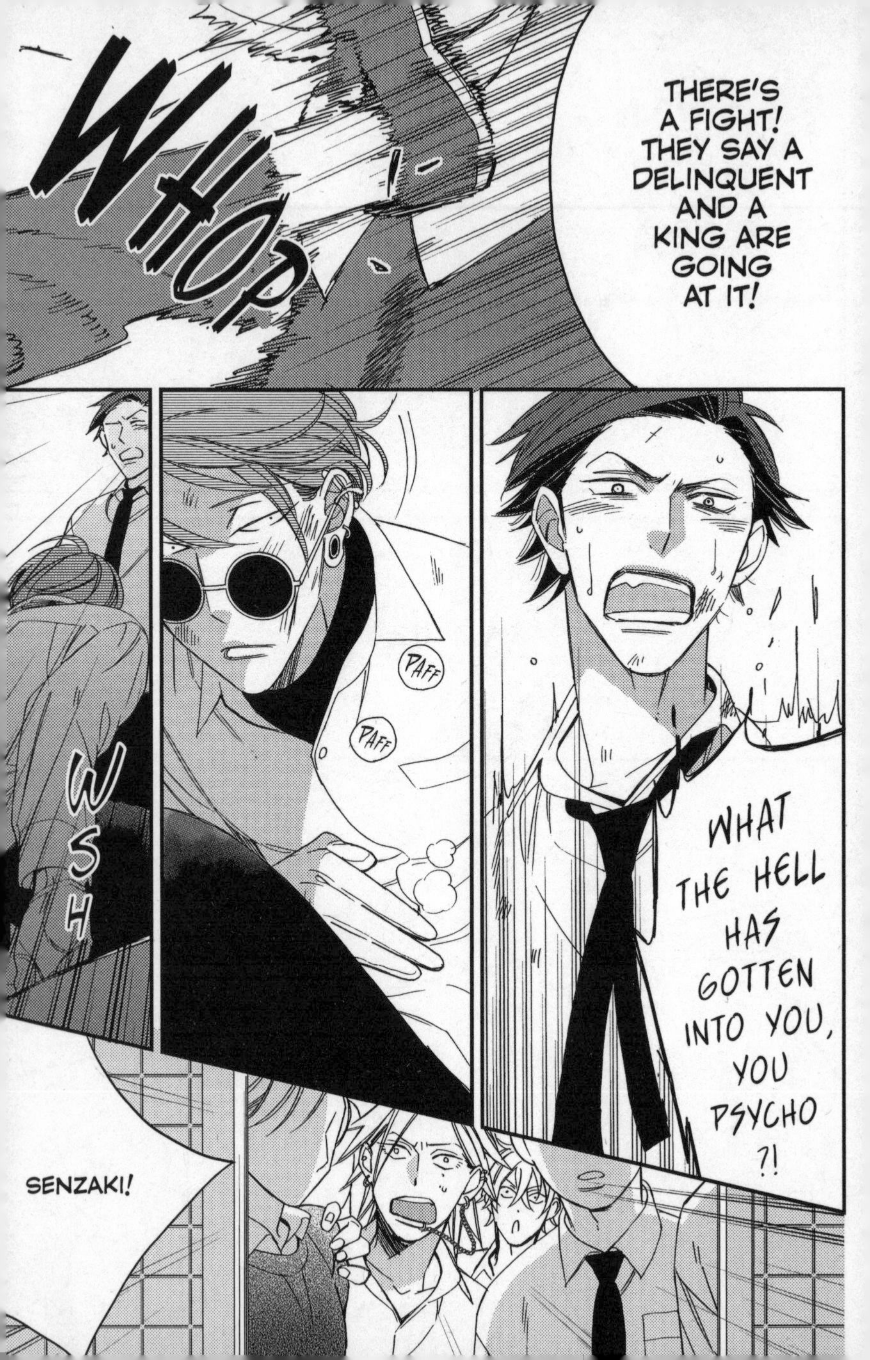
THERE'S A FIGHT! THEY SAY A DELINQUENT AND A KING ARE GOING AT IT!
WHOP
WHAT THE HELL HAS GOTTEN INTO YOU, YOU PSYCHO ?!
PAFF
PAFF
WSH
SENZAKI!

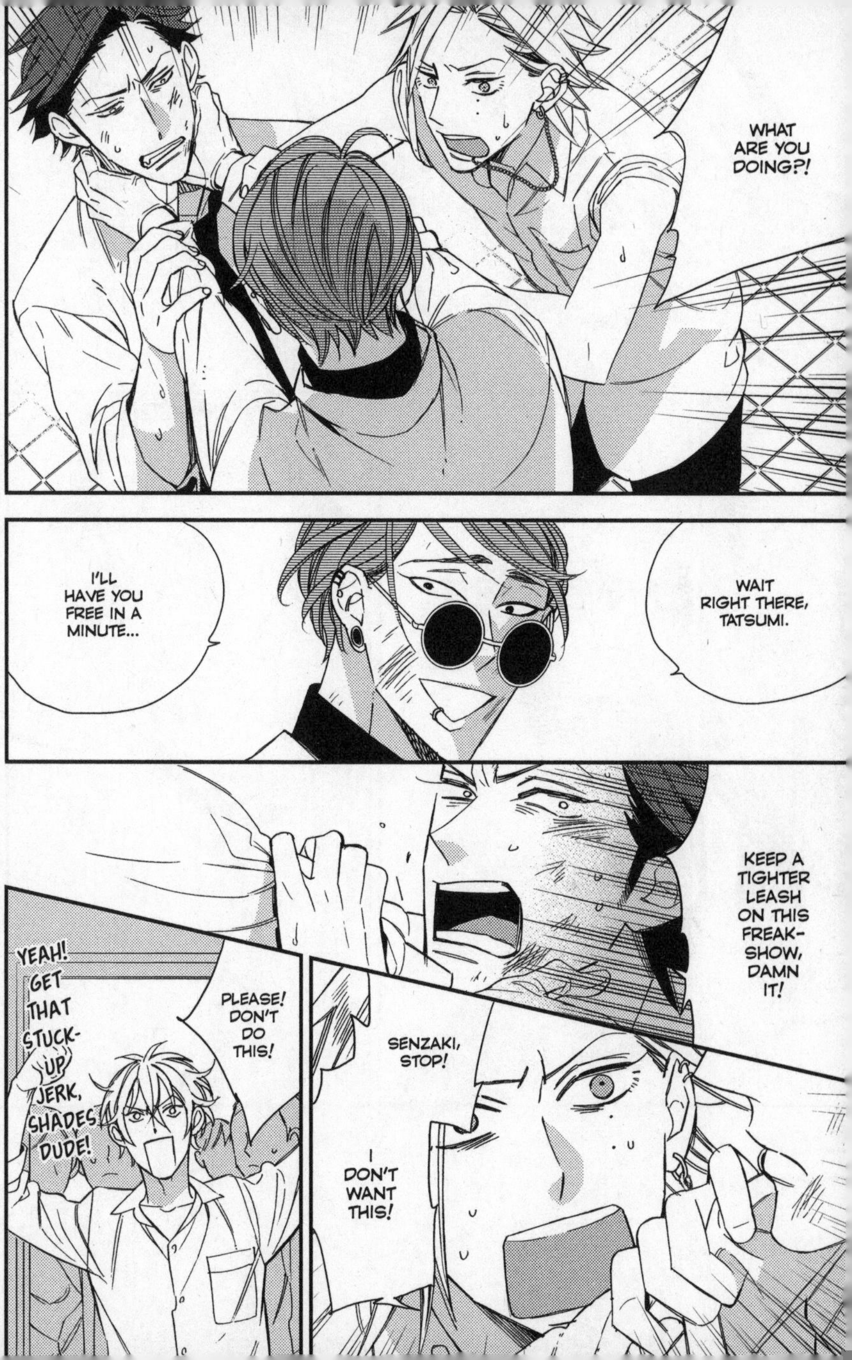
WHAT ARE YOU DOING?!
WAIT RIGHT THERE, TATSUMI.
I'LL HAVE YOU FREE IN A MINUTE...
KEEP A TIGHTER LEASH ON THIS FREAK-SHOW, DAMN IT!
SENZAKI, STOP!
I DON'T WANT THIS!
PLEASE! DON'T DO THIS!
YEAH! GET THAT STUCK-UP JERK, SHADES DUDE!

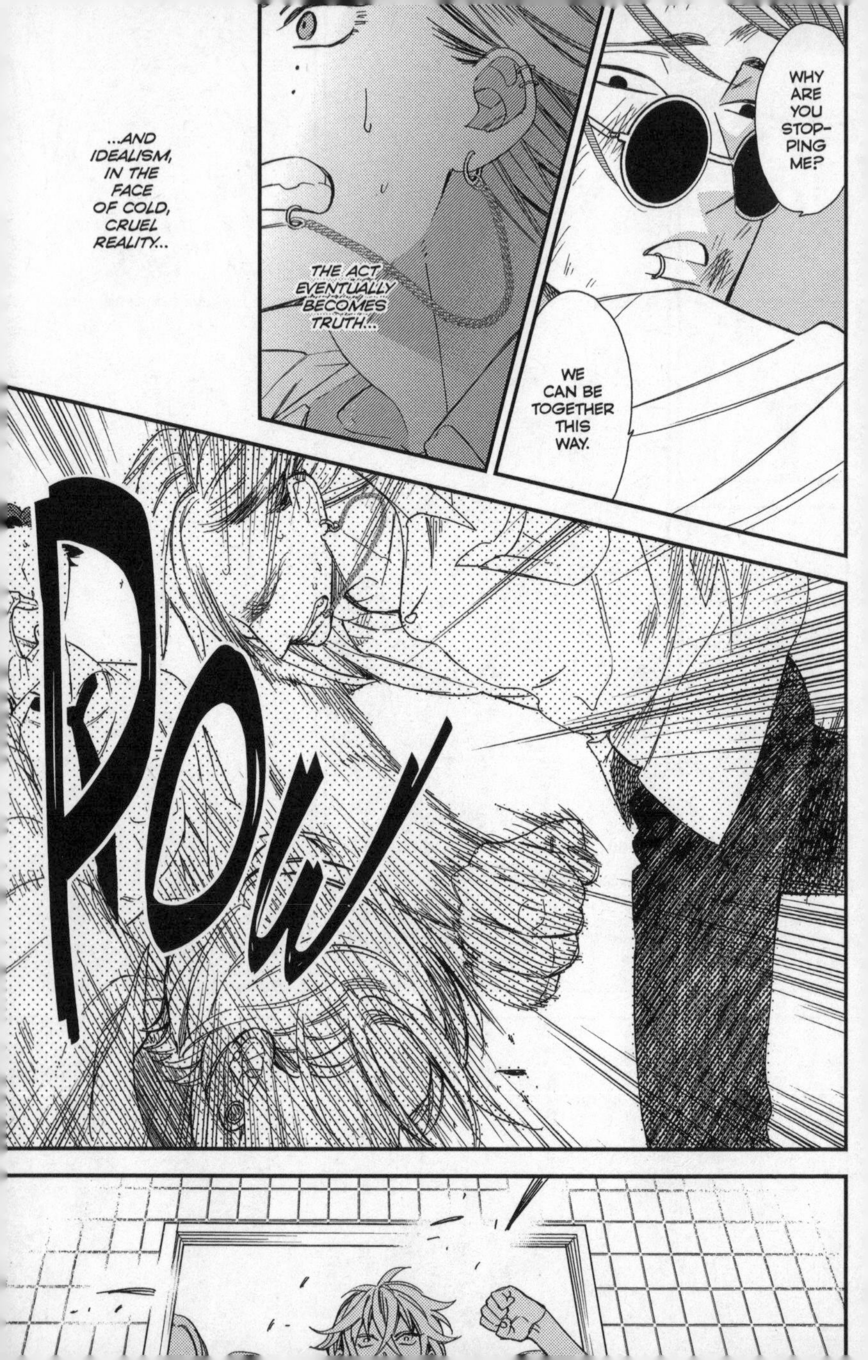
WHY ARE YOU STOPPING ME?
WE CAN BE TOGETHER THIS WAY.
THE ACT EVENTUALLY BECOMES TRUTH...
...AND IDEALISM, IN THE FACE OF COLD, CRUEL REALITY...
POW

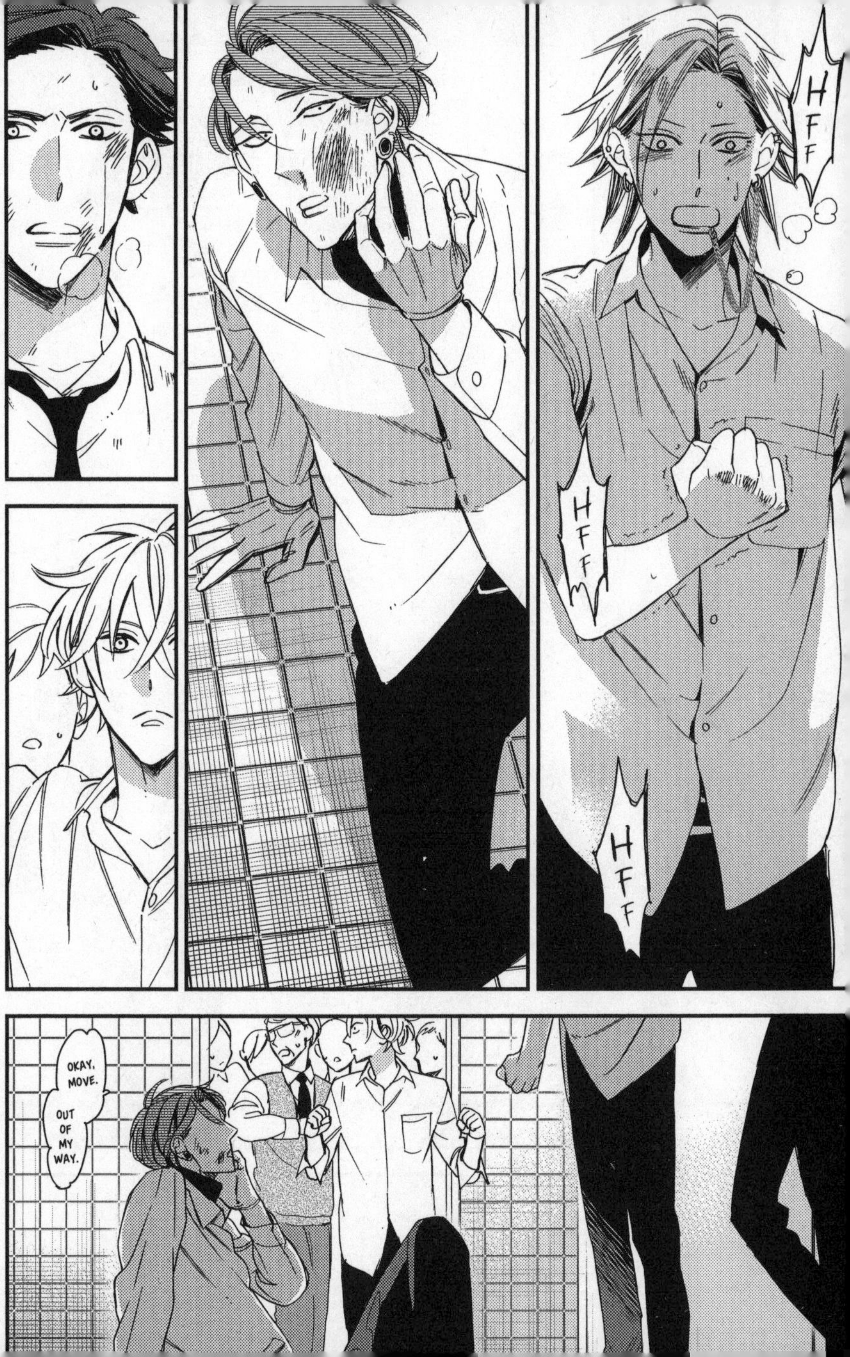
HFF
HFF
HFF
OKAY, MOVE.
OUT OF MY WAY.

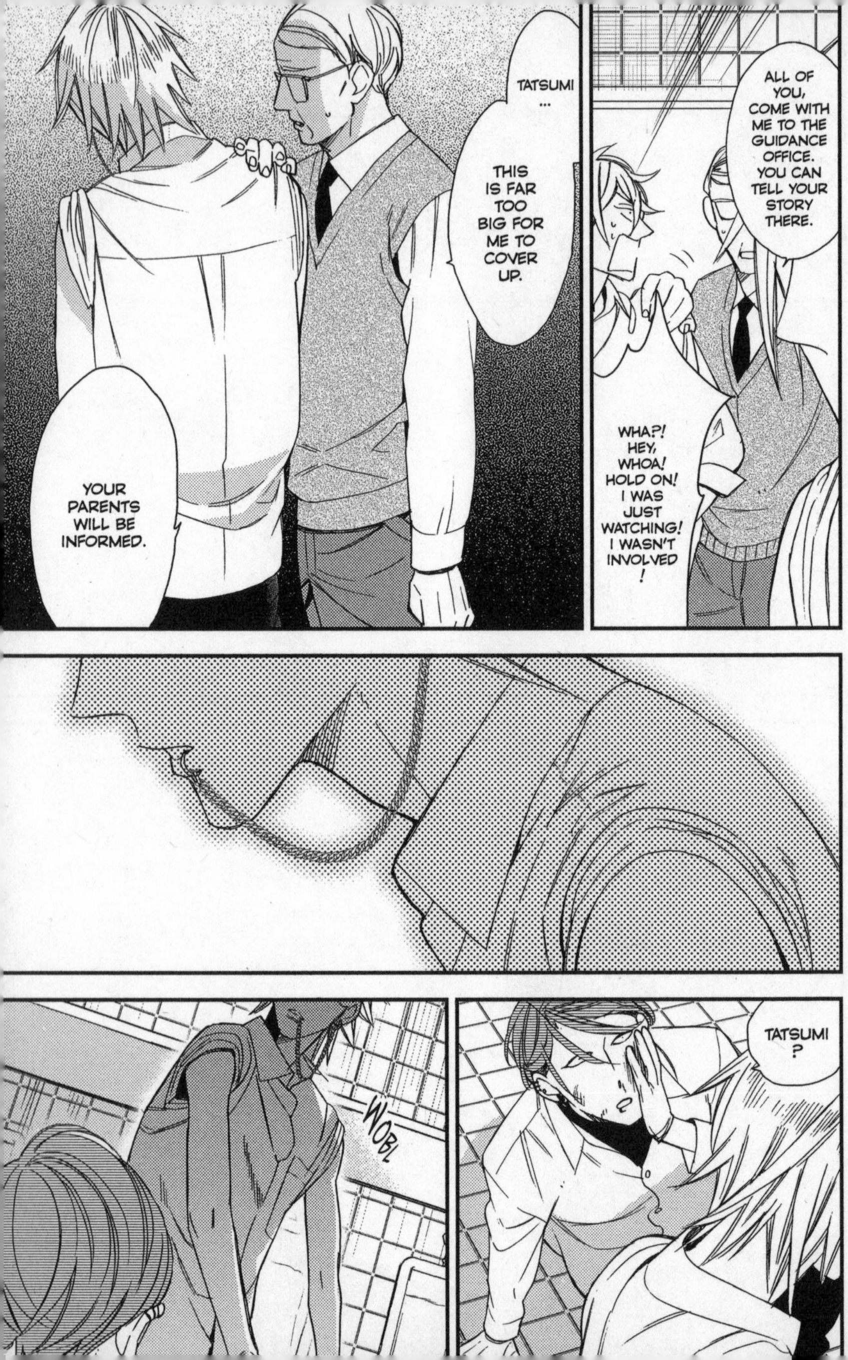
ALL OF YOU, COME WITH ME TO THE GUIDANCE OFFICE. YOU CAN TELL YOUR STORY THERE.
WHA?! HEY, WHOA! HOLD ON! I WAS JUST WATCHING! I WASN'T INVOLVED!
TATSUMI...
THIS IS FAR TOO BIG FOR ME TO COVER UP.
YOUR PARENTS WILL BE INFORMED.
TATSUMI?
WOBL

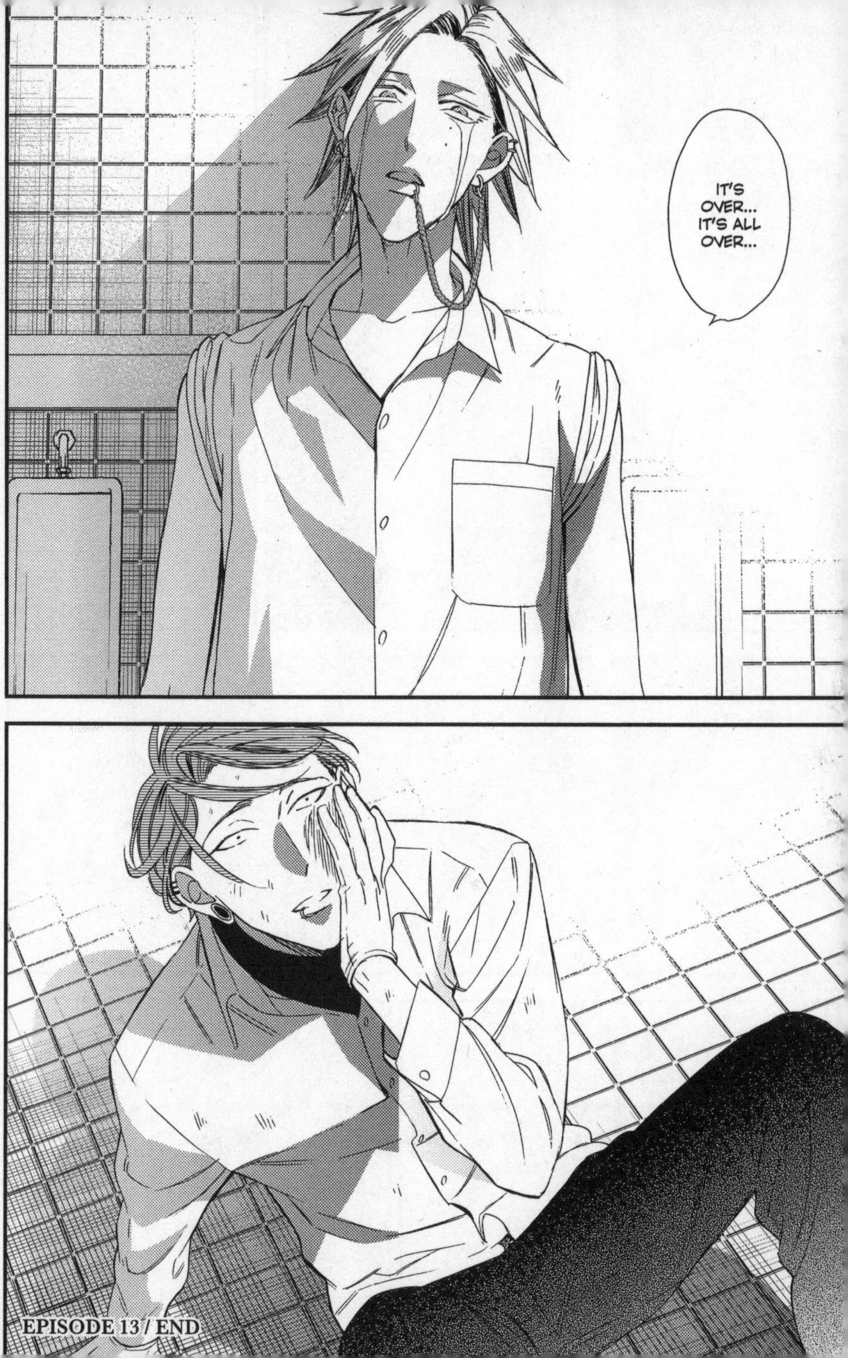
IT'S OVER... IT'S ALL OVER...
EPISODE 13 / END

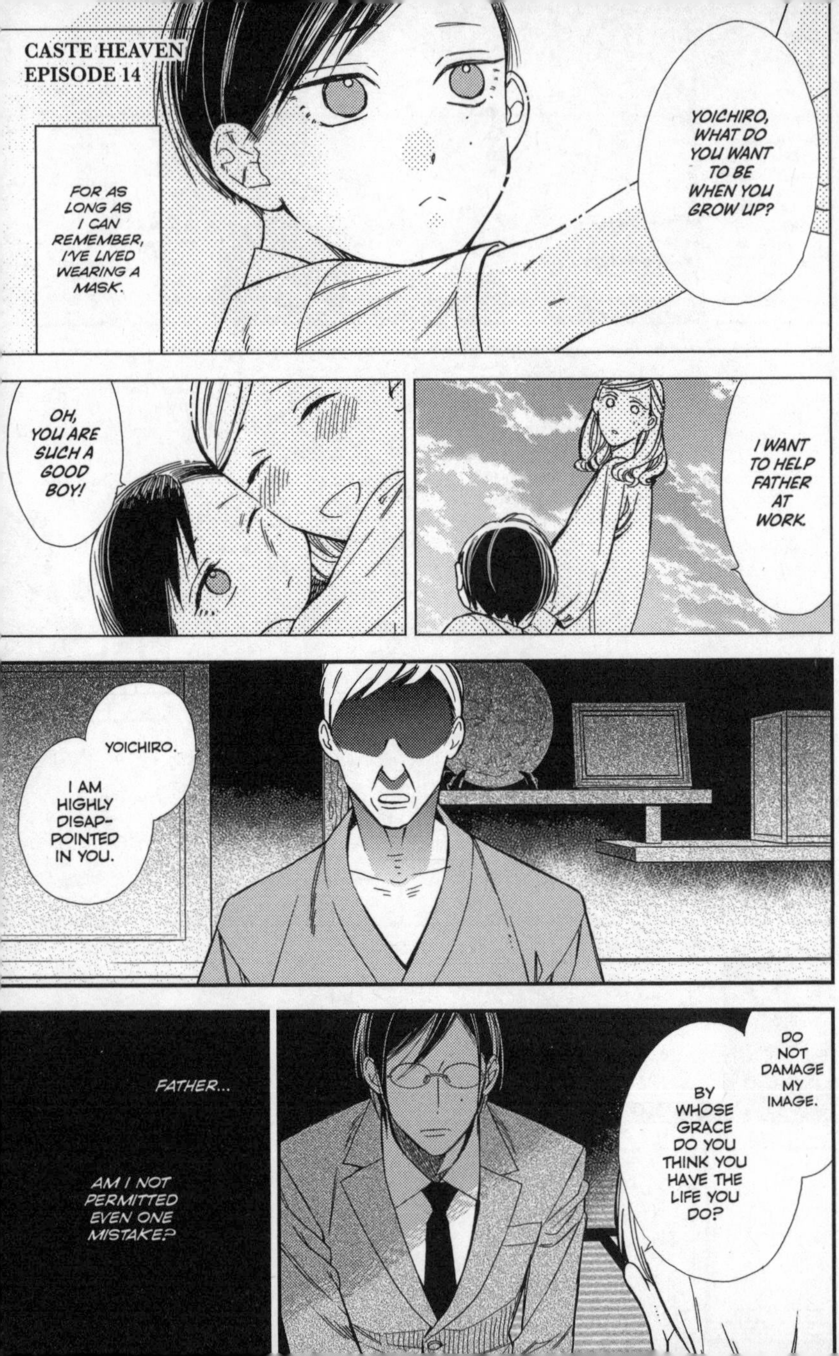
CASTE HEAVEN
EPISODE 14
YOICHIRO, WHAT DO YOU WANT TO BE WHEN YOU GROW UP?
FOR AS LONG AS I CAN REMEMBER, I'VE LIVED WEARING A MASK.
I WANT TO HELP FATHER AT WORK.
OH, YOU ARE SUCH A GOOD BOY!
YOICHIRO.
I AM HIGHLY DISAP-POINTED IN YOU.
DO NOT DAMAGE MY IMAGE.
BY WHOSE GRACE DO YOU THINK YOU HAVE THE LIFE YOU DO?
FATHER...
AM I NOT PERMITTED EVEN ONE MISTAKE?

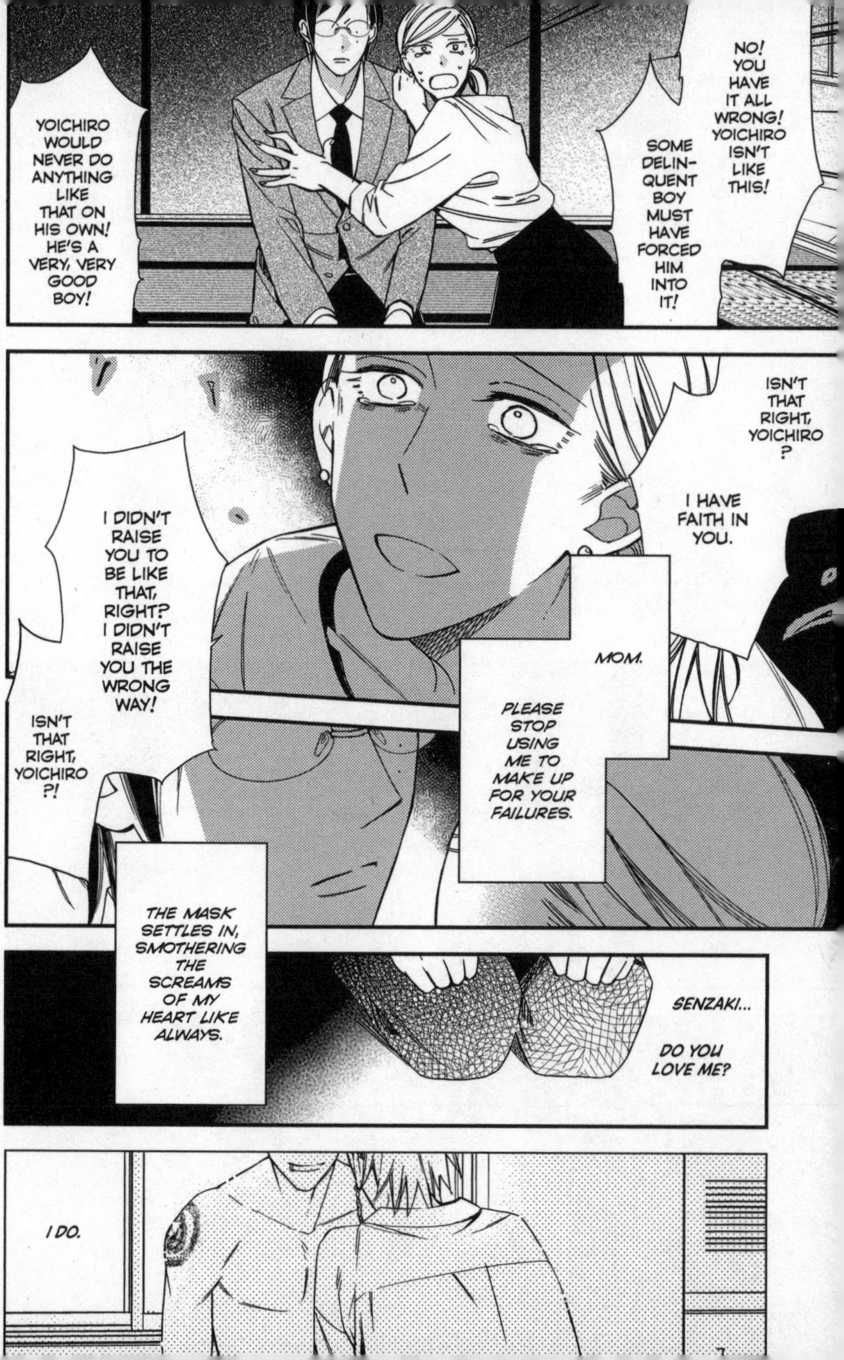
NO! YOU HAVE IT ALL WRONG! YOICHIRO ISN'T LIKE THIS!
SOME DELIN-QUENT BOY MUST HAVE FORCED HIM INTO IT!
YOICHIRO WOULD NEVER DO ANYTHING LIKE THAT ON HIS OWN! HE'S A VERY, VERY GOOD BOY!
ISN'T THAT RIGHT, YOICHIRO?
I HAVE FAITH IN YOU.
I DIDN'T RAISE YOU TO BE LIKE THAT, RIGHT? I DIDN'T RAISE YOU THE WRONG WAY!
ISN'T THAT RIGHT, YOICHIRO?!
MOM.
PLEASE STOP USING ME TO MAKE UP FOR YOUR FAILURES.
SENZAKI...
DO YOU LOVE ME?
THE MASK SETTLES IN, SMOTHERING THE SCREAMS OF MY HEART LIKE ALWAYS.
I DO.

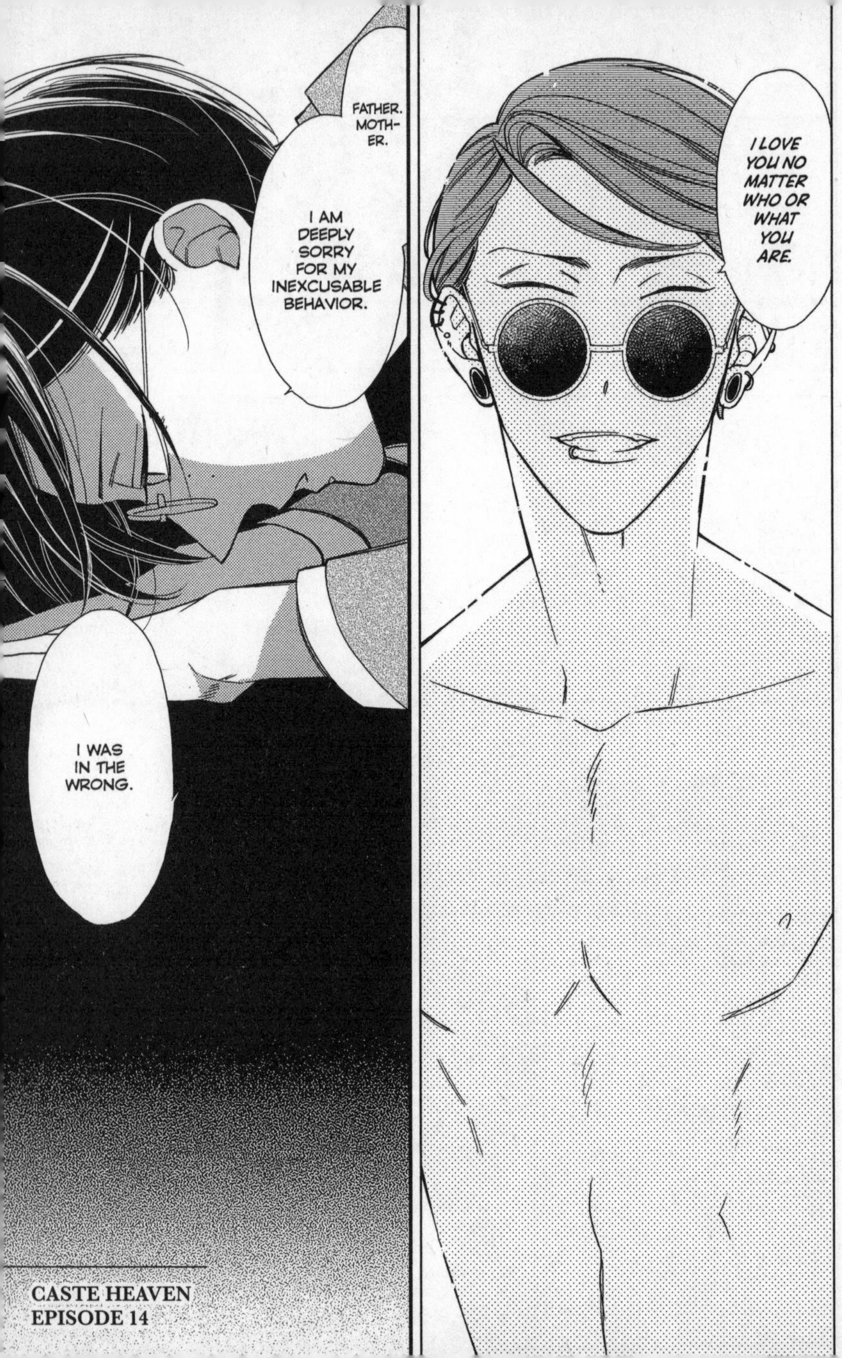
I LOVE YOU NO MATTER WHO OR WHAT YOU ARE.
FATHER. MOTH-ER.
I AM DEEPLY SORRY FOR MY INEXCUSABLE BEHAVIOR.
I WAS IN THE WRONG.
CASTE HEAVEN EPISODE 14

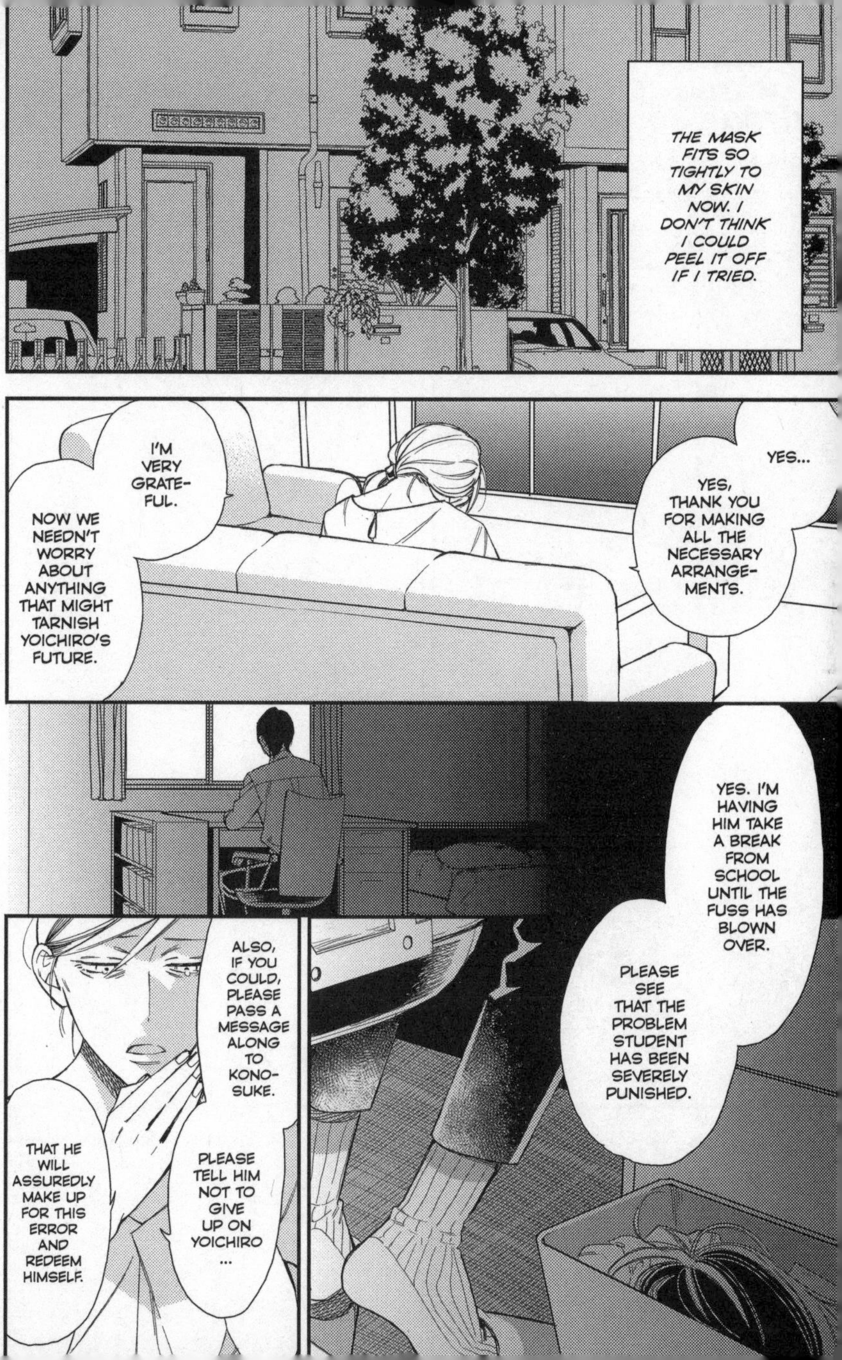
THE MASK FITS SO TIGHTLY TO MY SKIN NOW. I DON'T THINK I COULD PEEL IT OFF IF I TRIED.
YES...
YES, THANK YOU FOR MAKING ALL THE NECESSARY ARRANGE-MENTS.
I'M VERY GRATE-FUL.
NOW WE NEEDN'T WORRY ABOUT ANYTHING THAT MIGHT TARNISH YOICHIRO'S FUTURE.
YES. I'M HAVING HIM TAKE A BREAK FROM SCHOOL UNTIL THE FUSS HAS BLOWN OVER.
PLEASE SEE THAT THE PROBLEM STUDENT HAS BEEN SEVERELY PUNISHED.
ALSO, IF YOU COULD, PLEASE PASS A MESSAGE ALONG TO KONO-SUKE.
PLEASE TELL HIM NOT TO GIVE UP ON YOICHIRO ...
THAT HE WILL ASSUREDLY MAKE UP FOR THIS ERROR AND REDEEM HIMSELF.

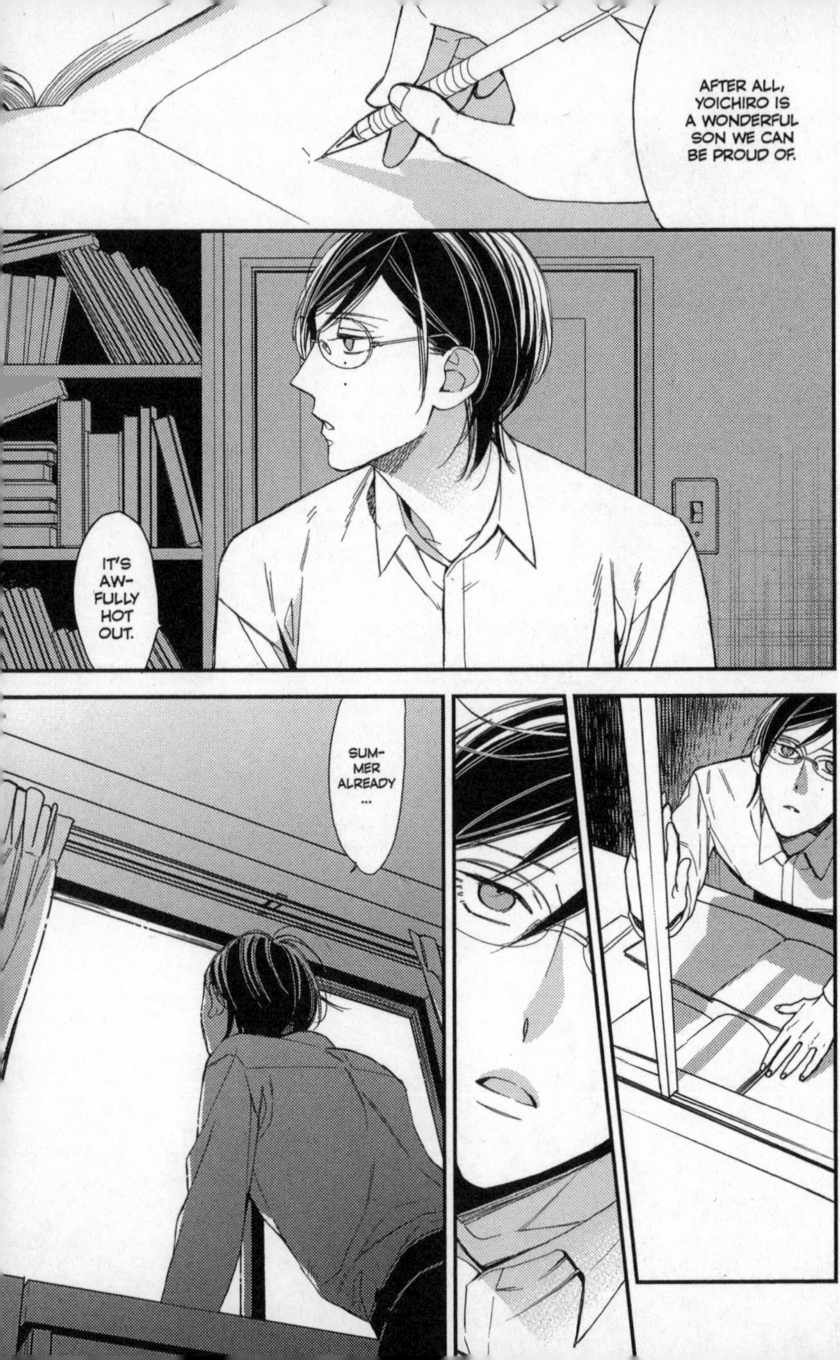
AFTER ALL, YOICHIRO IS A WONDERFUL SON WE CAN BE PROUD OF.
IT'S AW-FULLY HOT OUT.
SUM-MER ALREADY ...

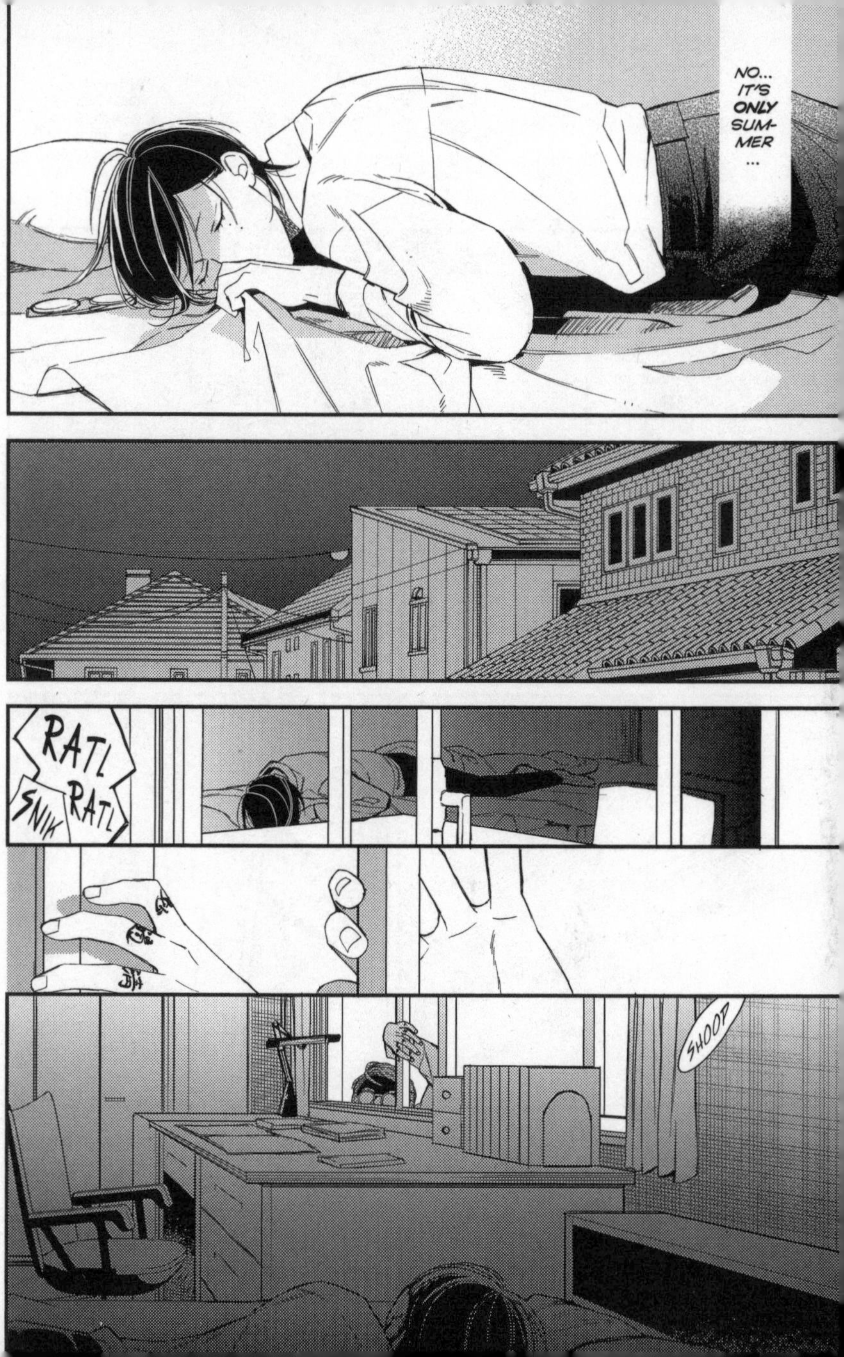
NO... IT'S ONLY SUMMER...
RATL
RATL
SNIK
SHOOP

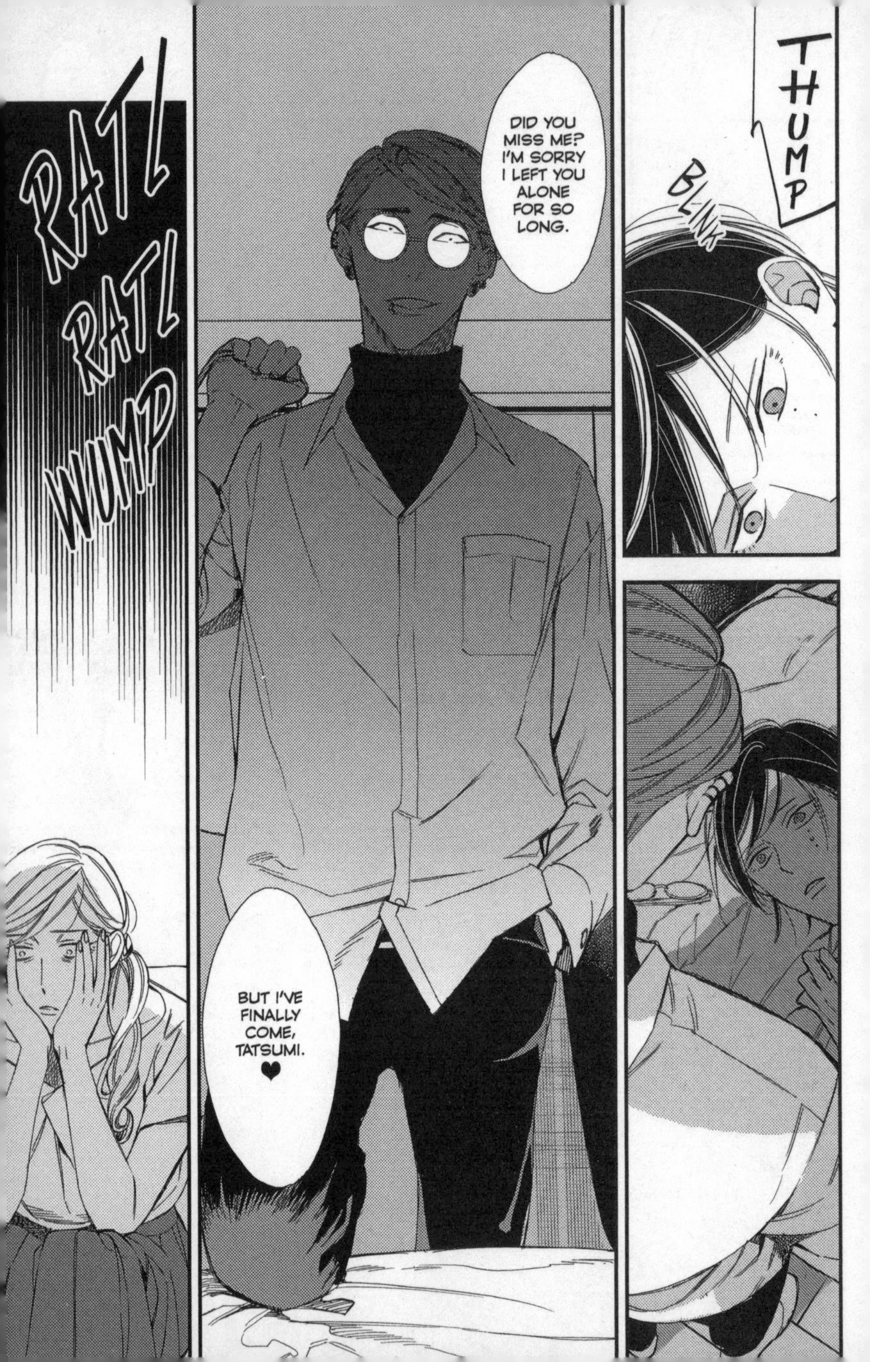
THUMP THUMP
BLINK
DID YOU MISS ME? I'M SORRY I LEFT YOU ALONE FOR SO LONG.
BUT I'VE FINALLY COME, TATSUMI. ♥
RATL RATL
WUMP

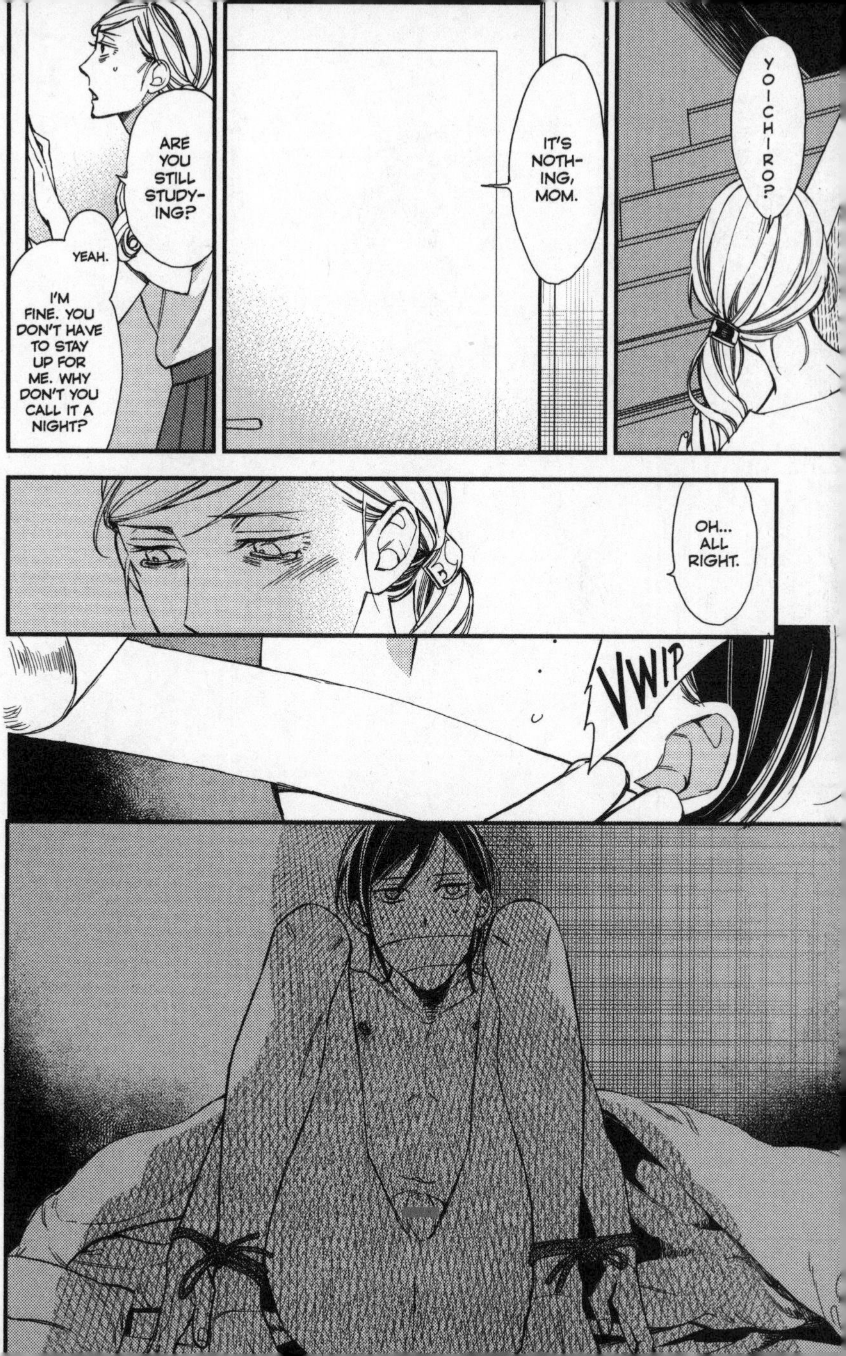
YOICHIRO?
IT'S NOTHING, MOM.
ARE YOU STILL STUDYING?
YEAH.
I'M FINE. YOU DON'T HAVE TO STAY UP FOR ME. WHY DON'T YOU CALL IT A NIGHT?
OH... ALL RIGHT.
VWIP

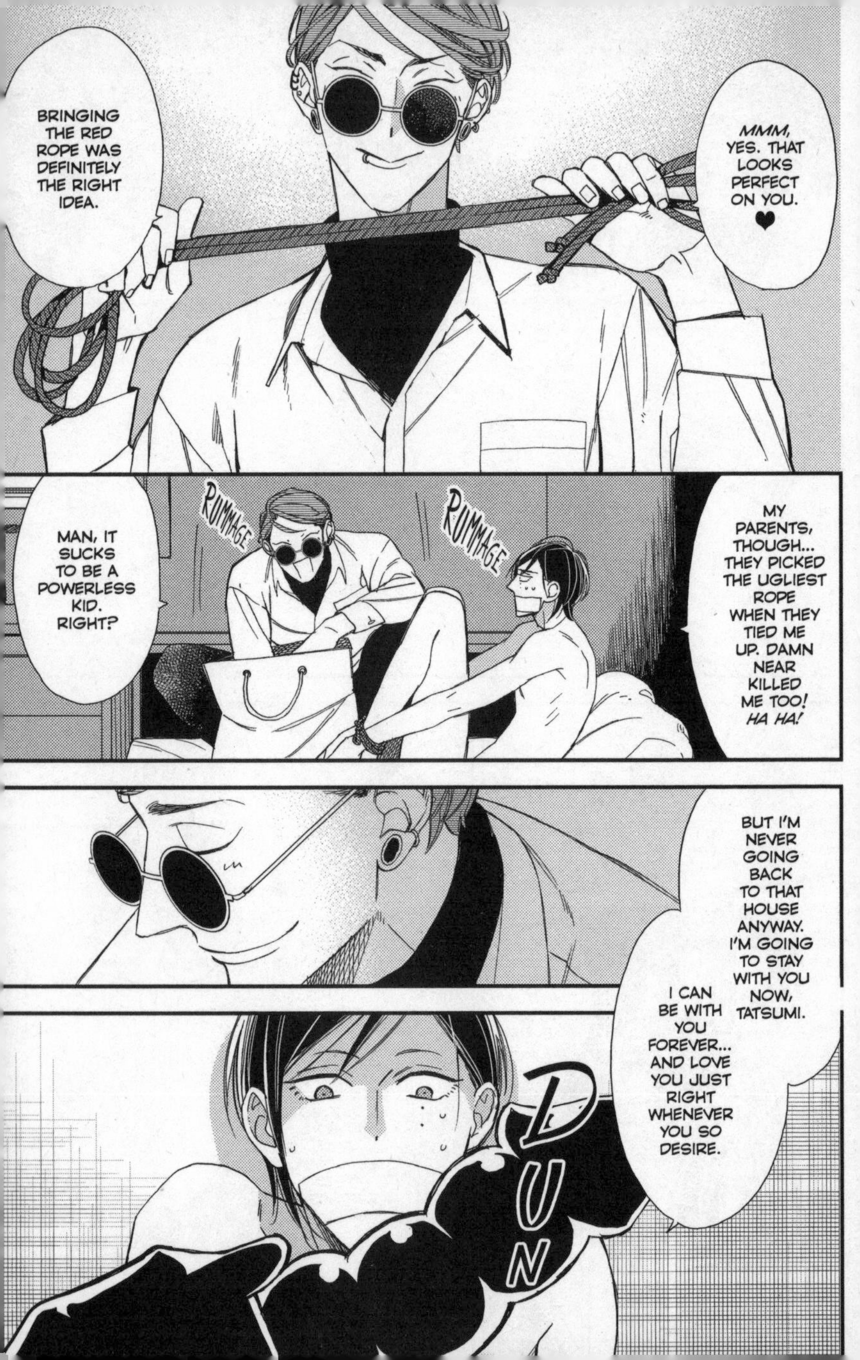
MMM, YES. THAT LOOKS PERFECT ON YOU. ♥
BRINGING THE RED ROPE WAS DEFINITELY THE RIGHT IDEA.
MY PARENTS, THOUGH... THEY PICKED THE UGLIEST ROPE WHEN THEY TIED ME UP. DAMN NEAR KILLED ME TOO! HA HA!
RUMMAGE
RUMMAGE
MAN, IT SUCKS TO BE A POWERLESS KID. RIGHT?
BUT I'M NEVER GOING BACK TO THAT HOUSE ANYWAY. I'M GOING TO STAY WITH YOU NOW, TATSUMI.
I CAN BE WITH YOU FOREVER... AND LOVE YOU JUST RIGHT WHENEVER YOU SO DESIRE.
DUN

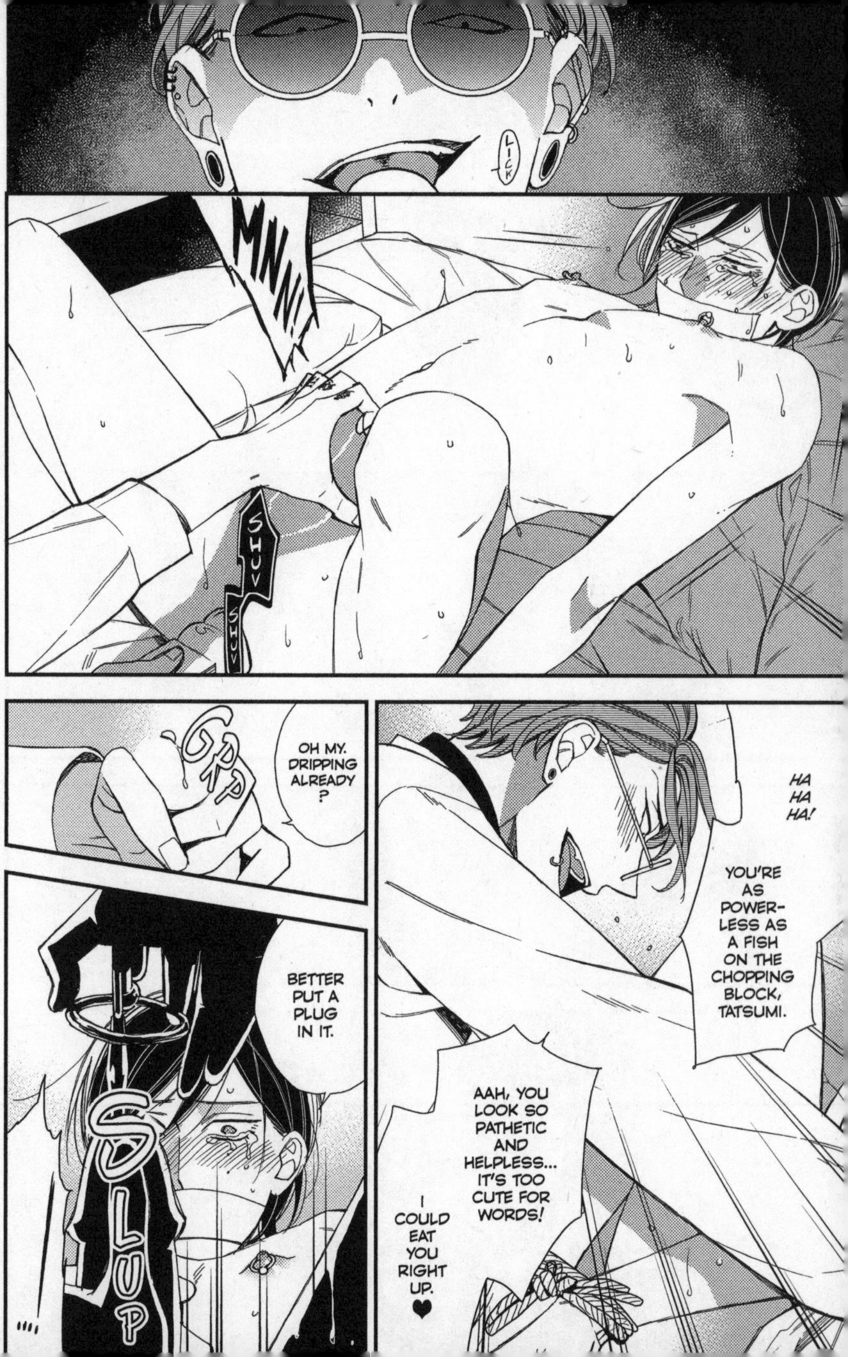
LICK
MNN!
SHUV
SHUV
HA HA HA!
YOU'RE AS POWERLESS AS A FISH ON THE CHOPPING BLOCK, TATSUMI.
AAH, YOU LOOK SO PATHETIC AND HELPLESS... IT'S TOO CUTE FOR WORDS!
I COULD EAT YOU RIGHT UP. ❤
GRP
OH MY. DRIPPING ALREADY?
BETTER PUT A PLUG IN IT.
SLLUP

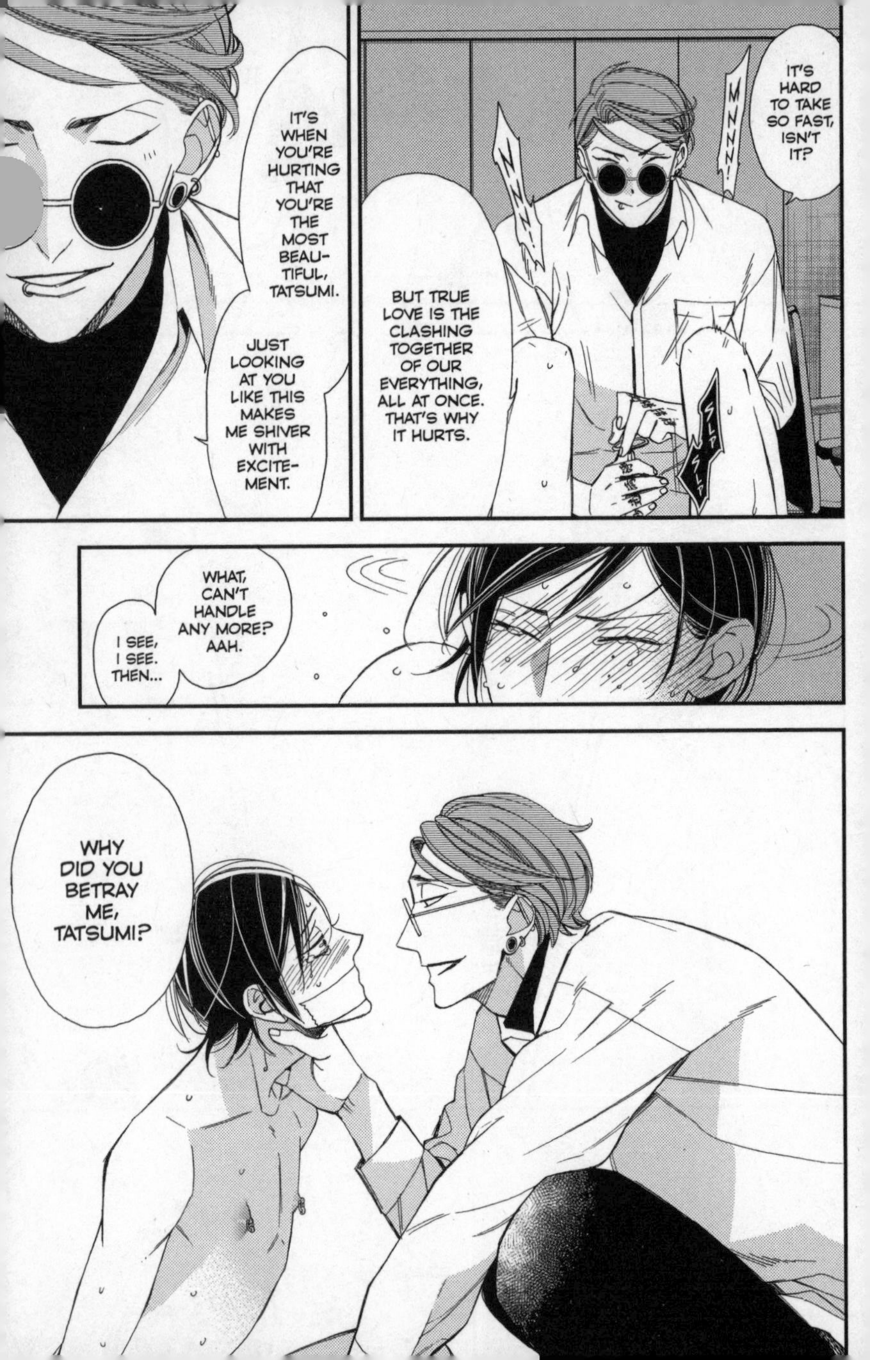
MNNN!
IT'S HARD TO TAKE SO FAST, ISN'T IT?
NNN!
SLP SLP
BUT TRUE LOVE IS THE CLASHING TOGETHER OF OUR EVERYTHING, ALL AT ONCE. THAT'S WHY IT HURTS.
IT'S WHEN YOU'RE HURTING THAT YOU'RE THE MOST BEAUTIFUL, TATSUMI.
JUST LOOKING AT YOU LIKE THIS MAKES ME SHIVER WITH EXCITEMENT.
WHAT, CAN'T HANDLE ANY MORE? AAH.
I SEE, I SEE. THEN...
WHY DID YOU BETRAY ME, TATSUMI?

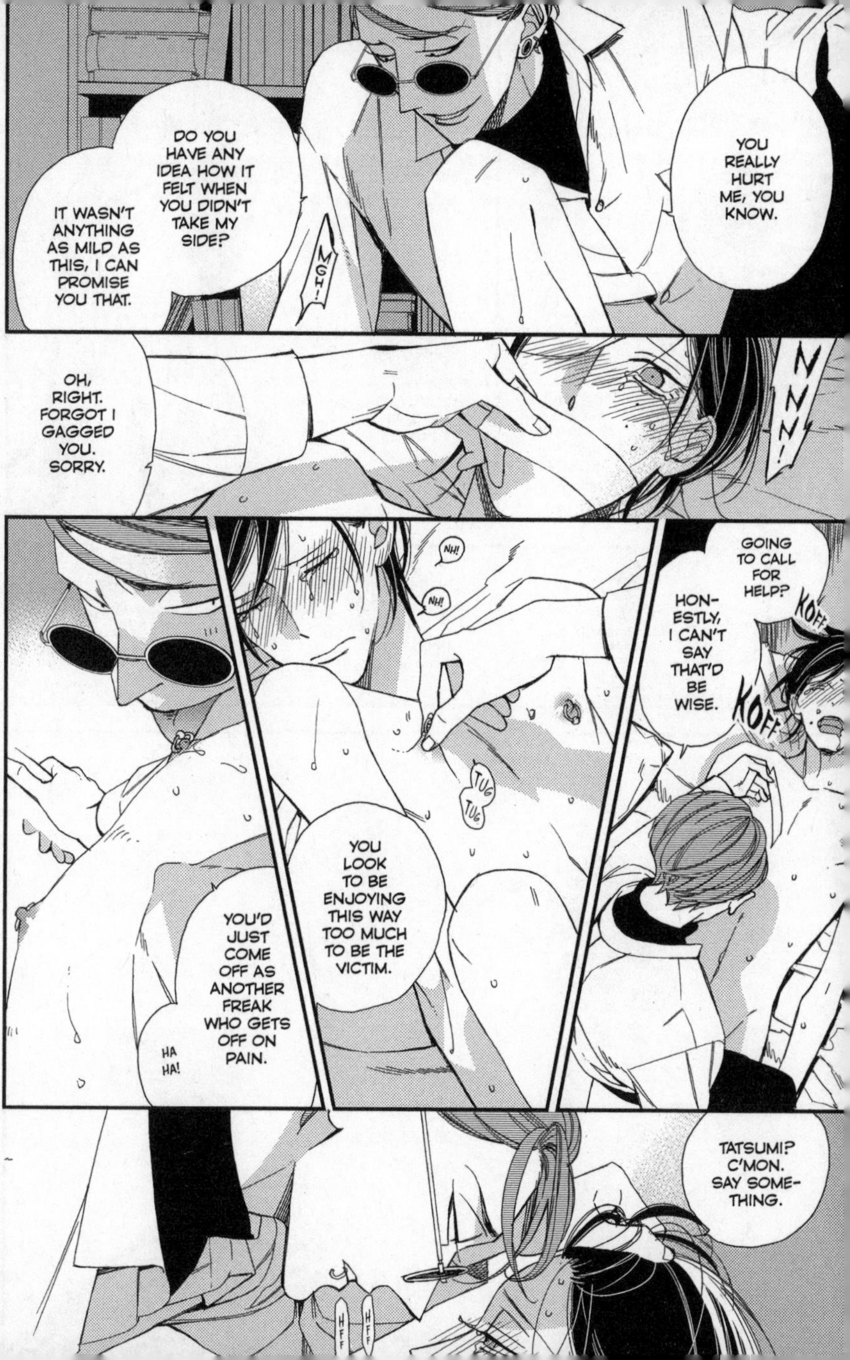
YOU REALLY HURT ME, YOU KNOW.
DO YOU HAVE ANY IDEA HOW IT FELT WHEN YOU DIDN'T TAKE MY SIDE?
MGH!
IT WASN'T ANYTHING AS MILD AS THIS, I CAN PROMISE YOU THAT.
NNN!
OH, RIGHT. FORGOT I GAGGED YOU. SORRY.
GOING TO CALL FOR HELP?
HON-ESTLY, I CAN'T SAY THAT'D BE WISE.
KOFF
KOFF
NH!
NH!
TUG TUG
YOU LOOK TO BE ENJOYING THIS WAY TOO MUCH TO BE THE VICTIM.
YOU'D JUST COME OFF AS ANOTHER FREAK WHO GETS OFF ON PAIN.
HA HA!
TATSUMI? C'MON. SAY SOME-THING.
HFF
HFF

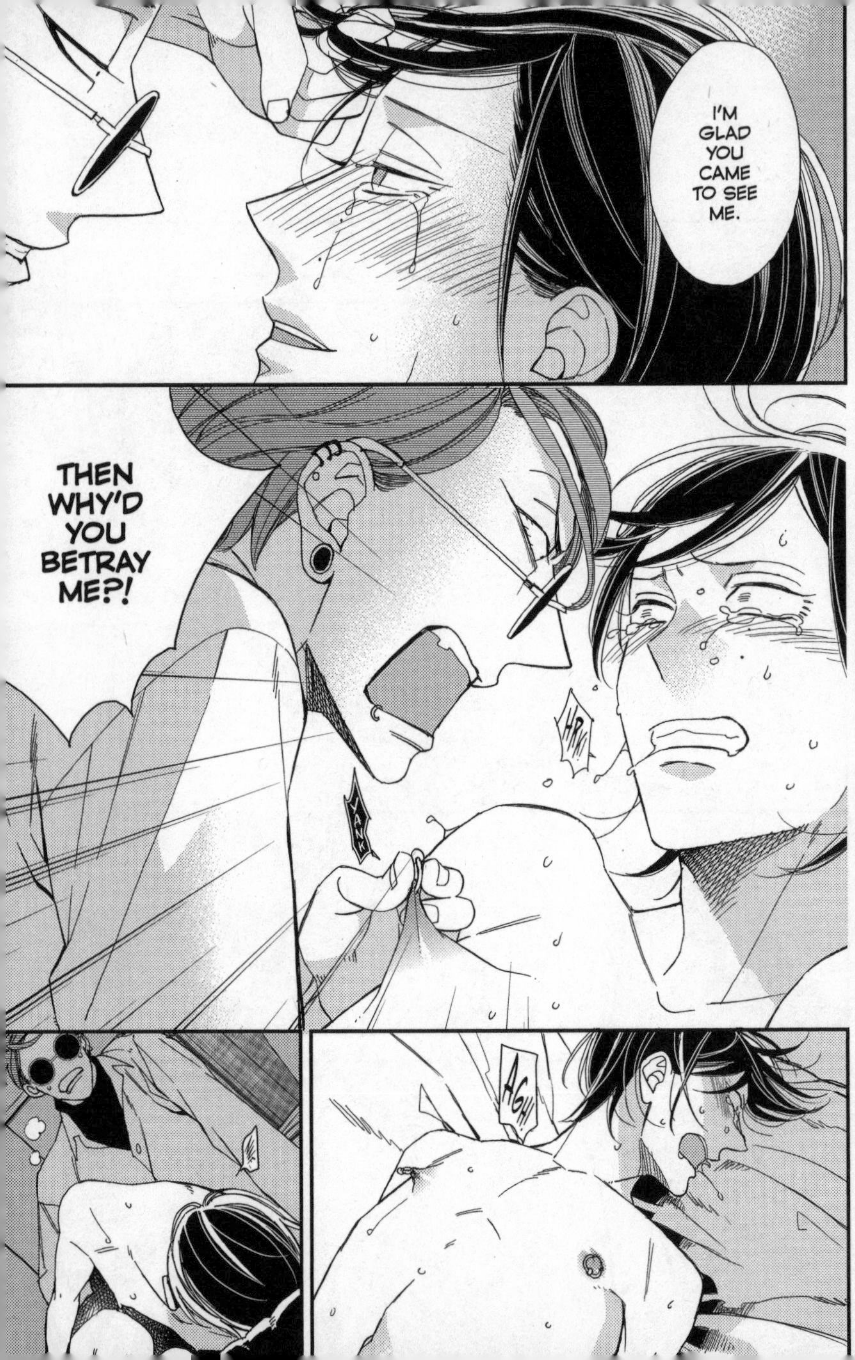
I'M GLAD YOU CAME TO SEE ME.
THEN WHY'D YOU BETRAY ME?!
HRK!
YANK
AGH!

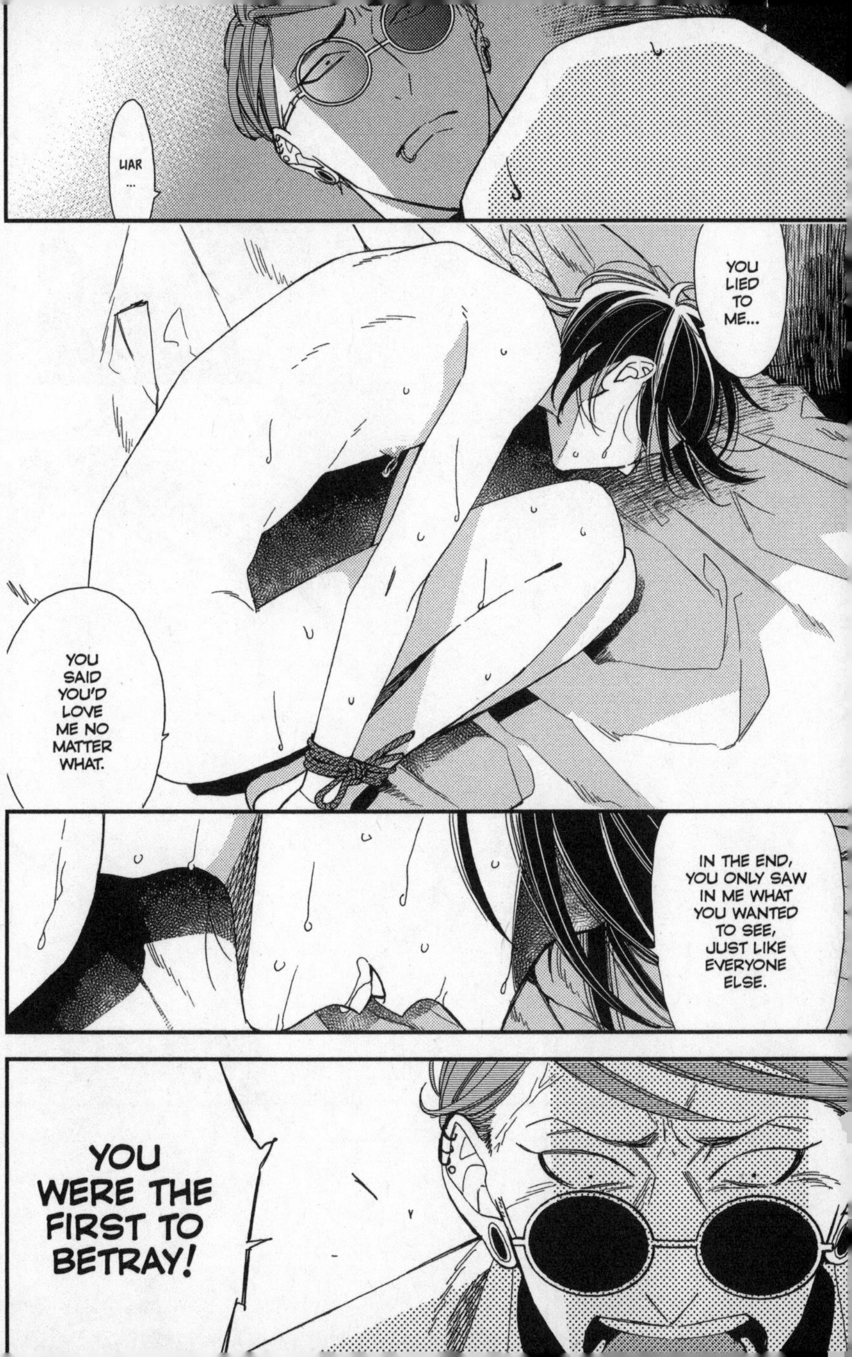
LIAR ...
YOU LIED TO ME...
YOU SAID YOU'D LOVE ME NO MATTER WHAT.
IN THE END, YOU ONLY SAW IN ME WHAT YOU WANTED TO SEE, JUST LIKE EVERYONE ELSE.
YOU WERE THE FIRST TO BETRAY!

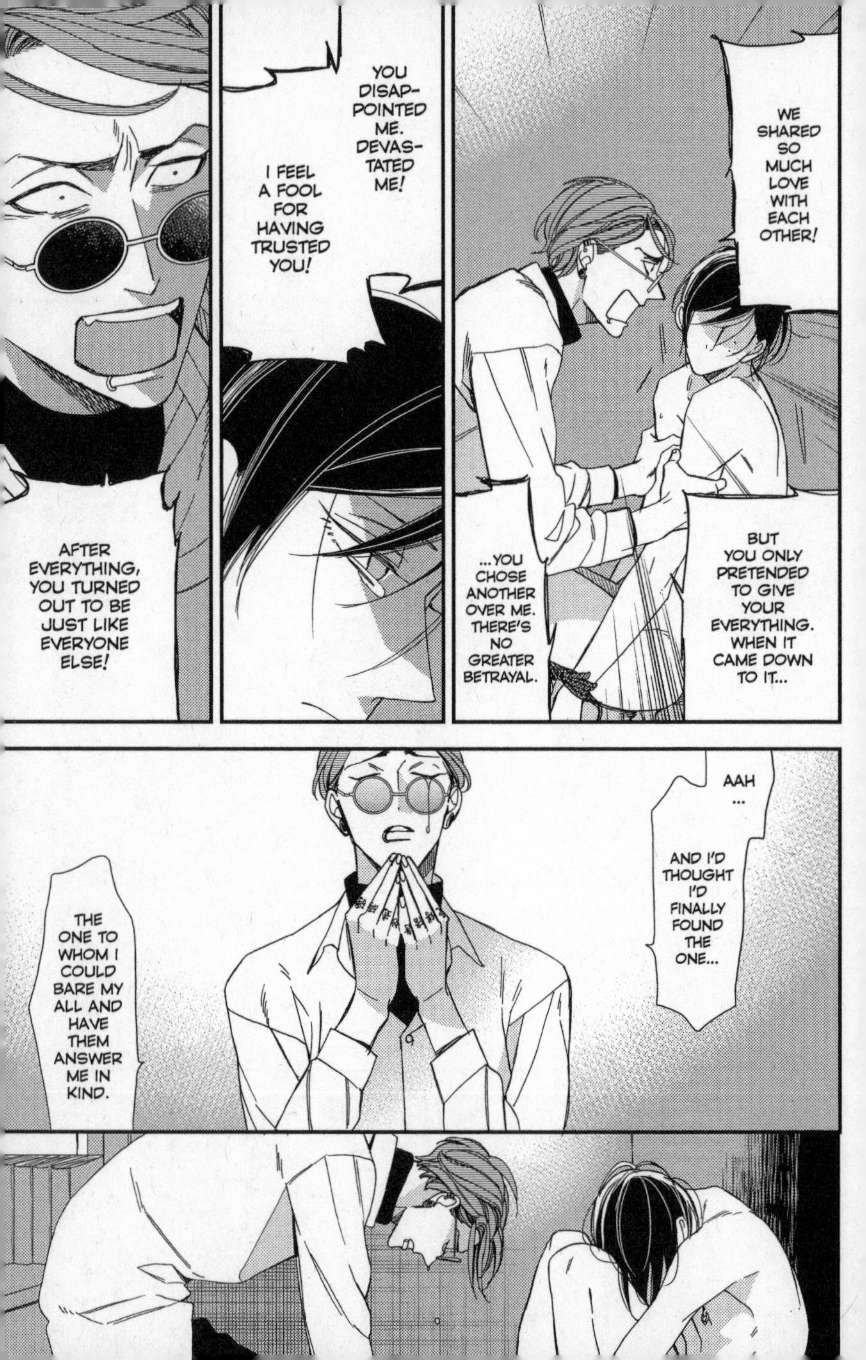
WE SHARED SO MUCH LOVE WITH EACH OTHER!
BUT YOU ONLY PRETENDED TO GIVE YOUR EVERYTHING. WHEN IT CAME DOWN TO IT...
...YOU CHOSE ANOTHER OVER ME. THERE'S NO GREATER BETRAYAL.
YOU DISAPPOINTED ME. DEVASTATED ME!
I FEEL A FOOL FOR HAVING TRUSTED YOU!
AFTER EVERYTHING, YOU TURNED OUT TO BE JUST LIKE EVERYONE ELSE!
AAH ...
AND I'D THOUGHT I'D FINALLY FOUND THE ONE...
THE ONE TO WHOM I COULD BARE MY ALL AND HAVE THEM ANSWER ME IN KIND.

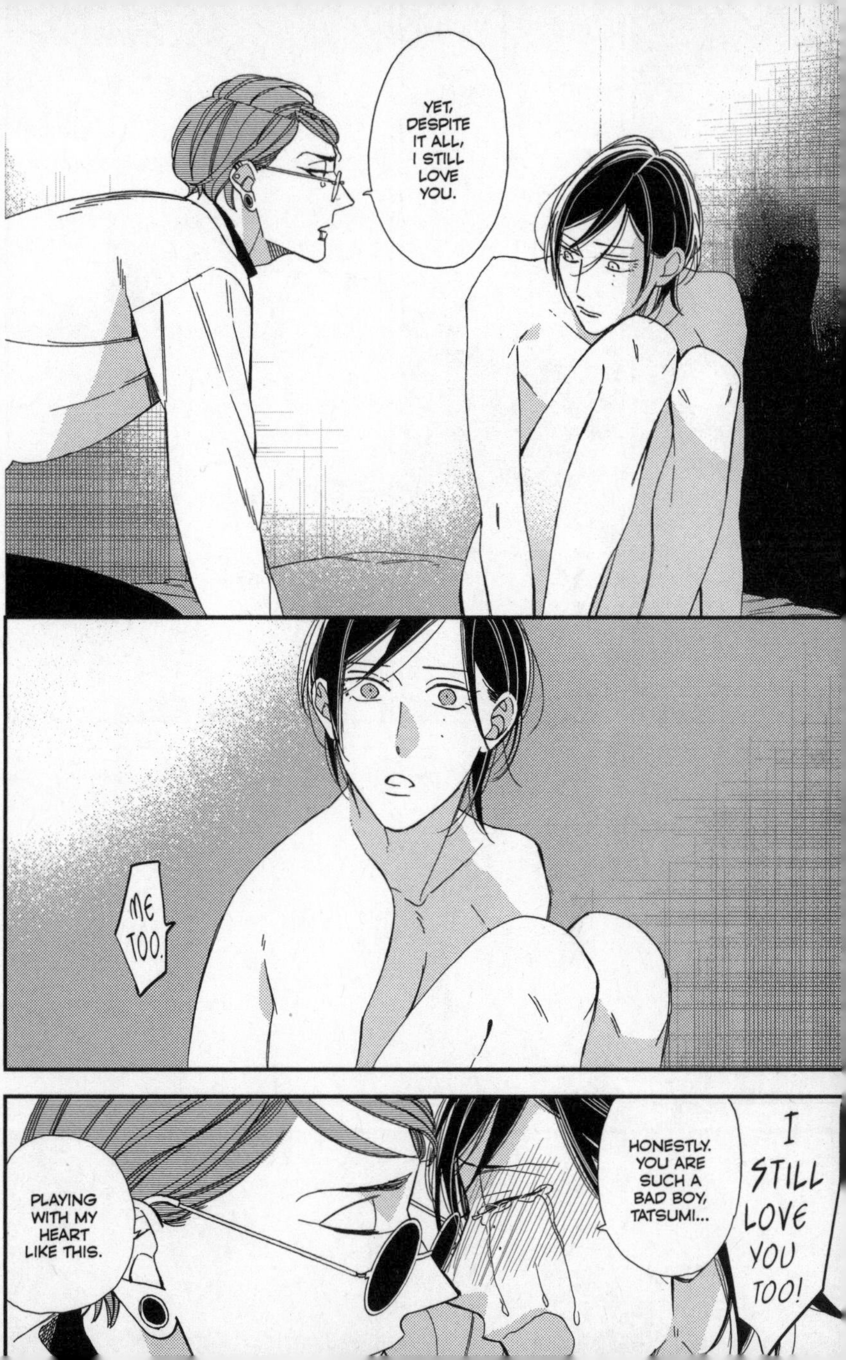
YET, DESPITE IT ALL, I STILL LOVE YOU.
ME TOO.
I STILL LOVE YOU TOO!
HONESTLY. YOU ARE SUCH A BAD BOY, TATSUMI...
PLAYING WITH MY HEART LIKE THIS.

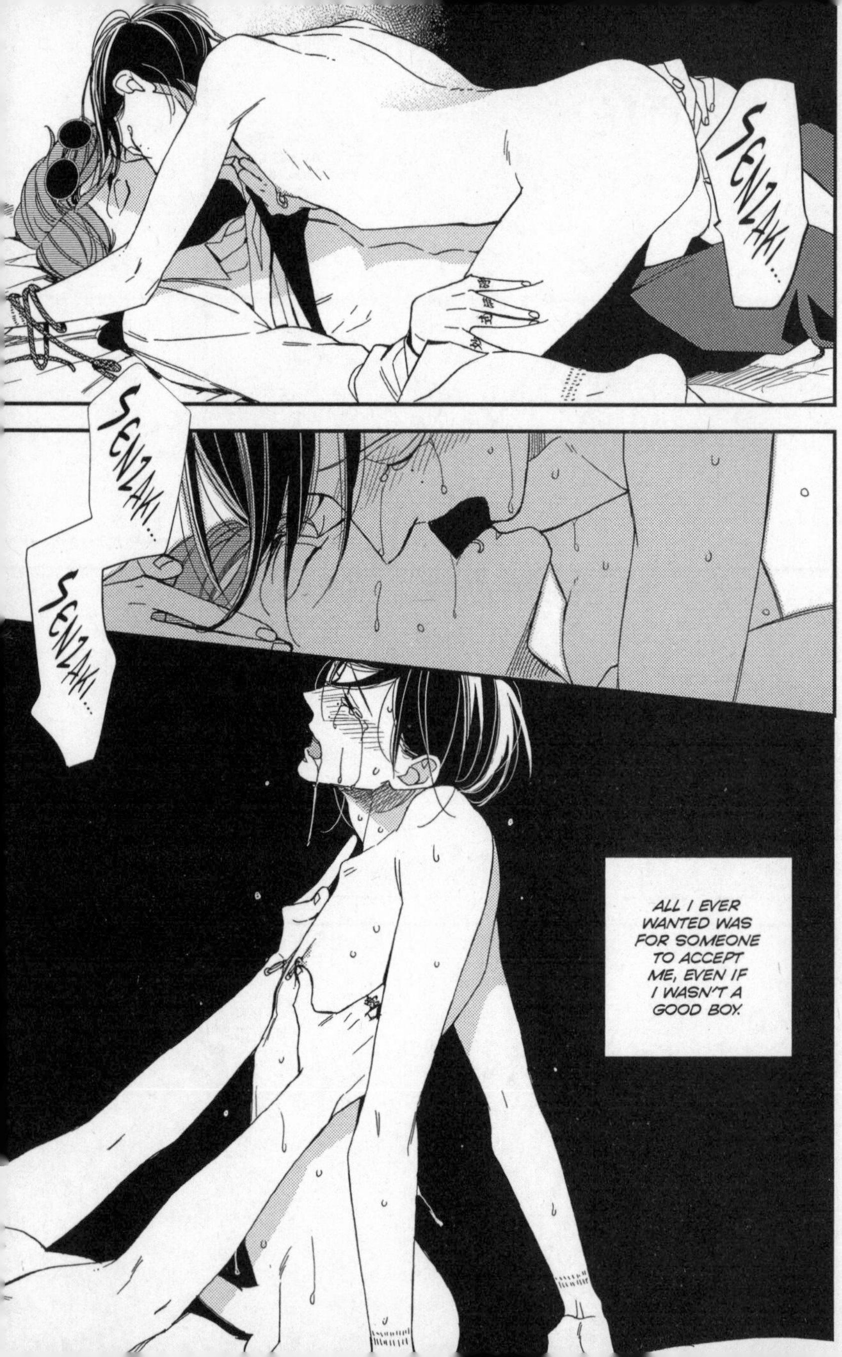
SENZAKI...
SENZAKI...
SENZAKI...
ALL I EVER WANTED WAS FOR SOMEONE TO ACCEPT ME, EVEN IF I WASN'T A GOOD BOY.

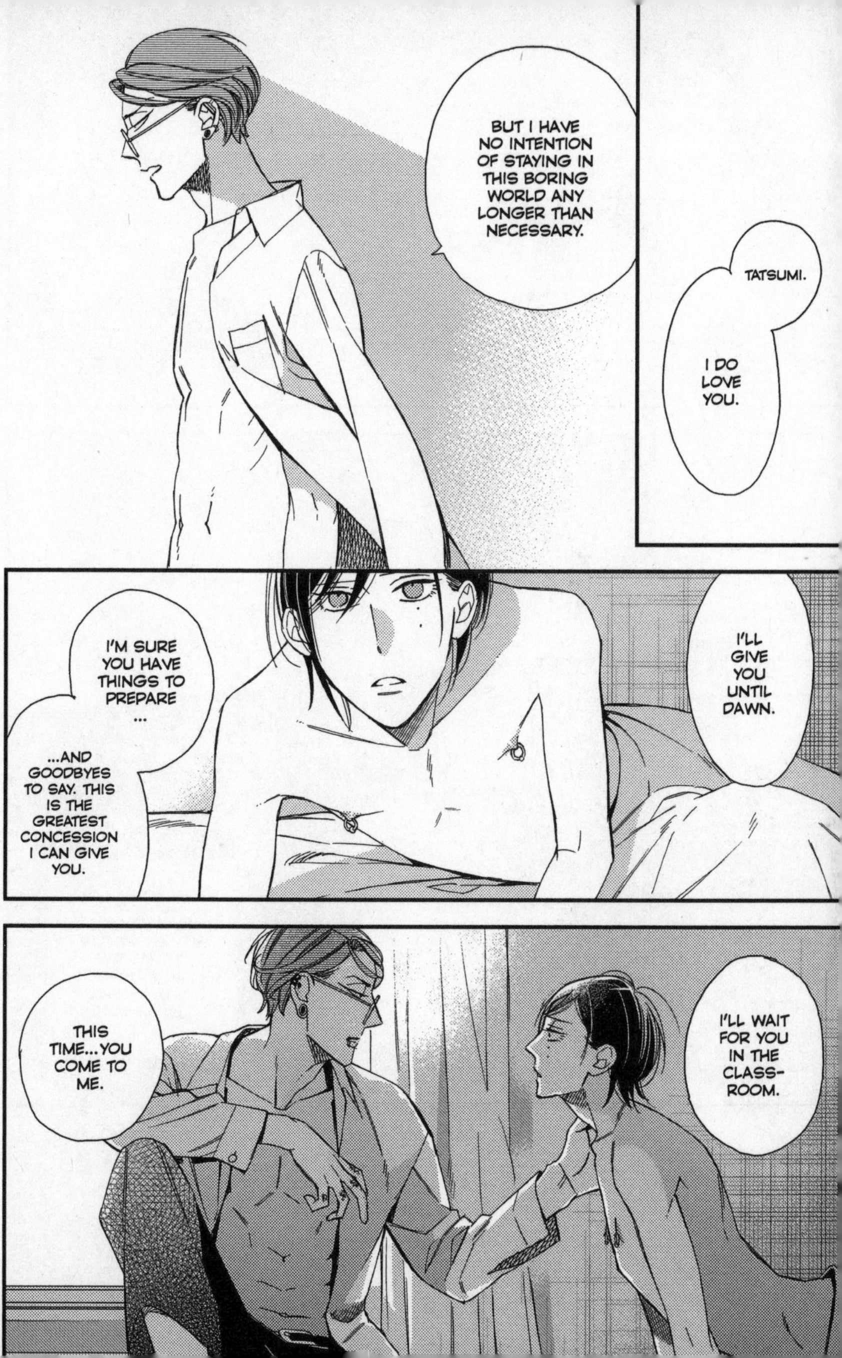
TATSUMI.
I DO LOVE YOU.
BUT I HAVE NO INTENTION OF STAYING IN THIS BORING WORLD ANY LONGER THAN NECESSARY.
I'LL GIVE YOU UNTIL DAWN.
I'M SURE YOU HAVE THINGS TO PREPARE ...
...AND GOODBYES TO SAY. THIS IS THE GREATEST CONCESSION I CAN GIVE YOU.
I'LL WAIT FOR YOU IN THE CLASS-ROOM.
THIS TIME...YOU COME TO ME.

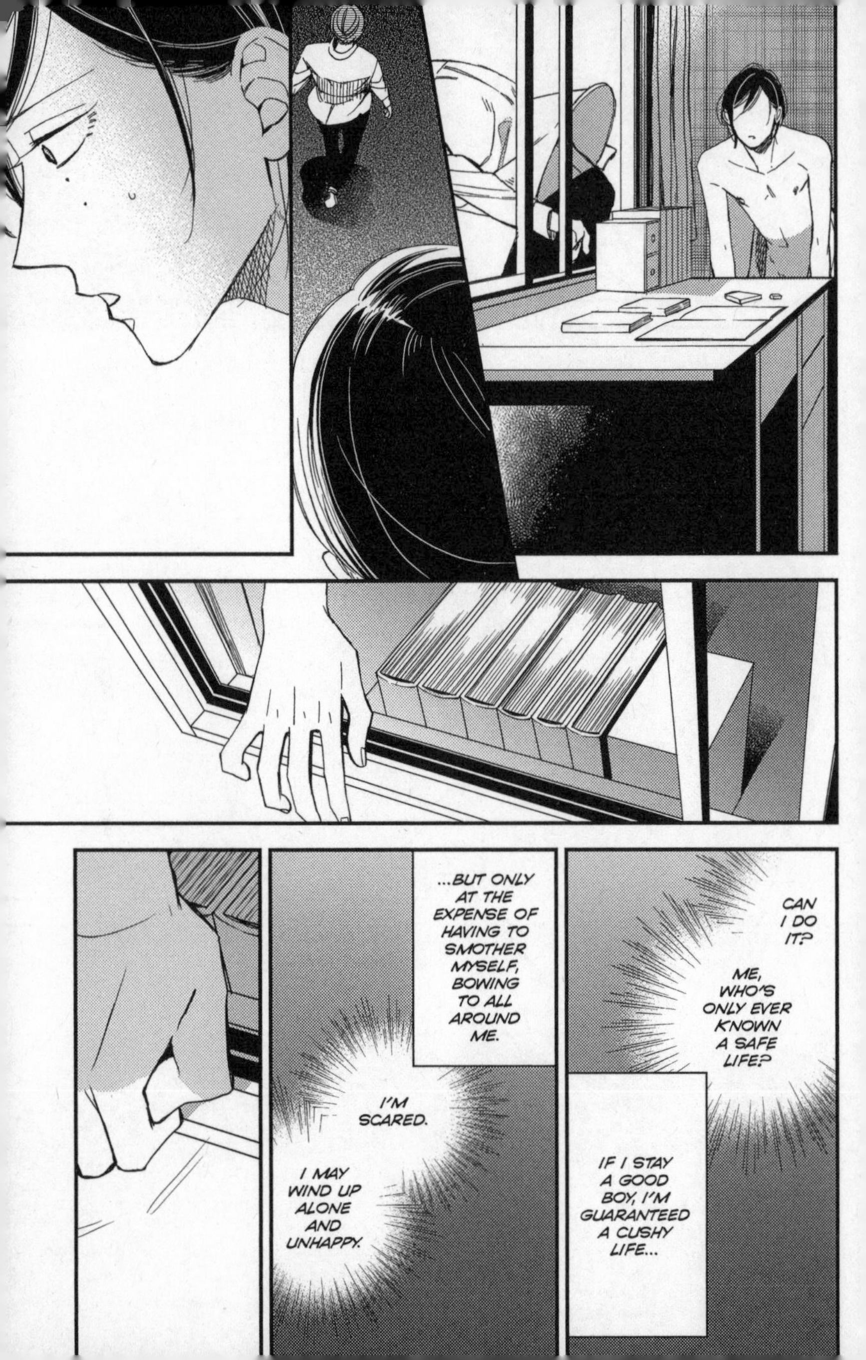
CAN I DO IT?
ME, WHO'S ONLY EVER KNOWN A SAFE LIFE?
IF I STAY A GOOD BOY, I'M GUARANTEED A CUSHY LIFE...
...BUT ONLY AT THE EXPENSE OF HAVING TO SMOTHER MYSELF, BOWING TO ALL AROUND ME.
I'M SCARED.
I MAY WIND UP ALONE AND UNHAPPY.

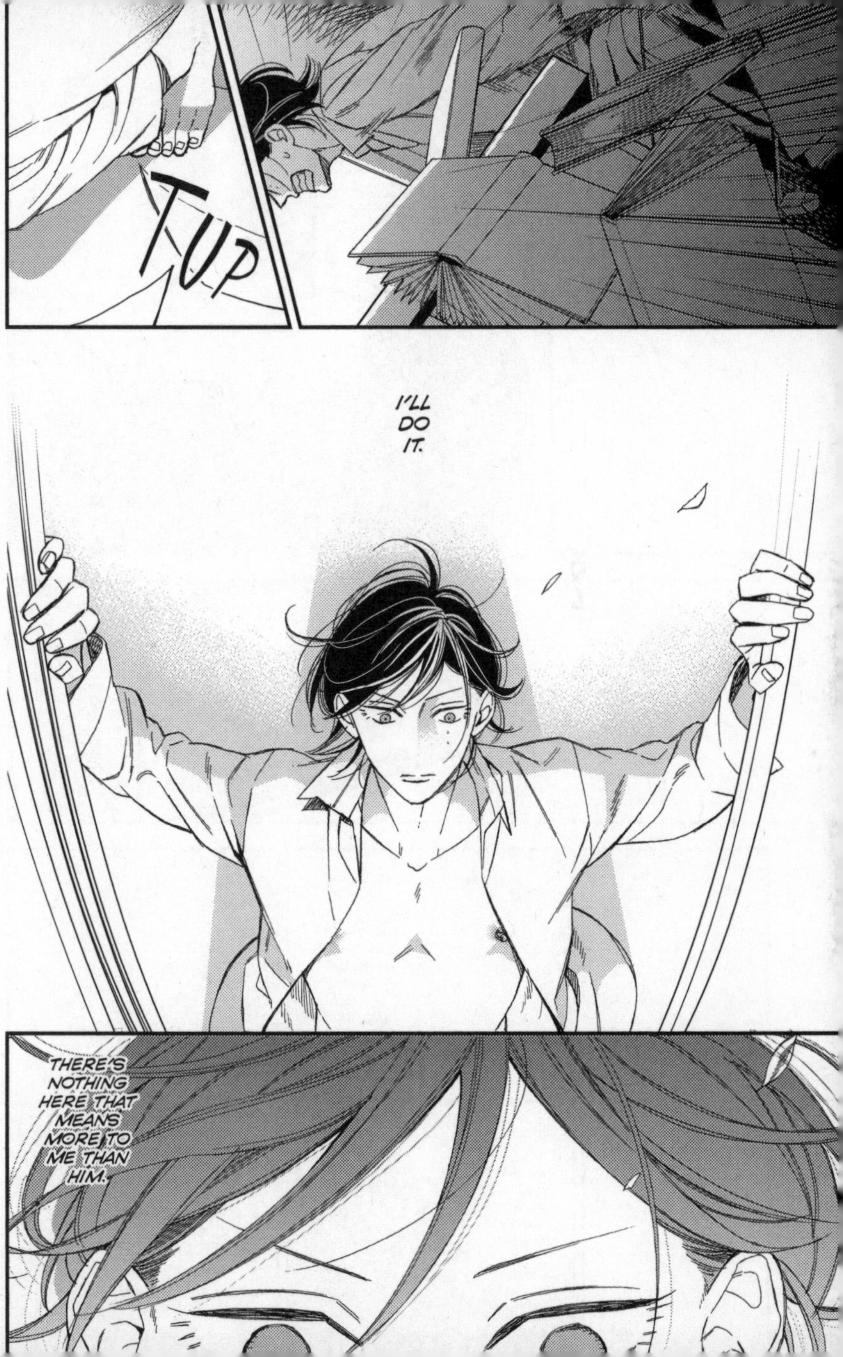
TUP
I'LL DO IT.
THERE'S NOTHING HERE THAT MEANS MORE TO ME THAN HIM.

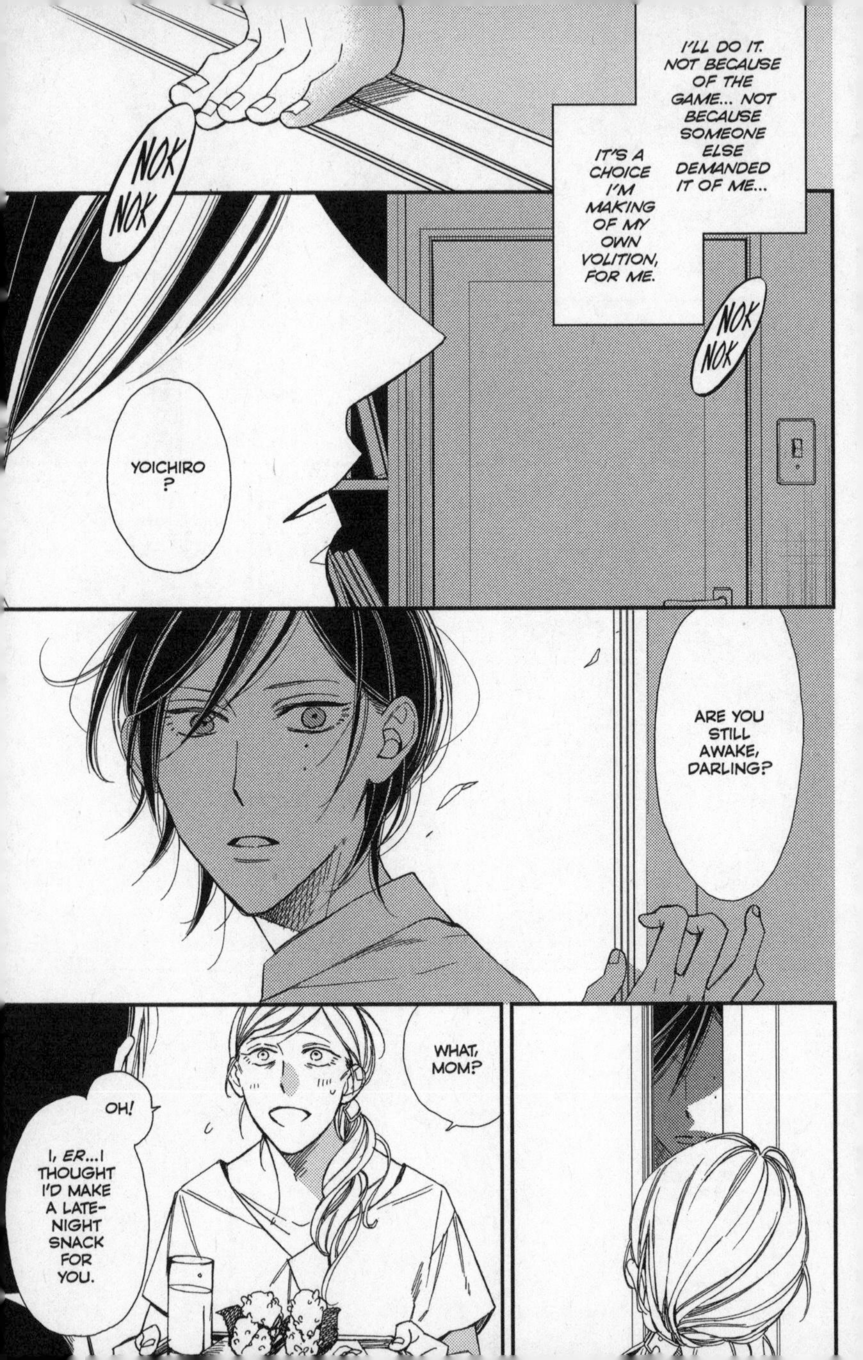
I'LL DO IT. NOT BECAUSE OF THE GAME... NOT BECAUSE SOMEONE ELSE DEMANDED IT OF ME...
IT'S A CHOICE I'M MAKING OF MY OWN VOLITION, FOR ME.
NOK NOK
NOK NOK
YOICHIRO?
ARE YOU STILL AWAKE, DARLING?
WHAT, MOM?
OH!
I, *ER*...I THOUGHT I'D MAKE A LATE-NIGHT SNACK FOR YOU.

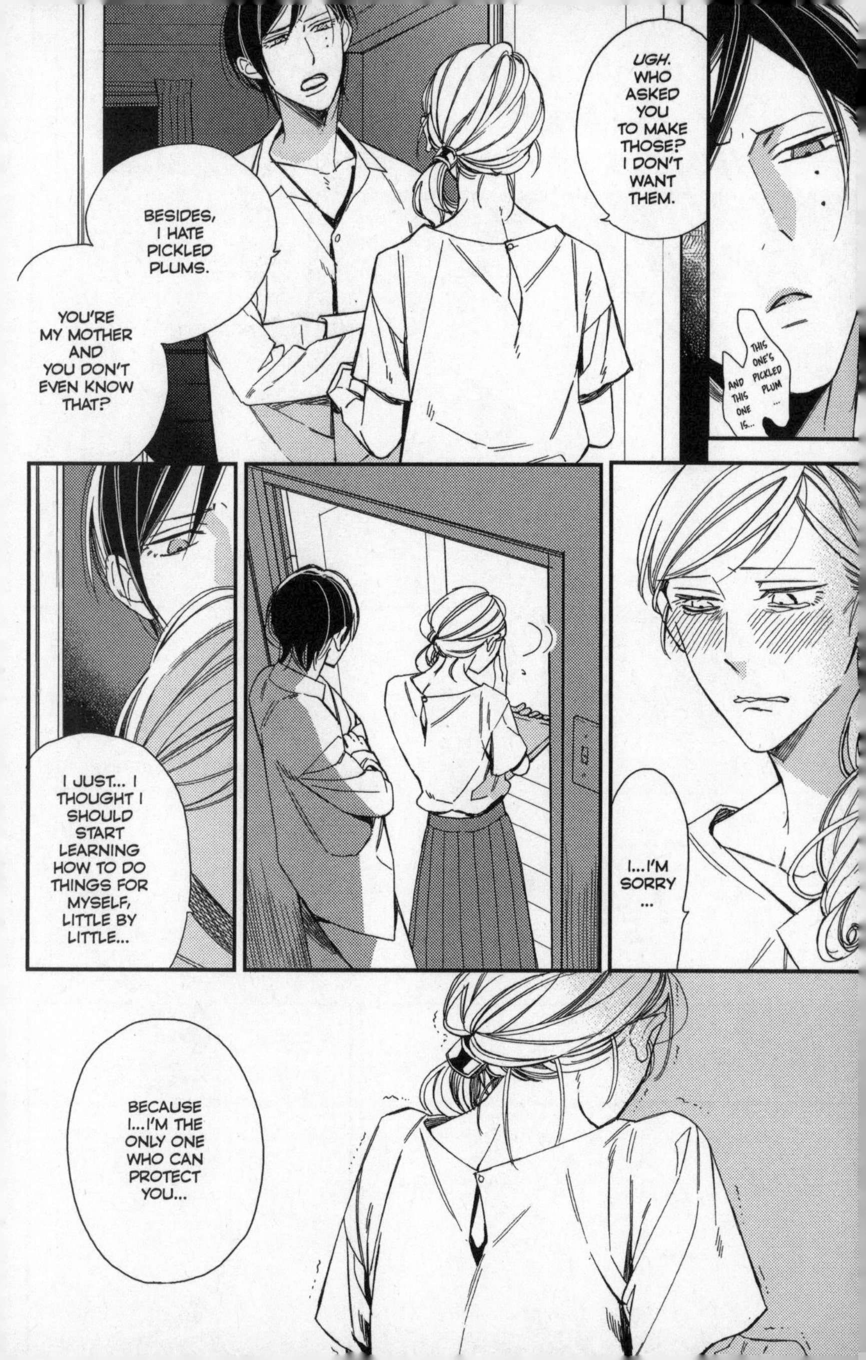
THIS ONE'S PICKLED PLUM... AND THIS ONE IS...
UGH. WHO ASKED YOU TO MAKE THOSE? I DON'T WANT THEM.
BESIDES, I HATE PICKLED PLUMS.
YOU'RE MY MOTHER AND YOU DON'T EVEN KNOW THAT?
I...I'M SORRY...
I JUST... I THOUGHT I SHOULD START LEARNING HOW TO DO THINGS FOR MYSELF, LITTLE BY LITTLE...
BECAUSE I...I'M THE ONLY ONE WHO CAN PROTECT YOU...

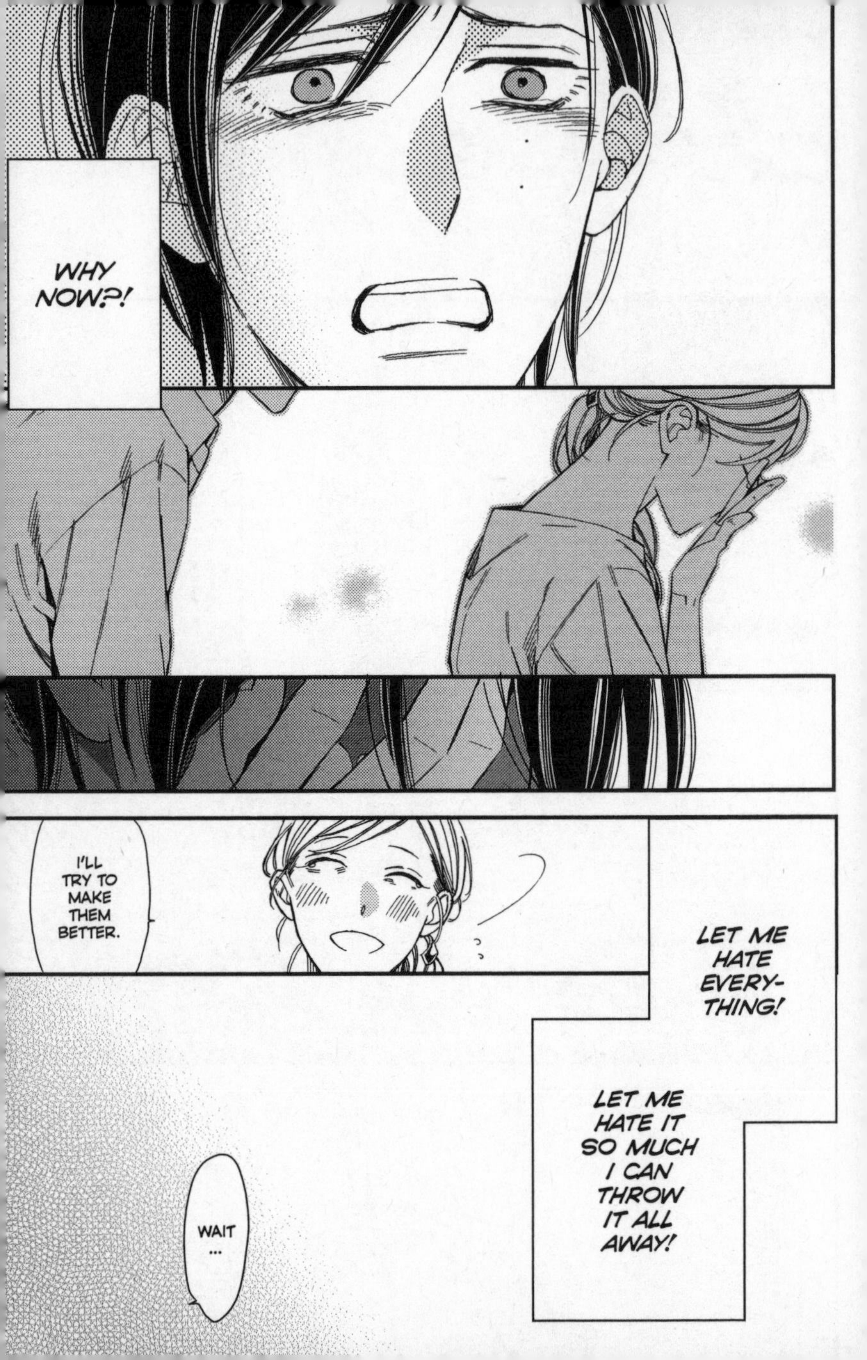
WHY NOW?!
LET ME HATE EVERYTHING!
I'LL TRY TO MAKE THEM BETTER.
LET ME HATE IT SO MUCH I CAN THROW IT ALL AWAY!
WAIT...

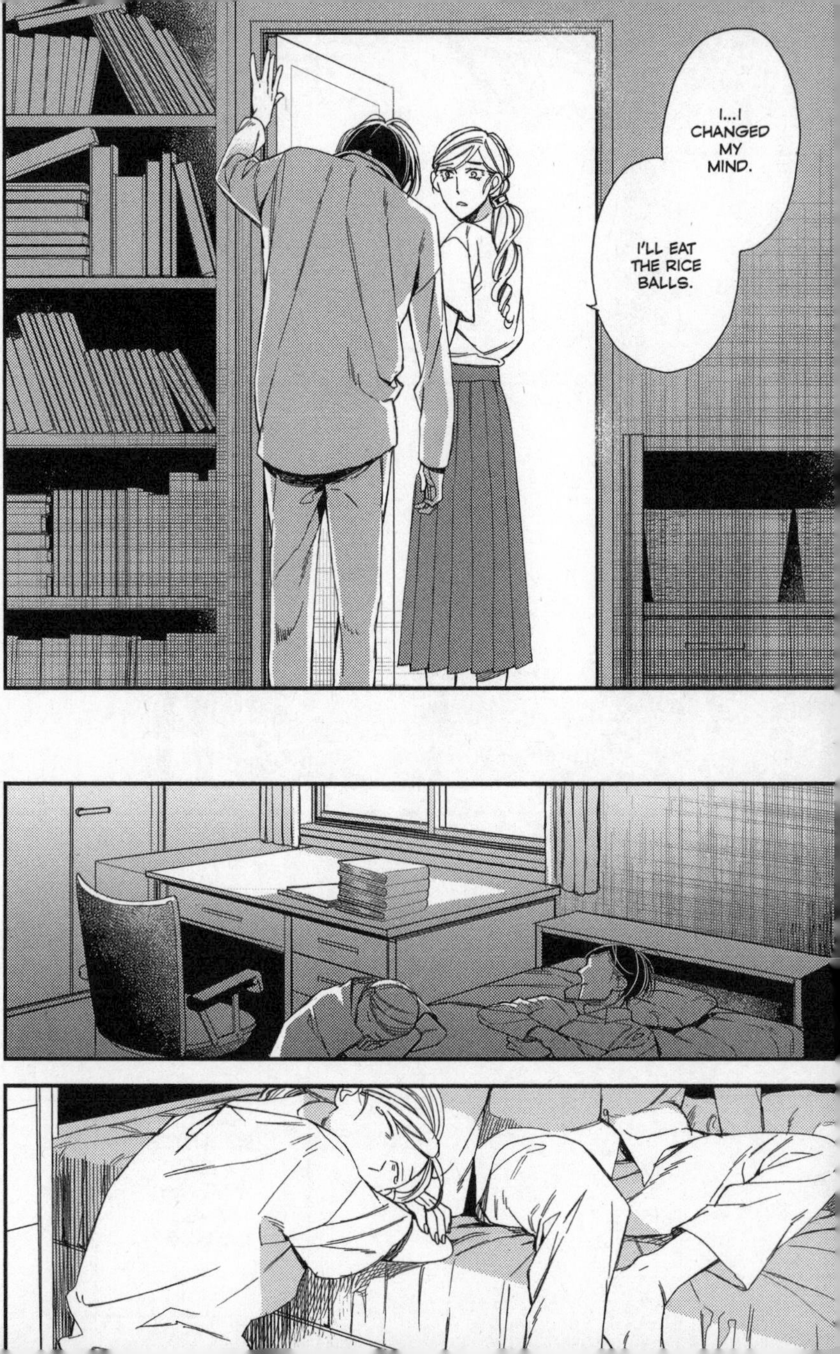
I...I CHANGED MY MIND.
I'LL EAT THE RICE BALLS.

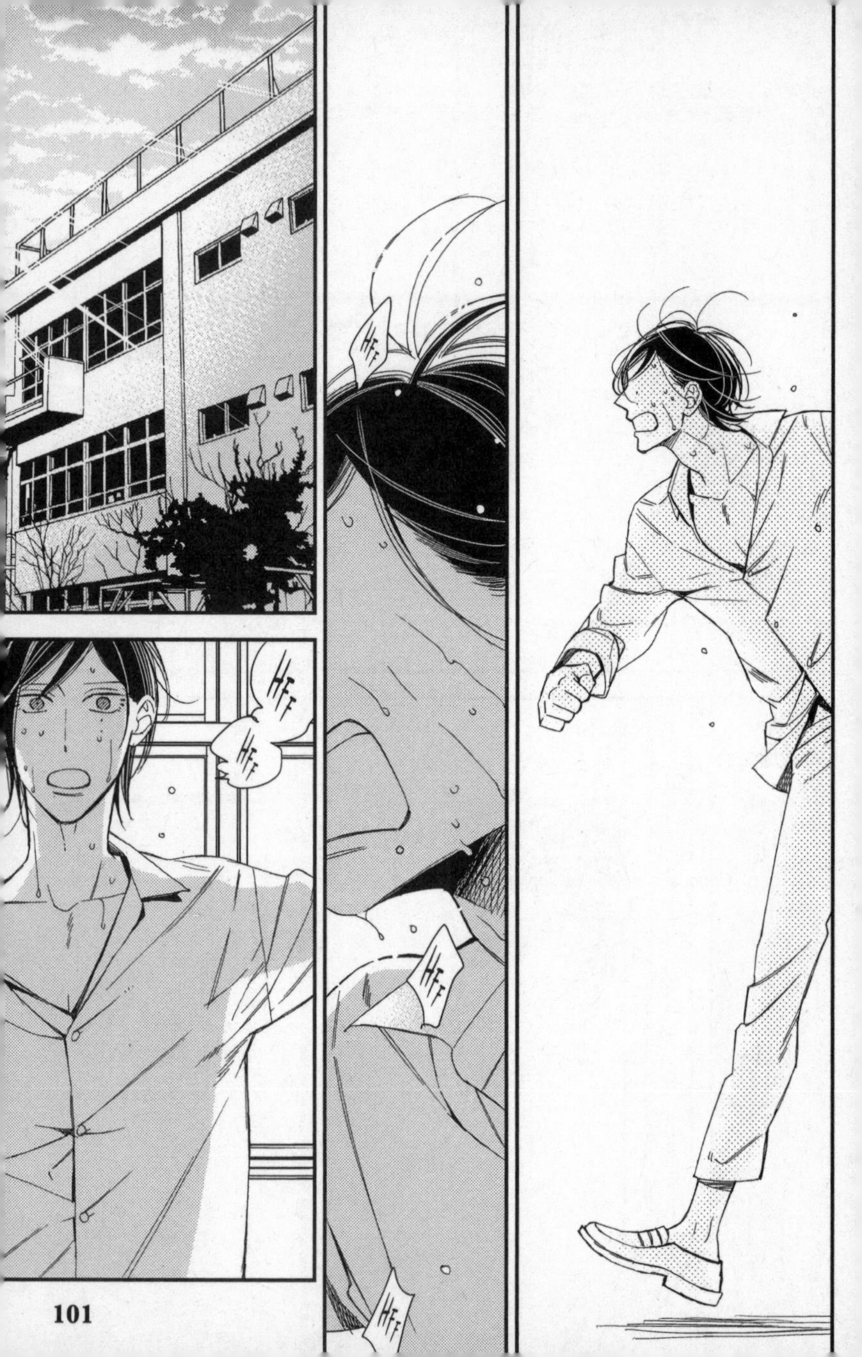
HFF
HFF
HFF
HFF
HFF

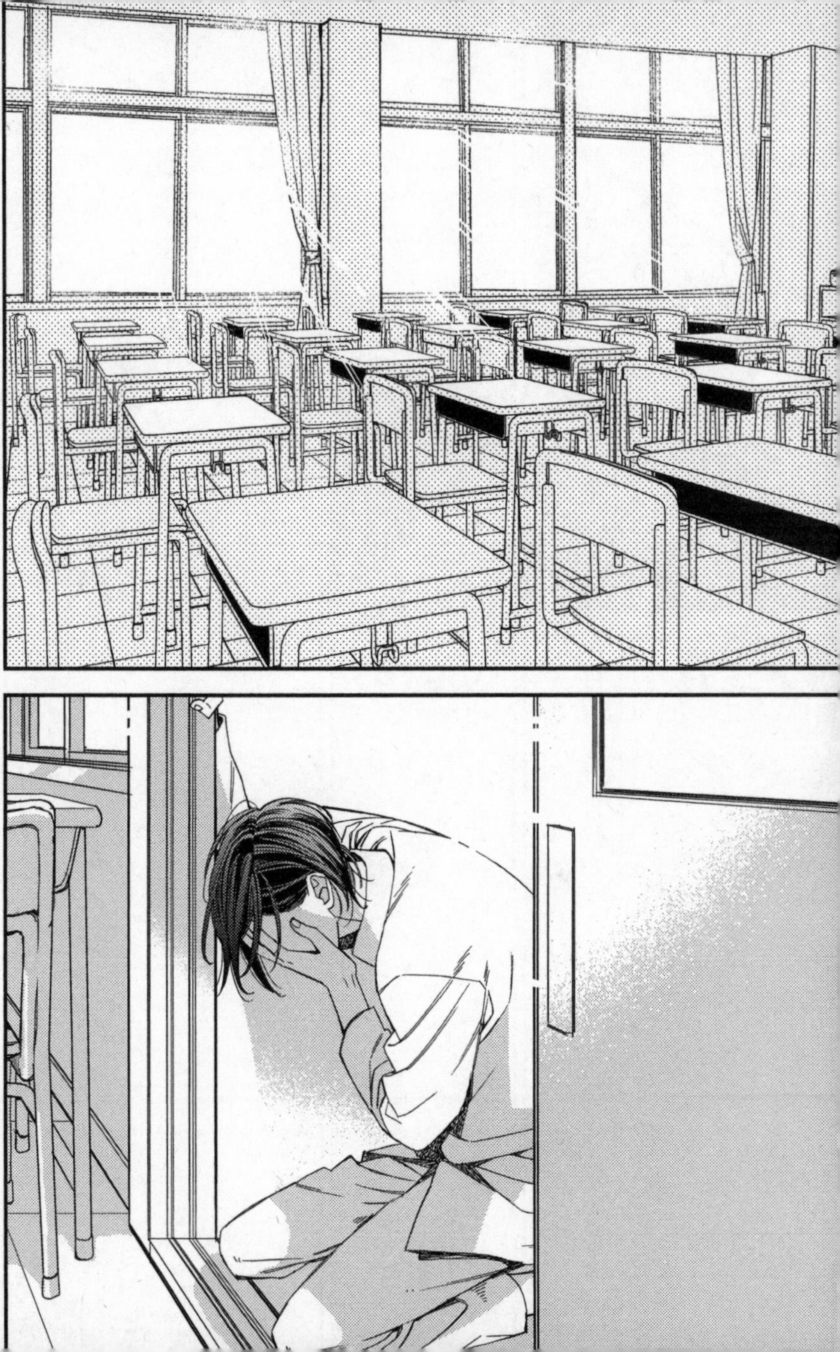

BY THE TIME I RETURNED TO SCHOOL, SENZAKI WAS GONE.

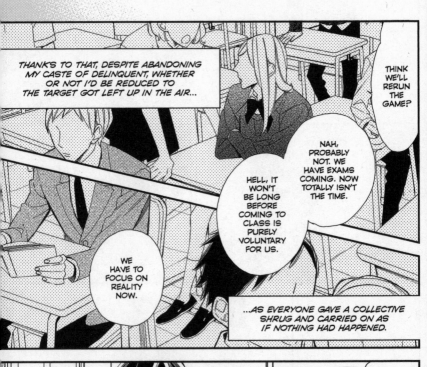

THANK'S TO THAT, DESPITE ABANDONING MY CASTE OF DELINQUENT, WHETHER OR NOT I'D BE REDUCED TO THE TARGET GOT LEFT UP IN THE AIR...

THINK WE'LL RERUN THE GAME?

NAH, PROBABLY NOT. WE HAVE EXAMS COMING. NOW TOTALLY ISN'T THE TIME.

HELL, IT WON'T BE LONG BEFORE COMING TO CLASS IS PURELY VOLUNTARY FOR US.

WE HAVE TO FOCUS ON REALITY NOW.

...AS EVERYONE GAVE A COLLECTIVE SHRUG AND CARRIED ON AS IF NOTHING HAD HAPPENED.

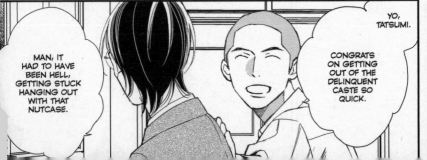

YO, TATSUMI.

CONGRATS ON GETTING OUT OF THE DELINQUENT CASTE SO QUICK.

MAN, IT HAD TO HAVE BEEN HELL, GETTING STUCK HANGING OUT WITH THAT NUTCASE.

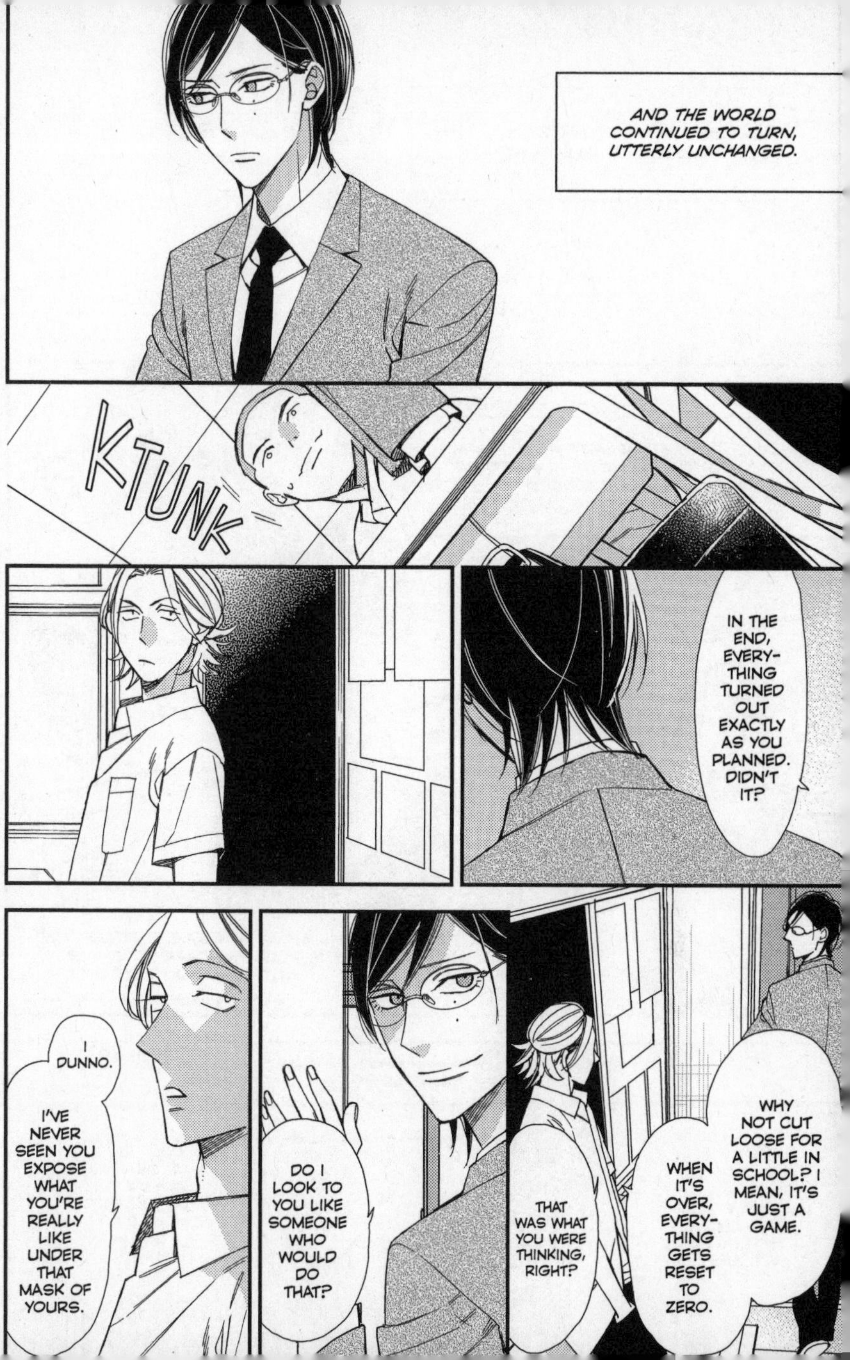
AND THE WORLD CONTINUED TO TURN, UTTERLY UNCHANGED.
KTUNK
IN THE END, EVERYTHING TURNED OUT EXACTLY AS YOU PLANNED. DIDN'T IT?
WHY NOT CUT LOOSE FOR A LITTLE IN SCHOOL? I MEAN, IT'S JUST A GAME.
WHEN IT'S OVER, EVERYTHING GETS RESET TO ZERO.
THAT WAS WHAT YOU WERE THINKING, RIGHT?
DO I LOOK TO YOU LIKE SOMEONE WHO WOULD DO THAT?
I DUNNO.
I'VE NEVER SEEN YOU EXPOSE WHAT YOU'RE REALLY LIKE UNDER THAT MASK OF YOURS.

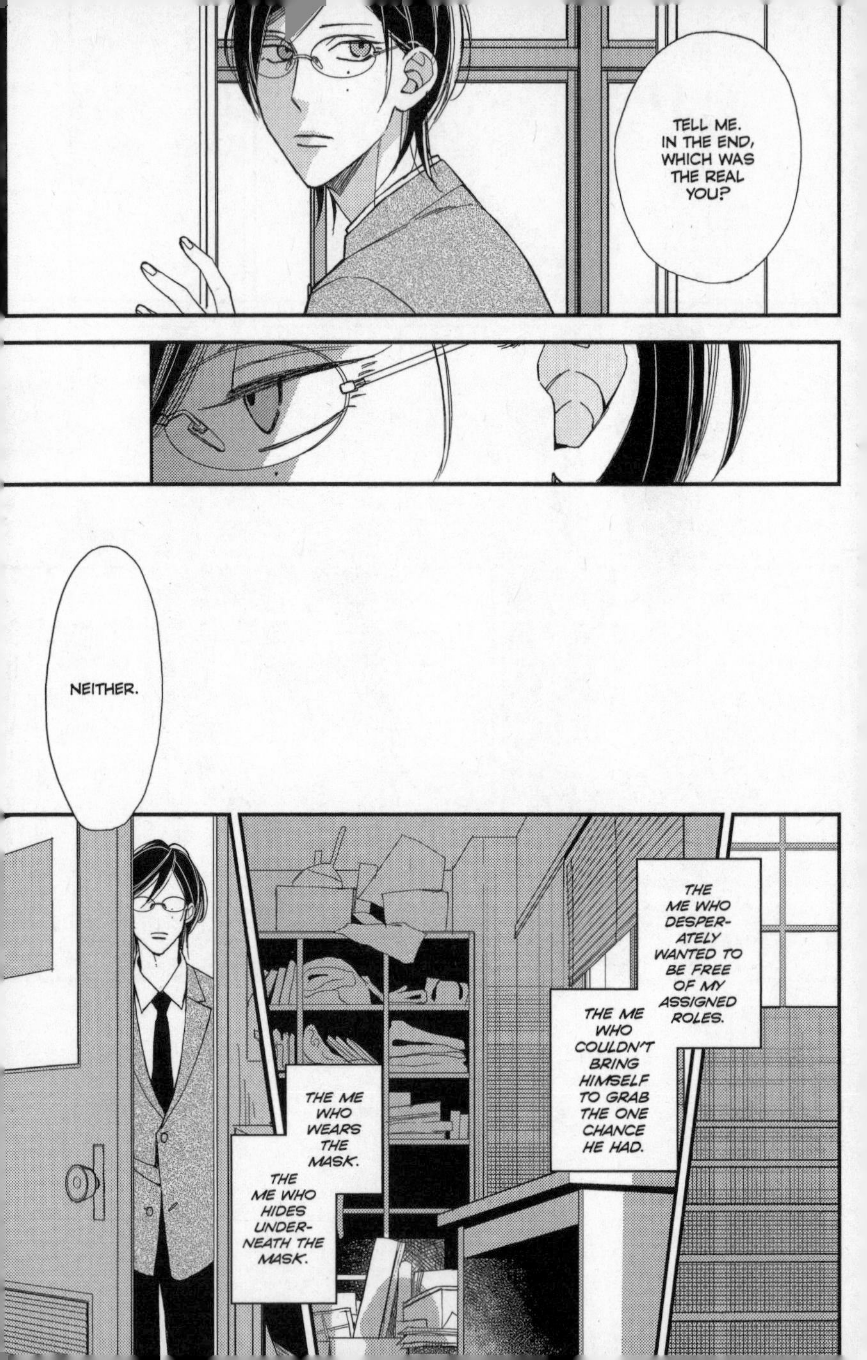
TELL ME. IN THE END, WHICH WAS THE REAL YOU?
NEITHER.
THE ME WHO DESPERATELY WANTED TO BE FREE OF MY ASSIGNED ROLES.
THE ME WHO COULDN'T BRING HIMSELF TO GRAB THE ONE CHANCE HE HAD.
THE ME WHO WEARS THE MASK.
THE ME WHO HIDES UNDERNEATH THE MASK.

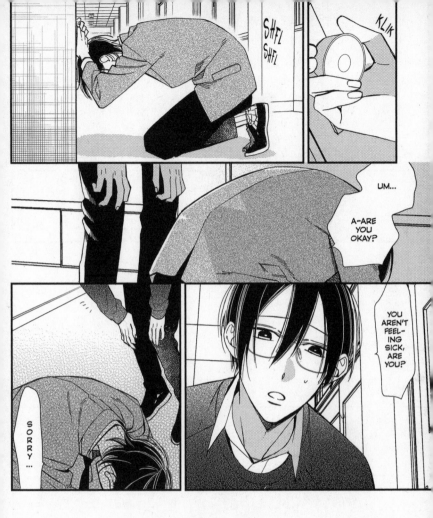

SHFL
SHFL

KLIK

UM...

A-ARE YOU OKAY?

YOU AREN'T FEEL- ING SICK, ARE YOU?

SORRY...

BOTH SO VERY DIFFERENT...
YET BOTH UNDENIABLY ME.

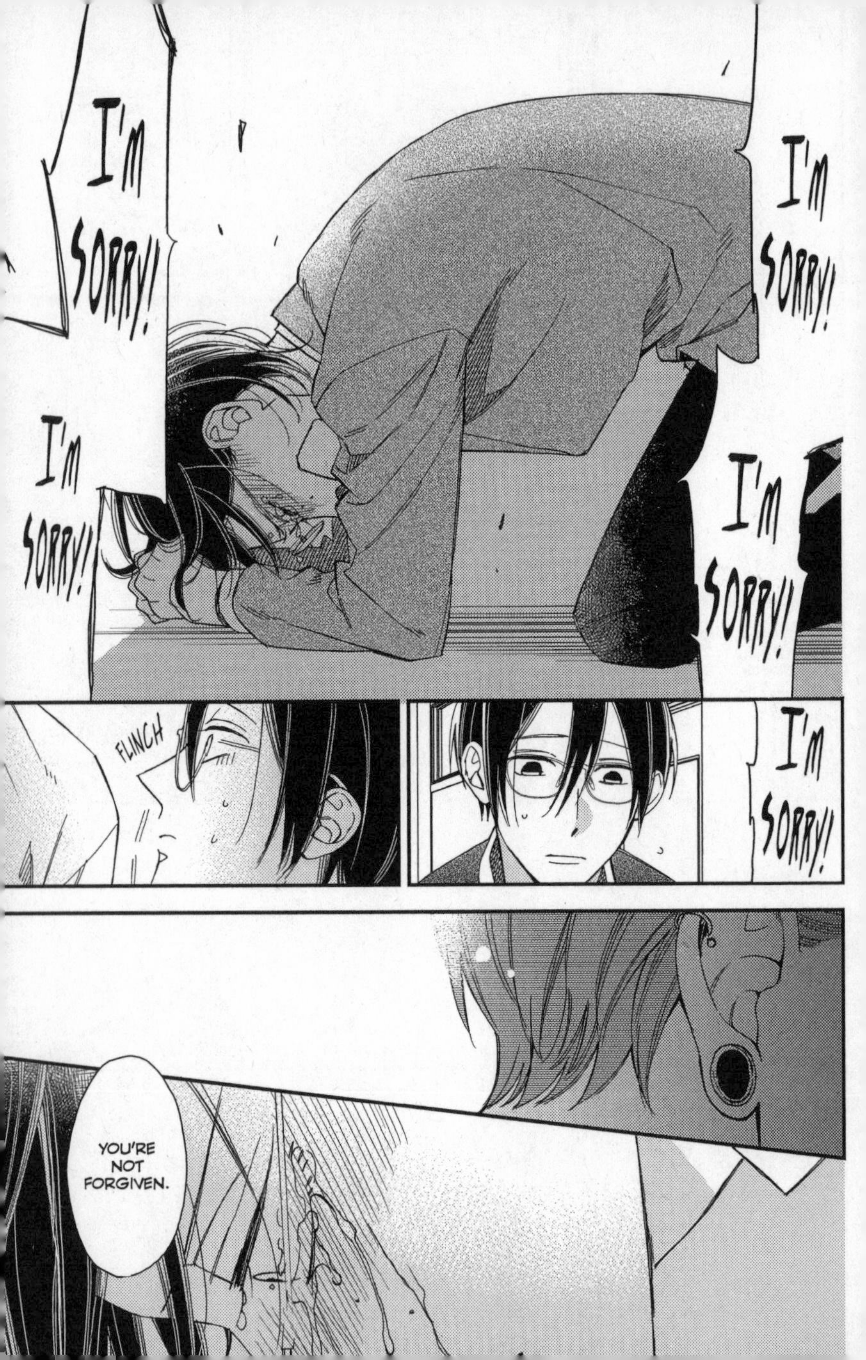
I'M SORRY!
I'M SORRY!
I'M SORRY!
I'M SORRY!
I'M SORRY!
FLINCH
YOU'RE NOT FORGIVEN.

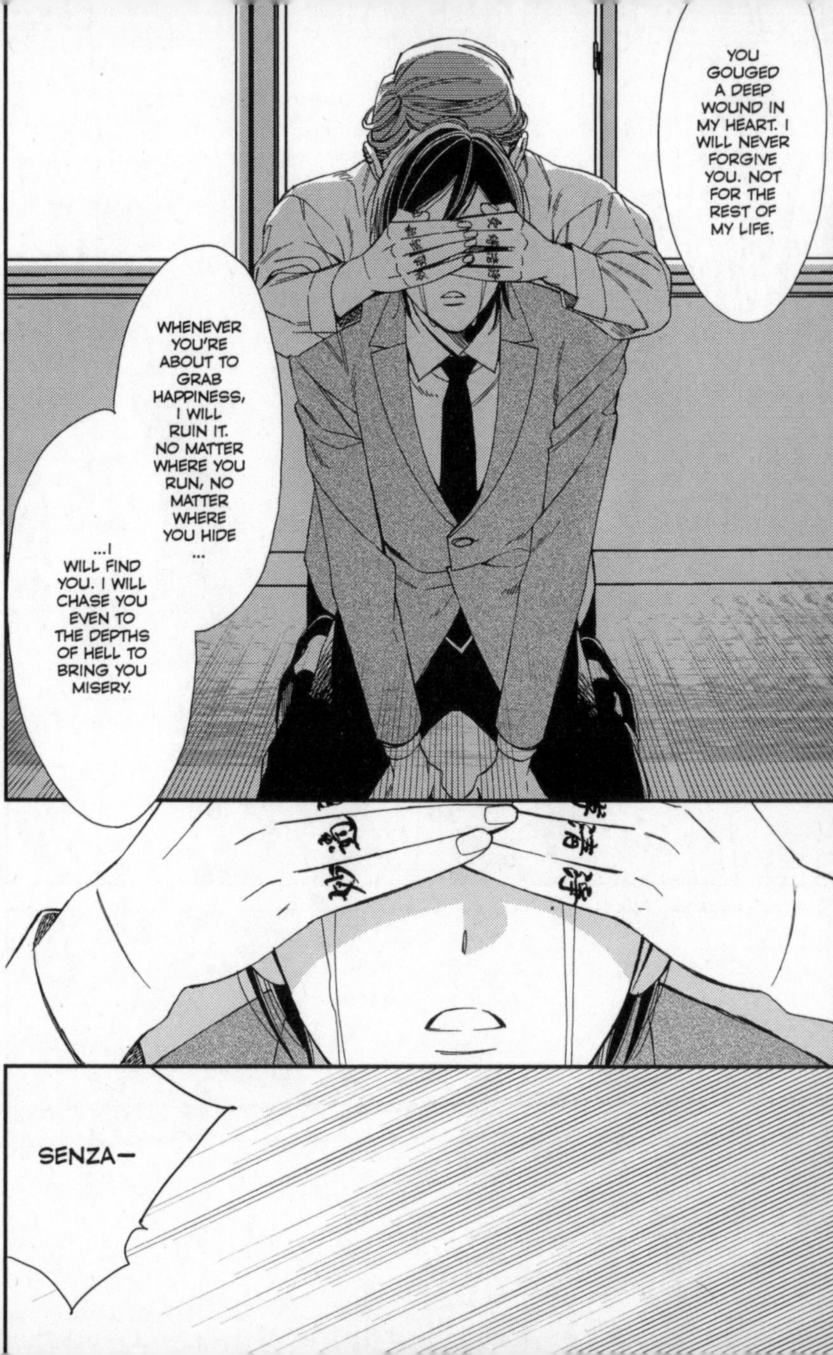
YOU GOUGED A DEEP WOUND IN MY HEART. I WILL NEVER FORGIVE YOU. NOT FOR THE REST OF MY LIFE.
WHENEVER YOU'RE ABOUT TO GRAB HAPPINESS, I WILL RUIN IT. NO MATTER WHERE YOU RUN, NO MATTER WHERE YOU HIDE ...
...I WILL FIND YOU. I WILL CHASE YOU EVEN TO THE DEPTHS OF HELL TO BRING YOU MISERY.
SENZA—

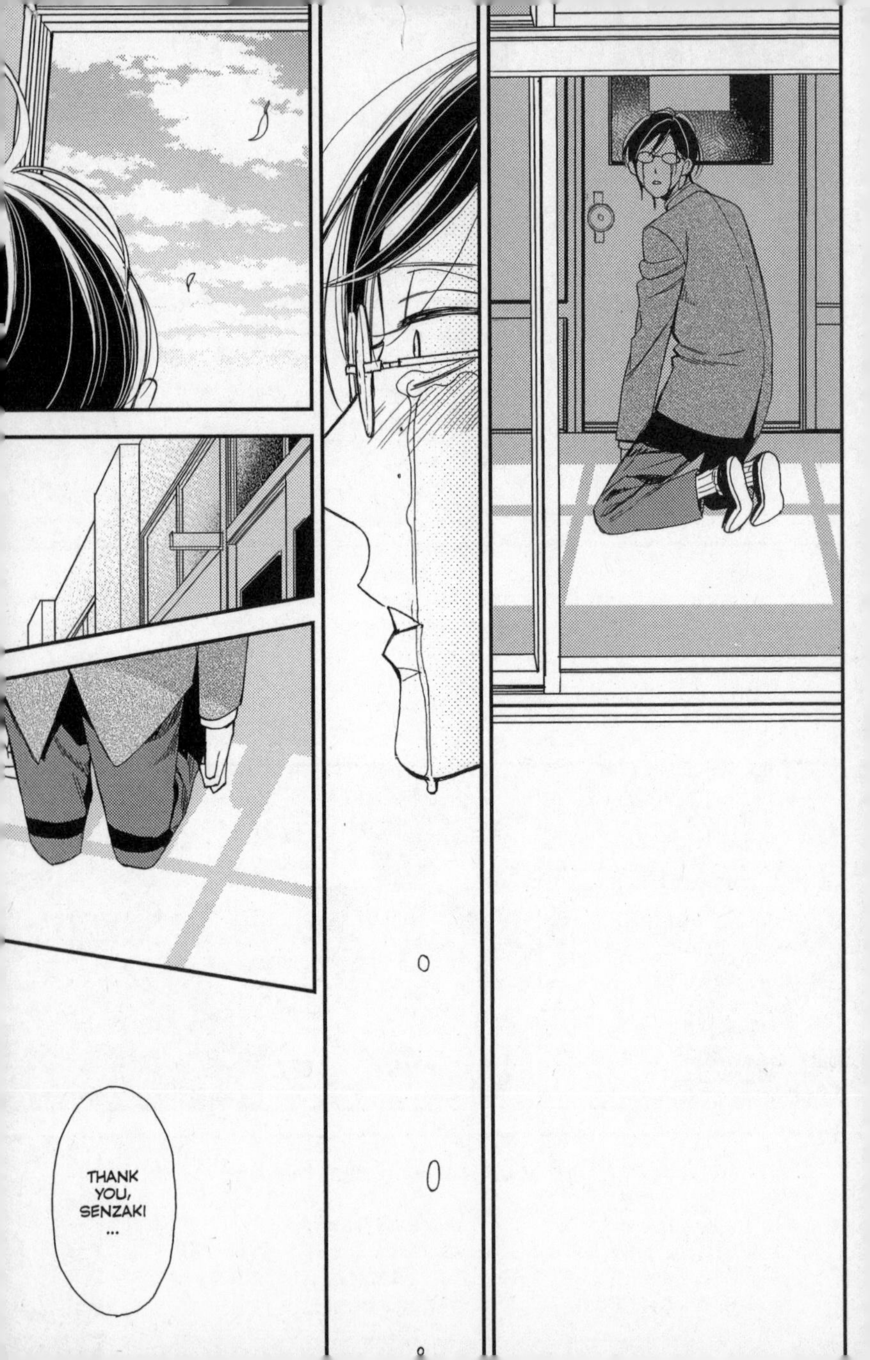
THANK YOU, SENZAKI ...

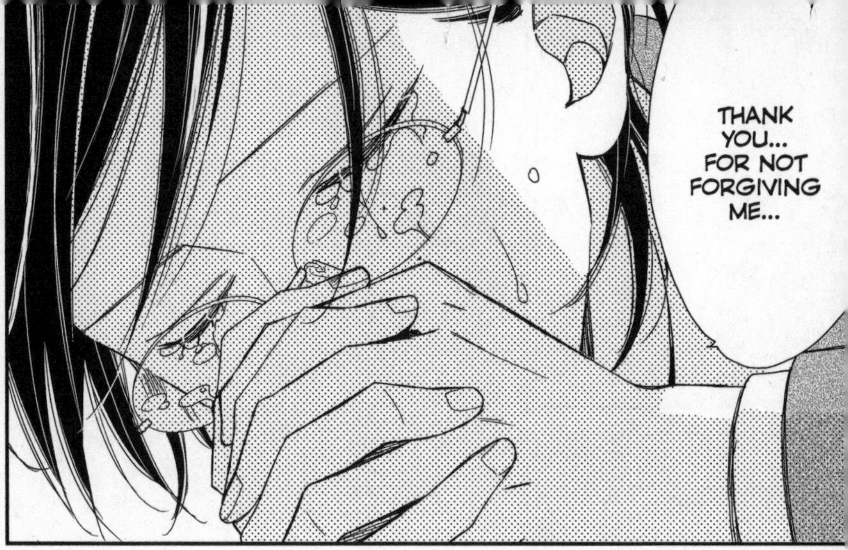
THANK YOU... FOR NOT FORGIVING ME...

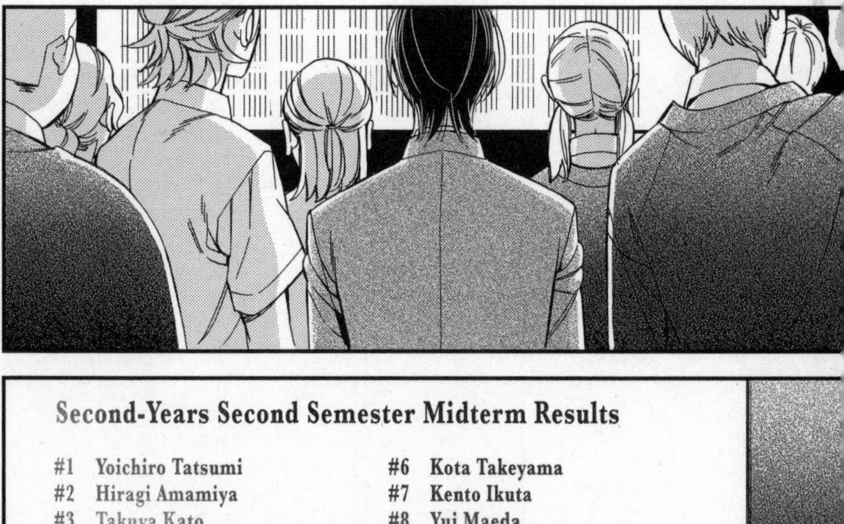

Second-Years Second Semester Midterm Results

#1	Yoichiro Tatsumi	#6	Kota Takeyama
#2	Hiragi Amamiya	#7	Kento Ikuta
#3	Takuya Kato	#8	Yui Maeda
#4	Daisuke Yamaguchi	#9	Aika Ohtaki
#5	Kotaro Kudo	#10	Misaki Sato

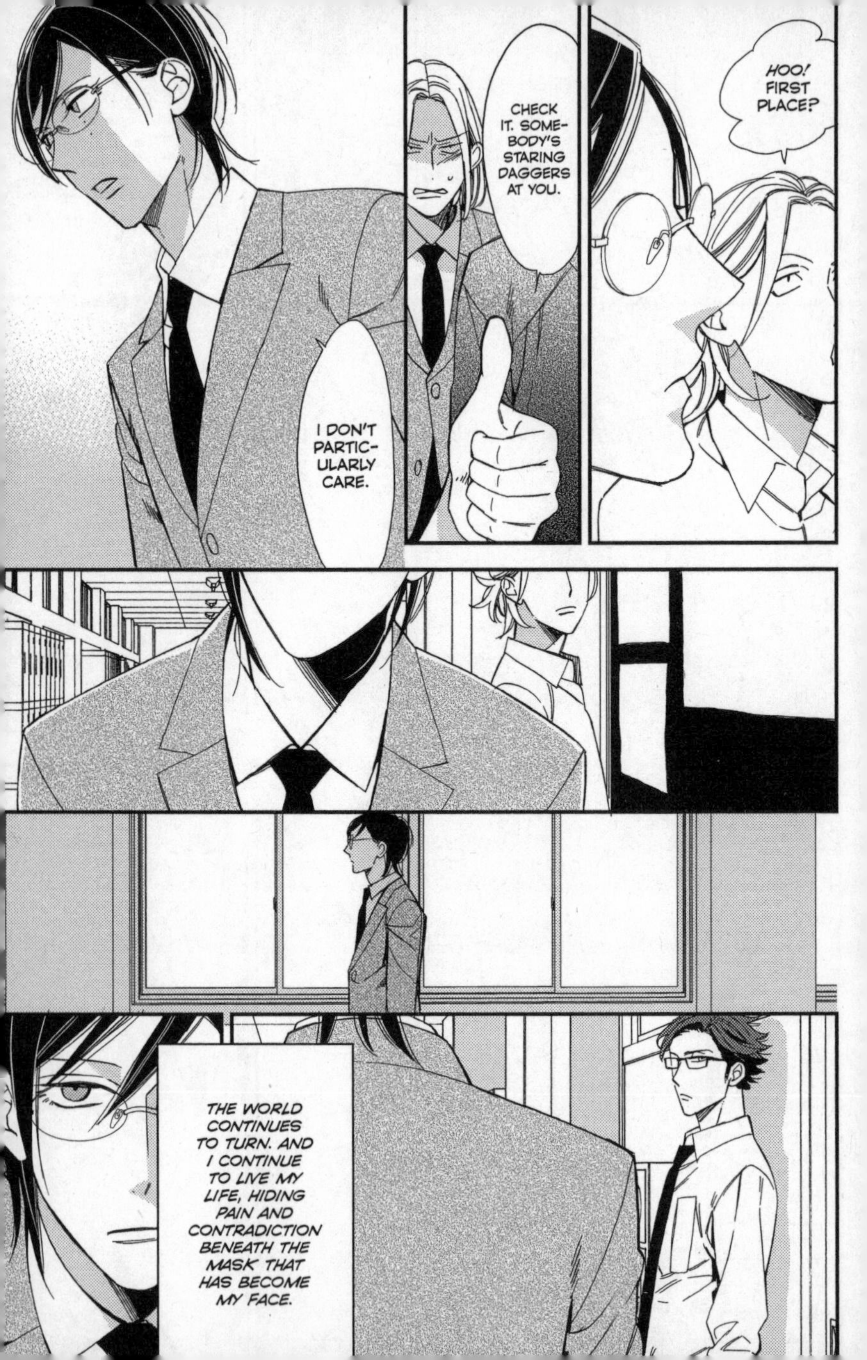
HOO! FIRST PLACE?
CHECK IT. SOMEBODY'S STARING DAGGERS AT YOU.
I DON'T PARTICULARLY CARE.
THE WORLD CONTINUES TO TURN. AND I CONTINUE TO LIVE MY LIFE, HIDING PAIN AND CONTRADICTION BENEATH THE MASK THAT HAS BECOME MY FACE.

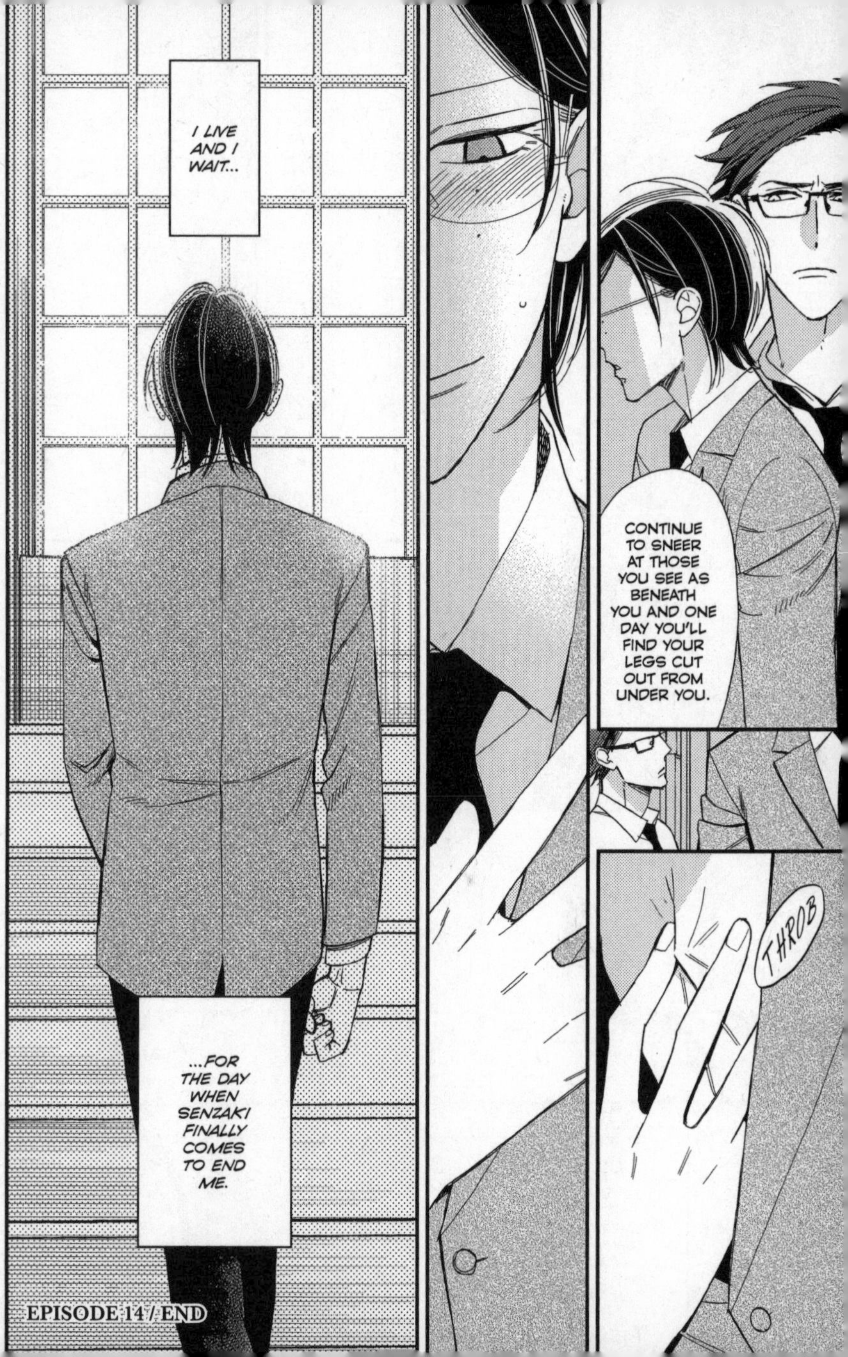
CONTINUE TO SNEER AT THOSE YOU SEE AS BENEATH YOU AND ONE DAY YOU'LL FIND YOUR LEGS CUT OUT FROM UNDER YOU.
THROB
I LIVE AND I WAIT...
...FOR THE DAY WHEN SENZAKI FINALLY COMES TO END ME.
EPISODE 14 / END

CASTE HEAVEN
EPISODE 15

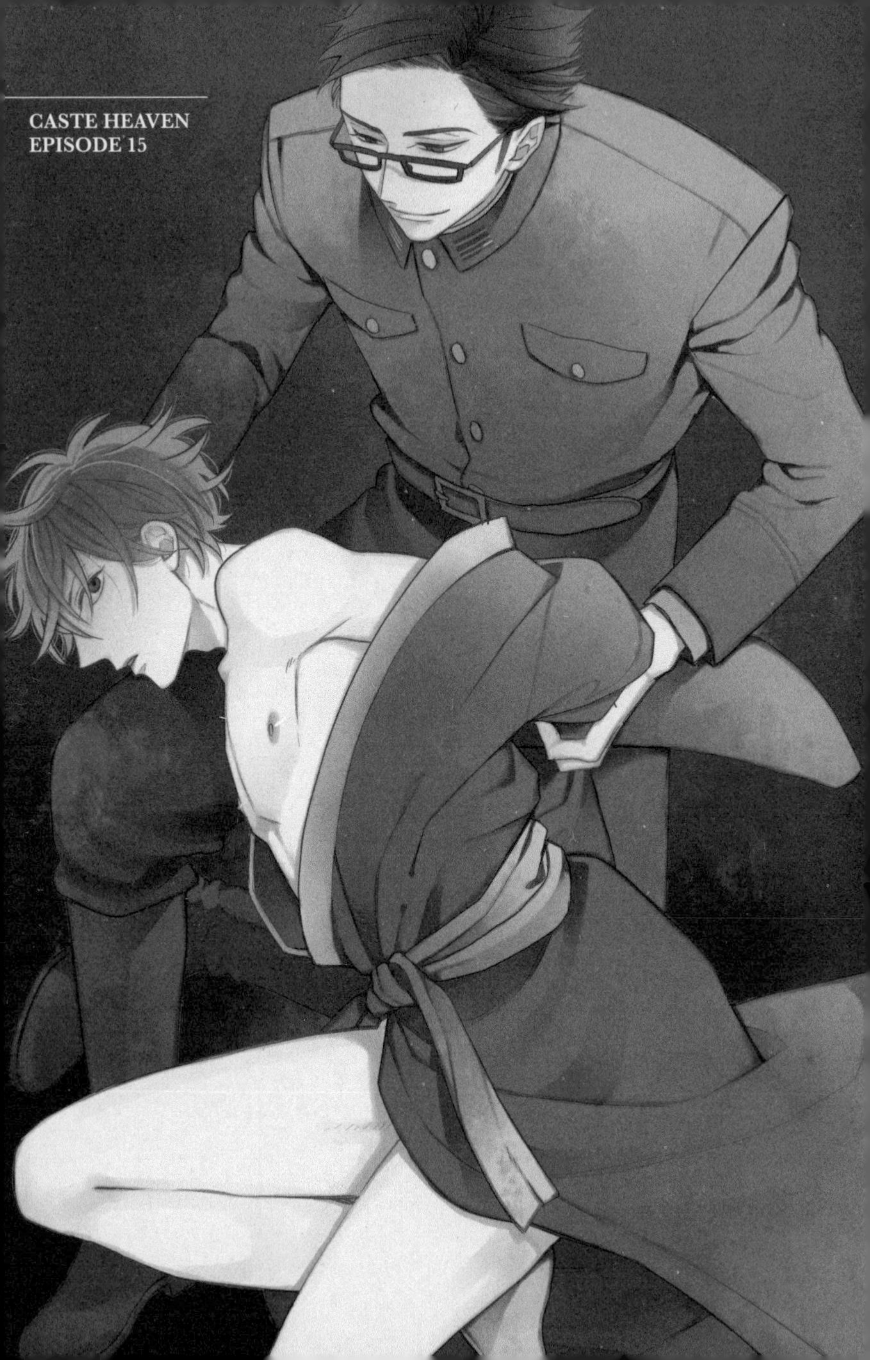

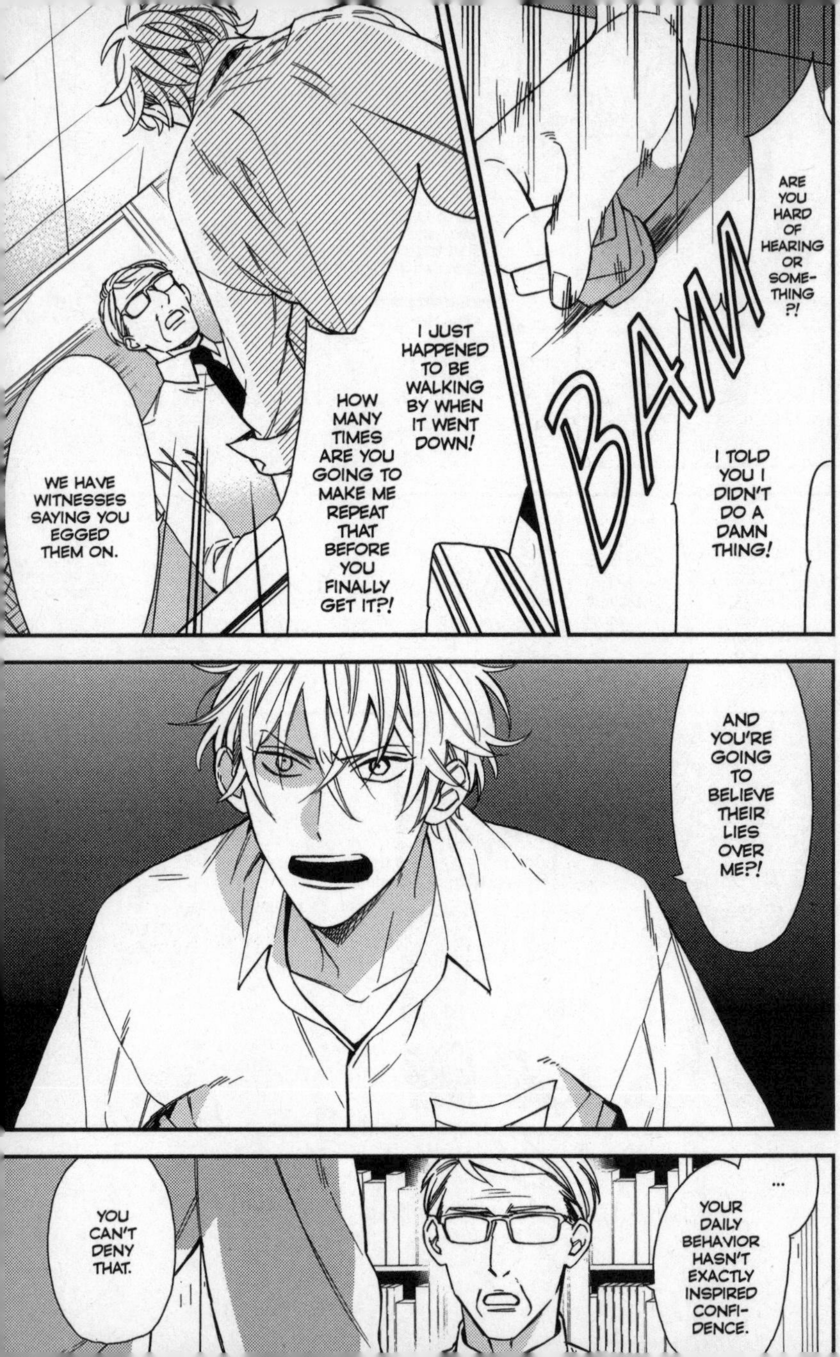
ARE YOU HARD OF HEARING OR SOME-THING?!
BAM
I TOLD YOU I DIDN'T DO A DAMN THING!
I JUST HAPPENED TO BE WALKING BY WHEN IT WENT DOWN!
HOW MANY TIMES ARE YOU GOING TO MAKE ME REPEAT THAT BEFORE YOU FINALLY GET IT?!
WE HAVE WITNESSES SAYING YOU EGGED THEM ON.
AND YOU'RE GOING TO BELIEVE THEIR LIES OVER ME?!
...
YOUR DAILY BEHAVIOR HASN'T EXACTLY INSPIRED CONFIDENCE.
YOU CAN'T DENY THAT.

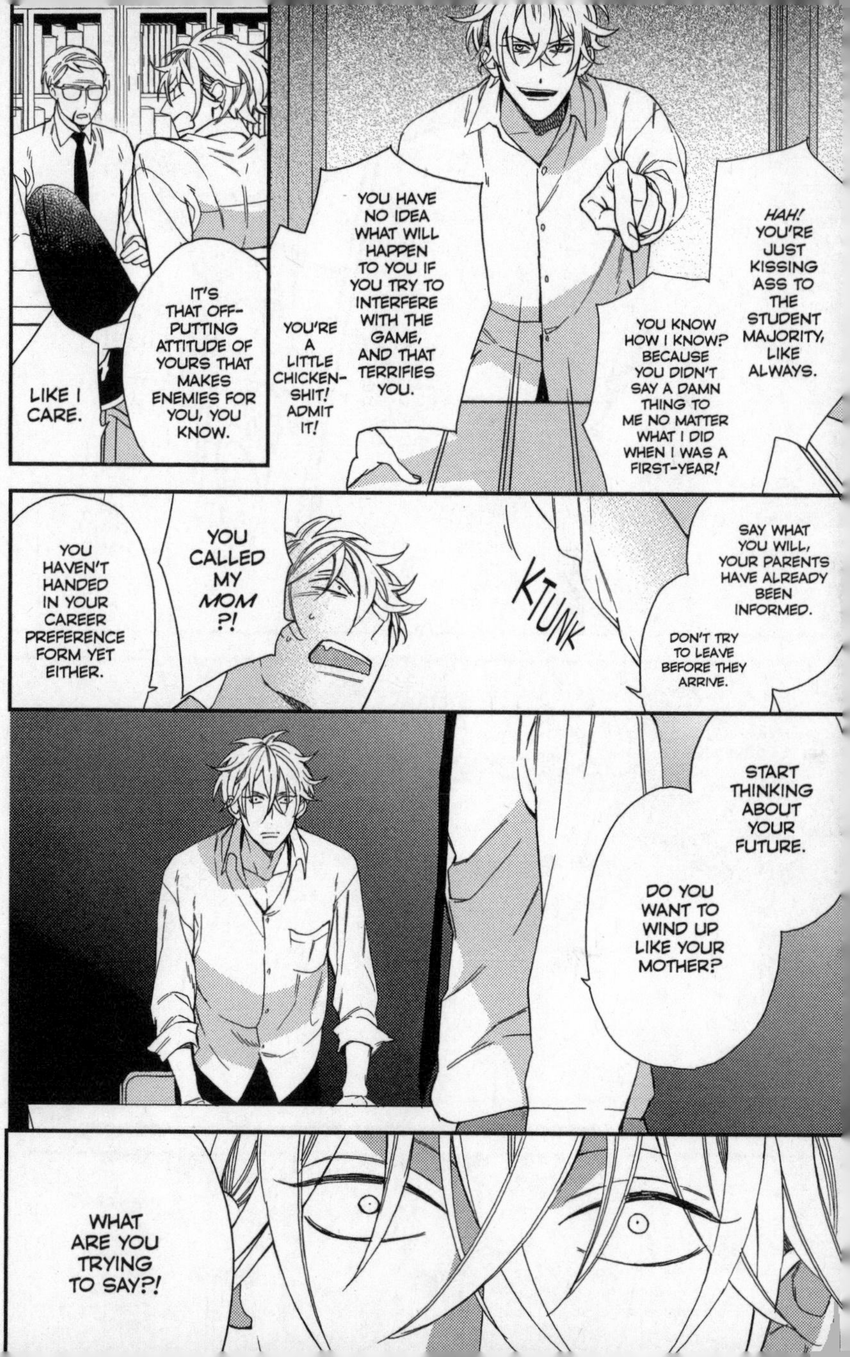
HAH! YOU'RE JUST KISSING ASS TO THE STUDENT MAJORITY, LIKE ALWAYS.
YOU KNOW HOW I KNOW? BECAUSE YOU DIDN'T SAY A DAMN THING TO ME NO MATTER WHAT I DID WHEN I WAS A FIRST-YEAR!
YOU HAVE NO IDEA WHAT WILL HAPPEN TO YOU IF YOU TRY TO INTERFERE WITH THE GAME, AND THAT TERRIFIES YOU.
YOU'RE A LITTLE CHICKEN-SHIT! ADMIT IT!
IT'S THAT OFF-PUTTING ATTITUDE OF YOURS THAT MAKES ENEMIES FOR YOU, YOU KNOW.
LIKE I CARE.
SAY WHAT YOU WILL, YOUR PARENTS HAVE ALREADY BEEN INFORMED.
DON'T TRY TO LEAVE BEFORE THEY ARRIVE.
KTUNK
YOU CALLED MY *MOM* ?!
YOU HAVEN'T HANDED IN YOUR CAREER PREFERENCE FORM YET EITHER.
START THINKING ABOUT YOUR FUTURE.
DO YOU WANT TO WIND UP LIKE YOUR MOTHER?
WHAT ARE YOU TRYING TO SAY?!

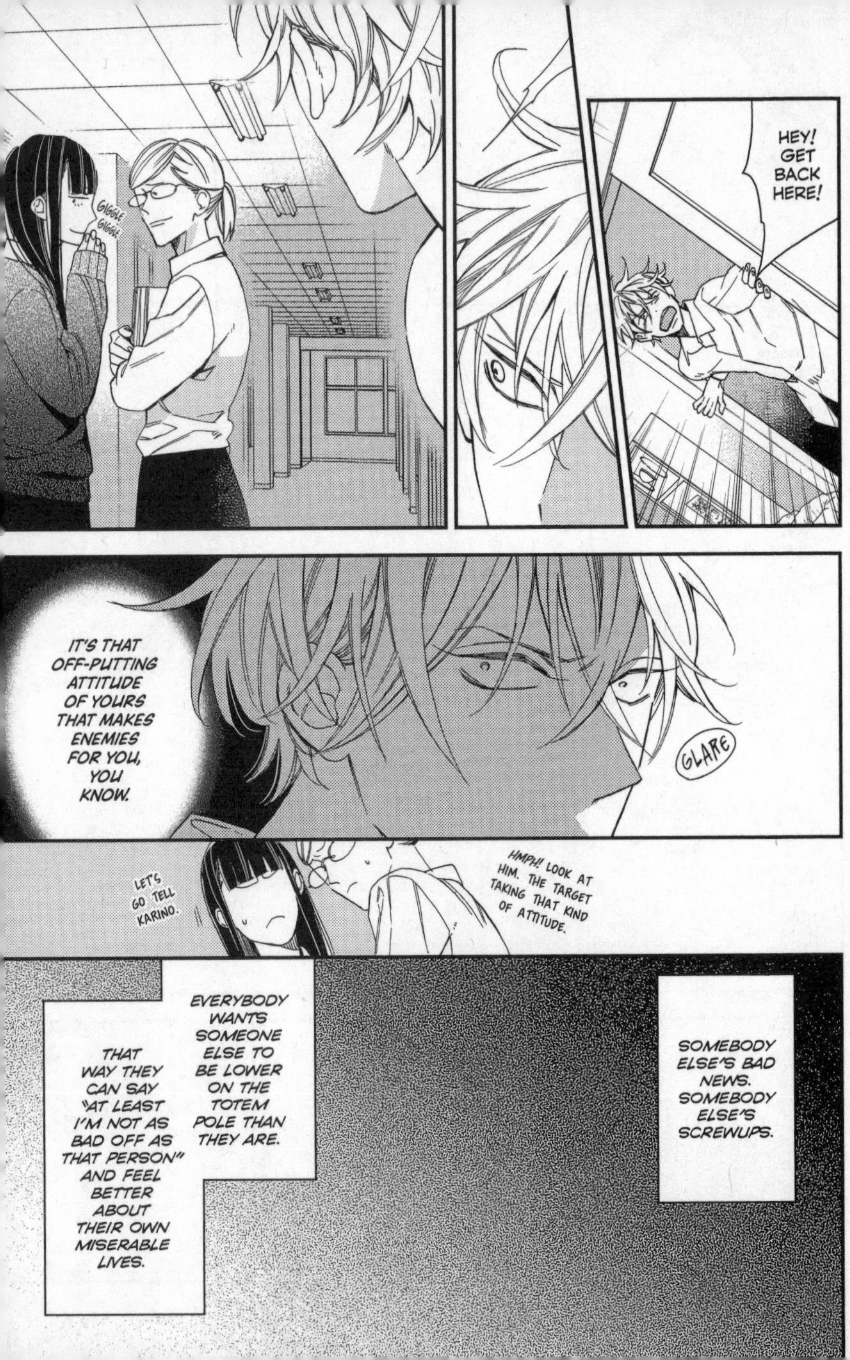
HEY! GET BACK HERE!
GIGGLE GIGGLE
IT'S THAT OFF-PUTTING ATTITUDE OF YOURS THAT MAKES ENEMIES FOR YOU, YOU KNOW.
GLARE
HMPH! LOOK AT HIM. THE TARGET TAKING THAT KIND OF ATTITUDE.
LET'S GO TELL KARINO.
SOMEBODY ELSE'S BAD NEWS. SOMEBODY ELSE'S SCREWUPS.
EVERYBODY WANTS SOMEONE ELSE TO BE LOWER ON THE TOTEM POLE THAN THEY ARE.
THAT WAY THEY CAN SAY "AT LEAST I'M NOT AS BAD OFF AS THAT PERSON" AND FEEL BETTER ABOUT THEIR OWN MISERABLE LIVES.

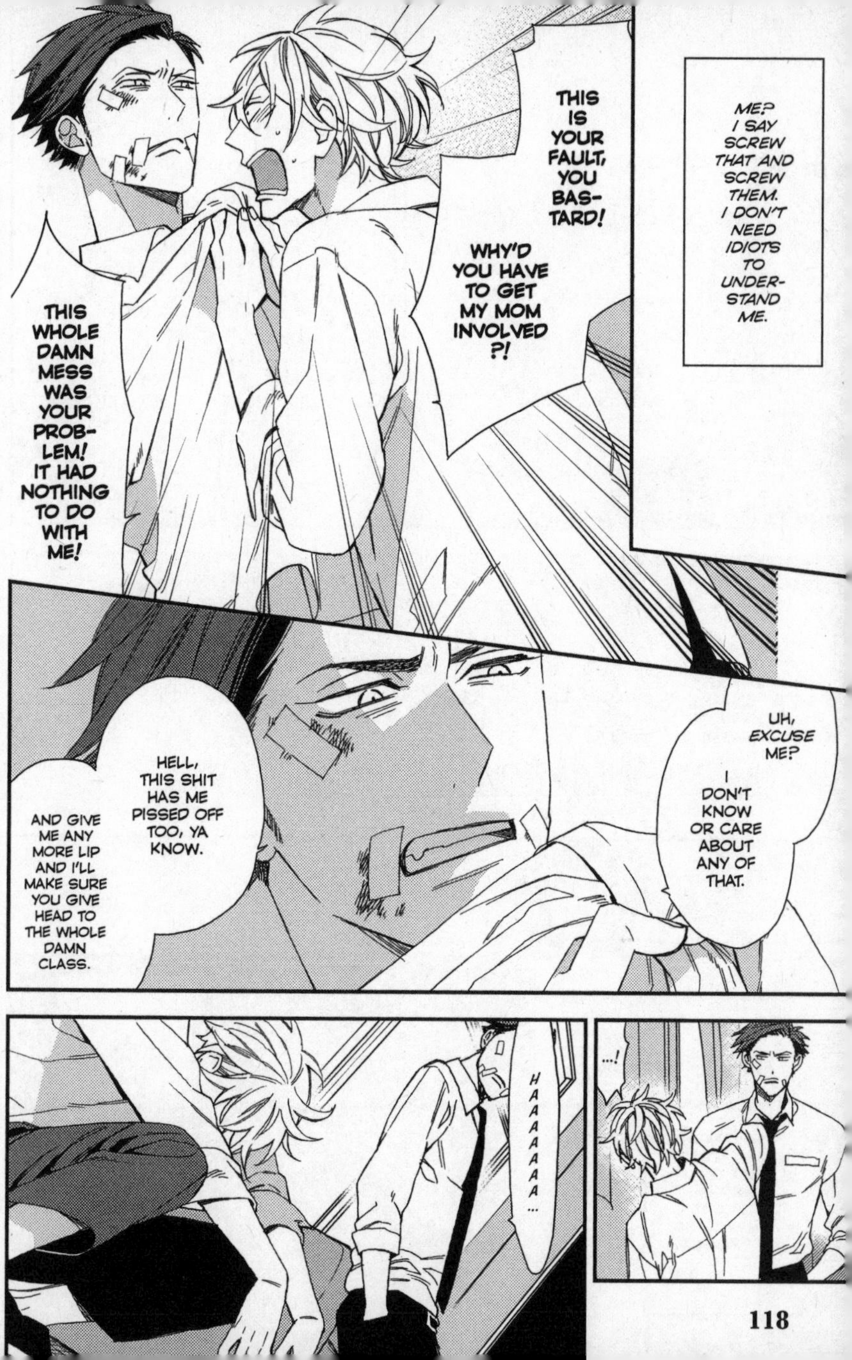
ME? I SAY SCREW THAT AND SCREW THEM. I DON'T NEED IDIOTS TO UNDER-STAND ME.
THIS IS YOUR FAULT, YOU BAS-TARD!
WHY'D YOU HAVE TO GET MY MOM INVOLVED?!
THIS WHOLE DAMN MESS WAS YOUR PROB-LEM! IT HAD NOTHING TO DO WITH ME!
UH, *EXCUSE* ME? I DON'T KNOW OR CARE ABOUT ANY OF THAT.
HELL, THIS SHIT HAS ME PISSED OFF TOO, YA KNOW.
AND GIVE ME ANY MORE LIP AND I'LL MAKE SURE YOU GIVE HEAD TO THE WHOLE DAMN CLASS.
...!
HAAAAAAA...

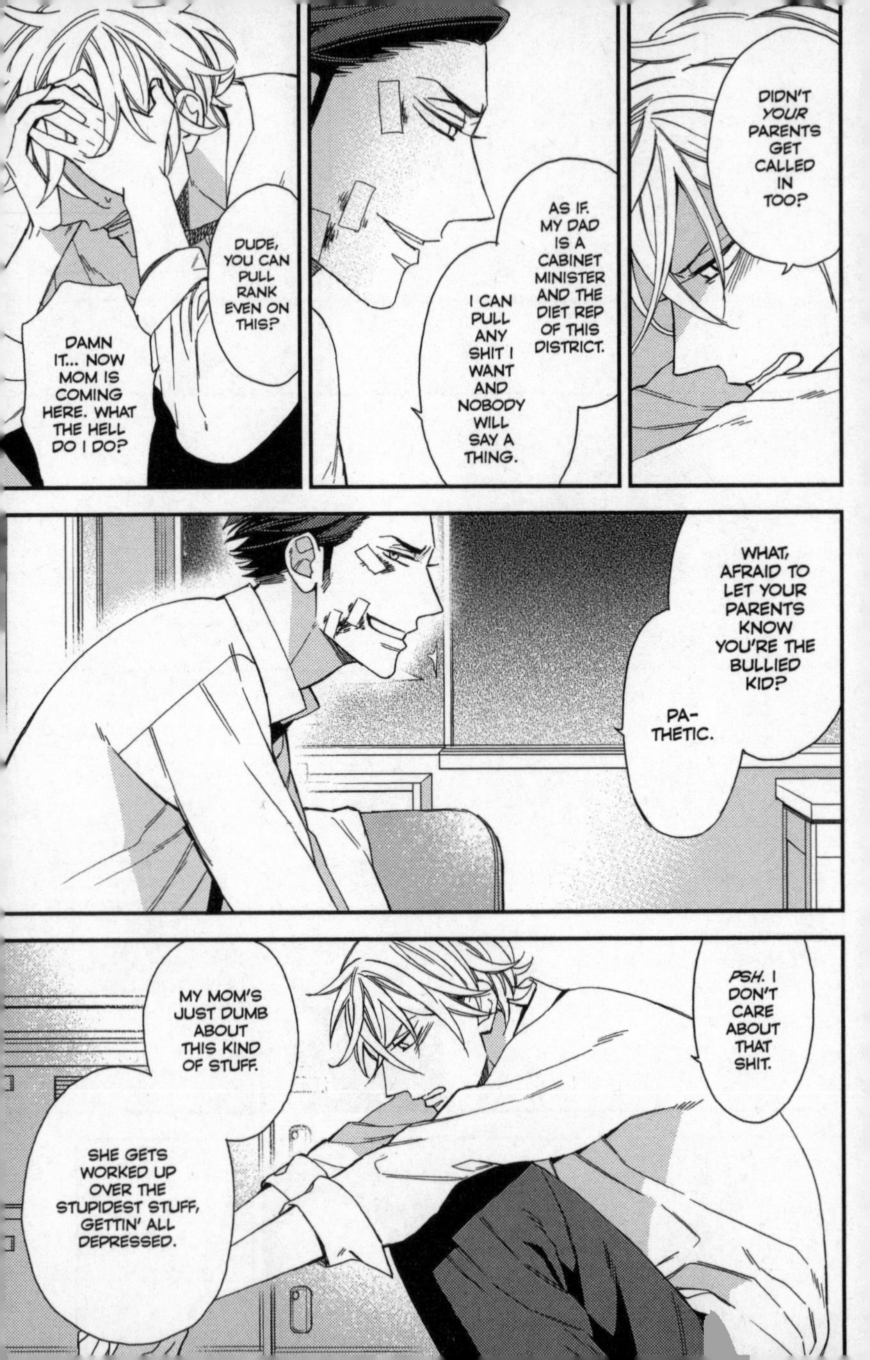
DIDN'T *YOUR* PARENTS GET CALLED IN TOO?
AS IF. MY DAD IS A CABINET MINISTER AND THE DIET REP OF THIS DISTRICT.
I CAN PULL ANY SHIT I WANT AND NOBODY WILL SAY A THING.
DUDE, YOU CAN PULL RANK EVEN ON THIS?
DAMN IT... NOW MOM IS COMING HERE. WHAT THE HELL DO I DO?
WHAT, AFRAID TO LET YOUR PARENTS KNOW YOU'RE THE BULLIED KID?
PA-THETIC.
PSH. I DON'T CARE ABOUT THAT SHIT.
MY MOM'S JUST DUMB ABOUT THIS KIND OF STUFF.
SHE GETS WORKED UP OVER THE STUPIDEST STUFF, GETTIN' ALL DEPRESSED.

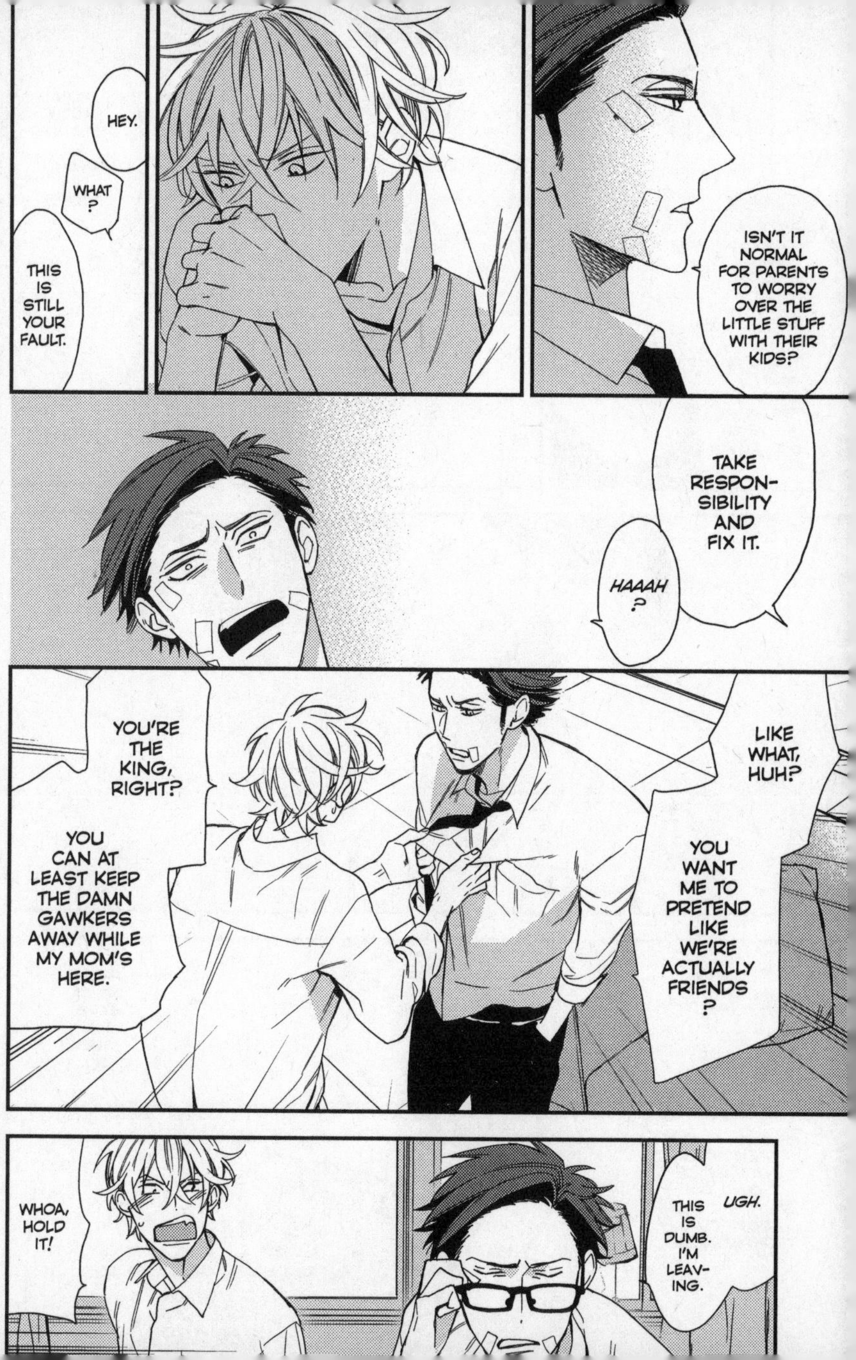
ISN'T IT NORMAL FOR PARENTS TO WORRY OVER THE LITTLE STUFF WITH THEIR KIDS?
HEY.
WHAT?
THIS IS STILL YOUR FAULT.
TAKE RESPONSIBILITY AND FIX IT.
HAAAH?
LIKE WHAT, HUH?
YOU WANT ME TO PRETEND LIKE WE'RE ACTUALLY FRIENDS?
YOU'RE THE KING, RIGHT?
YOU CAN AT LEAST KEEP THE DAMN GAWKERS AWAY WHILE MY MOM'S HERE.
UGH.
THIS IS DUMB. I'M LEAVING.
WHOA, HOLD IT!

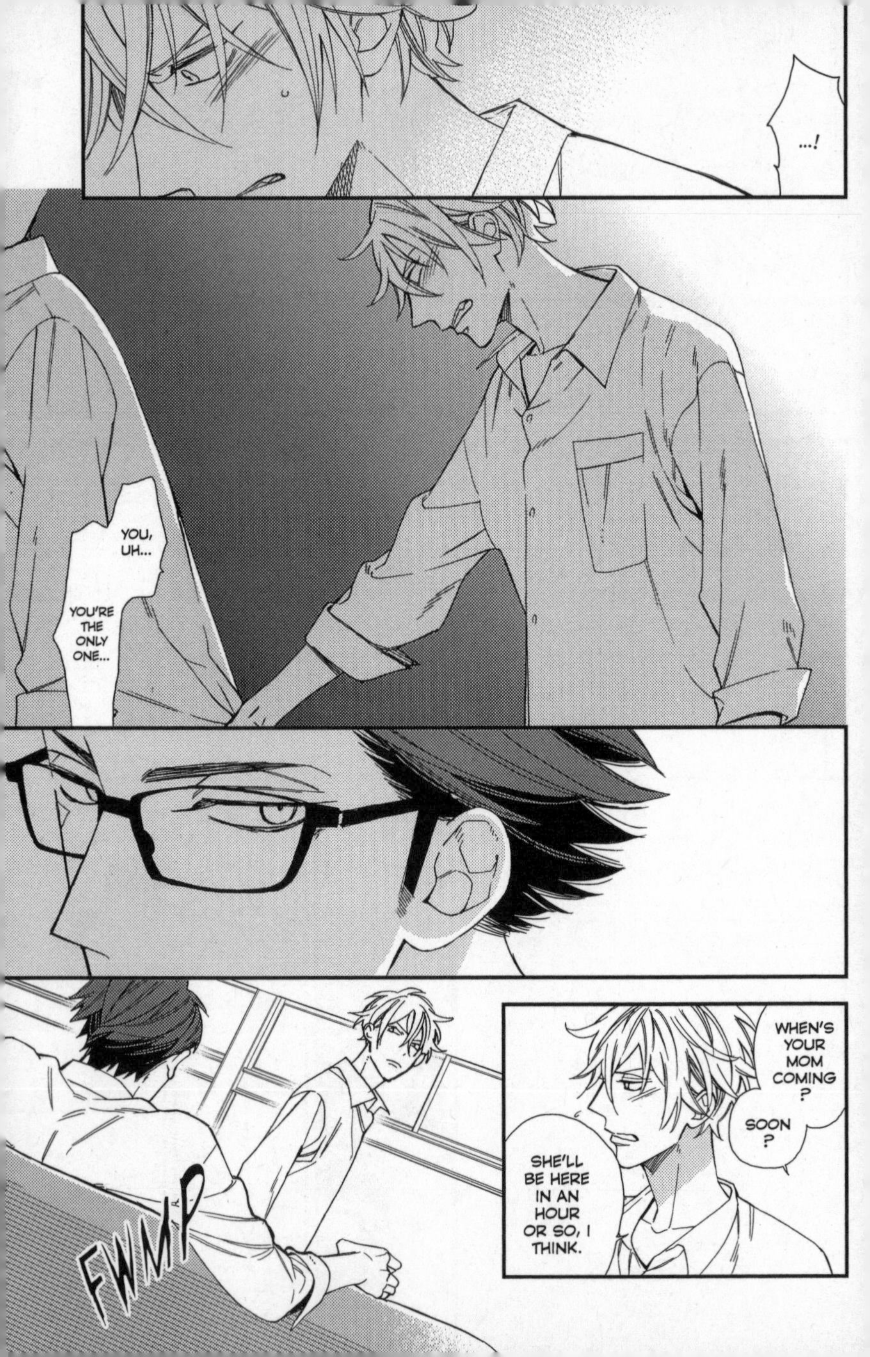
...!
YOU, UH...
YOU'RE THE ONLY ONE...
WHEN'S YOUR MOM COMING?
SOON?
SHE'LL BE HERE IN AN HOUR OR SO, I THINK.
FWMP

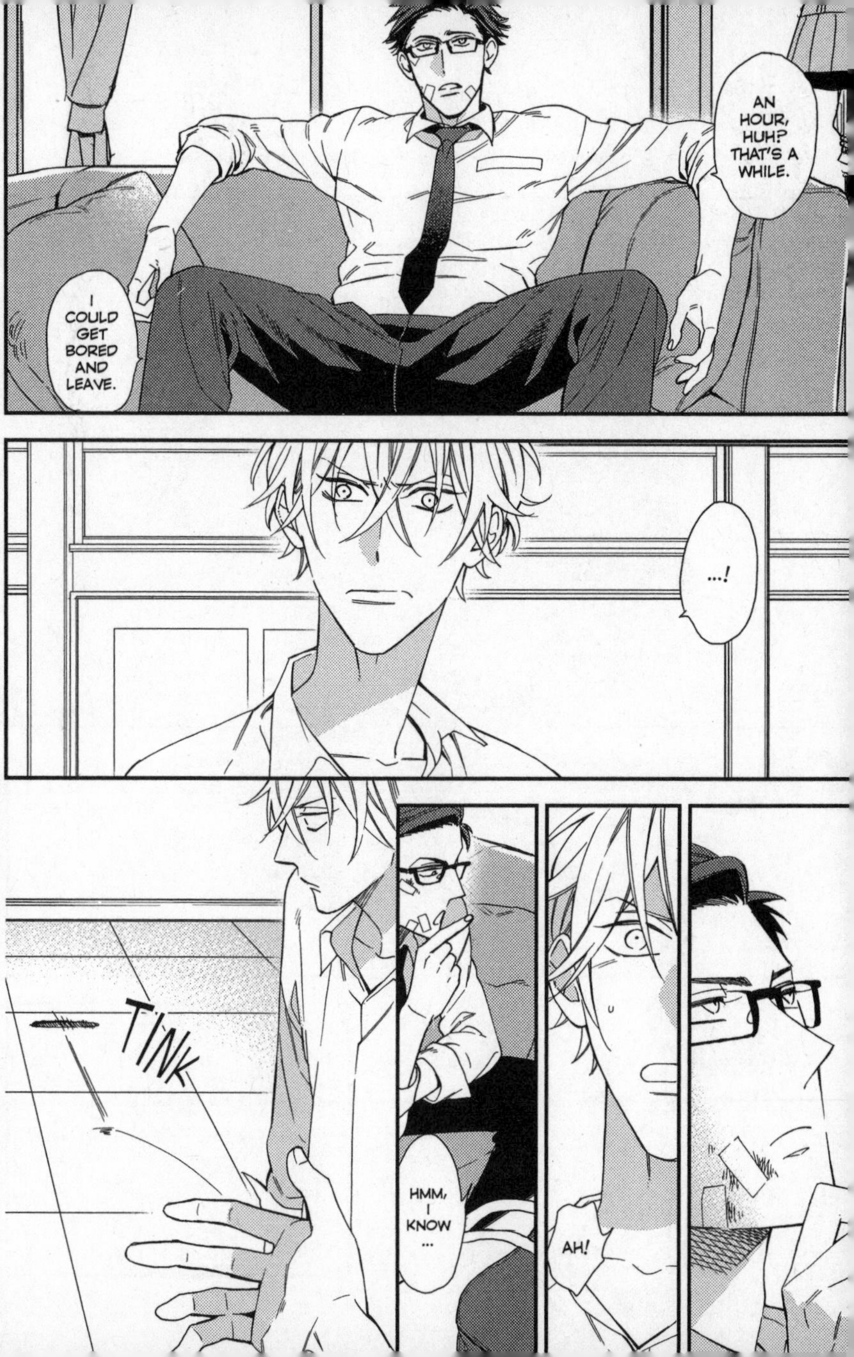
AN HOUR, HUH? THAT'S A WHILE.
I COULD GET BORED AND LEAVE.
...!
AH!
HMM, I KNOW ...
TINK

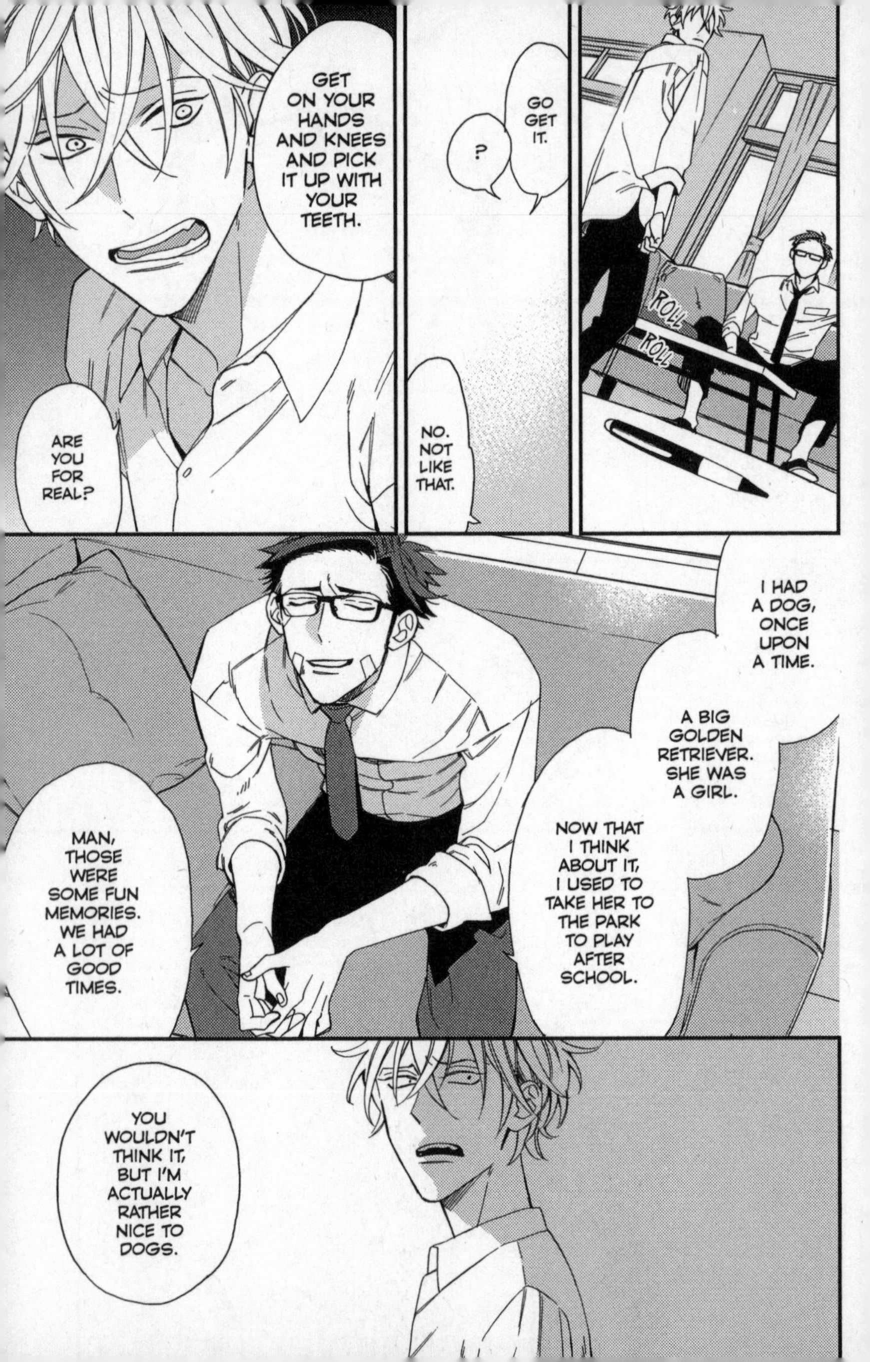
ROLL
ROLL
GO GET IT.
?
NO. NOT LIKE THAT.
GET ON YOUR HANDS AND KNEES AND PICK IT UP WITH YOUR TEETH.
ARE YOU FOR REAL?
I HAD A DOG, ONCE UPON A TIME.
A BIG GOLDEN RETRIEVER. SHE WAS A GIRL.
NOW THAT I THINK ABOUT IT, I USED TO TAKE HER TO THE PARK TO PLAY AFTER SCHOOL.
MAN, THOSE WERE SOME FUN MEMORIES. WE HAD A LOT OF GOOD TIMES.
YOU WOULDN'T THINK IT, BUT I'M ACTUALLY RATHER NICE TO DOGS.

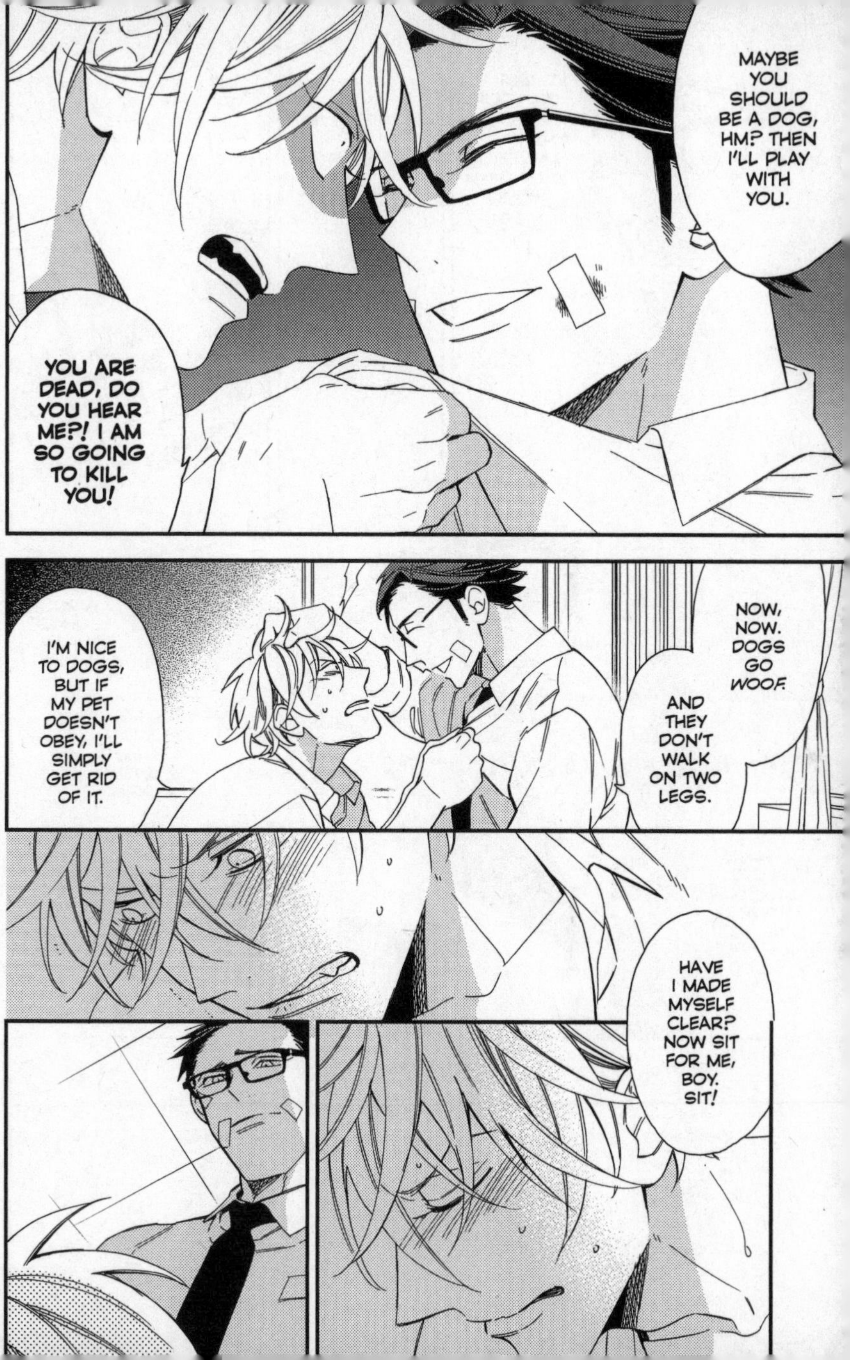
MAYBE YOU SHOULD BE A DOG, HM? THEN I'LL PLAY WITH YOU.
YOU ARE DEAD, DO YOU HEAR ME?! I AM SO GOING TO KILL YOU!
NOW, NOW. DOGS GO *WOOF.*
AND THEY DON'T WALK ON TWO LEGS.
I'M NICE TO DOGS, BUT IF MY PET DOESN'T OBEY, I'LL SIMPLY GET RID OF IT.
HAVE I MADE MYSELF CLEAR? NOW SIT FOR ME, BOY. SIT!

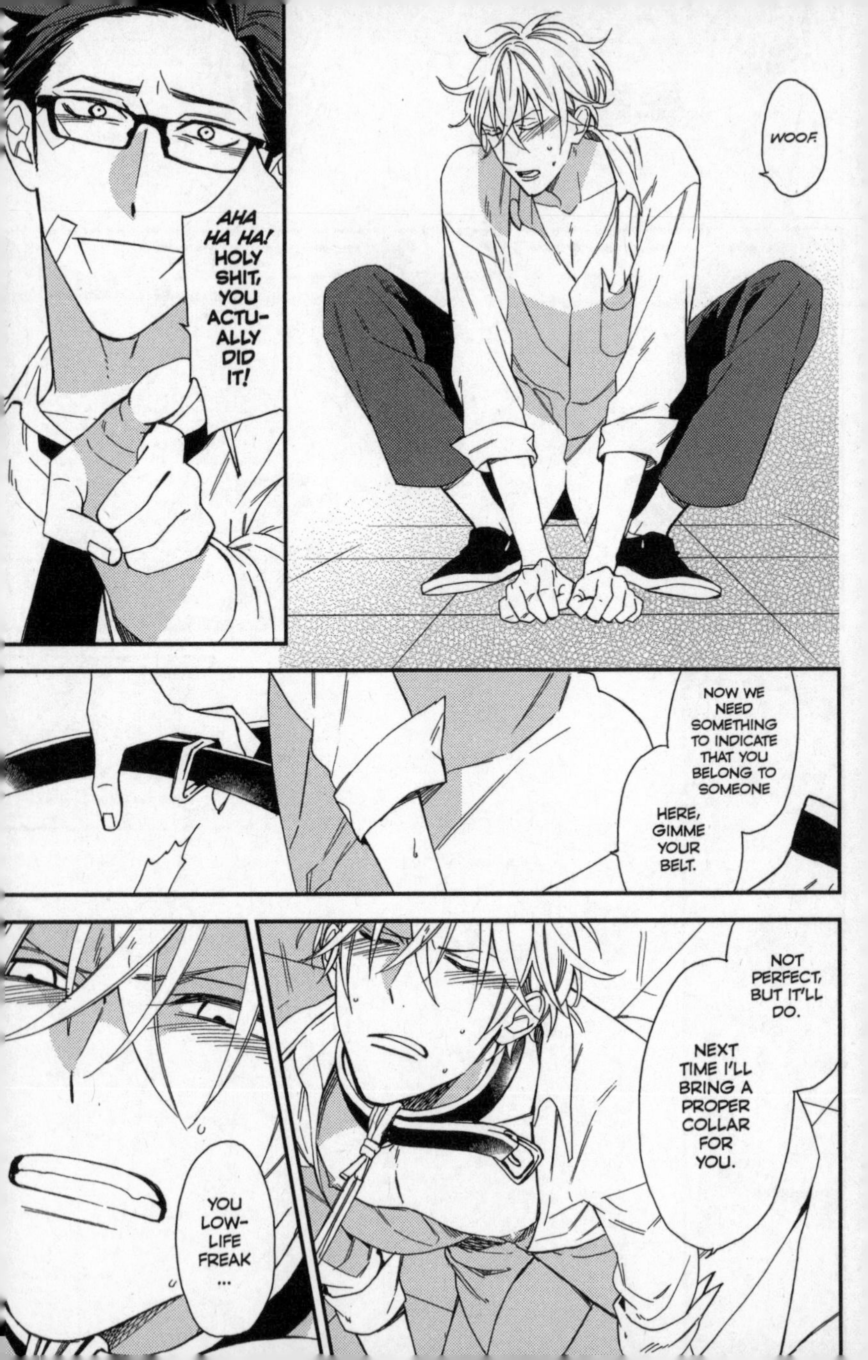
WOOF.
AHA HA HA! HOLY SHIT, YOU ACTU-ALLY DID IT!
NOW WE NEED SOMETHING TO INDICATE THAT YOU BELONG TO SOMEONE
HERE, GIMME YOUR BELT.
NOT PERFECT, BUT IT'LL DO.
NEXT TIME I'LL BRING A PROPER COLLAR FOR YOU.
YOU LOW-LIFE FREAK ...

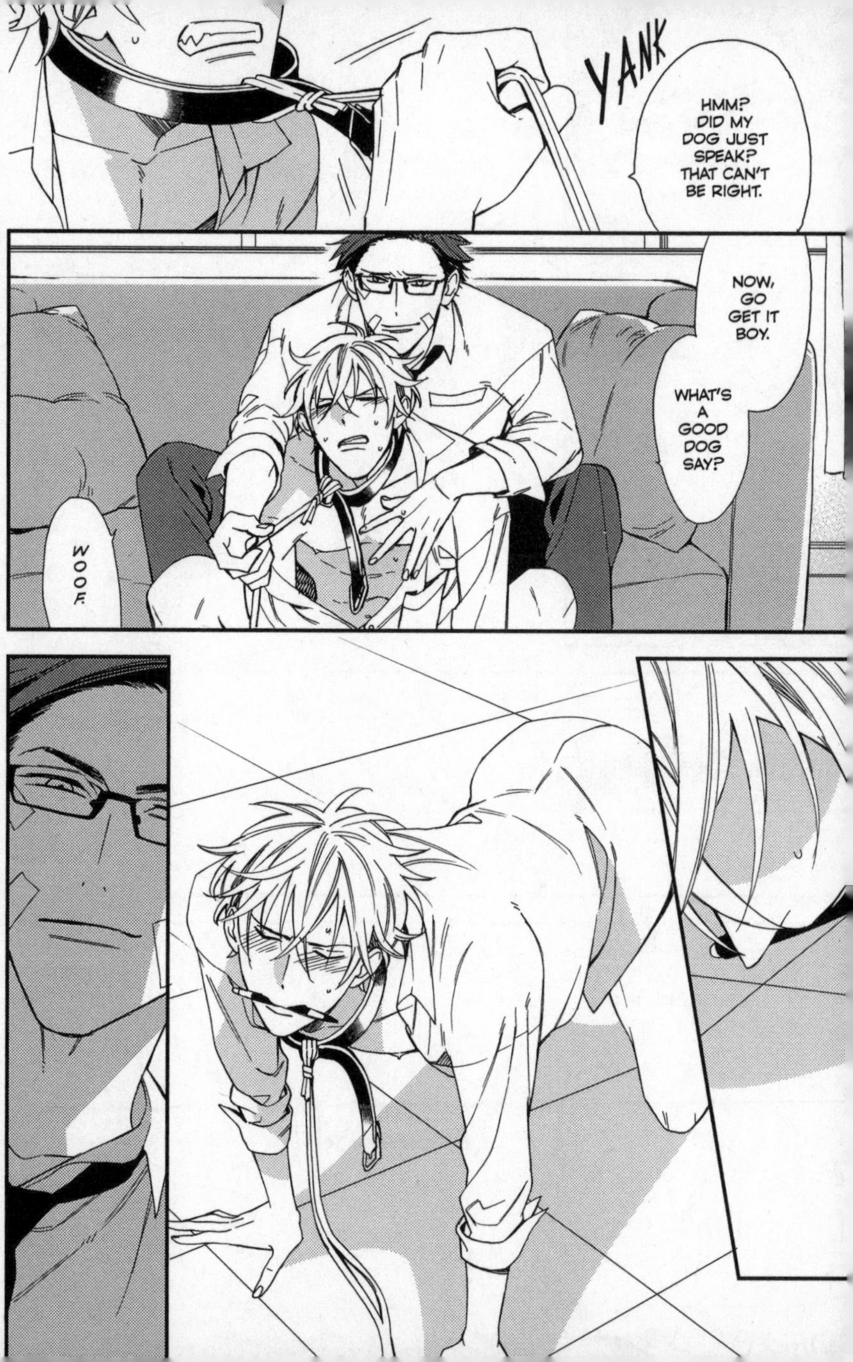
YANK
HMM? DID MY DOG JUST SPEAK? THAT CAN'T BE RIGHT.
NOW, GO GET IT BOY.
WHAT'S A GOOD DOG SAY?
WOOF.

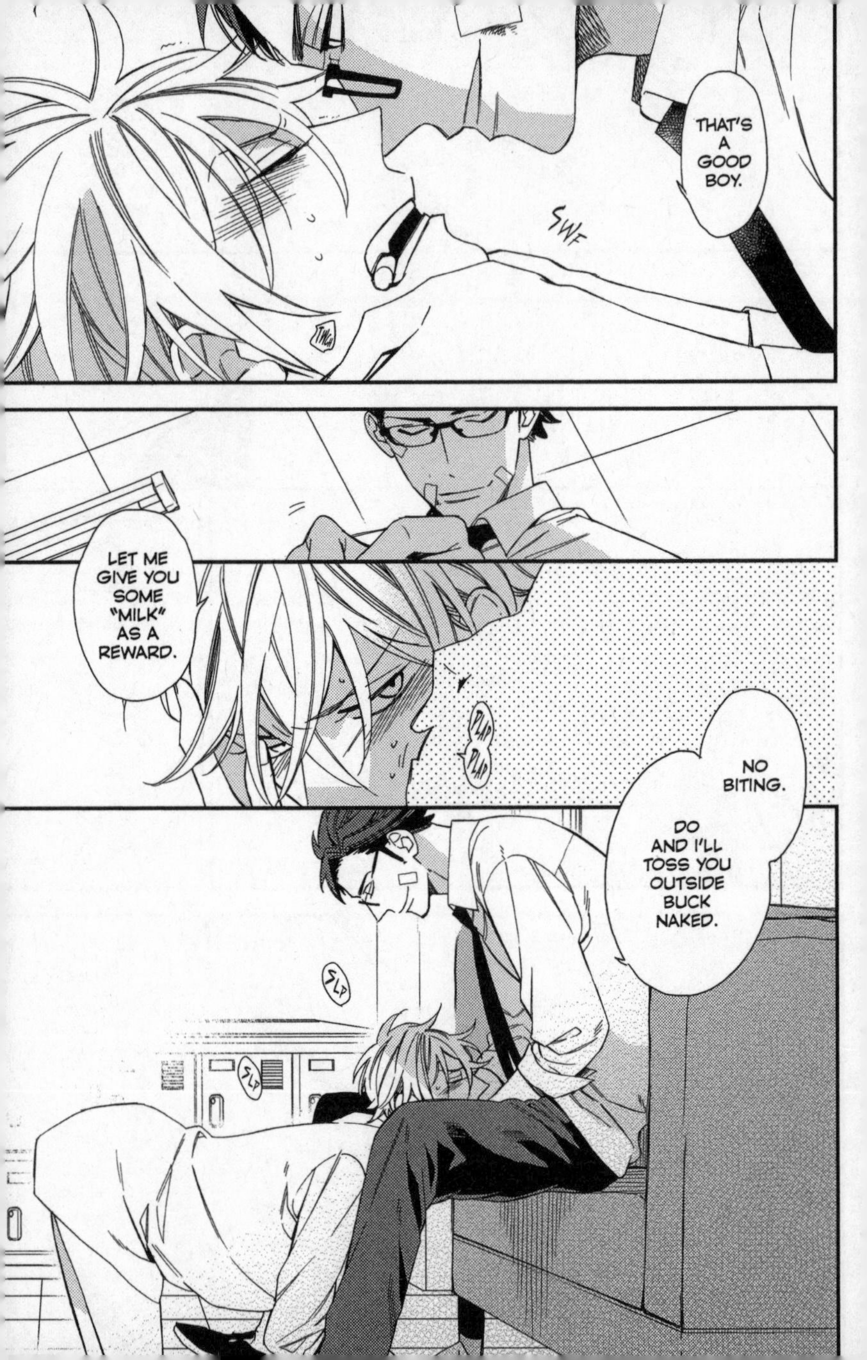
THAT'S A GOOD BOY.
SWF
TWCH
LET ME GIVE YOU SOME "MILK" AS A REWARD.
PLAP PLAP
NO BITING.
DO AND I'LL TOSS YOU OUTSIDE BUCK NAKED.
SLP
SLP

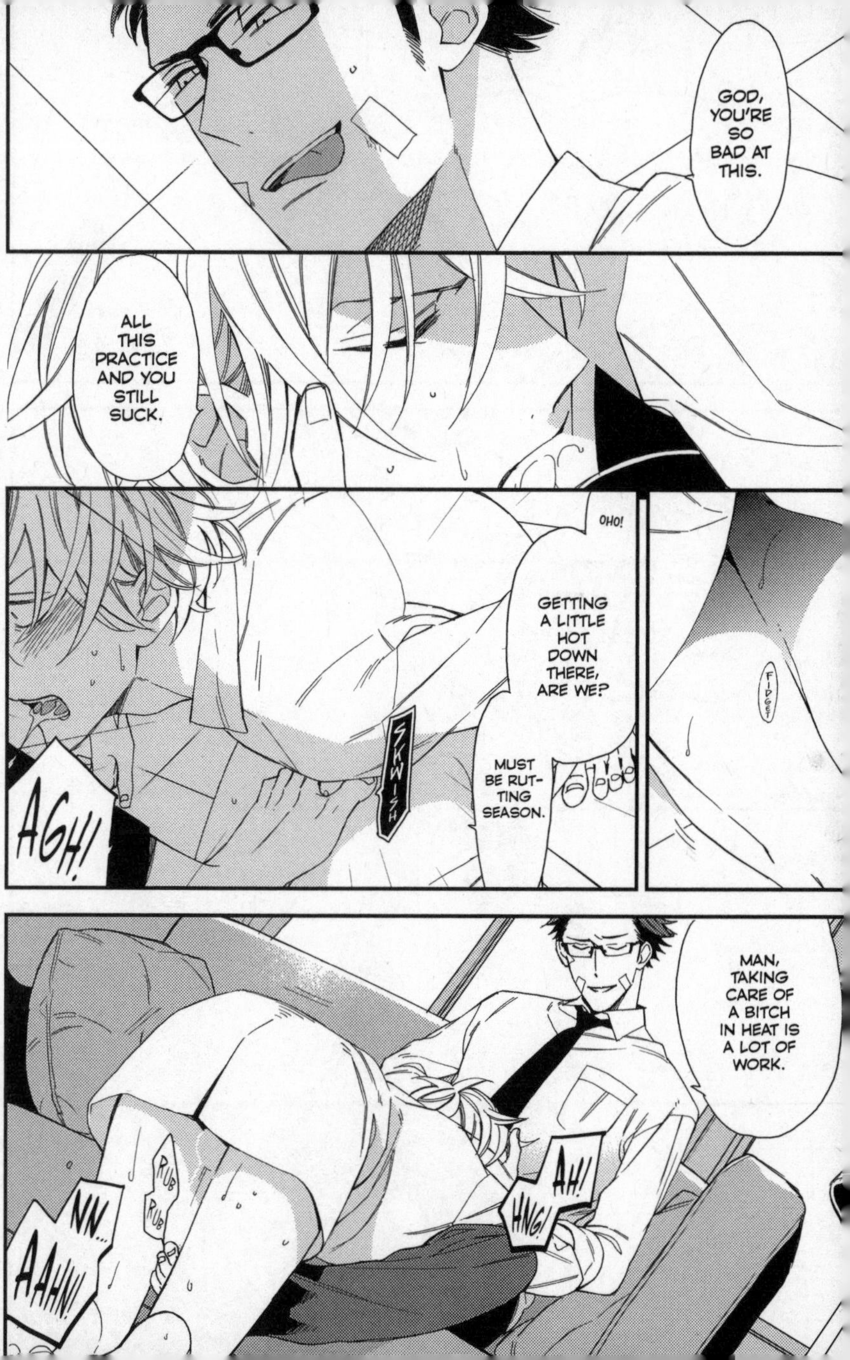
GOD, YOU'RE SO BAD AT THIS.
ALL THIS PRACTICE AND YOU STILL SUCK.
FIDGET
OHO!
GETTING A LITTLE HOT DOWN THERE, ARE WE?
MUST BE RUT-TING SEASON.
SKWISH
AGH!
MAN, TAKING CARE OF A BITCH IN HEAT IS A LOT OF WORK.
AH!
HNG!
RUB RUB
NN... AAHN!

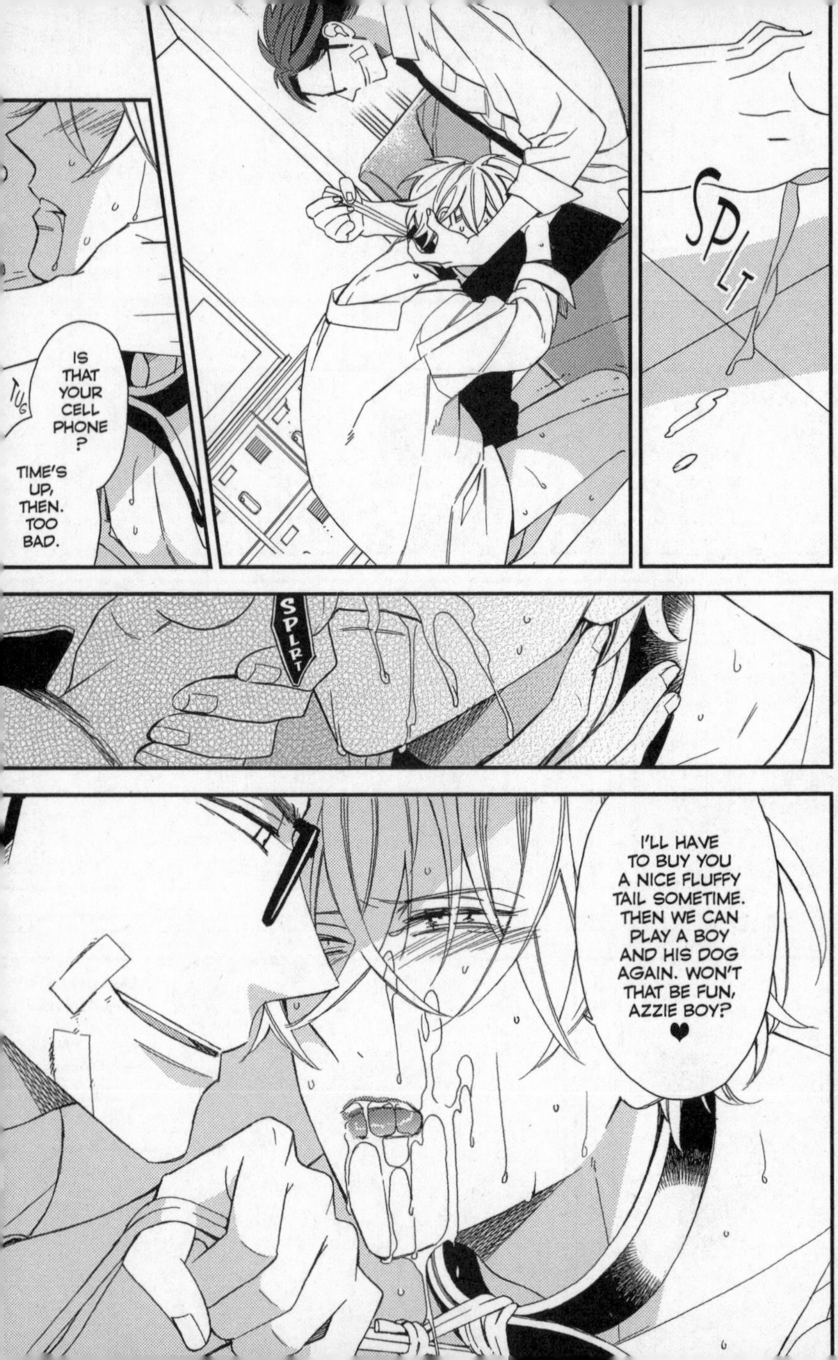
SPLT
TUG
IS THAT YOUR CELL PHONE?
TIME'S UP, THEN. TOO BAD.
SPLRT
I'LL HAVE TO BUY YOU A NICE FLUFFY TAIL SOMETIME. THEN WE CAN PLAY A BOY AND HIS DOG AGAIN. WON'T THAT BE FUN, AZZIE BOY? ♥

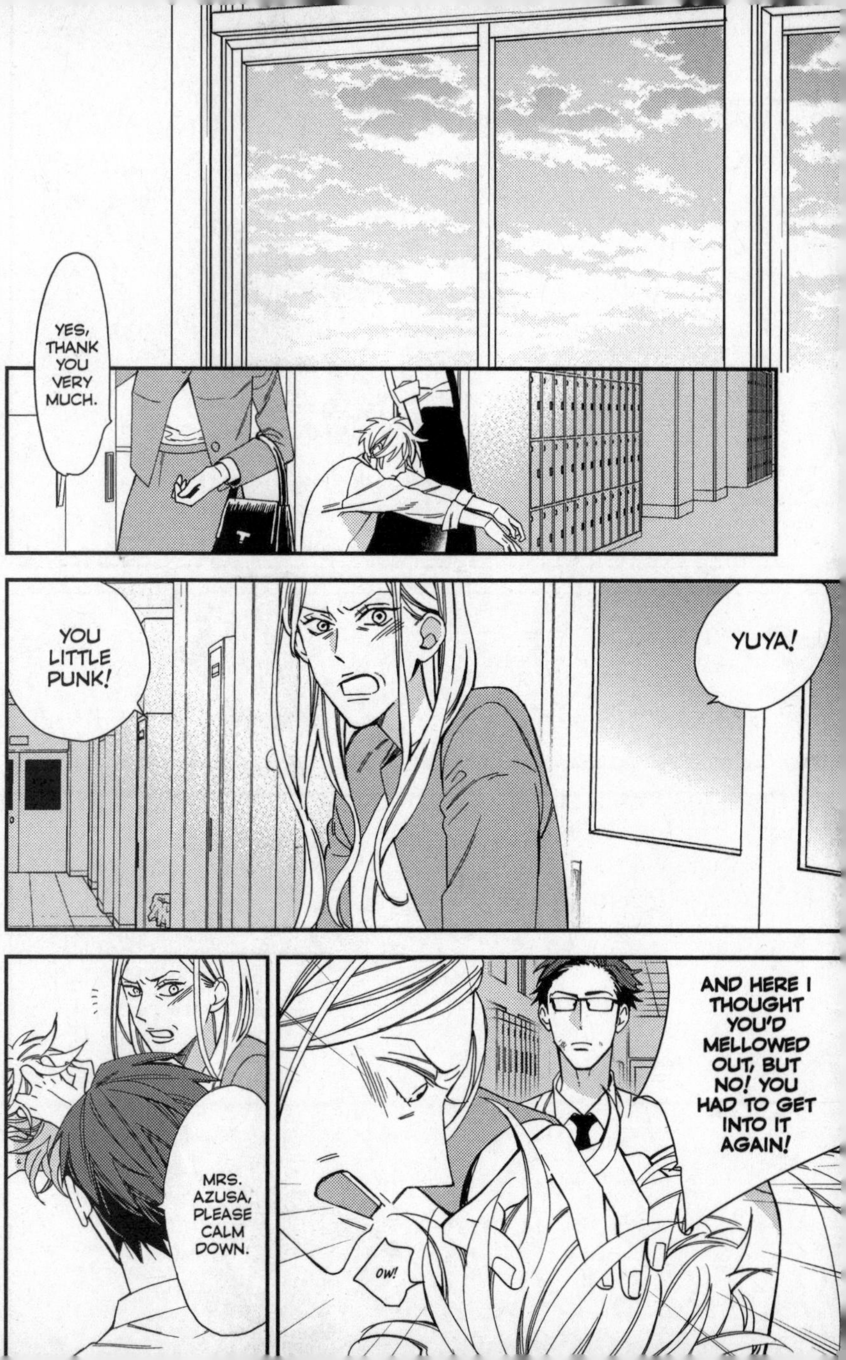
YES, THANK YOU VERY MUCH.
YUYA!
YOU LITTLE PUNK!
AND HERE I THOUGHT YOU'D MELLOWED OUT, BUT NO! YOU HAD TO GET INTO IT AGAIN!
OW!
MRS. AZUSA, PLEASE CALM DOWN.

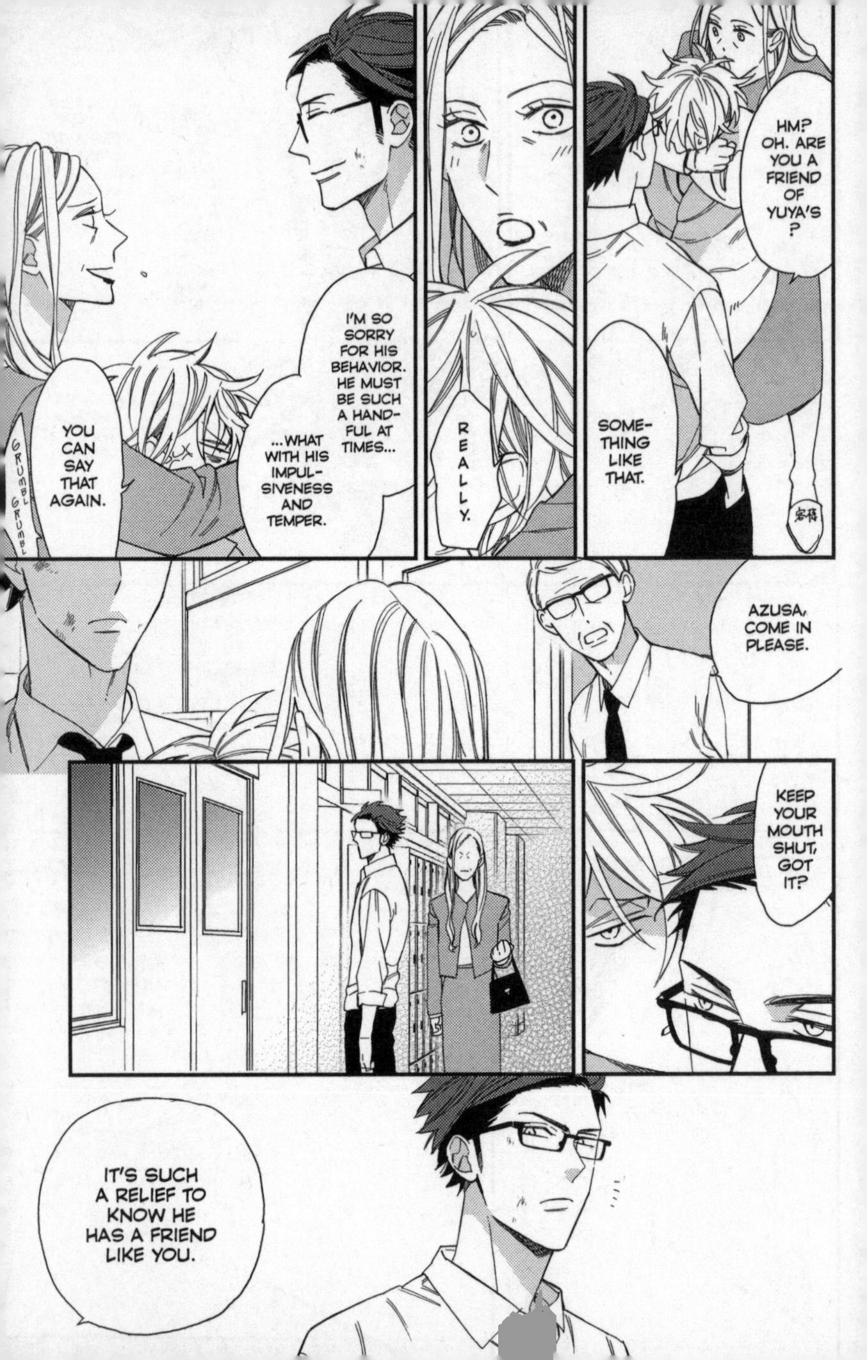
HM? OH. ARE YOU A FRIEND OF YUYA'S?
SOME-THING LIKE THAT.
REALLY.
I'M SO SORRY FOR HIS BEHAVIOR. HE MUST BE SUCH A HAND-FUL AT TIMES...
...WHAT WITH HIS IMPUL-SIVENESS AND TEMPER.
YOU CAN SAY THAT AGAIN.
GRUMBL GRUMBL
AZUSA, COME IN PLEASE.
KEEP YOUR MOUTH SHUT, GOT IT?
IT'S SUCH A RELIEF TO KNOW HE HAS A FRIEND LIKE YOU.

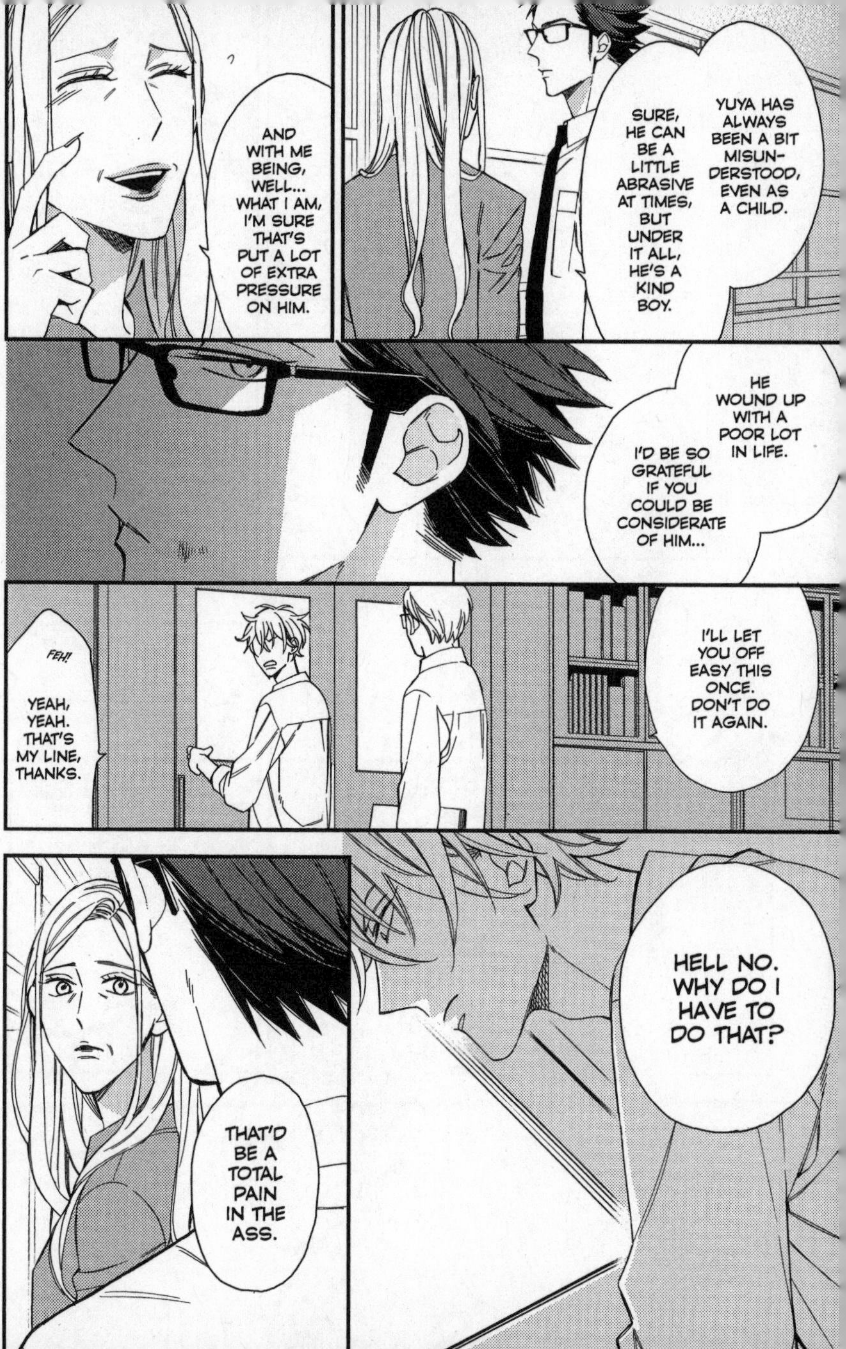
YUYA HAS ALWAYS BEEN A BIT MISUNDERSTOOD, EVEN AS A CHILD.
SURE, HE CAN BE A LITTLE ABRASIVE AT TIMES, BUT UNDER IT ALL, HE'S A KIND BOY.
AND WITH ME BEING, WELL... WHAT I AM, I'M SURE THAT'S PUT A LOT OF EXTRA PRESSURE ON HIM.
HE WOUND UP WITH A POOR LOT IN LIFE.
I'D BE SO GRATEFUL IF YOU COULD BE CONSIDERATE OF HIM...
I'LL LET YOU OFF EASY THIS ONCE. DON'T DO IT AGAIN.
FEH!
YEAH, YEAH. THAT'S MY LINE, THANKS.
HELL NO. WHY DO I HAVE TO DO THAT?
THAT'D BE A TOTAL PAIN IN THE ASS.

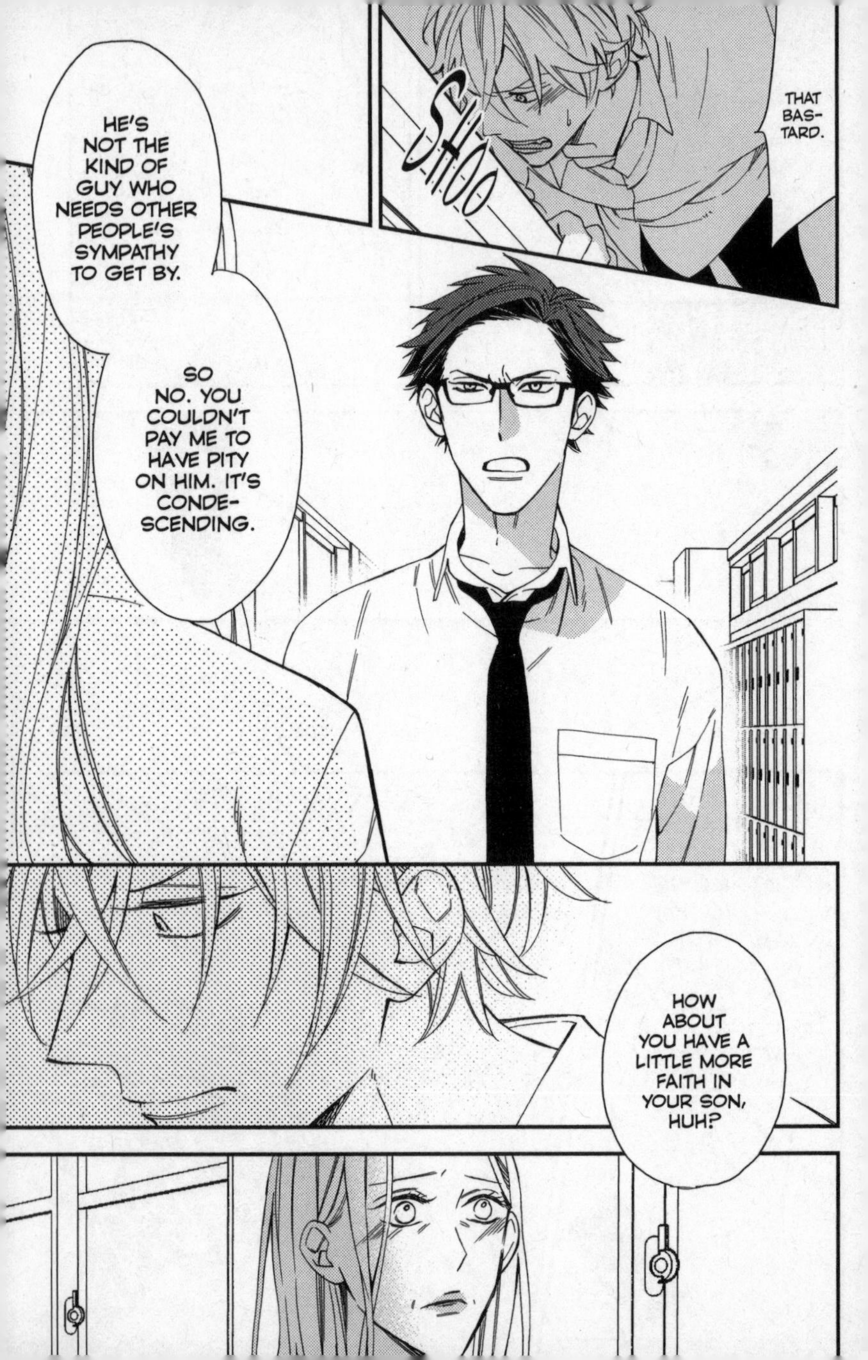
SHOO
THAT BASTARD.
HE'S NOT THE KIND OF GUY WHO NEEDS OTHER PEOPLE'S SYMPATHY TO GET BY.
SO NO. YOU COULDN'T PAY ME TO HAVE PITY ON HIM. IT'S CONDESCENDING.
HOW ABOUT YOU HAVE A LITTLE MORE FAITH IN YOUR SON, HUH?

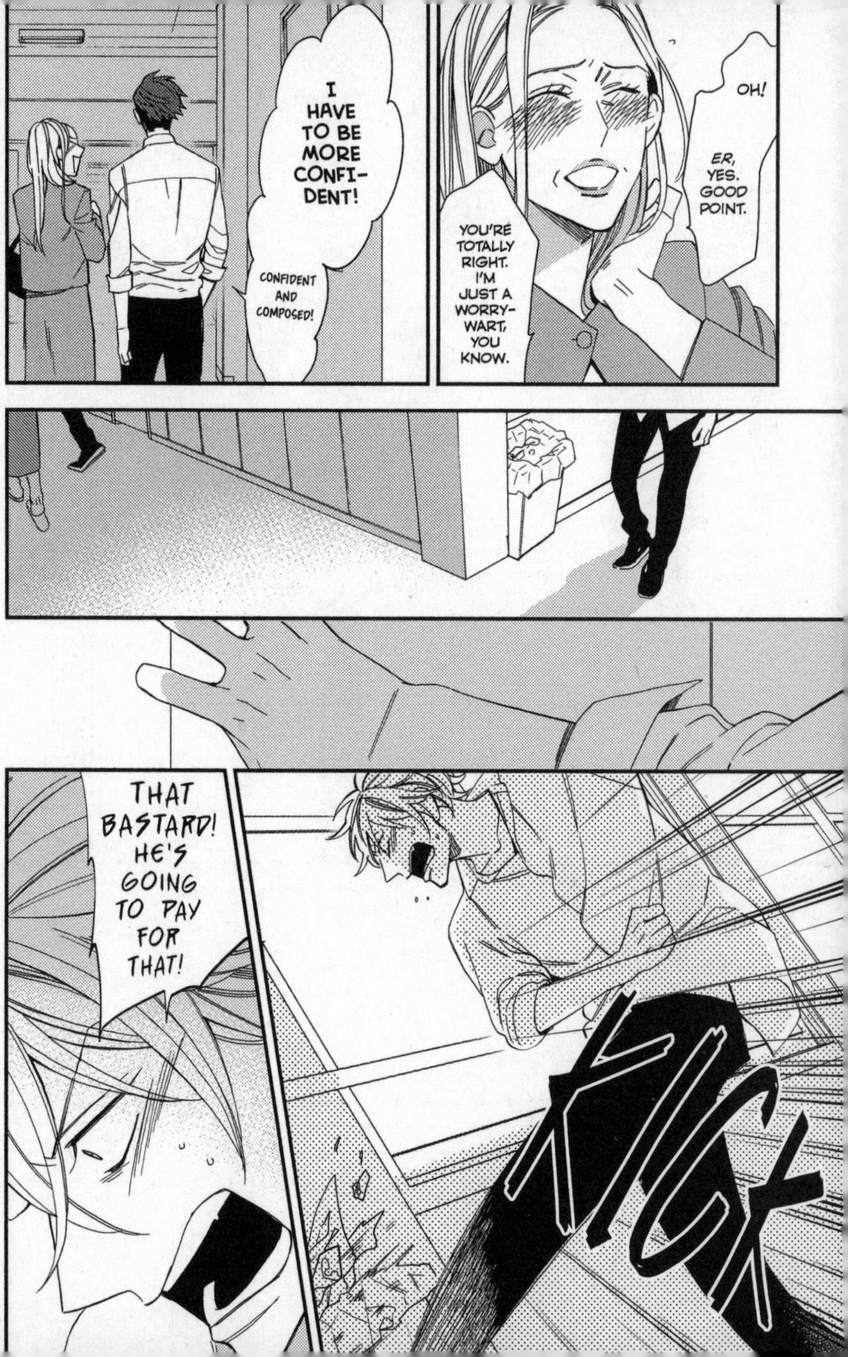
OH!
ER, YES. GOOD POINT.
YOU'RE TOTALLY RIGHT. I'M JUST A WORRY-WART, YOU KNOW.
I HAVE TO BE MORE CONFI-DENT!
CONFIDENT AND COMPOSED!
KICK
THAT BASTARD! HE'S GOING TO PAY FOR THAT!

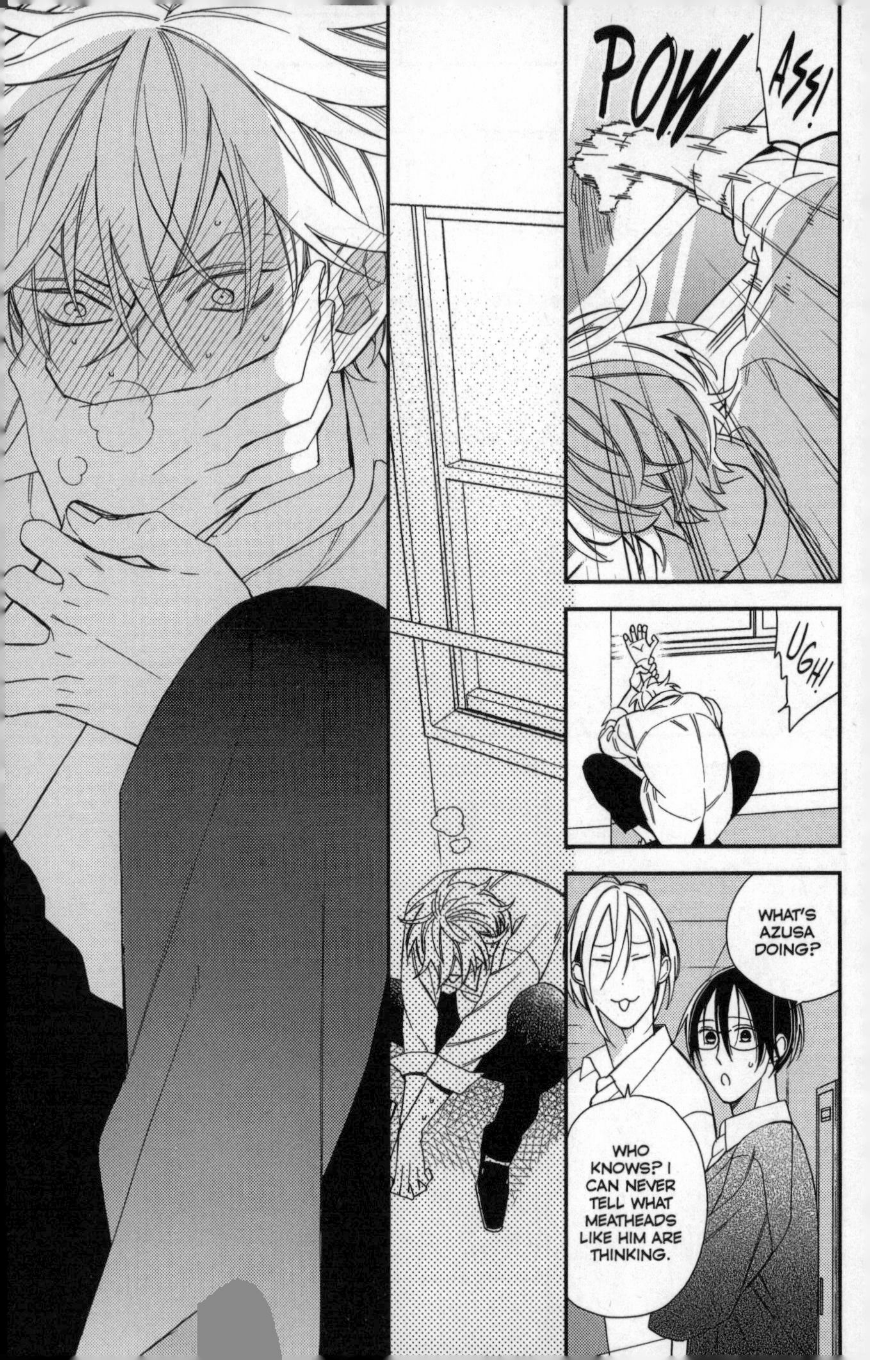
POW
ASS!
UGH!
WHAT'S AZUSA DOING?
WHO KNOWS? I CAN NEVER TELL WHAT MEATHEADS LIKE HIM ARE THINKING.

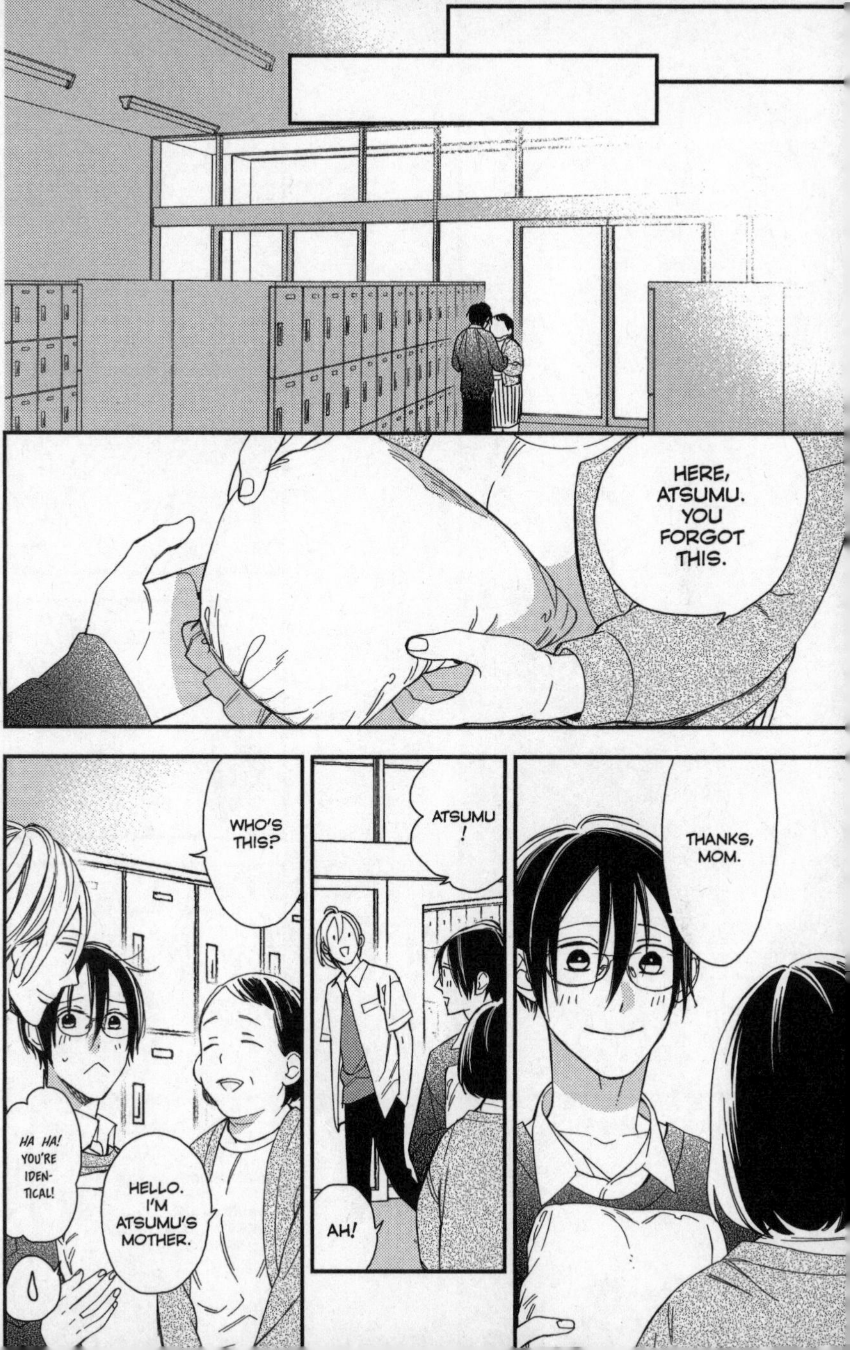
HERE, ATSUMU. YOU FORGOT THIS.
THANKS, MOM.
ATSUMU!
AH!
WHO'S THIS?
HELLO. I'M ATSUMU'S MOTHER.
HA HA! YOU'RE IDEN-TICAL!

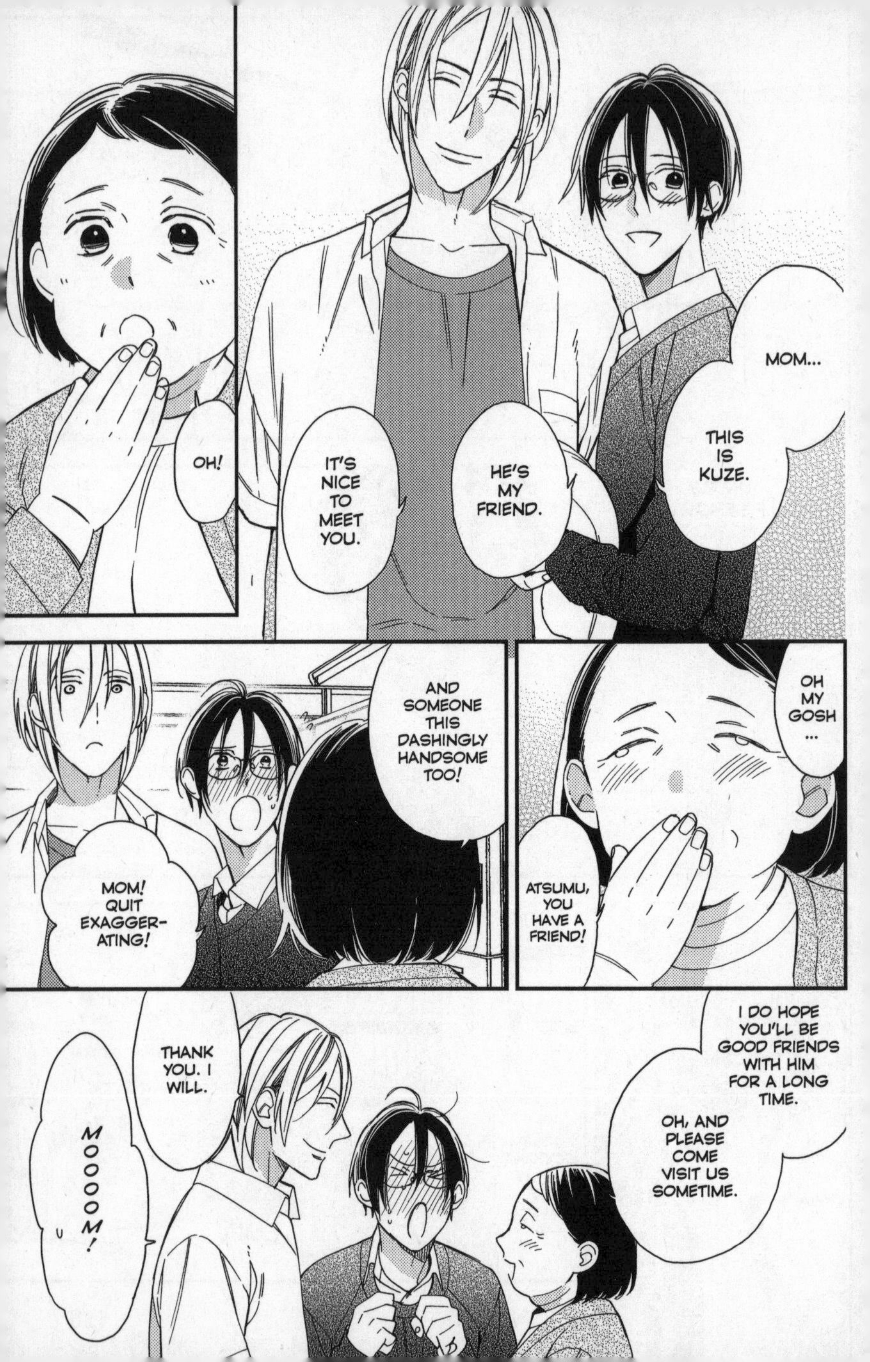
MOM...
THIS IS KUZE.
HE'S MY FRIEND.
IT'S NICE TO MEET YOU.
OH!
OH MY GOSH ...
ATSUMU, YOU HAVE A FRIEND!
AND SOMEONE THIS DASHINGLY HANDSOME TOO!
MOM! QUIT EXAGGER-ATING!
I DO HOPE YOU'LL BE GOOD FRIENDS WITH HIM FOR A LONG TIME.
OH, AND PLEASE COME VISIT US SOMETIME.
THANK YOU. I WILL.
MOOOOOM!

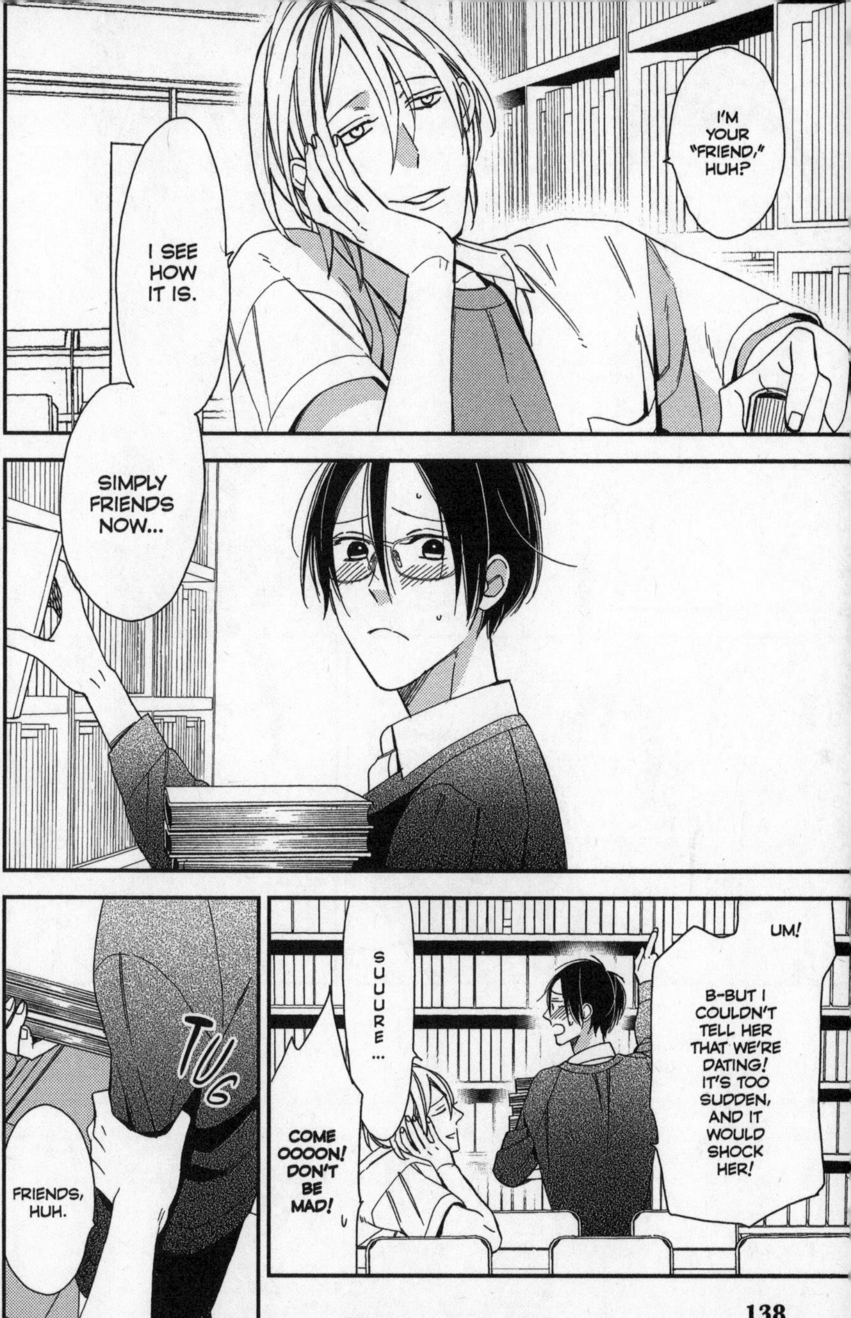
I'M YOUR "FRIEND," HUH?
I SEE HOW IT IS.
SIMPLY FRIENDS NOW...
UM!
B-BUT I COULDN'T TELL HER THAT WE'RE DATING! IT'S TOO SUDDEN, AND IT WOULD SHOCK HER!
SUUURE...
COME OOOON! DON'T BE MAD!
TUG
FRIENDS, HUH.

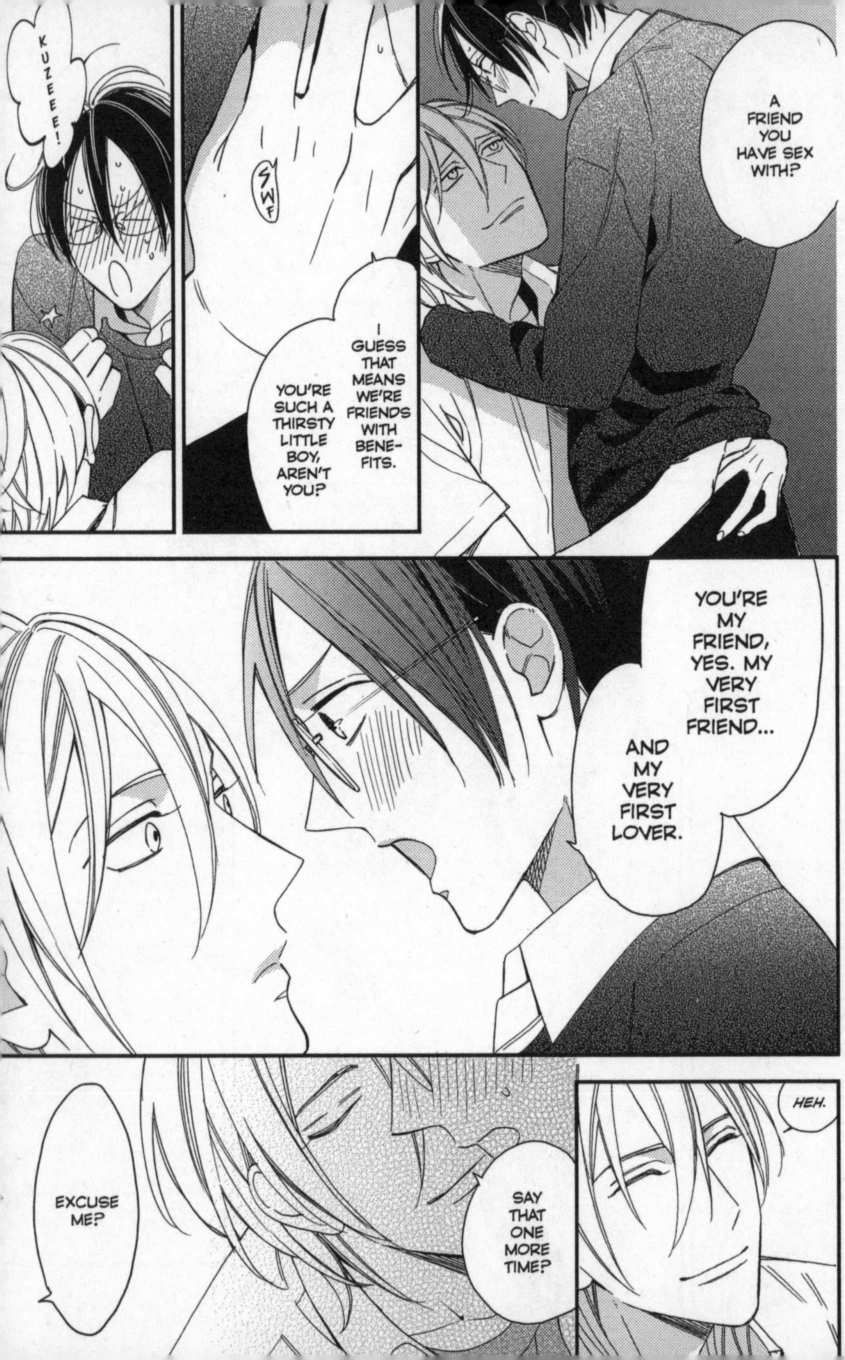
A FRIEND YOU HAVE SEX WITH?
SWF
I GUESS THAT MEANS WE'RE FRIENDS WITH BENE-FITS.
YOU'RE SUCH A THIRSTY LITTLE BOY, AREN'T YOU?
KUZEEE!
YOU'RE MY FRIEND, YES. MY VERY FIRST FRIEND...
AND MY VERY FIRST LOVER.
HEH.
SAY THAT ONE MORE TIME?
EXCUSE ME?

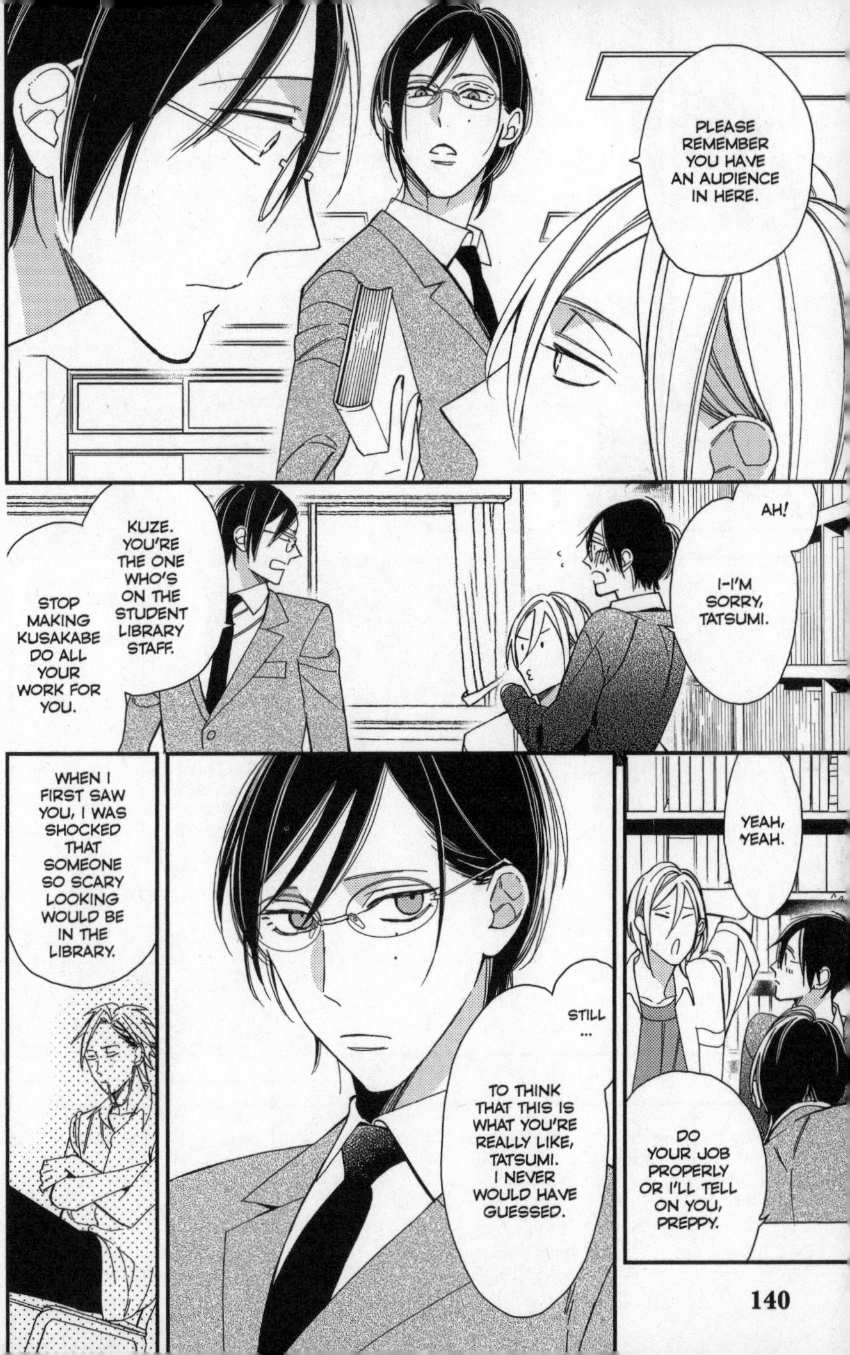
PLEASE REMEMBER YOU HAVE AN AUDIENCE IN HERE.
AH!
I-I'M SORRY, TATSUMI.
KUZE. YOU'RE THE ONE WHO'S ON THE STUDENT LIBRARY STAFF.
STOP MAKING KUSAKABE DO ALL YOUR WORK FOR YOU.
YEAH, YEAH.
DO YOUR JOB PROPERLY OR I'LL TELL ON YOU, PREPPY.
STILL...
TO THINK THAT THIS IS WHAT YOU'RE REALLY LIKE, TATSUMI. I NEVER WOULD HAVE GUESSED.
WHEN I FIRST SAW YOU, I WAS SHOCKED THAT SOMEONE SO SCARY LOOKING WOULD BE IN THE LIBRARY.

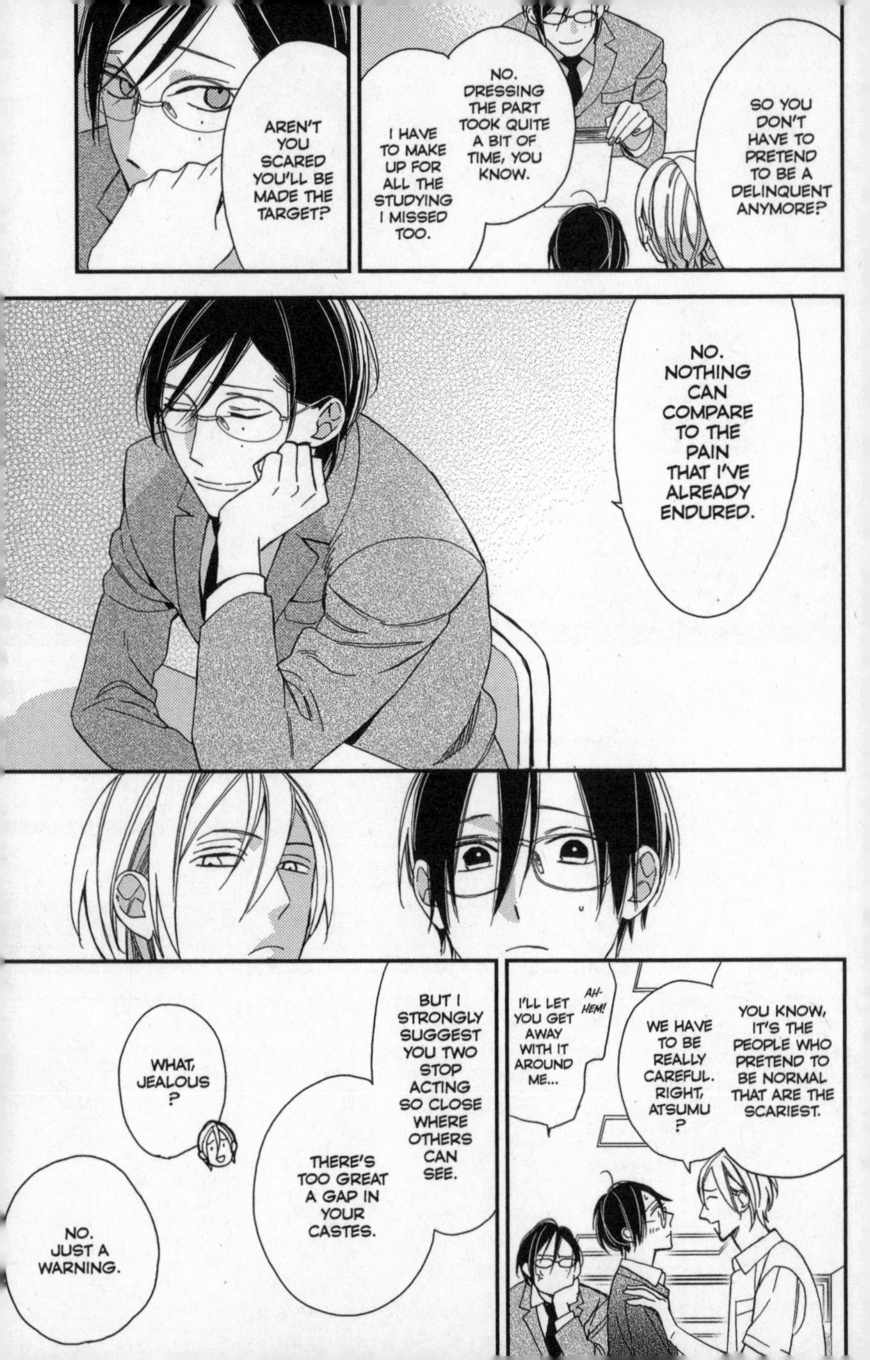
SO YOU DON'T HAVE TO PRETEND TO BE A DELINQUENT ANYMORE?
NO. DRESSING THE PART TOOK QUITE A BIT OF TIME, YOU KNOW.
I HAVE TO MAKE UP FOR ALL THE STUDYING I MISSED TOO.
AREN'T YOU SCARED YOU'LL BE MADE THE TARGET?
NO. NOTHING CAN COMPARE TO THE PAIN THAT I'VE ALREADY ENDURED.
YOU KNOW, IT'S THE PEOPLE WHO PRETEND TO BE NORMAL THAT ARE THE SCARIEST.
WE HAVE TO BE REALLY CAREFUL. RIGHT, ATSUMU?
AH-HEM!
I'LL LET YOU GET AWAY WITH IT AROUND ME...
BUT I STRONGLY SUGGEST YOU TWO STOP ACTING SO CLOSE WHERE OTHERS CAN SEE.
THERE'S TOO GREAT A GAP IN YOUR CASTES.
WHAT, JEALOUS?
NO. JUST A WARNING.

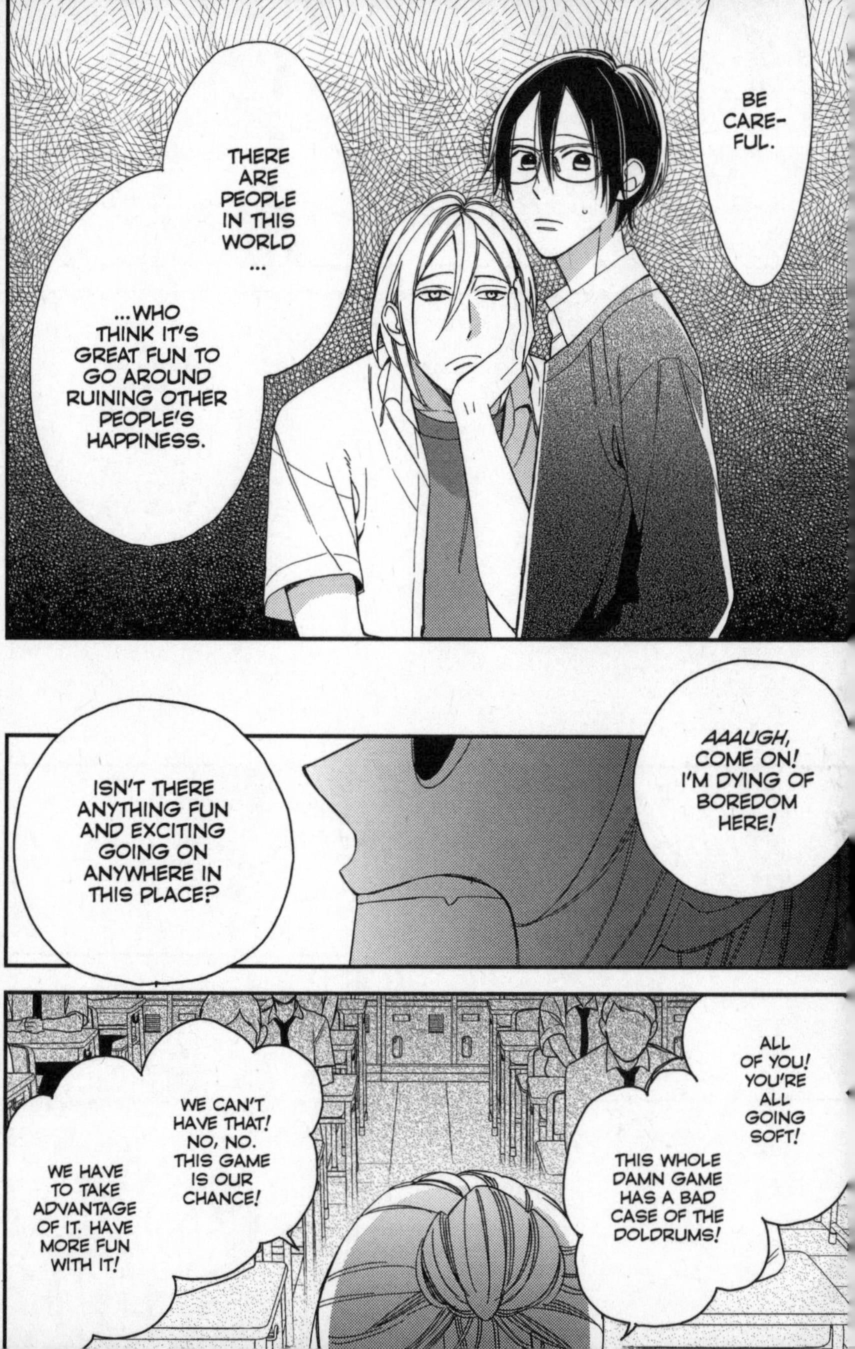
BE CARE-FUL.
THERE ARE PEOPLE IN THIS WORLD...
...WHO THINK IT'S GREAT FUN TO GO AROUND RUINING OTHER PEOPLE'S HAPPINESS.
AAAUGH, COME ON! I'M DYING OF BOREDOM HERE!
ISN'T THERE ANYTHING FUN AND EXCITING GOING ON ANYWHERE IN THIS PLACE?
ALL OF YOU! YOU'RE ALL GOING SOFT!
THIS WHOLE DAMN GAME HAS A BAD CASE OF THE DOLDRUMS!
WE CAN'T HAVE THAT! NO, NO. THIS GAME IS OUR CHANCE!
WE HAVE TO TAKE ADVANTAGE OF IT. HAVE MORE FUN WITH IT!

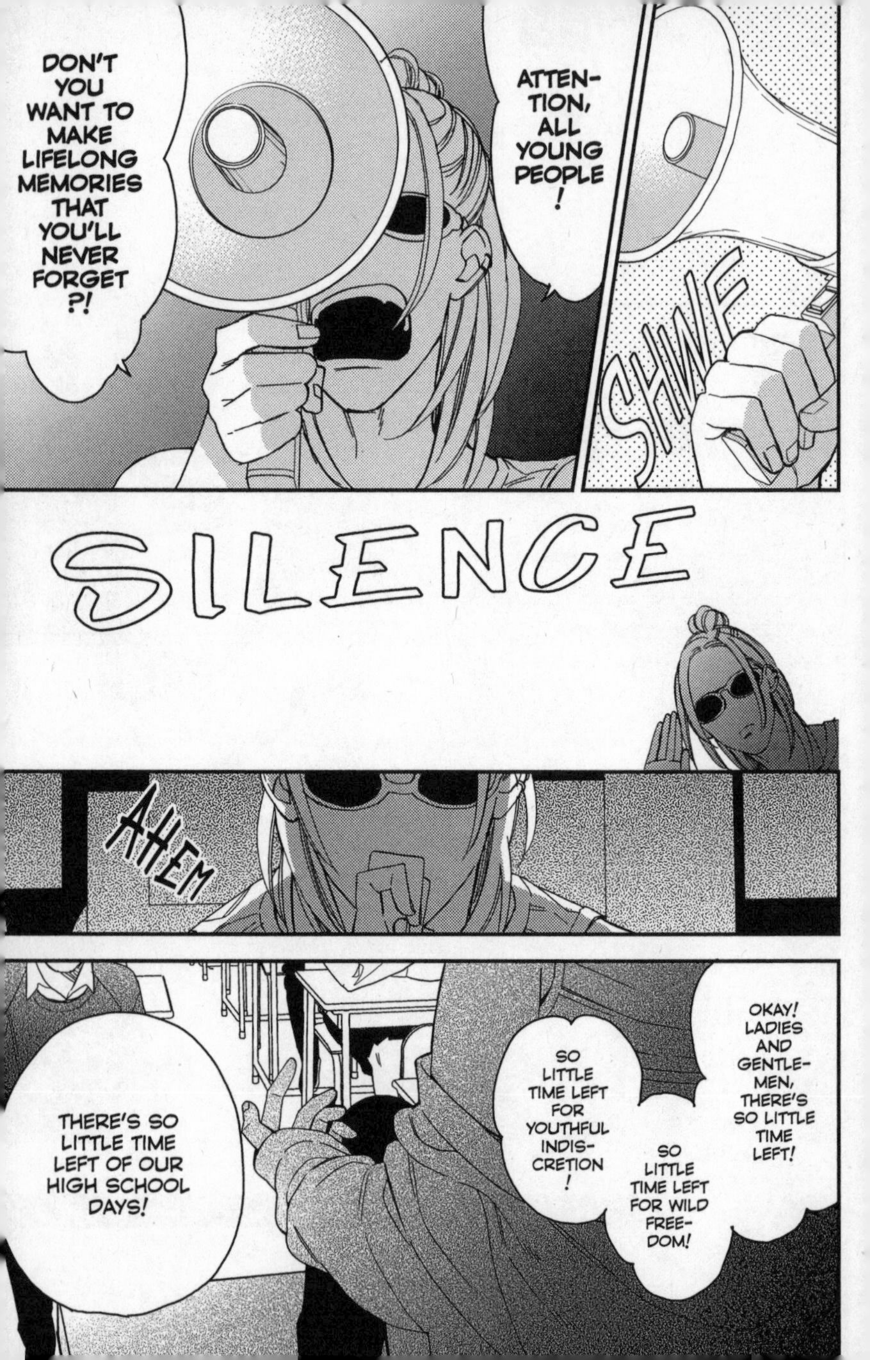
ATTENTION, ALL YOUNG PEOPLE!
SHWF
DON'T YOU WANT TO MAKE LIFELONG MEMORIES THAT YOU'LL NEVER FORGET?!
SILENCE
AHEM
OKAY! LADIES AND GENTLEMEN, THERE'S SO LITTLE TIME LEFT!
SO LITTLE TIME LEFT FOR WILD FREEDOM!
SO LITTLE TIME LEFT FOR YOUTHFUL INDISCRETION!
THERE'S SO LITTLE TIME LEFT OF OUR HIGH SCHOOL DAYS!

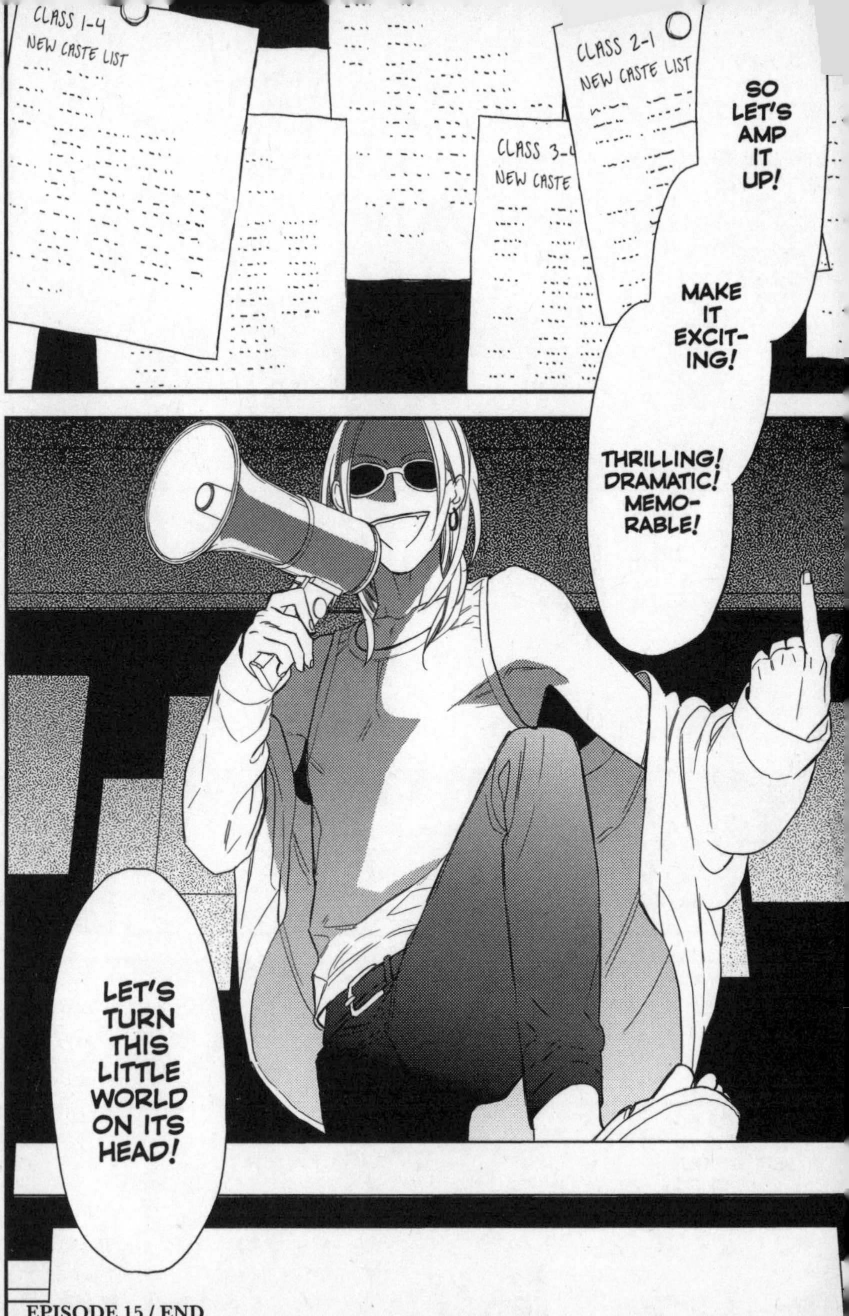
CLASS 2-1
NEW CASTE LIST
CLASS 3-
NEW CASTE
CLASS 1-4
NEW CASTE LIST
SO LET'S AMP IT UP!
MAKE IT EXCIT-ING!
THRILLING! DRAMATIC! MEMO-RABLE!
LET'S TURN THIS LITTLE WORLD ON ITS HEAD!

EPISODE 15 / END

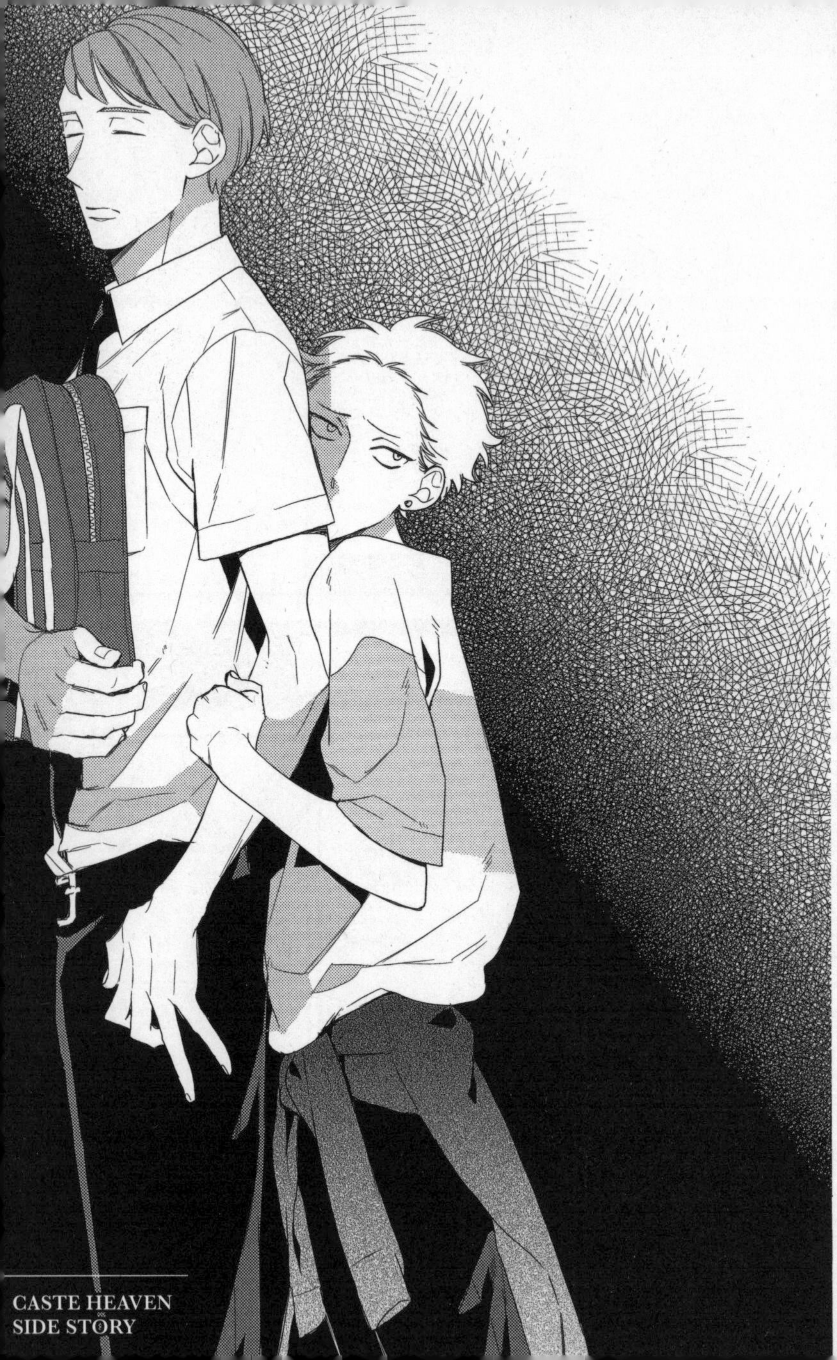
CASTE HEAVEN
SIDE STORY

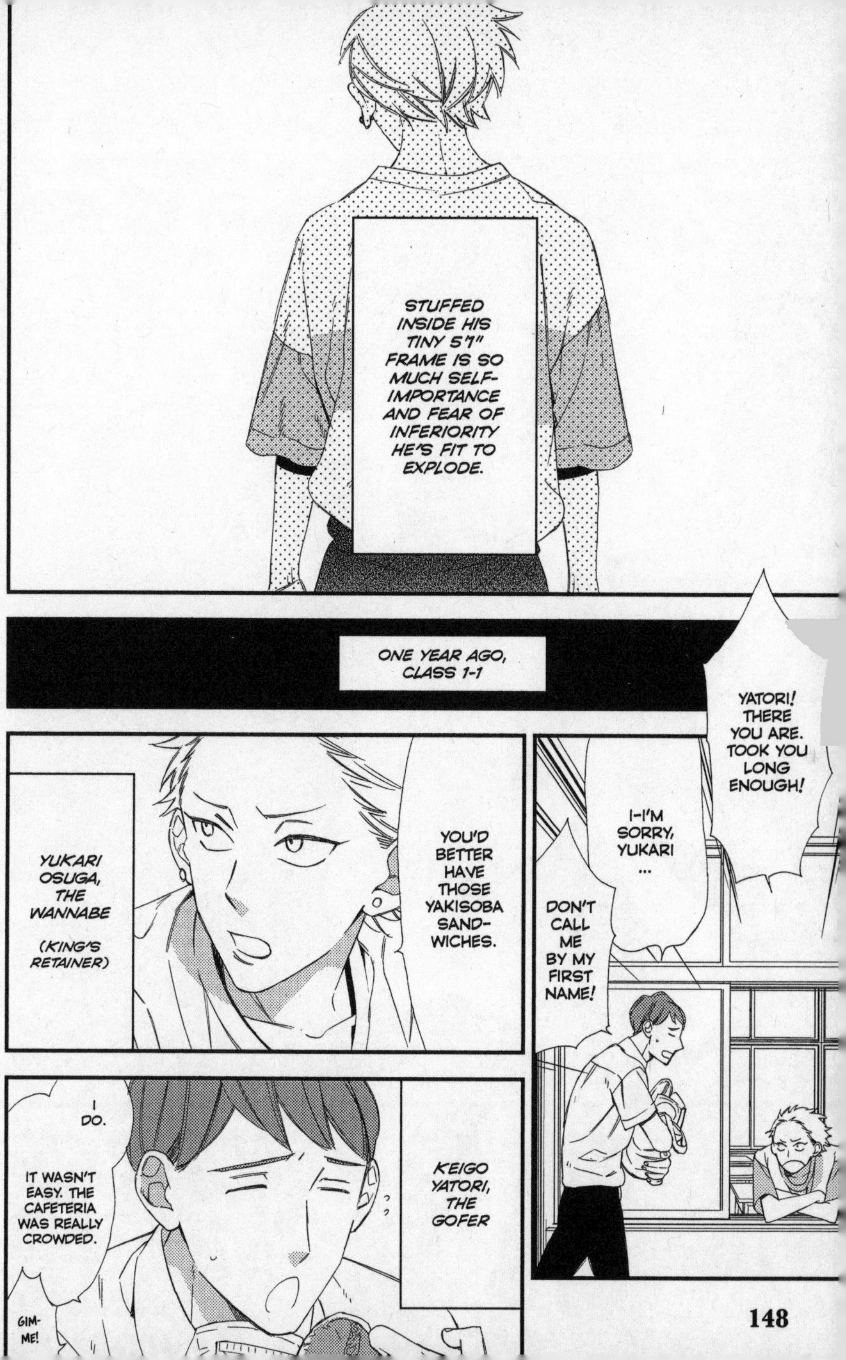
STUFFED INSIDE HIS TINY 5'7" FRAME IS SO MUCH SELF-IMPORTANCE AND FEAR OF INFERIORITY HE'S FIT TO EXPLODE.
ONE YEAR AGO, CLASS 1-1
YATORI! THERE YOU ARE. TOOK YOU LONG ENOUGH!
I-I'M SORRY, YUKARI...
DON'T CALL ME BY MY FIRST NAME!
YOU'D BETTER HAVE THOSE YAKISOBA SANDWICHES.
YUKARI OSUGA, THE WANNABE
(KING'S RETAINER)
KEIGO YATORI, THE GOFER
I DO.
IT WASN'T EASY. THE CAFETERIA WAS REALLY CROWDED.
GIMME!

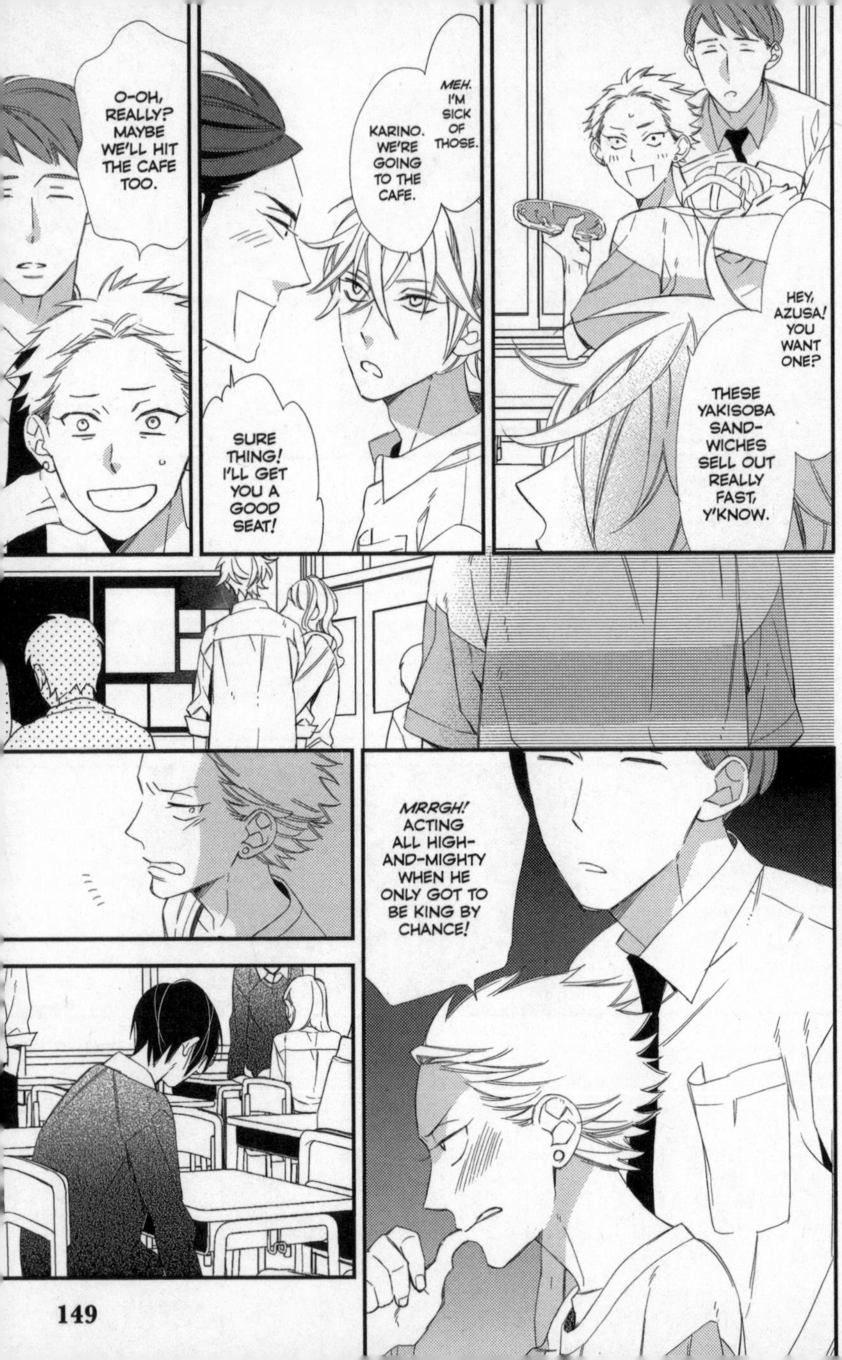
HEY, AZUSA! YOU WANT ONE?
THESE YAKISOBA SANDWICHES SELL OUT REALLY FAST, Y'KNOW.
MEH. I'M SICK OF THOSE.
KARINO. WE'RE GOING TO THE CAFE.
SURE THING! I'LL GET YOU A GOOD SEAT!
O-OH, REALLY? MAYBE WE'LL HIT THE CAFE TOO.
MRRGH! ACTING ALL HIGH-AND-MIGHTY WHEN HE ONLY GOT TO BE KING BY CHANCE!

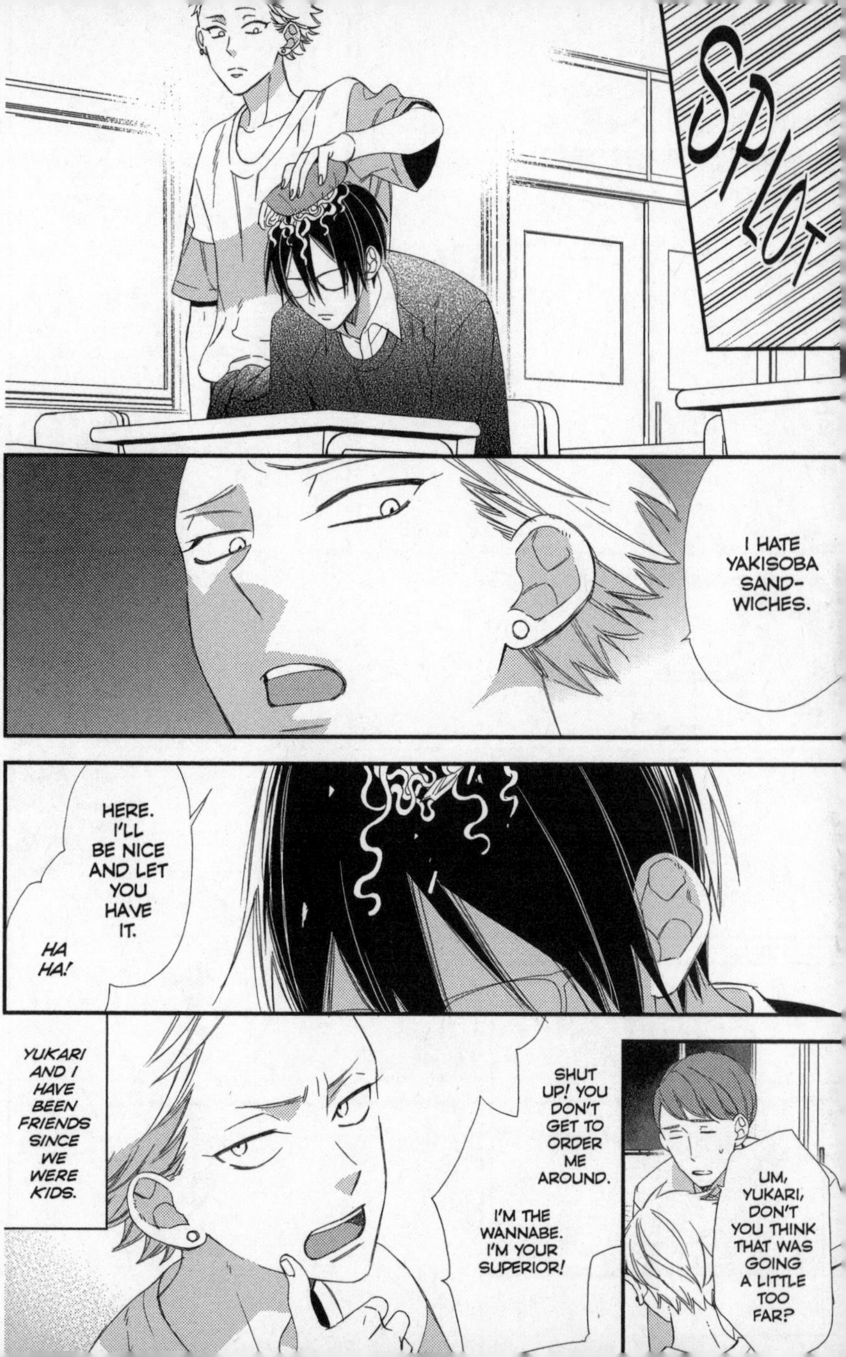
SPLOT
I HATE YAKISOBA SANDWICHES.
HERE. I'LL BE NICE AND LET YOU HAVE IT.
HA HA!
UM, YUKARI, DON'T YOU THINK THAT WAS GOING A LITTLE TOO FAR?
SHUT UP! YOU DON'T GET TO ORDER ME AROUND.
I'M THE WANNABE. I'M YOUR SUPERIOR!
YUKARI AND I HAVE BEEN FRIENDS SINCE WE WERE KIDS.

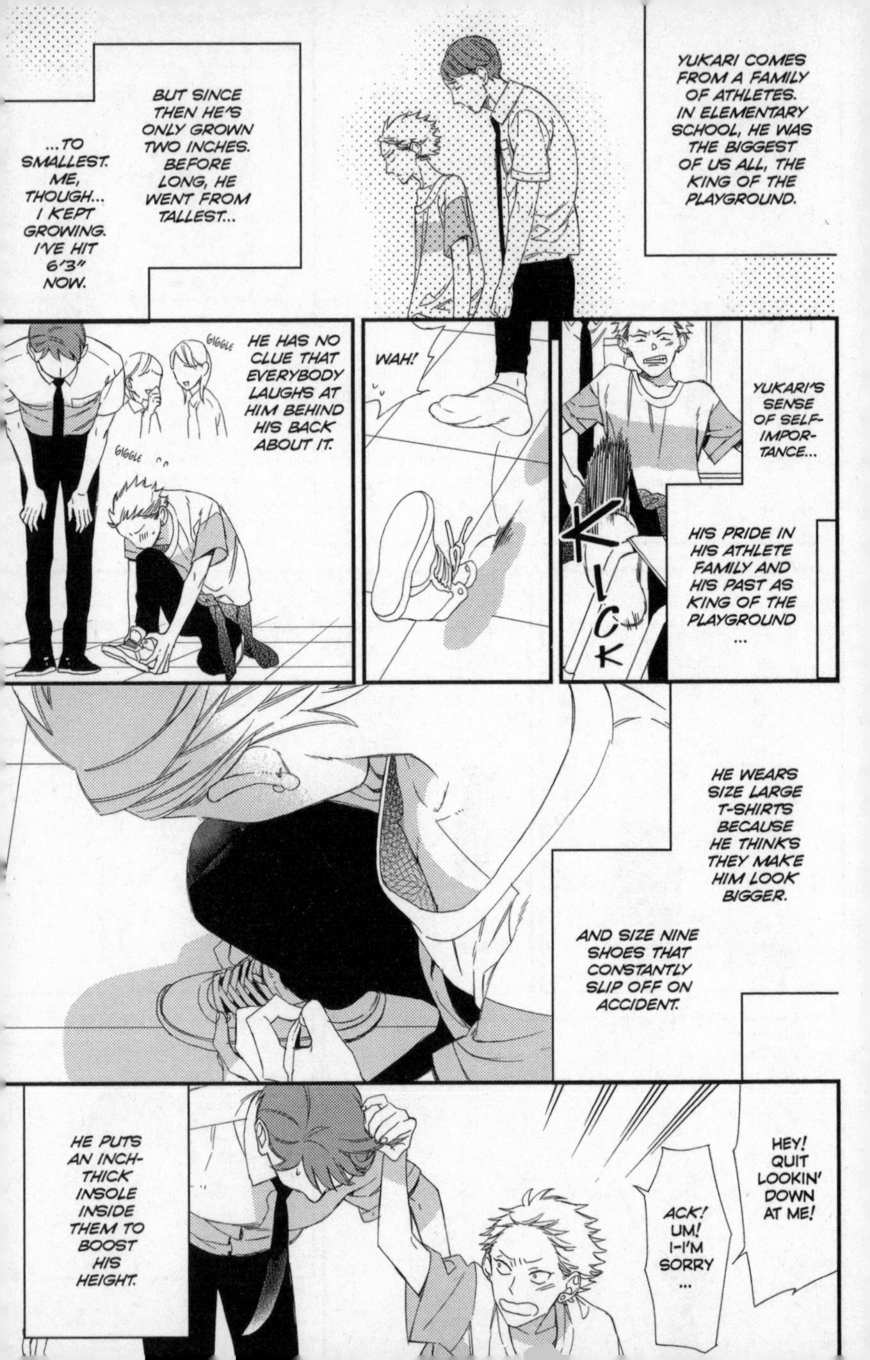
YUKARI COMES FROM A FAMILY OF ATHLETES. IN ELEMENTARY SCHOOL, HE WAS THE BIGGEST OF US ALL, THE KING OF THE PLAYGROUND.
BUT SINCE THEN HE'S ONLY GROWN TWO INCHES. BEFORE LONG, HE WENT FROM TALLEST...
...TO SMALLEST. ME, THOUGH... I KEPT GROWING. I'VE HIT 6'3" NOW.
YUKARI'S SENSE OF SELF-IMPORTANCE...
HIS PRIDE IN HIS ATHLETE FAMILY AND HIS PAST AS KING OF THE PLAYGROUND...
KICK
WAH!
HE HAS NO CLUE THAT EVERYBODY LAUGHS AT HIM BEHIND HIS BACK ABOUT IT.
GIGGLE
GIGGLE
HE WEARS SIZE LARGE T-SHIRTS BECAUSE HE THINKS THEY MAKE HIM LOOK BIGGER.
AND SIZE NINE SHOES THAT CONSTANTLY SLIP OFF ON ACCIDENT.
HEY! QUIT LOOKIN' DOWN AT ME!
ACK! UM! I-I'M SORRY...
HE PUTS AN INCH-THICK INSOLE INSIDE THEM TO BOOST HIS HEIGHT.

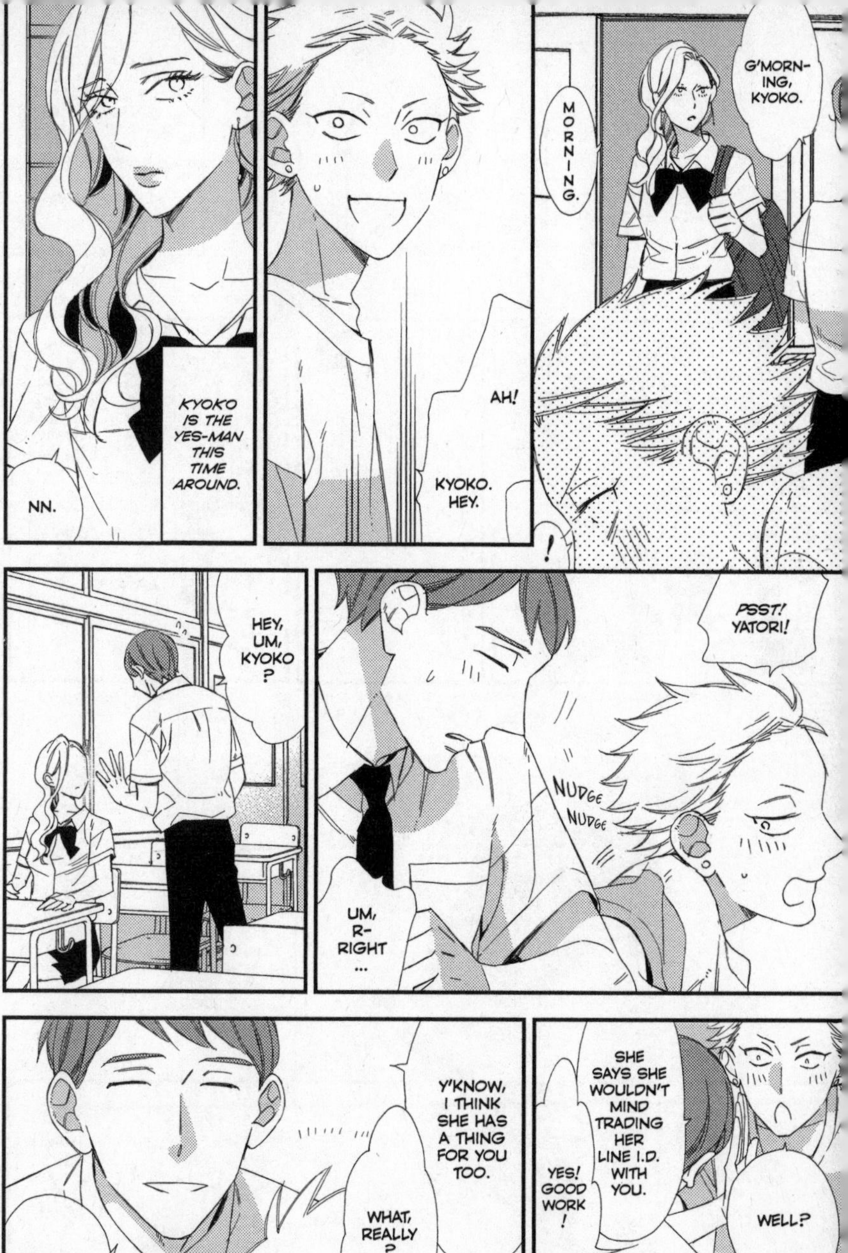
G'MORNING, KYOKO.
MORNING.
!
AH!
KYOKO. HEY.
KYOKO IS THE YES-MAN THIS TIME AROUND.
NN.
PSST! YATORI!
NUDGE NUDGE
UM, R-RIGHT...
HEY, UM, KYOKO?
WELL?
SHE SAYS SHE WOULDN'T MIND TRADING HER LINE I.D. WITH YOU.
YES! GOOD WORK!
Y'KNOW, I THINK SHE HAS A THING FOR YOU TOO.
WHAT, REALLY?
YEAH. REALLY.

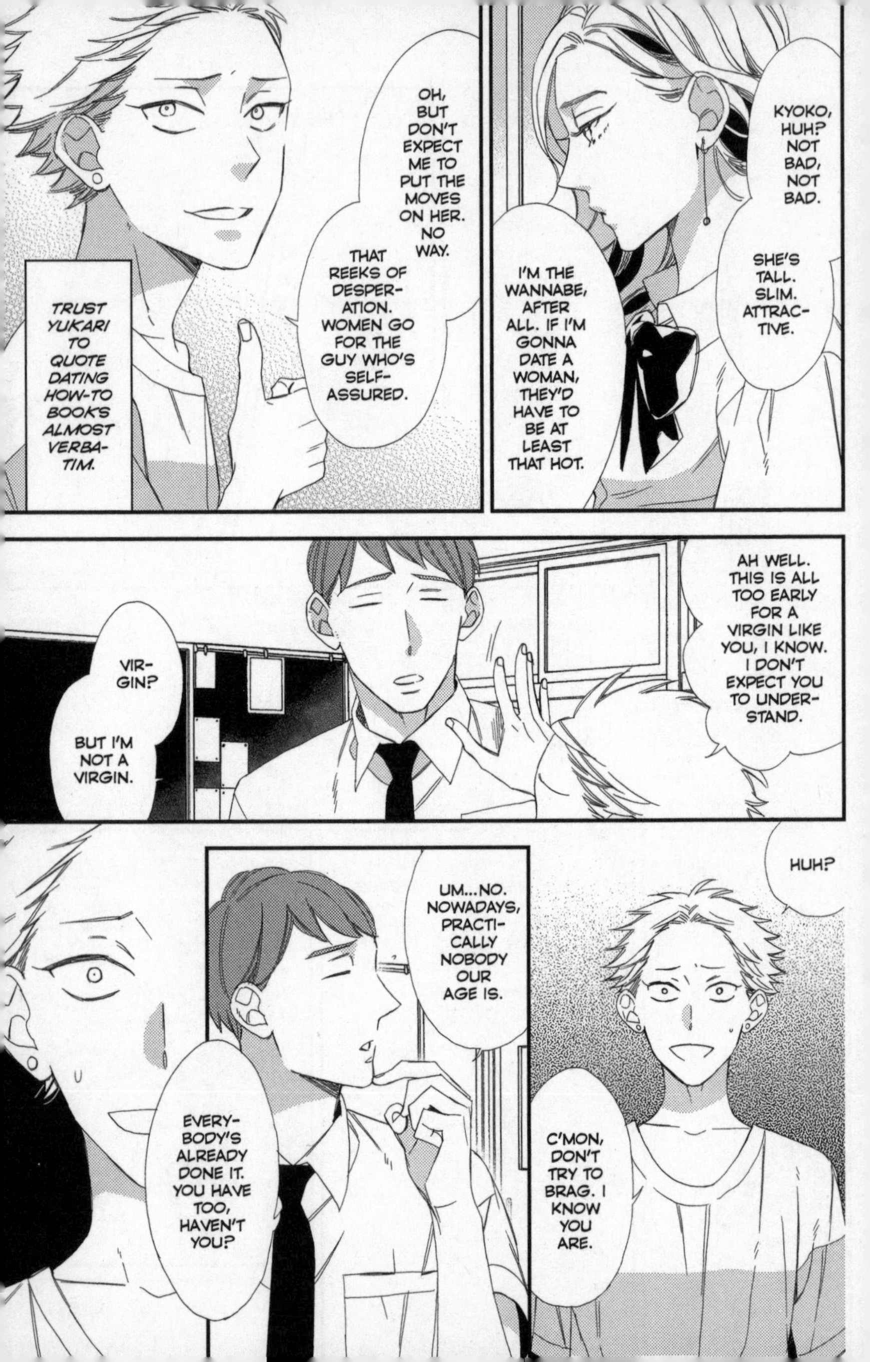
KYOKO, HUH? NOT BAD, NOT BAD.
SHE'S TALL. SLIM. ATTRACTIVE.
I'M THE WANNABE, AFTER ALL. IF I'M GONNA DATE A WOMAN, THEY'D HAVE TO BE AT LEAST THAT HOT.
OH, BUT DON'T EXPECT ME TO PUT THE MOVES ON HER. NO WAY.
THAT REEKS OF DESPERATION. WOMEN GO FOR THE GUY WHO'S SELF-ASSURED.
TRUST YUKARI TO QUOTE DATING HOW-TO BOOKS ALMOST VERBATIM.
AH WELL. THIS IS ALL TOO EARLY FOR A VIRGIN LIKE YOU, I KNOW. I DON'T EXPECT YOU TO UNDERSTAND.
VIRGIN?
BUT I'M NOT A VIRGIN.
HUH?
C'MON, DON'T TRY TO BRAG. I KNOW YOU ARE.
UM...NO. NOWADAYS, PRACTICALLY NOBODY OUR AGE IS.
EVERYBODY'S ALREADY DONE IT. YOU HAVE TOO, HAVEN'T YOU?

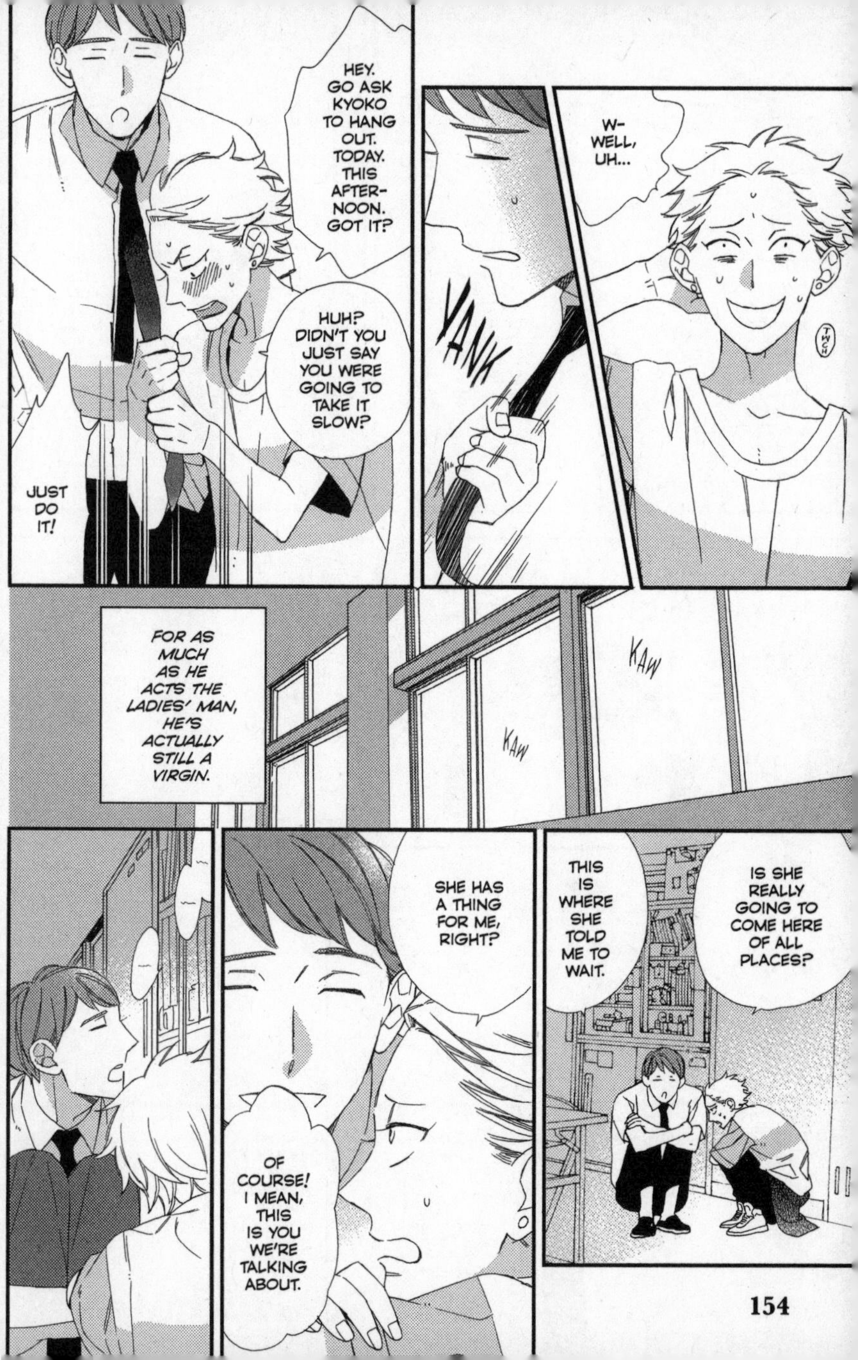
W-
WELL,
UH...
TWCH
YANK
HEY. GO ASK KYOKO TO HANG OUT. TODAY. THIS AFTER-NOON. GOT IT?
HUH? DIDN'T YOU JUST SAY YOU WERE GOING TO TAKE IT SLOW?
JUST DO IT!
KAW
KAW
FOR AS MUCH AS HE ACTS THE LADIES' MAN, HE'S ACTUALLY STILL A VIRGIN.
IS SHE REALLY GOING TO COME HERE OF ALL PLACES?
THIS IS WHERE SHE TOLD ME TO WAIT.
SHE HAS A THING FOR ME, RIGHT?
OF COURSE! I MEAN, THIS IS YOU WE'RE TALKING ABOUT.

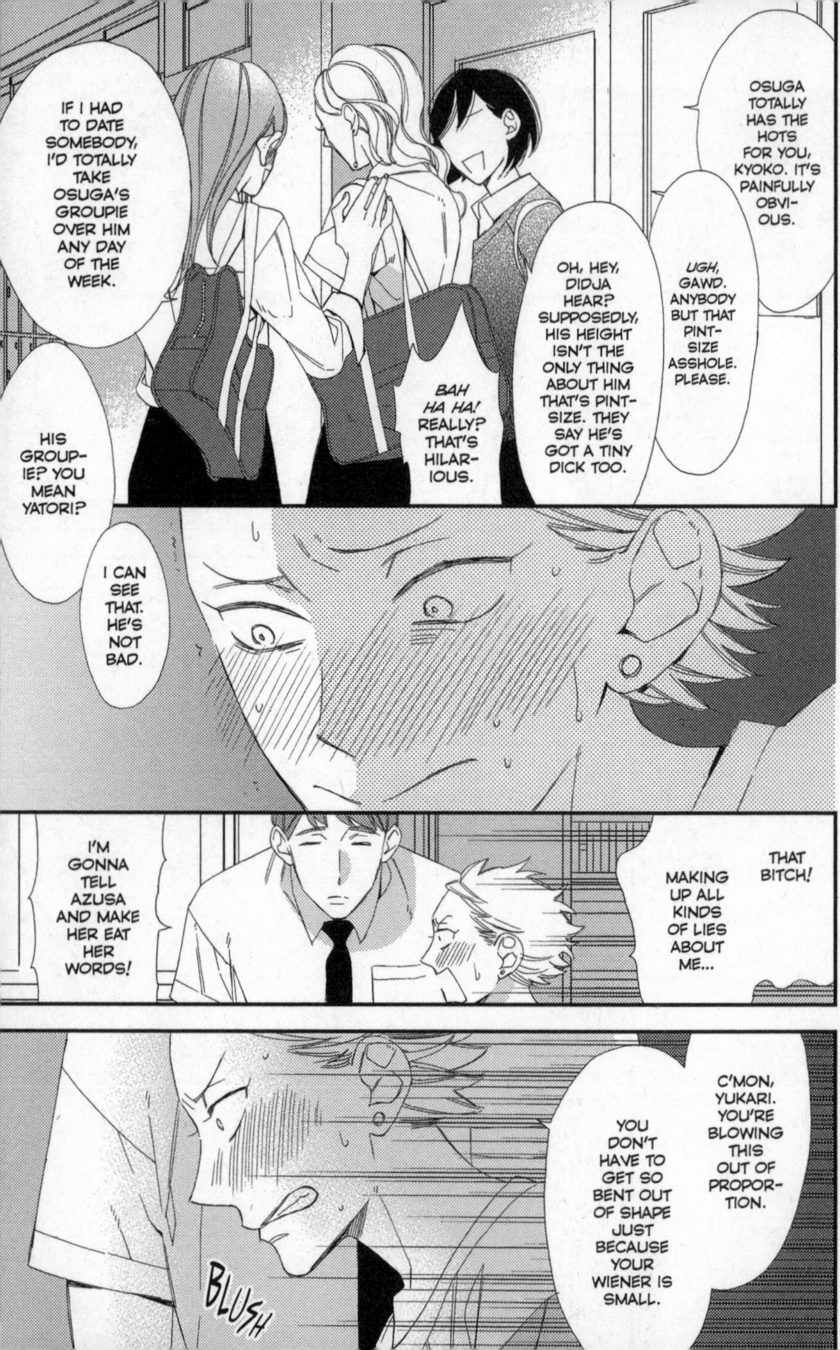
OSUGA TOTALLY HAS THE HOTS FOR YOU, KYOKO. IT'S PAINFULLY OBVIOUS.
UGH, GAWD. ANYBODY BUT THAT PINT-SIZE ASSHOLE. PLEASE.
OH, HEY, DIDJA HEAR? SUPPOSEDLY, HIS HEIGHT ISN'T THE ONLY THING ABOUT HIM THAT'S PINT-SIZE. THEY SAY HE'S GOT A TINY DICK TOO.
BAH HA HA! REALLY? THAT'S HILARIOUS.
IF I HAD TO DATE SOMEBODY, I'D TOTALLY TAKE OSUGA'S GROUPIE OVER HIM ANY DAY OF THE WEEK.
HIS GROUPIE? YOU MEAN YATORI?
I CAN SEE THAT. HE'S NOT BAD.
THAT BITCH!
MAKING UP ALL KINDS OF LIES ABOUT ME...
I'M GONNA TELL AZUSA AND MAKE HER EAT HER WORDS!
C'MON, YUKARI. YOU'RE BLOWING THIS OUT OF PROPORTION.
YOU DON'T HAVE TO GET SO BENT OUT OF SHAPE JUST BECAUSE YOUR WIENER IS SMALL.
BLUSH

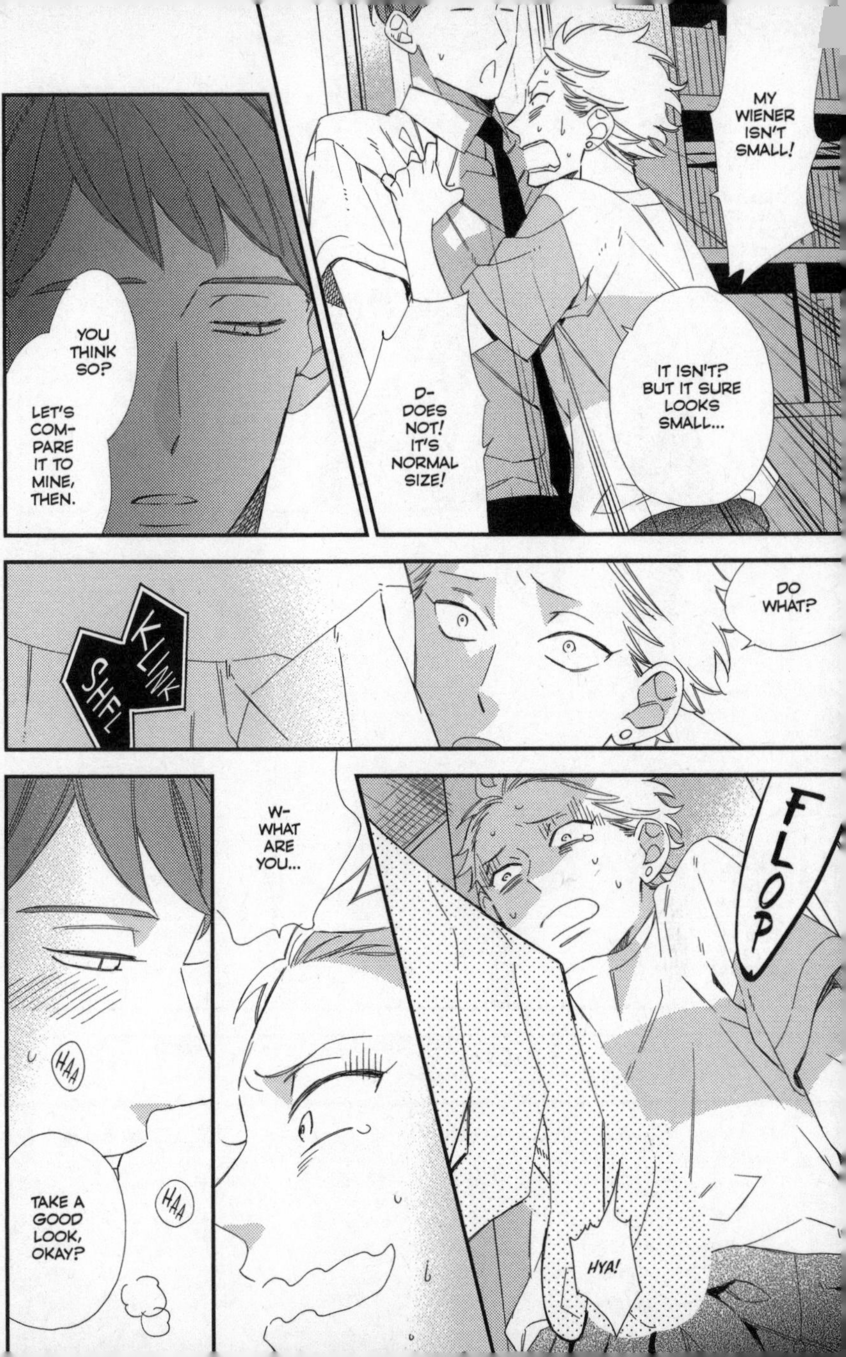
MY WIENER ISN'T SMALL!
IT ISN'T? BUT IT SURE LOOKS SMALL...
D-DOES NOT! IT'S NORMAL SIZE!
YOU THINK SO?
LET'S COMPARE IT TO MINE, THEN.
DO WHAT?
KLINK
SHFL
FLOP
W-WHAT ARE YOU...
HYA!
HAA
HAA
TAKE A GOOD LOOK, OKAY?

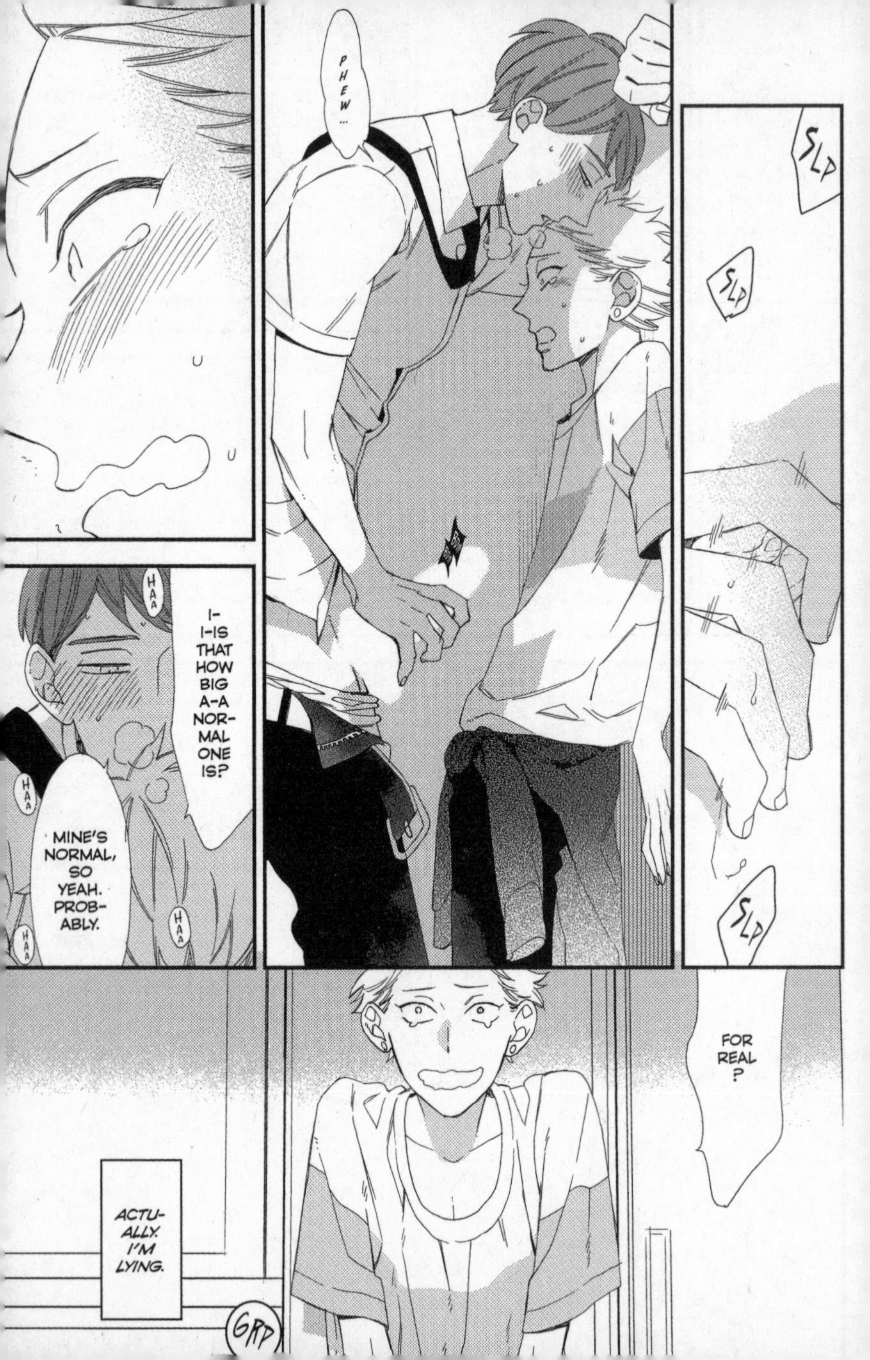
SLP
SLP
SLP
PHEW...
HAA
I- I-IS THAT HOW BIG A-A NORMAL ONE IS?
HAA
MINE'S NORMAL, SO YEAH. PROBABLY.
HAA
HAA
FOR REAL?
ACTUALLY. I'M LYING.
GRP

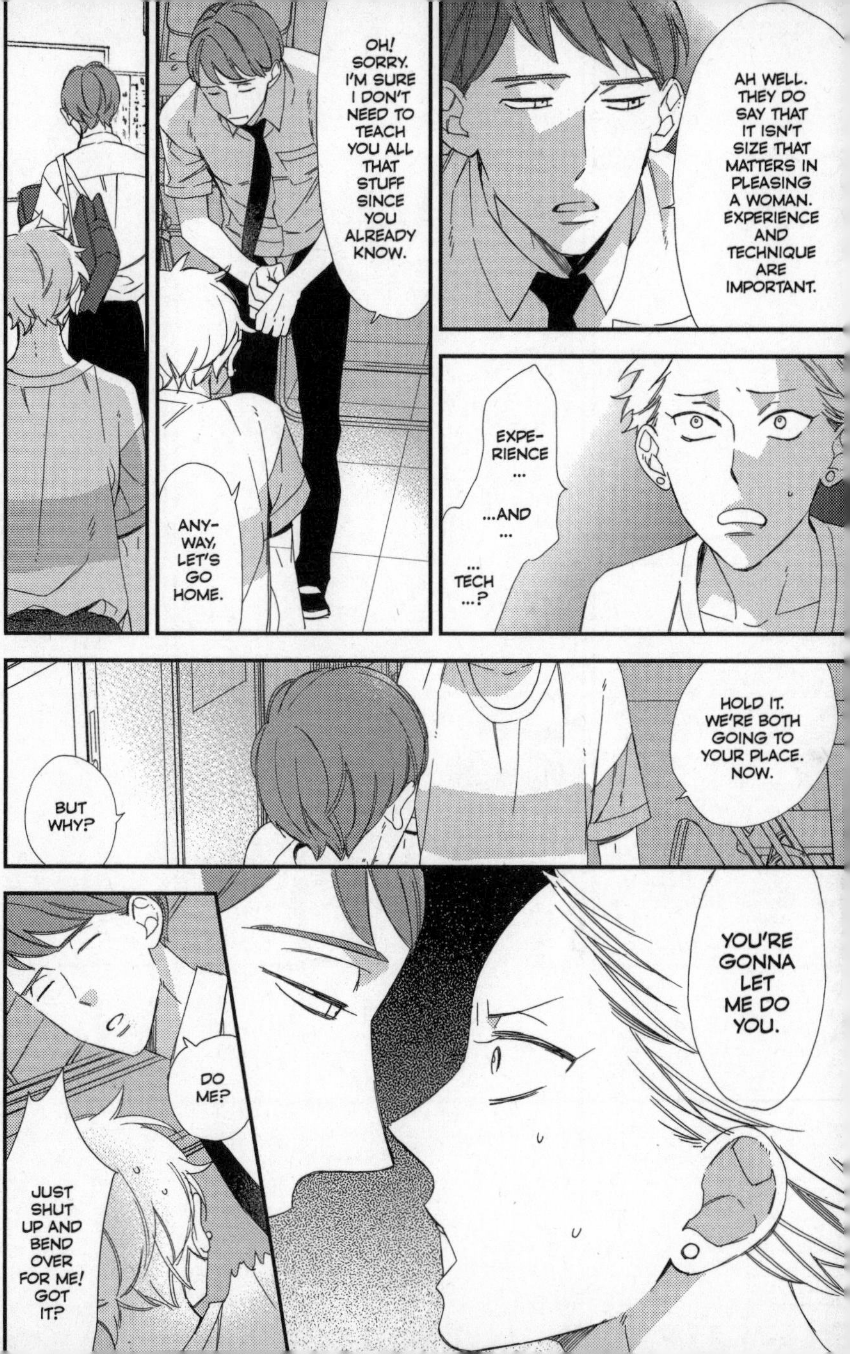
AH WELL. THEY DO SAY THAT IT ISN'T SIZE THAT MATTERS IN PLEASING A WOMAN. EXPERIENCE AND TECHNIQUE ARE IMPORTANT.
EXPE-RIENCE ...
...AND ...
...TECH ...?
OH! SORRY. I'M SURE I DON'T NEED TO TEACH YOU ALL THAT STUFF SINCE YOU ALREADY KNOW.
ANY-WAY, LET'S GO HOME.
HOLD IT. WE'RE BOTH GOING TO YOUR PLACE. NOW.
BUT WHY?
YOU'RE GONNA LET ME DO YOU.
DO ME?
JUST SHUT UP AND BEND OVER FOR ME! GOT IT?

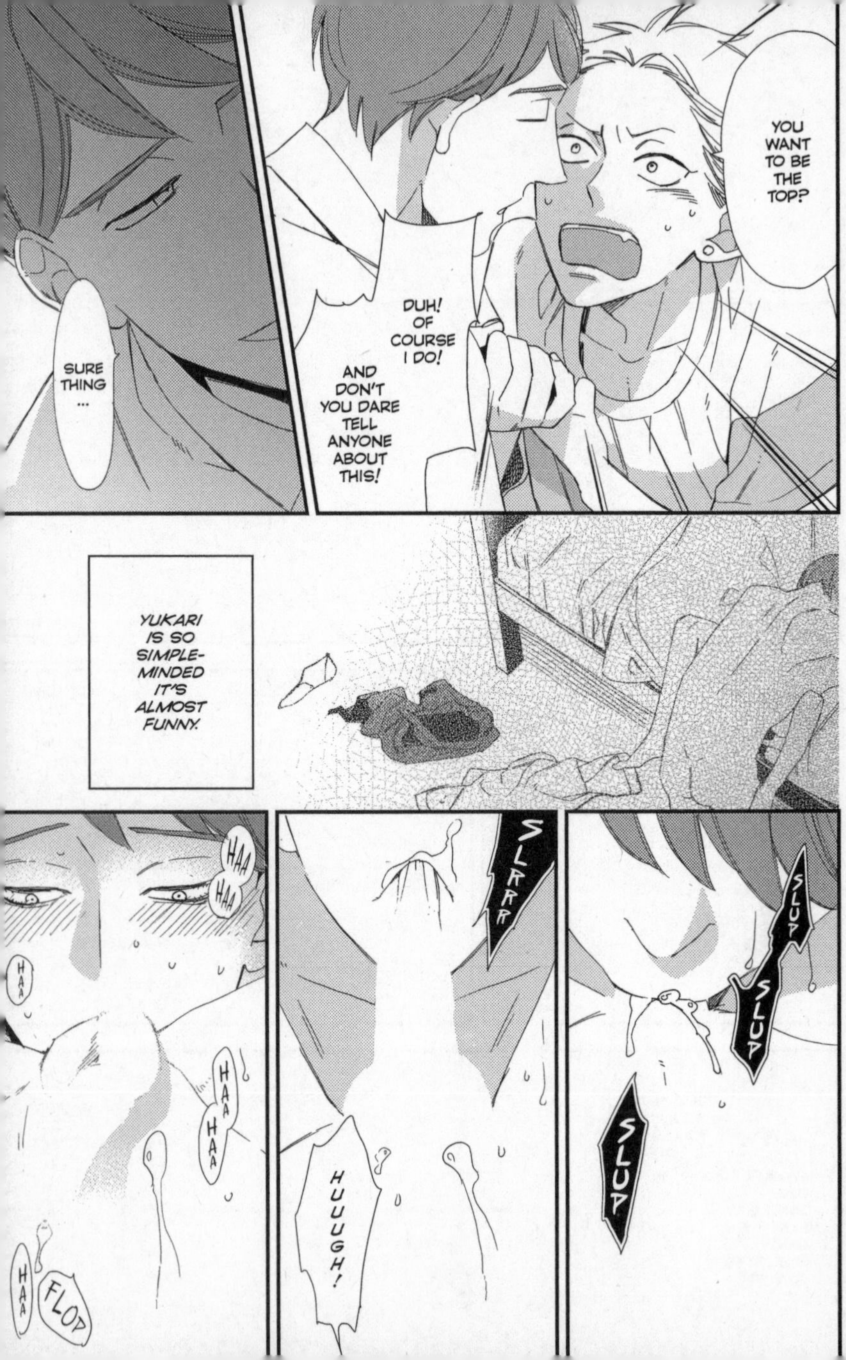
YOU WANT TO BE THE TOP?
DUH! OF COURSE I DO!
AND DON'T YOU DARE TELL ANYONE ABOUT THIS!
SURE THING ...
YUKARI IS SO SIMPLE-MINDED IT'S ALMOST FUNNY.
SLUP
SLUP
SLUP
SLRRR
HUUUGH!
HAA
HAA
HAA
HAA
HAA
HAA
FLOP

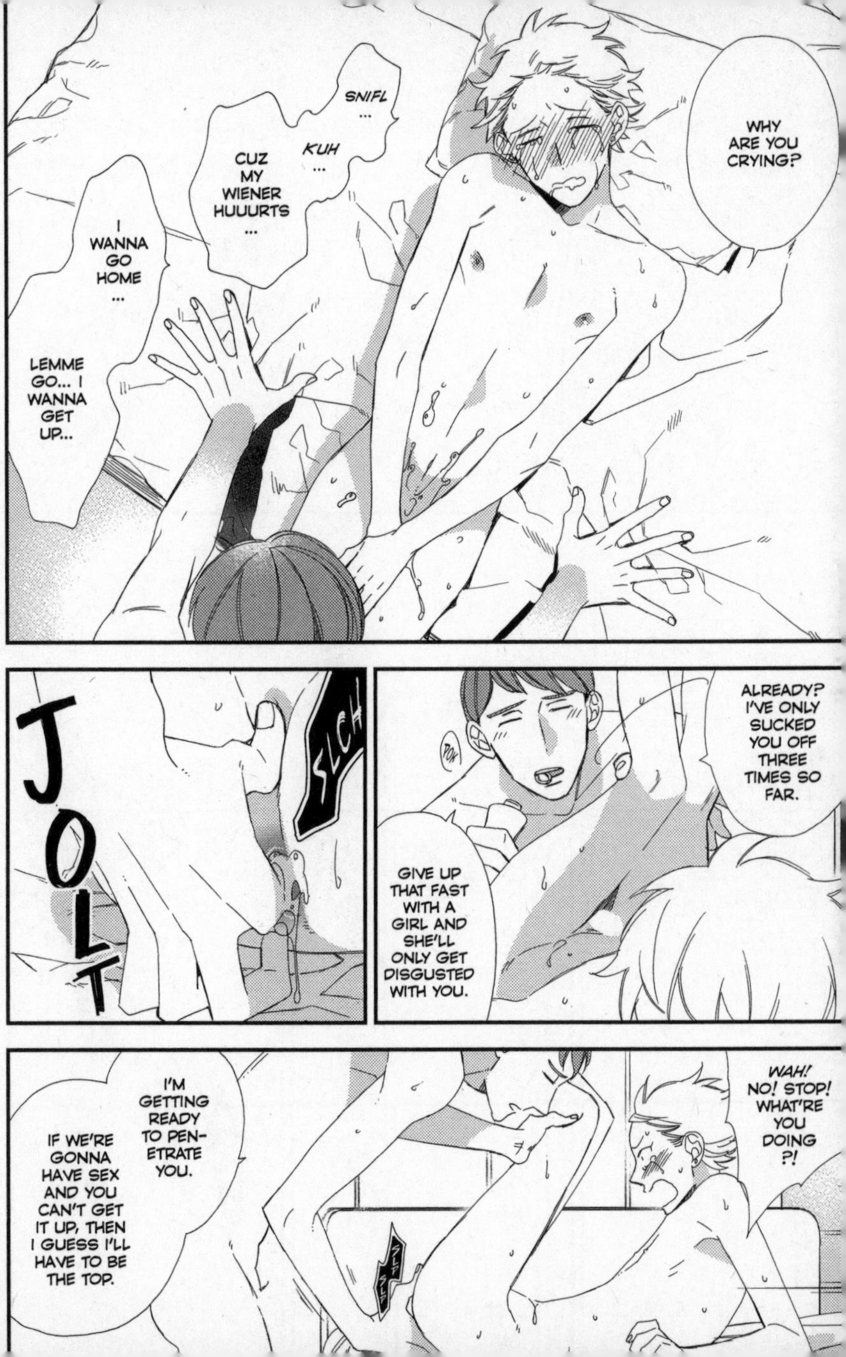
WHY ARE YOU CRYING?
SNIFL ...
KUH ...
CUZ MY WIENER HUUURTS ...
I WANNA GO HOME ...
LEMME GO... I WANNA GET UP...
ALREADY? I'VE ONLY SUCKED YOU OFF THREE TIMES SO FAR.
POK
GIVE UP THAT FAST WITH A GIRL AND SHE'LL ONLY GET DISGUSTED WITH YOU.
SLCH
JOLT
WAH! NO! STOP! WHAT'RE YOU DOING ?!
I'M GETTING READY TO PEN-ETRATE YOU.
IF WE'RE GONNA HAVE SEX AND YOU CAN'T GET IT UP, THEN I GUESS I'LL HAVE TO BE THE TOP.
SLP SLP

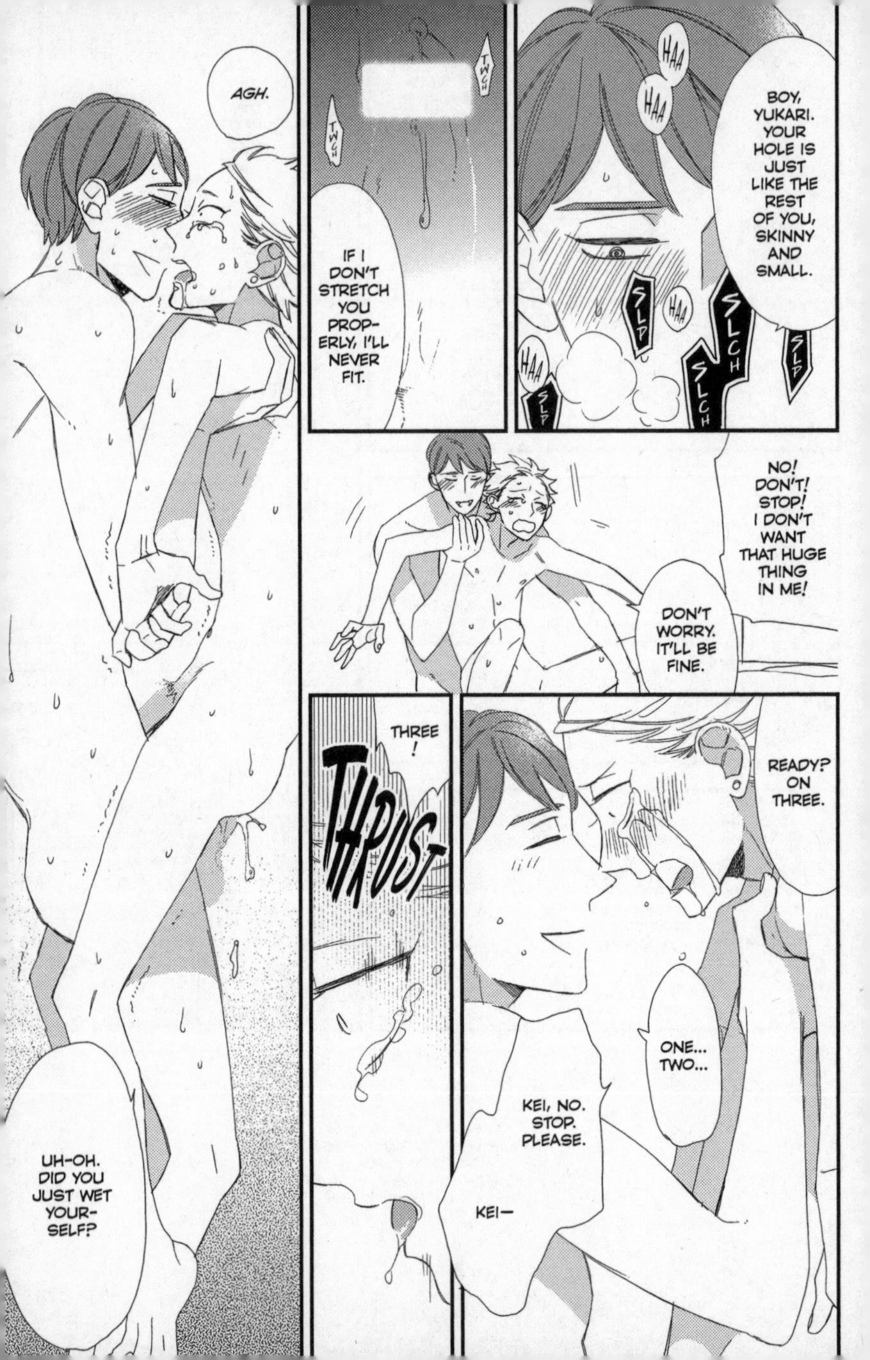
HAA
HAA
BOY, YUKARI. YOUR HOLE IS JUST LIKE THE REST OF YOU, SKINNY AND SMALL.
HAA
HAA
SLP
SLCH
SLCH
SLP
SLP
TWCH
TWCH
IF I DON'T STRETCH YOU PROP-ERLY, I'LL NEVER FIT.
NO! DON'T! STOP! I DON'T WANT THAT HUGE THING IN ME!
DON'T WORRY. IT'LL BE FINE.
READY? ON THREE.
ONE... TWO...
KEI, NO. STOP. PLEASE.
KEI—
THREE!
THRUST
AGH.
UH-OH. DID YOU JUST WET YOUR-SELF?

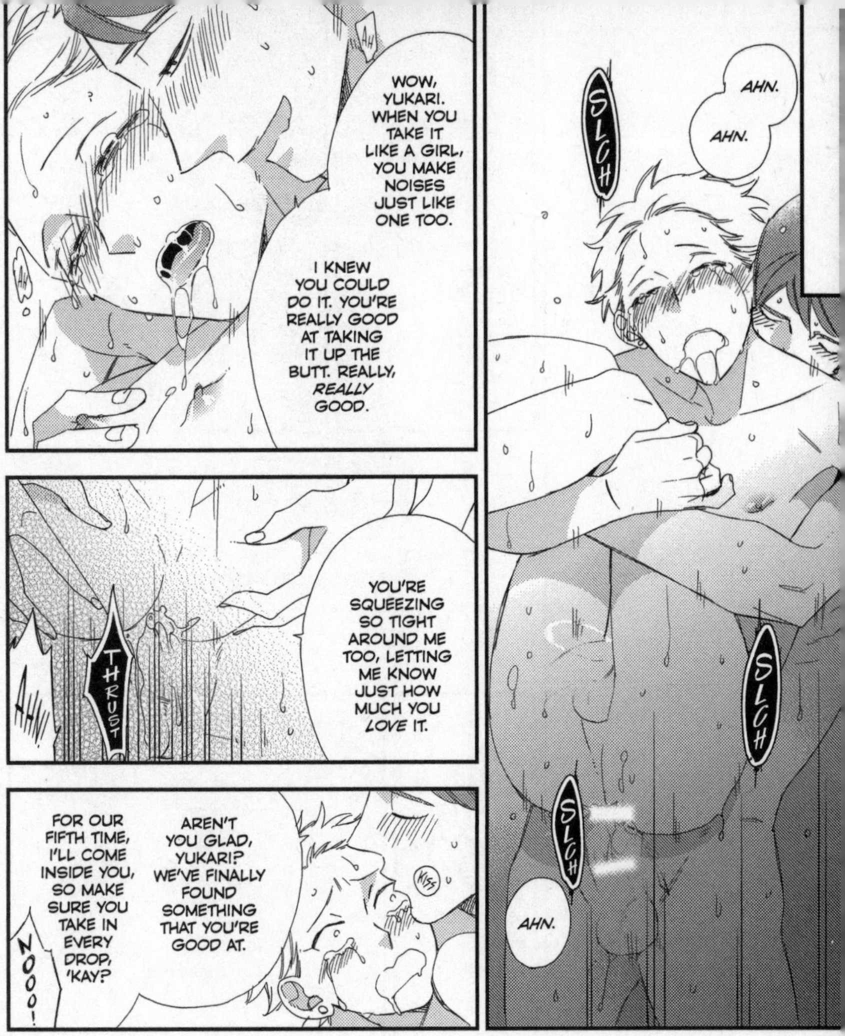
AHN.
AHN.
SLCH
SLCH
SLCH
AHN.
AH
WOW, YUKARI. WHEN YOU TAKE IT LIKE A GIRL, YOU MAKE NOISES JUST LIKE ONE TOO.
I KNEW YOU COULD DO IT. YOU'RE REALLY GOOD AT TAKING IT UP THE BUTT. REALLY, *REALLY* GOOD.
AH
YOU'RE SQUEEZING SO TIGHT AROUND ME TOO, LETTING ME KNOW JUST HOW MUCH YOU *LOVE* IT.
THRUST
AHN!
KISS
AREN'T YOU GLAD, YUKARI? WE'VE FINALLY FOUND SOMETHING THAT YOU'RE GOOD AT.
FOR OUR FIFTH TIME, I'LL COME INSIDE YOU, SO MAKE SURE YOU TAKE IN EVERY DROP, 'KAY?
NOOO!

I'M SURE YUKARI WILL NEVER GET NAKED IN FRONT OF OTHER PEOPLE AGAIN. AND I DOUBT HE'LL EVER HAVE SEX WITH A WOMAN EITHER.

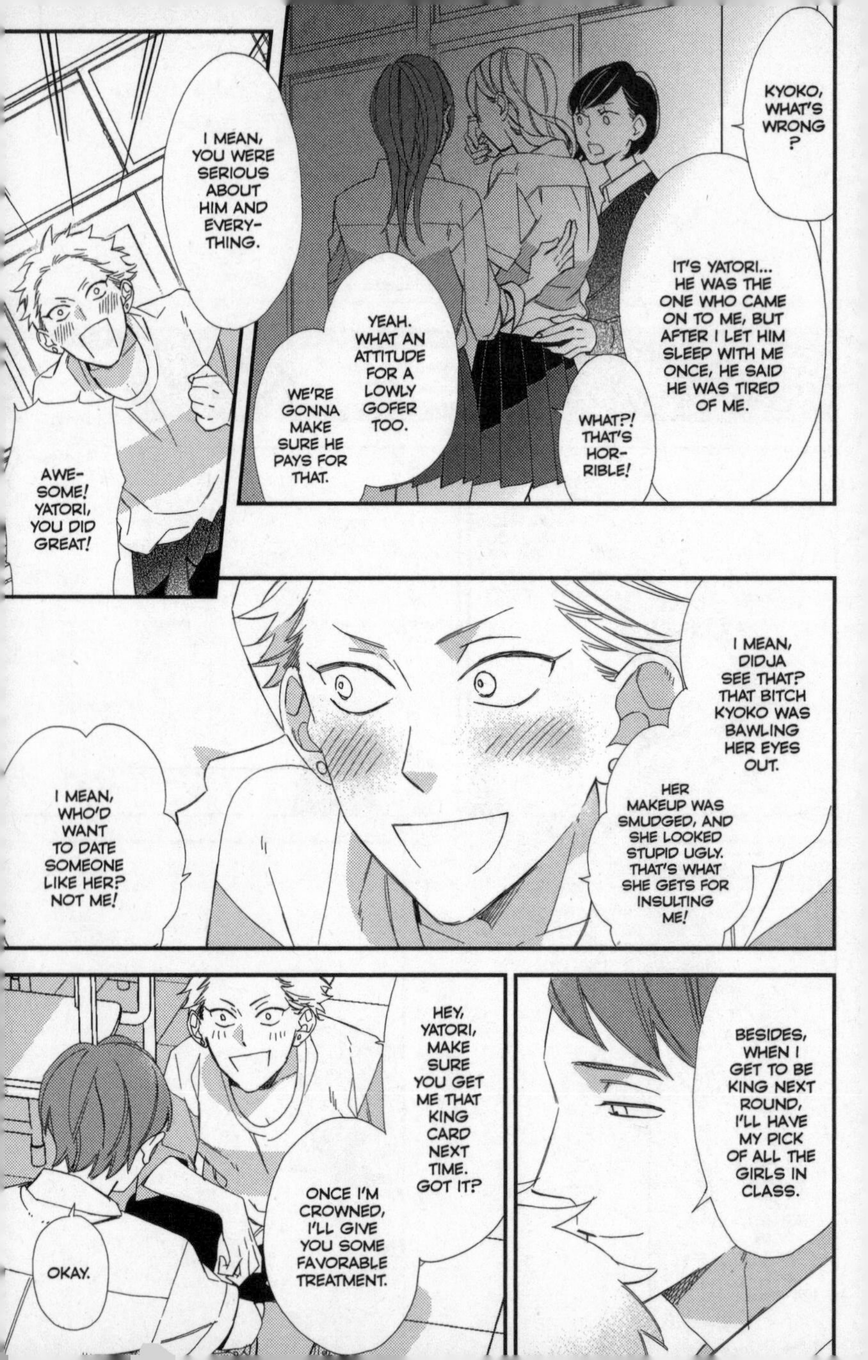
KYOKO, WHAT'S WRONG?
IT'S YATORI... HE WAS THE ONE WHO CAME ON TO ME, BUT AFTER I LET HIM SLEEP WITH ME ONCE, HE SAID HE WAS TIRED OF ME.
WHAT?! THAT'S HOR-RIBLE!
YEAH. WHAT AN ATTITUDE FOR A LOWLY GOFER TOO.
WE'RE GONNA MAKE SURE HE PAYS FOR THAT.
I MEAN, YOU WERE SERIOUS ABOUT HIM AND EVERY-THING.
AWE-SOME! YATORI, YOU DID GREAT!
I MEAN, DIDJA SEE THAT? THAT BITCH KYOKO WAS BAWLING HER EYES OUT.
HER MAKEUP WAS SMUDGED, AND SHE LOOKED STUPID UGLY. THAT'S WHAT SHE GETS FOR INSULTING ME!
I MEAN, WHO'D WANT TO DATE SOMEONE LIKE HER? NOT ME!
BESIDES, WHEN I GET TO BE KING NEXT ROUND, I'LL HAVE MY PICK OF ALL THE GIRLS IN CLASS.
HEY, YATORI, MAKE SURE YOU GET ME THAT KING CARD NEXT TIME. GOT IT?
ONCE I'M CROWNED, I'LL GIVE YOU SOME FAVORABLE TREATMENT.
OKAY.

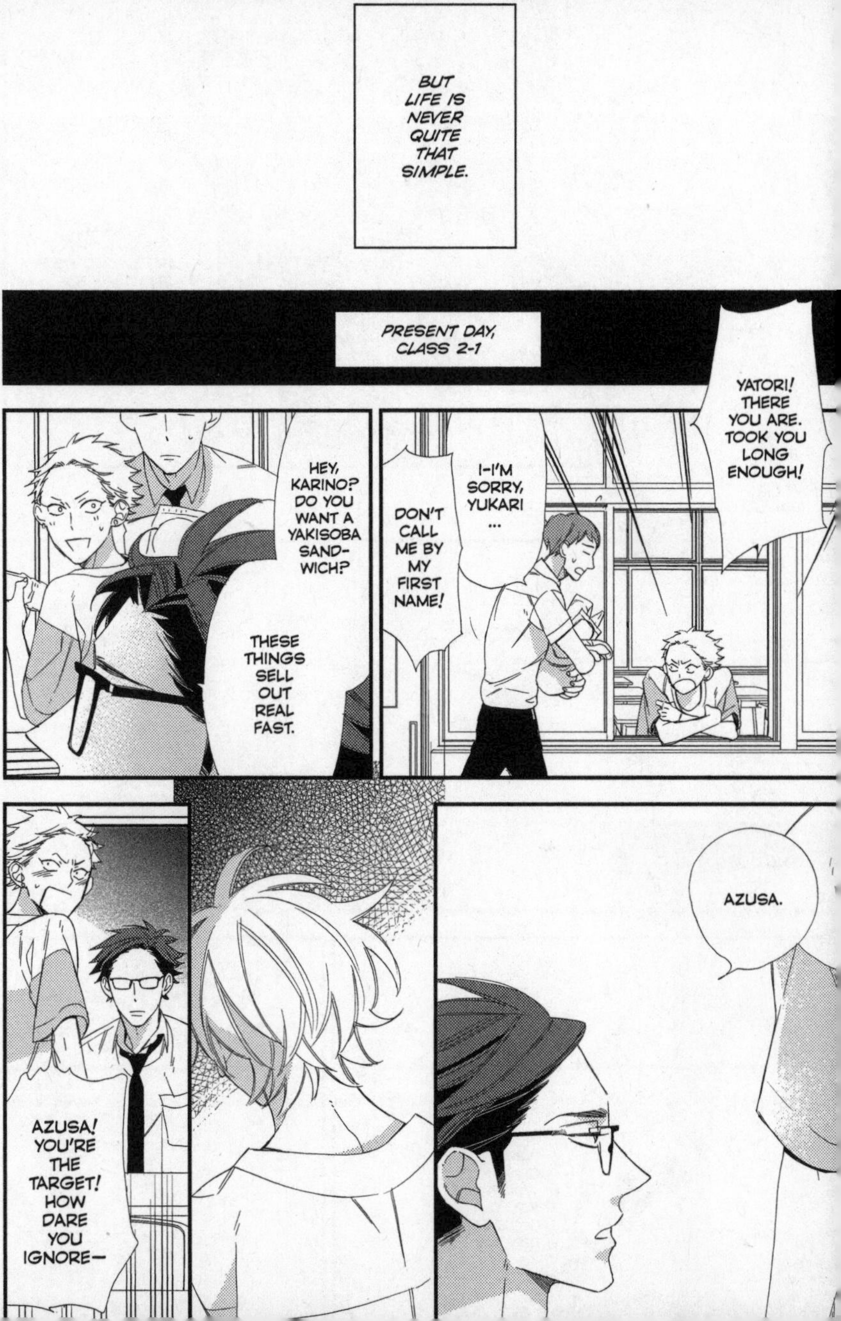
BUT LIFE IS NEVER QUITE THAT SIMPLE.
PRESENT DAY, CLASS 2-1
YATORI! THERE YOU ARE. TOOK YOU LONG ENOUGH!
I-I'M SORRY, YUKARI ...
DON'T CALL ME BY MY FIRST NAME!
HEY, KARINO? DO YOU WANT A YAKISOBA SAND-WICH?
THESE THINGS SELL OUT REAL FAST.
AZUSA.
AZUSA! YOU'RE THE TARGET! HOW DARE YOU IGNORE—

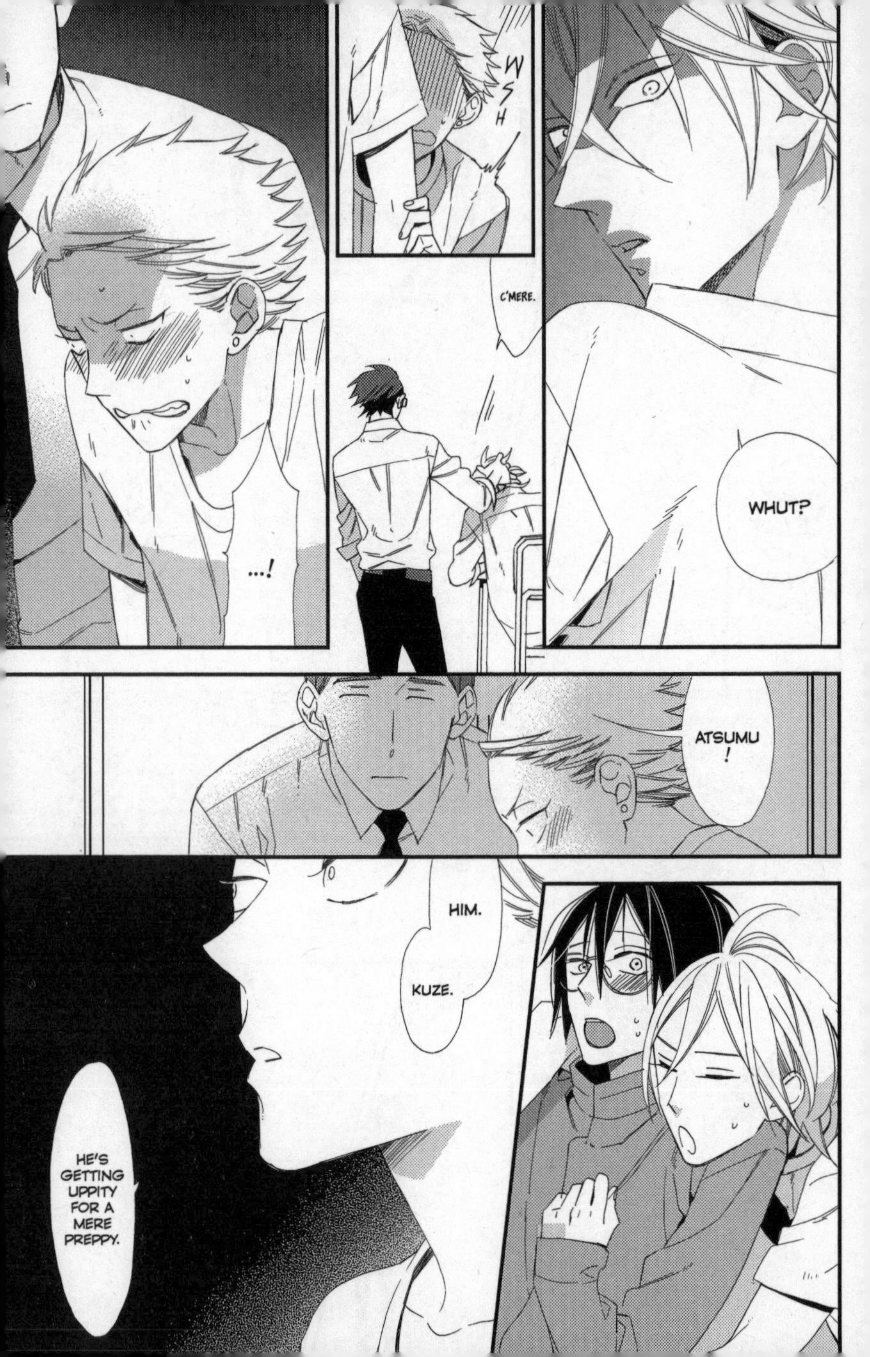
WSH
C'MERE.
WHUT?
...!
ATSUMU!
HIM.
KUZE.
HE'S GETTING UPPITY FOR A MERE PREPPY.

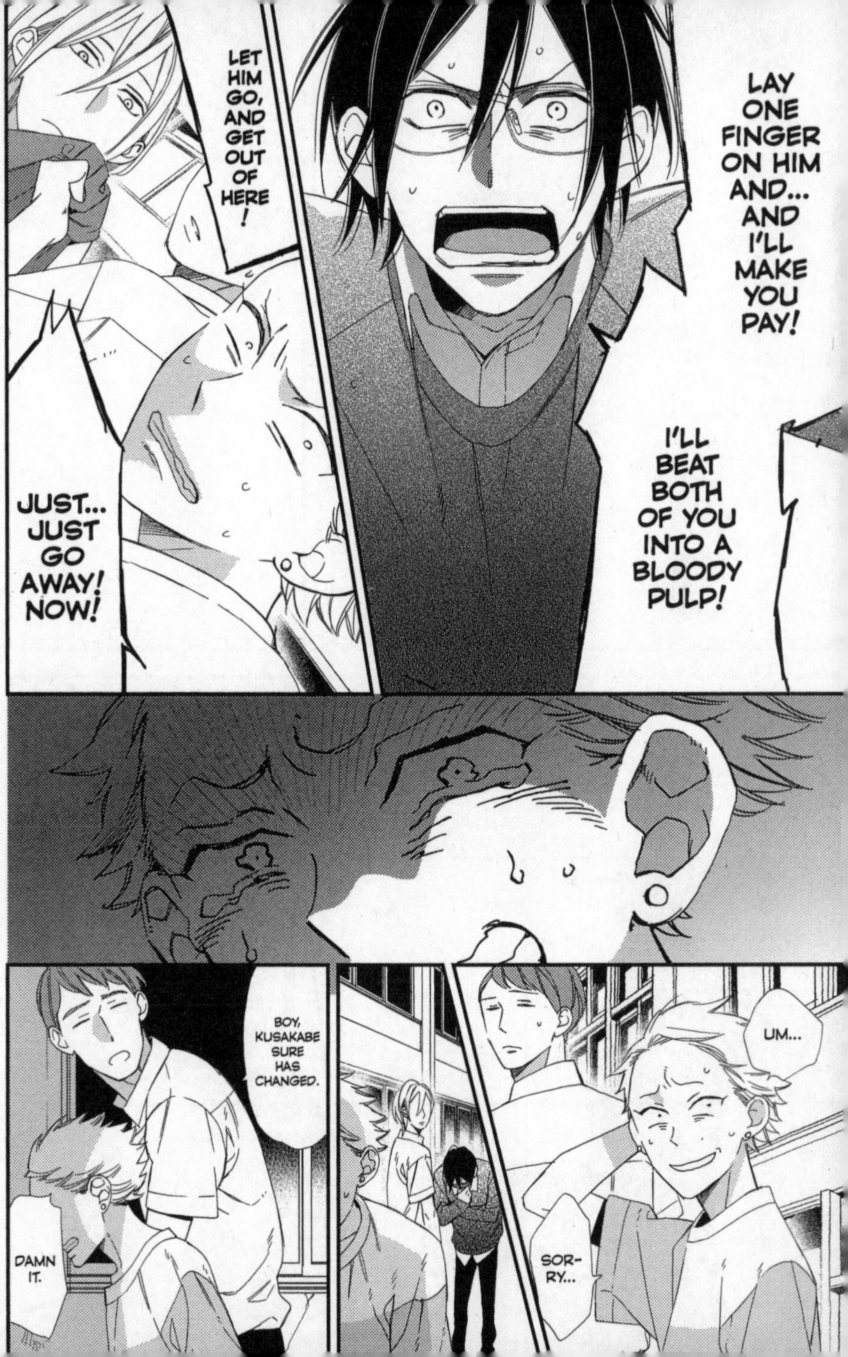
LAY ONE FINGER ON HIM AND... AND I'LL MAKE YOU PAY!
I'LL BEAT BOTH OF YOU INTO A BLOODY PULP!
LET HIM GO, AND GET OUT OF HERE!
JUST... JUST GO AWAY! NOW!
UM...
SOR-RY...
BOY, KUSAKABE SURE HAS CHANGED.
DAMN IT.

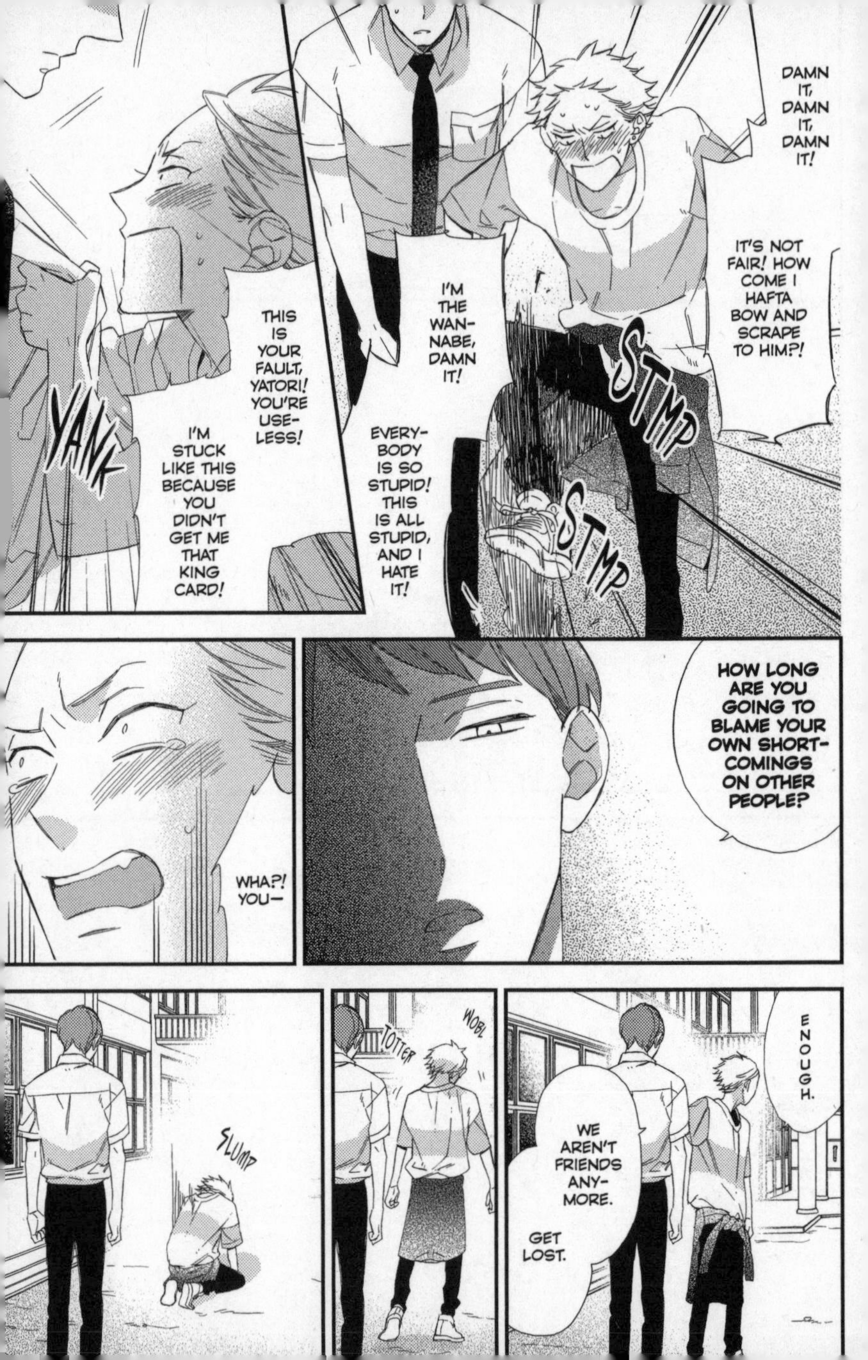
DAMN IT, DAMN IT, DAMN IT!
IT'S NOT FAIR! HOW COME I HAFTA BOW AND SCRAPE TO HIM?!
STMP
STMP
I'M THE WAN-NABE, DAMN IT!
EVERY-BODY IS SO STUPID! THIS IS ALL STUPID, AND I HATE IT!
THIS IS YOUR FAULT, YATORI! YOU'RE USE-LESS!
I'M STUCK LIKE THIS BECAUSE YOU DIDN'T GET ME THAT KING CARD!
YANK
HOW LONG ARE YOU GOING TO BLAME YOUR OWN SHORT-COMINGS ON OTHER PEOPLE?
WHA?! YOU—
ENOUGH.
WE AREN'T FRIENDS ANY-MORE.
GET LOST.
WOBL
TOTTER
SLUMP

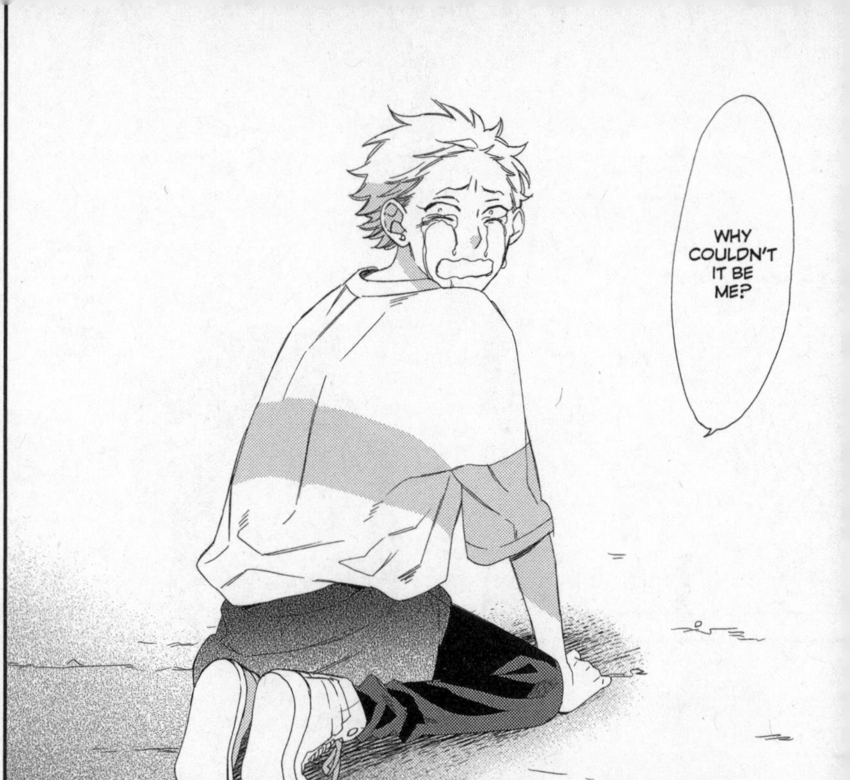
WHY COULDN'T IT BE ME?

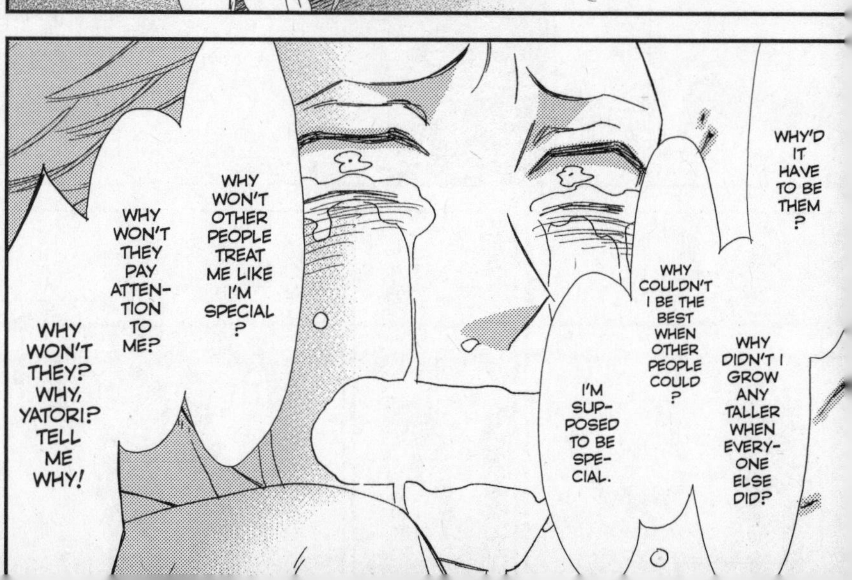
WHY'D IT HAVE TO BE THEM?
WHY DIDN'T I GROW ANY TALLER WHEN EVERYONE ELSE DID?
WHY COULDN'T I BE THE BEST WHEN OTHER PEOPLE COULD?
I'M SUPPOSED TO BE SPECIAL.
WHY WON'T OTHER PEOPLE TREAT ME LIKE I'M SPECIAL?
WHY WON'T THEY PAY ATTENTION TO ME?
WHY WON'T THEY? WHY, YATORI? TELL ME WHY!

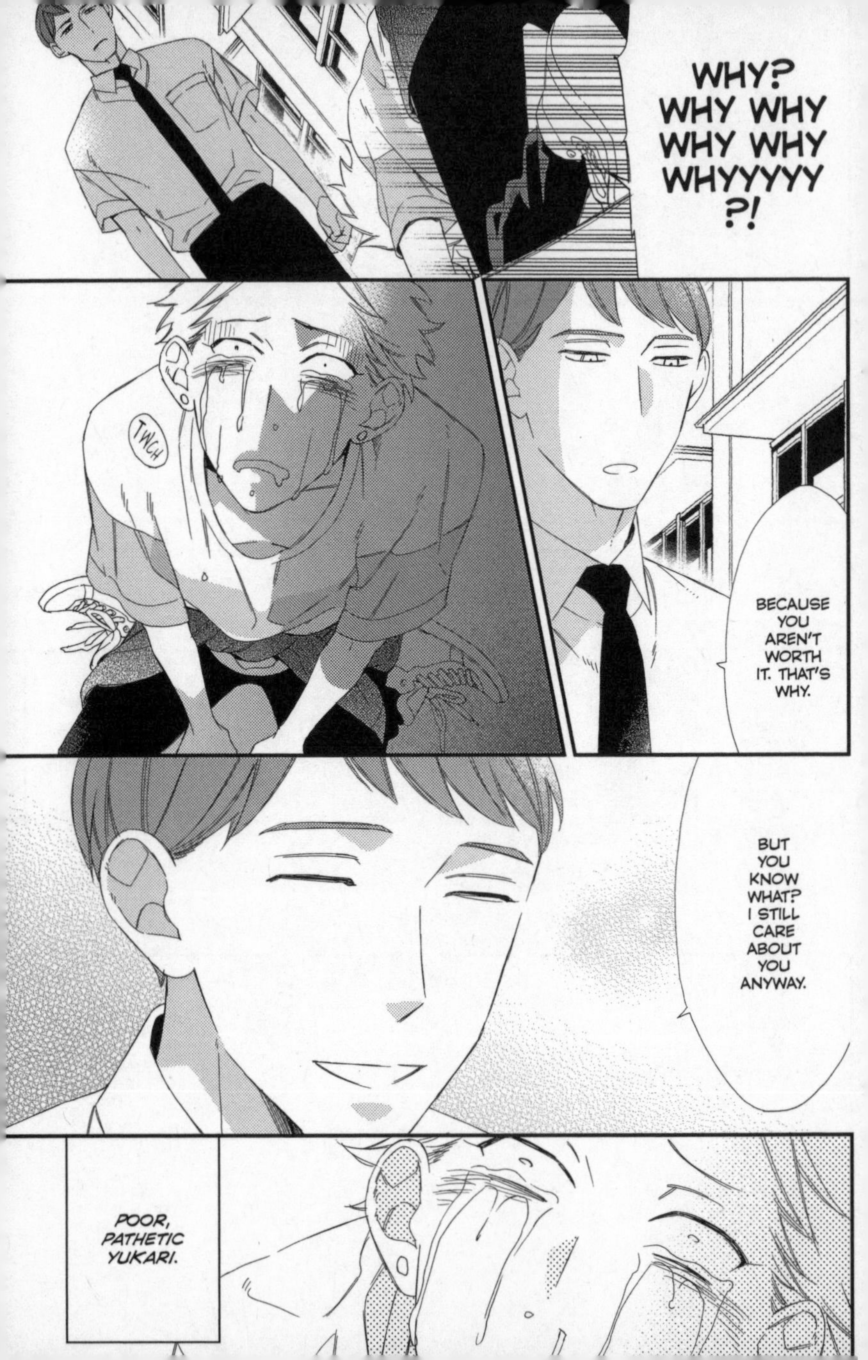
WHY? WHY WHY WHY WHY WHYYYYY ?!
BECAUSE YOU AREN'T WORTH IT. THAT'S WHY.
TWCH
BUT YOU KNOW WHAT? I STILL CARE ABOUT YOU ANYWAY.
POOR, PATHETIC YUKARI.

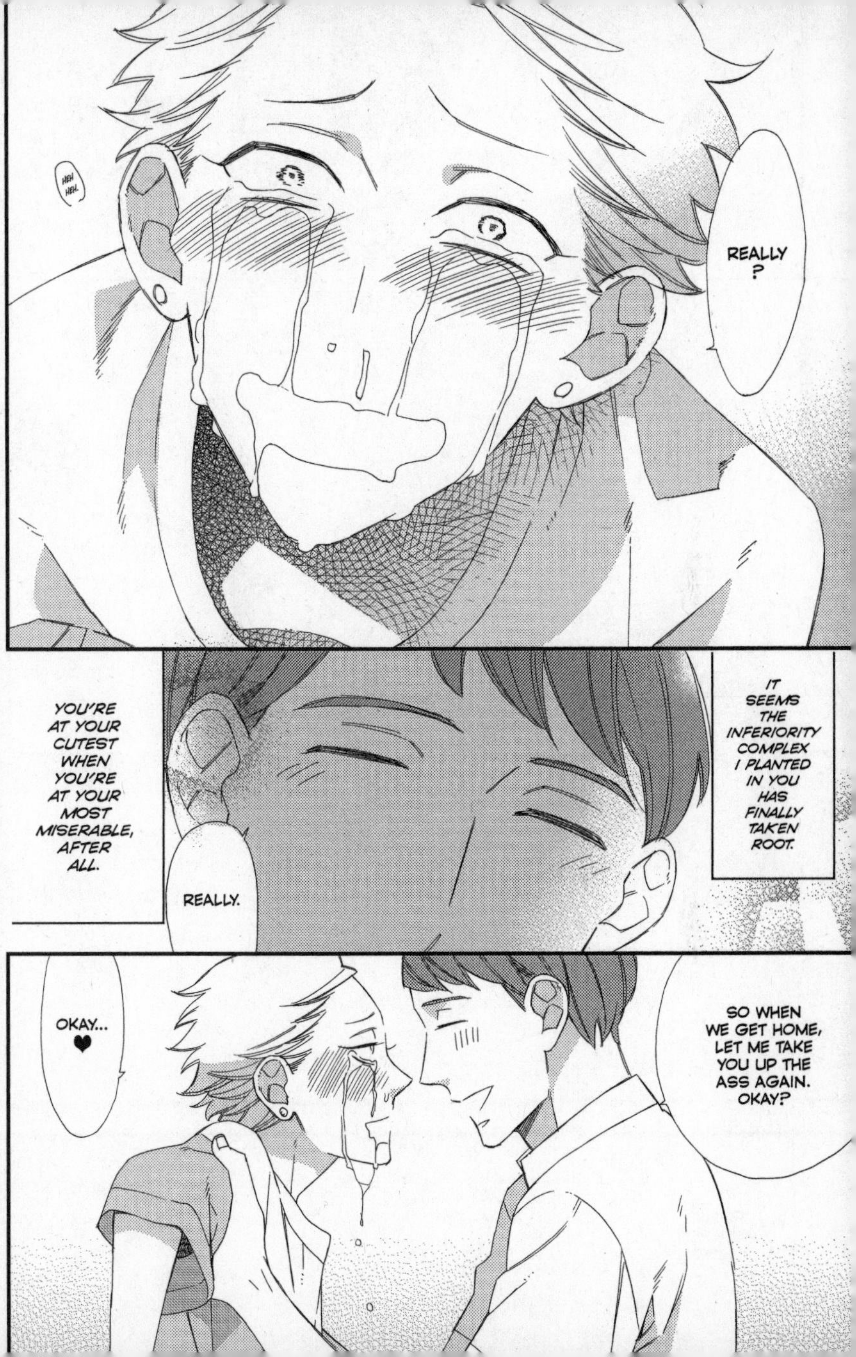
REALLY?
HEH HEH.
IT SEEMS THE INFERIORITY COMPLEX I PLANTED IN YOU HAS FINALLY TAKEN ROOT.
REALLY.
YOU'RE AT YOUR CUTEST WHEN YOU'RE AT YOUR MOST MISERABLE, AFTER ALL.
SO WHEN WE GET HOME, LET ME TAKE YOU UP THE ASS AGAIN. OKAY?
OKAY... ♥

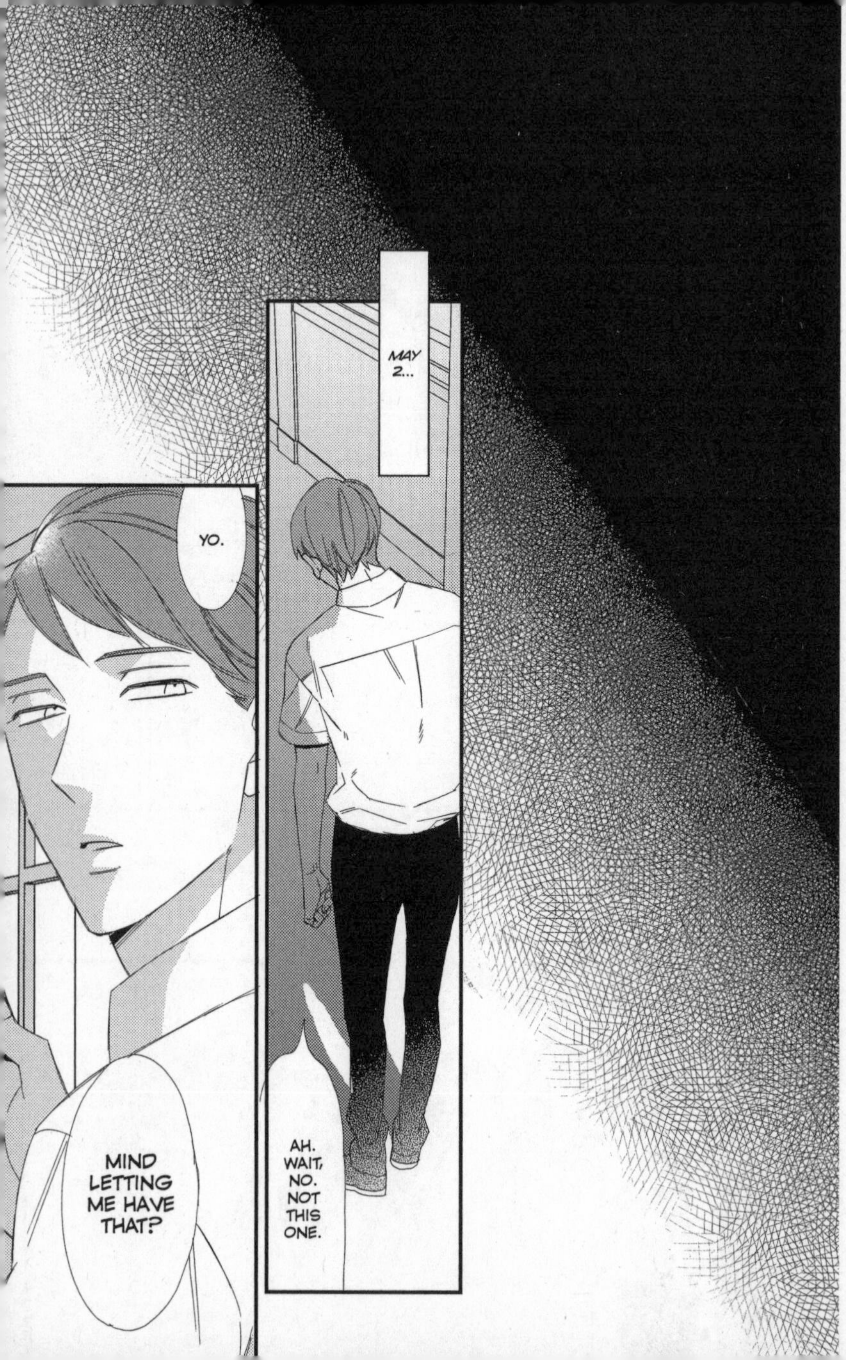
MAY 2...
AH. WAIT, NO. NOT THIS ONE.
YO.
MIND LETTING ME HAVE THAT?

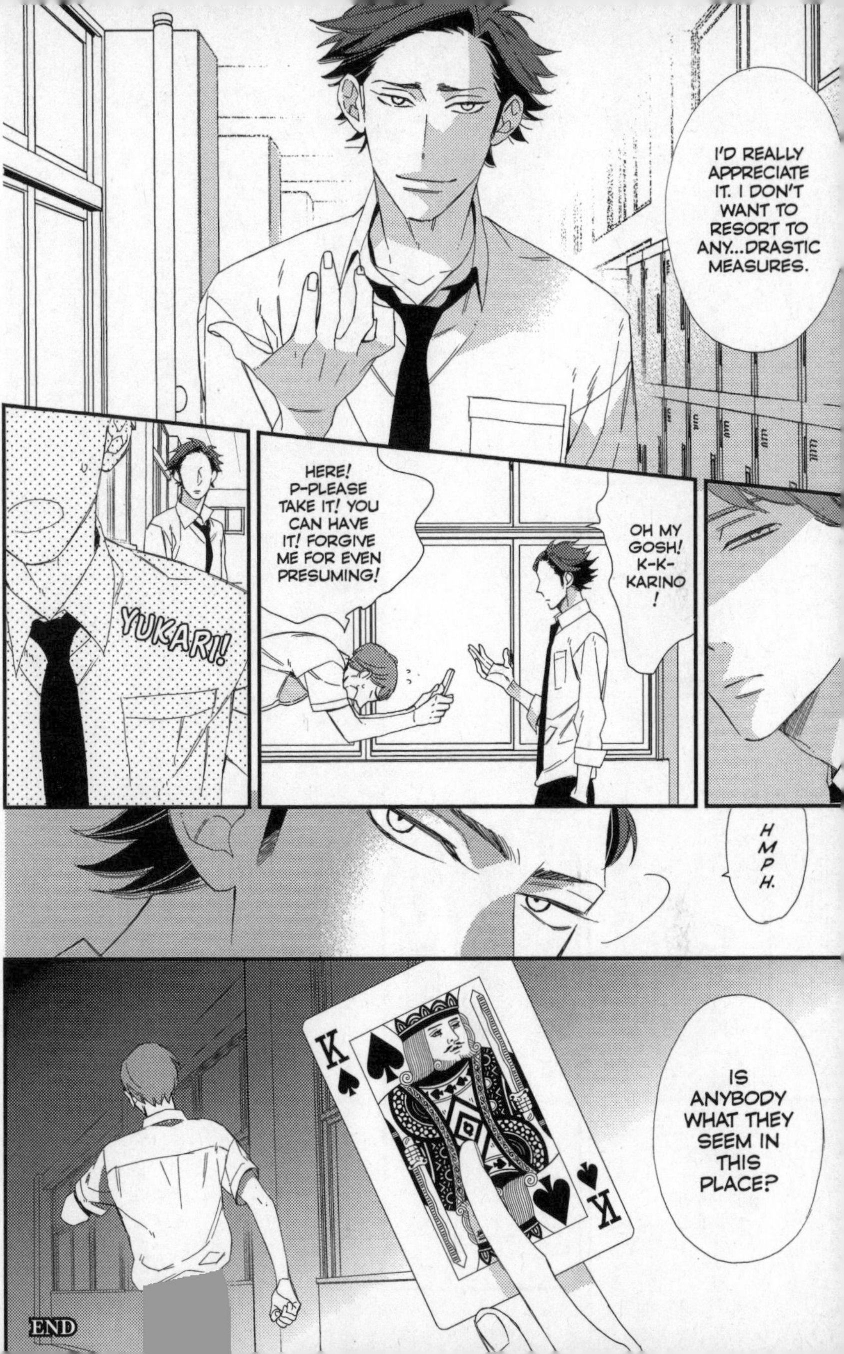
I'D REALLY APPRECIATE IT. I DON'T WANT TO RESORT TO ANY...DRASTIC MEASURES.
OH MY GOSH! K-K-KARINO!
HERE! P-PLEASE TAKE IT! YOU CAN HAVE IT! FORGIVE ME FOR EVEN PRESUMING!
YUKARI!
HMPH.
IS ANYBODY WHAT THEY SEEM IN THIS PLACE?
END

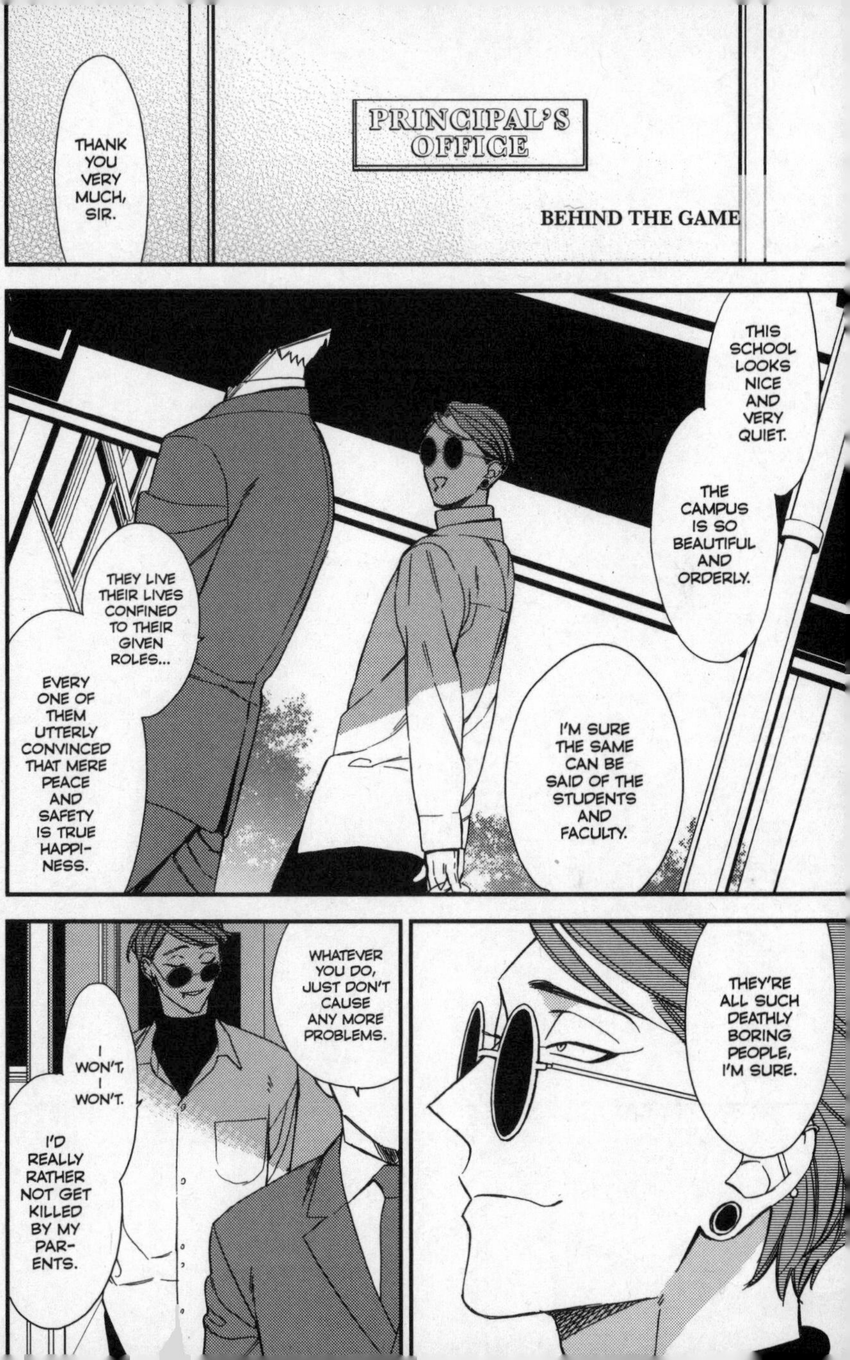
PRINCIPAL'S OFFICE
BEHIND THE GAME
THANK YOU VERY MUCH, SIR.
THIS SCHOOL LOOKS NICE AND VERY QUIET.
THE CAMPUS IS SO BEAUTIFUL AND ORDERLY.
I'M SURE THE SAME CAN BE SAID OF THE STUDENTS AND FACULTY.
THEY LIVE THEIR LIVES CONFINED TO THEIR GIVEN ROLES...
EVERY ONE OF THEM UTTERLY CONVINCED THAT MERE PEACE AND SAFETY IS TRUE HAPPI-NESS.
THEY'RE ALL SUCH DEATHLY BORING PEOPLE, I'M SURE.
WHATEVER YOU DO, JUST DON'T CAUSE ANY MORE PROBLEMS.
I WON'T, I WON'T.
I'D REALLY RATHER NOT GET KILLED BY MY PAR-ENTS.

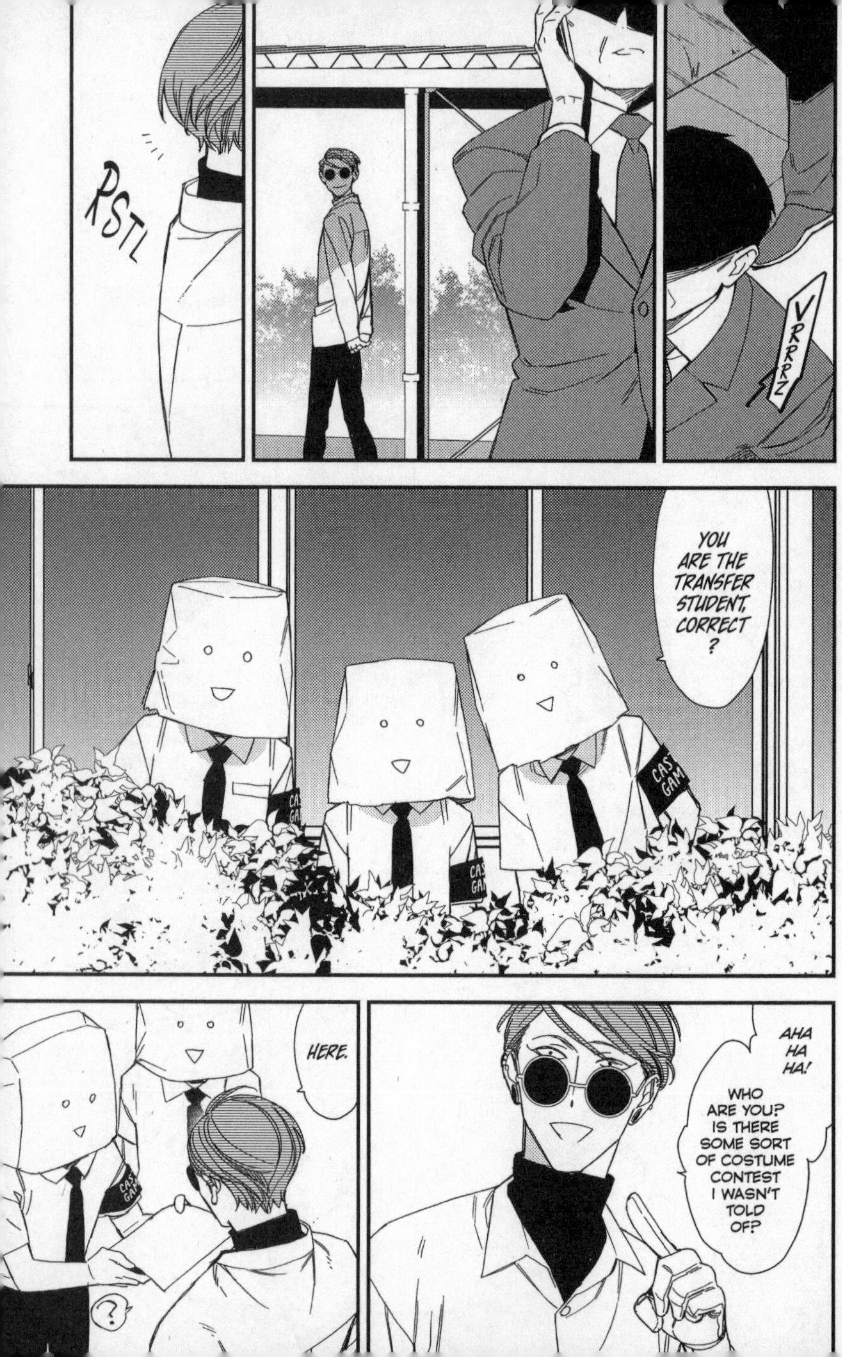
VRRRZ
RSTL
YOU ARE THE TRANSFER STUDENT, CORRECT?
AHA HA HA!
WHO ARE YOU? IS THERE SOME SORT OF COSTUME CONTEST I WASN'T TOLD OF?
HERE.
?

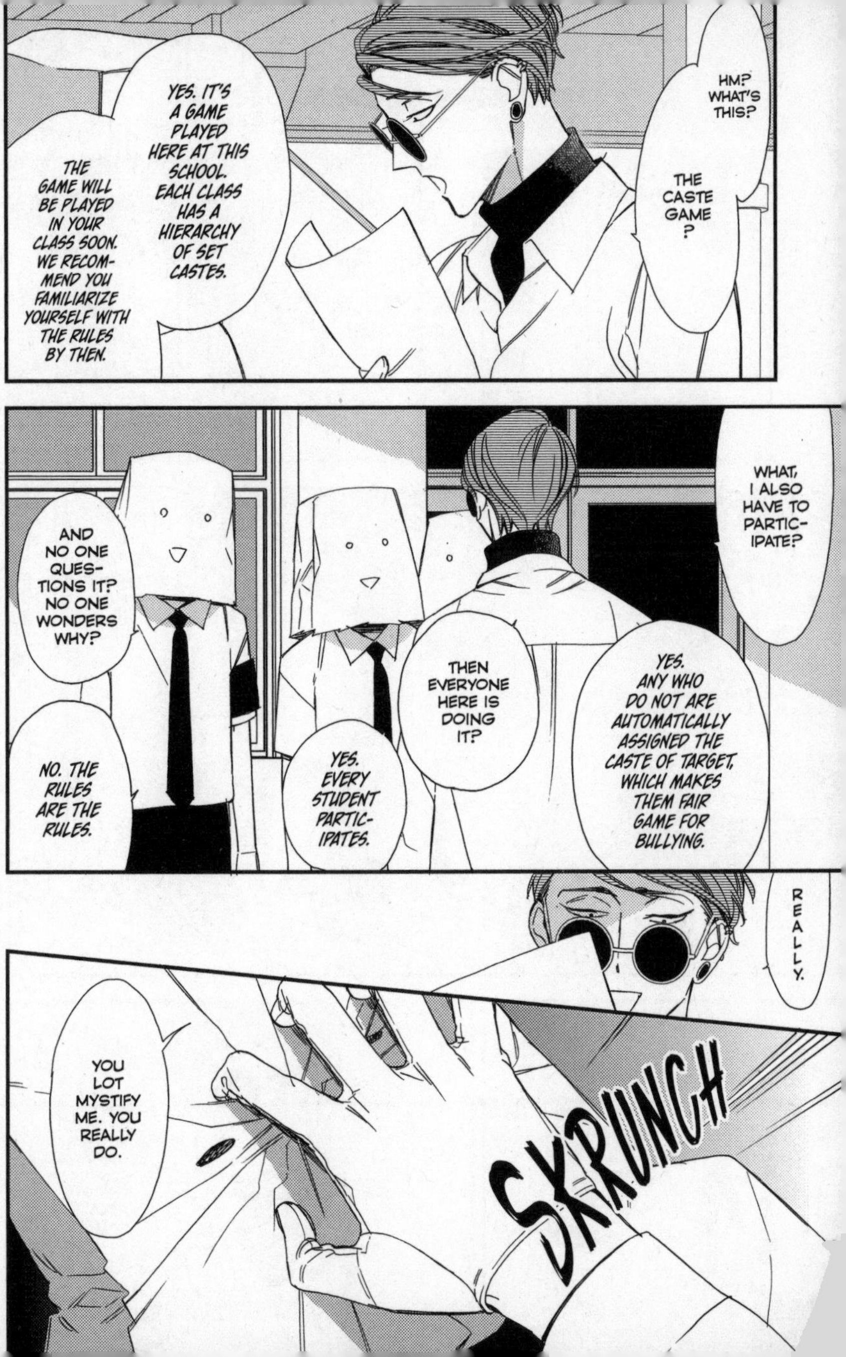
HM? WHAT'S THIS? THE CASTE GAME ?
YES. IT'S A GAME PLAYED HERE AT THIS SCHOOL. EACH CLASS HAS A HIERARCHY OF SET CASTES.
THE GAME WILL BE PLAYED IN YOUR CLASS SOON. WE RECOMMEND YOU FAMILIARIZE YOURSELF WITH THE RULES BY THEN.
WHAT, I ALSO HAVE TO PARTICIPATE?
YES. ANY WHO DO NOT ARE AUTOMATICALLY ASSIGNED THE CASTE OF TARGET, WHICH MAKES THEM FAIR GAME FOR BULLYING.
THEN EVERYONE HERE IS DOING IT?
YES. EVERY STUDENT PARTICIPATES.
AND NO ONE QUESTIONS IT? NO ONE WONDERS WHY?
NO. THE RULES ARE THE RULES.
REALLY.
YOU LOT MYSTIFY ME. YOU REALLY DO.
SKRUNCH

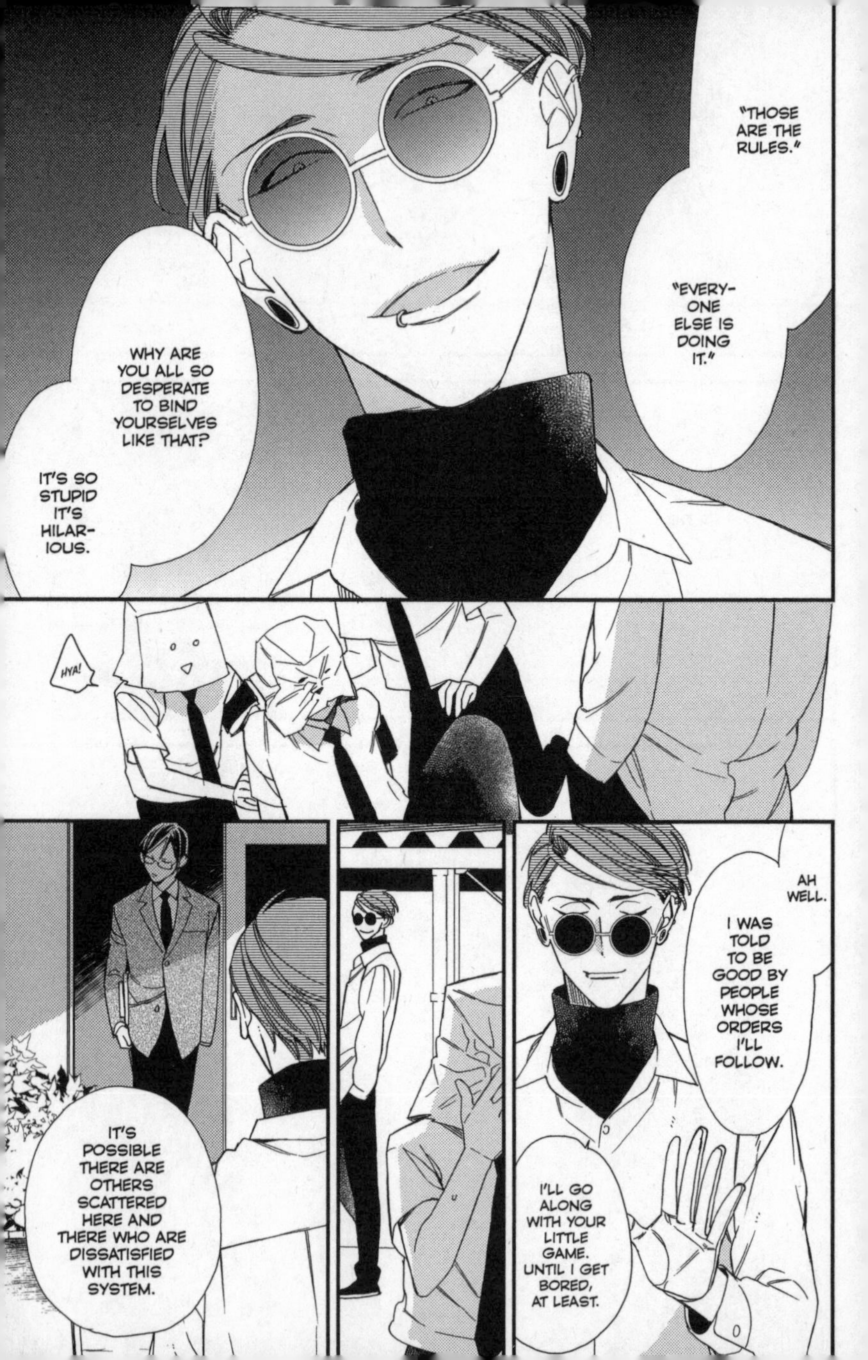
"THOSE ARE THE RULES."
"EVERY-ONE ELSE IS DOING IT."
WHY ARE YOU ALL SO DESPERATE TO BIND YOURSELVES LIKE THAT?
IT'S SO STUPID IT'S HILAR-IOUS.
HYA!
AH WELL.
I WAS TOLD TO BE GOOD BY PEOPLE WHOSE ORDERS I'LL FOLLOW.
I'LL GO ALONG WITH YOUR LITTLE GAME. UNTIL I GET BORED, AT LEAST.
IT'S POSSIBLE THERE ARE OTHERS SCATTERED HERE AND THERE WHO ARE DISSATISFIED WITH THIS SYSTEM.

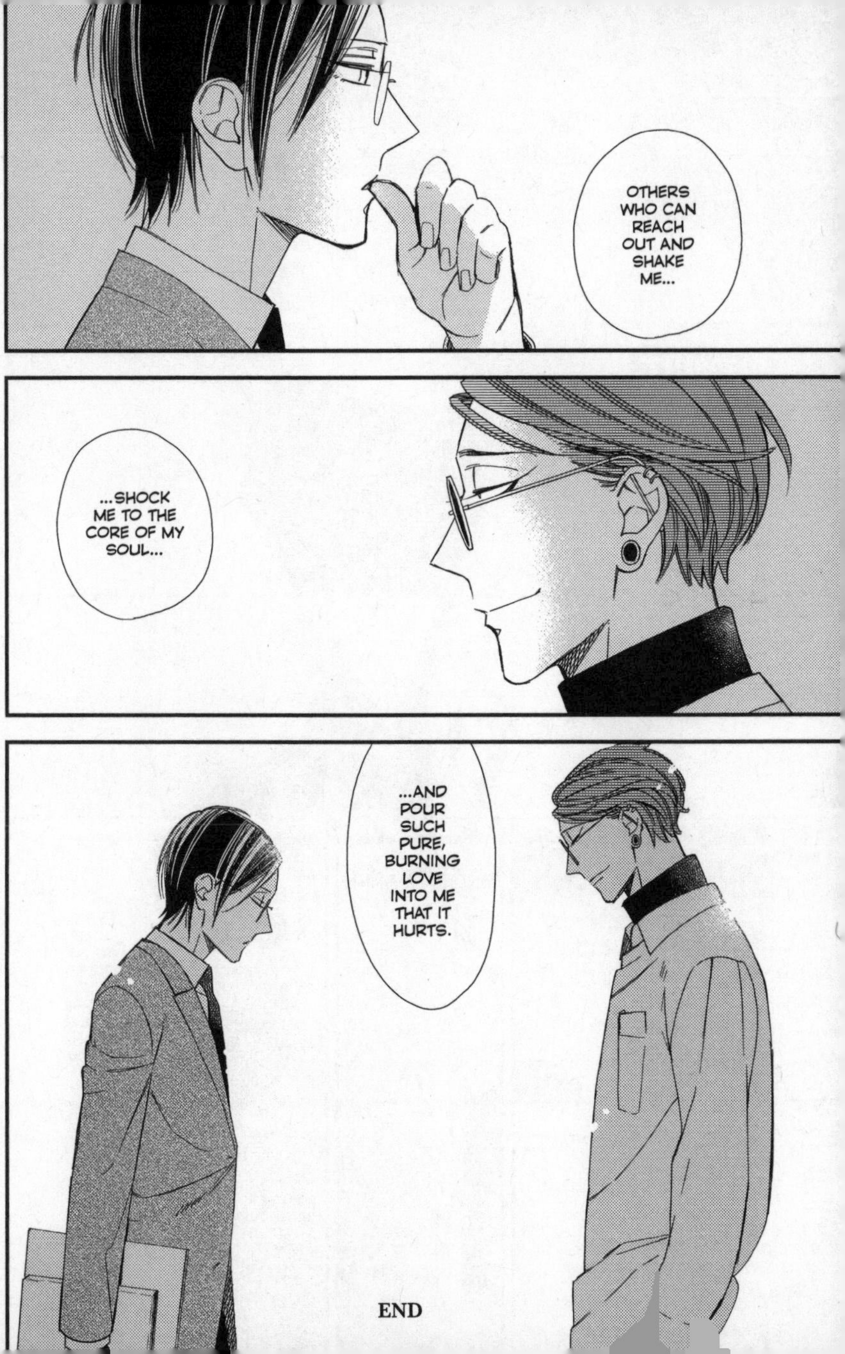
OTHERS WHO CAN REACH OUT AND SHAKE ME...
...SHOCK ME TO THE CORE OF MY SOUL...
...AND POUR SUCH PURE, BURNING LOVE INTO ME THAT IT HURTS.
END

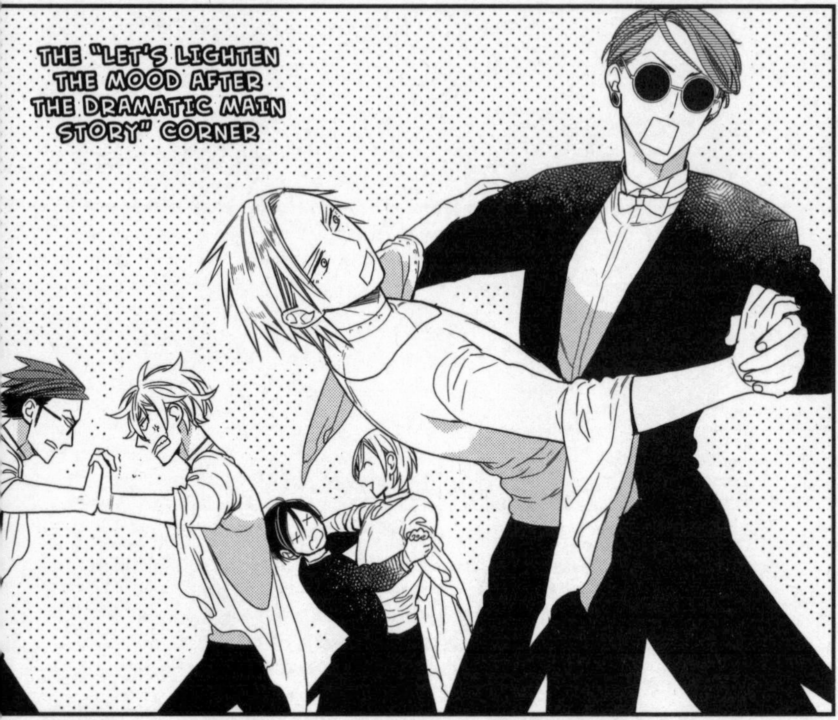
THE "LET'S LIGHTEN THE MOOD AFTER THE DRAMATIC MAIN STORY" CORNER

I BELIEVE THAT ALMOST EVERYONE BELONGS TO SOME COMMUNITY OR ANOTHER AND THAT THEY LIVE THEIR LIVES ACCORDING TO THE UNIQUE VALUES AND RULES ESPOUSED BY THAT COMMUNITY.

CASTE HEAVEN IS THE STORY OF THE STUDENTS WHO LIVE WITHIN THE CLOSED COMMUNITY OF A CERTAIN SCHOOL. THESE STUDENTS ALL BELIEVE IT'S NORMAL FOR THEM TO LIVE THEIR LIVES THERE, AND SENZAKI JUST HAPPENS TO BE A VISITOR WHO DROPPED BY.

IT'S KIND OF LIKE WHAT HAPPENS WHEN A HERD OF DOMESTIC ANIMALS SUDDENLY FINDS ONE OF THEIR WILD COUSINS IN THEIR MIDST.

I THOUGHT LONG AND HARD ABOUT WHAT TO DO WITH SENZAKI AND TATSUMI. IN THE END, SENZAKI COULDN'T BRING HIMSELF TO FULLY ASSIMILATE INTO THE CASTE COMMUNITY, AND TATSUMI COULDN'T MAKE THE DECISION TO LEAVE IT COMPLETELY BEHIND. EVEN IF THEY COULD HAVE, I DON'T THINK IT WOULD HAVE WORKED OUT FOR THEM.

WITH THIS, SENZAKI/TATSUMI COMES TO AN END. THERE ARE STILL A HANDFUL OF STORIES ABOUT THEM I'D LIKE TO TELL, BUT THOSE CAN'T HAPPEN UNTIL THE STORY OF *CASTE HEAVEN* HAS WRAPPED UP. I HOPE SOMEDAY I'LL HAVE THE CHANCE TO PRESENT THEM TO YOU.

I FIGURED A SHORT EXPLANATION WAS IN ORDER FOR THIS VOLUME, SO THIS CORNER TURNED OUT TO BE A BIT MORE SERIOUS THAN USUAL. STARTING NEXT VOLUME, KARINO AND AZUSA'S STORY WILL TAKE ITS NEXT STEP FORWARD. THANK YOU VERY MUCH FOR FOLLOWING *CASTE HEAVEN* THIS FAR.

CHISE OGAWA

About the Author

Chise Ogawa made her manga debut with *Ouji no Hakoniwa*. Her beautiful art style captivates readers, as does her wide storytelling range—from serious stories that explore the dark recesses of the human psyche to character-driven rom-coms. You can find out more about Chise Ogawa on her Twitter page, **@ogawaccc**.

Caste Heaven
Volume 3
SuBLime Manga Edition

Story and Art by **Chise Ogawa**

Translation—**Adrienne Beck**
Touch-Up Art and Lettering—**Deborah Fisher**
Cover and Graphic Design—**Shawn Carrico**
Editor—**Jennifer LeBlanc**

Caste Heaven © 2017 Chise Ogawa
Original Cover Design: UCHIKAWADESIGN
Originally published in Japan in 2017 by Libre Inc.
English translation rights arranged with Libre Inc.

libre

Published by SuBLime Manga
P.O. Box 77010
San Francisco, CA 94107

10 9 8 7 6 5 4 3 2 1
First printing, September 2020

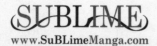

www.SuBLimeManga.com

For more information

on all our products, along with the most up-to-date news on releases, series announcements, and contests, please visit us at:

 SuBLimeManga.com

 twitter.com/**SuBLimeManga**

 facebook.com/**SuBLimeManga**

 instagram.com/**SuBLimeManga**

 SuBLimeManga.tumblr.com

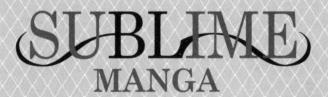

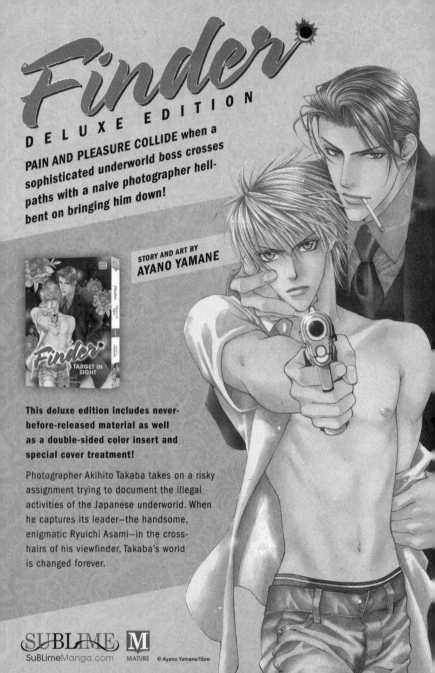

Finder

DELUXE EDITION

PAIN AND PLEASURE COLLIDE when a sophisticated underworld boss crosses paths with a naive photographer hell-bent on bringing him down!

**STORY AND ART BY
AYANO YAMANE**

This deluxe edition includes never-before-released material as well as a double-sided color insert and special cover treatment!

Photographer Akihito Takaba takes on a risky assignment trying to document the illegal activities of the Japanese underworld. When he captures its leader—the handsome, enigmatic Ryuichi Asami—in the cross-hairs of his viewfinder, Takaba's world is changed forever.

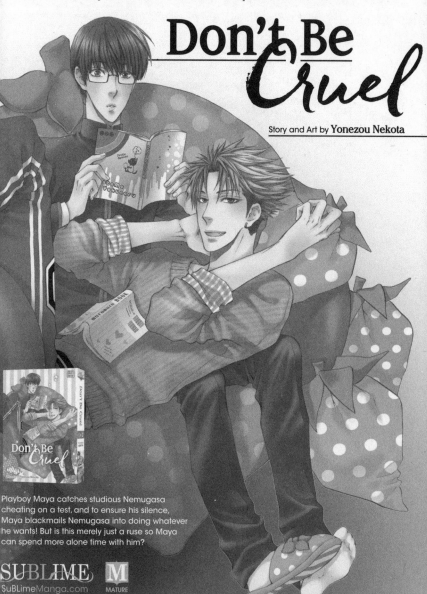

When a playboy falls for a nerd,
chemistry results in an explosive reaction!

Don't Be Cruel

Story and Art by **Yonezou Nekota**

Playboy Maya catches studious Nemugasa
cheating on a test, and to ensure his silence,
Maya blackmails Nemugasa into doing whatever
he wants! But is this merely just a ruse so Maya
can spend more alone time with him?

J A C K A S S !

STORY AND ART BY **SCARLET BERIKO**

WHEN THE PANTY HOSE GO ON, ALL BETS ARE OFF BETWEEN THESE BEST GUY FRIENDS!

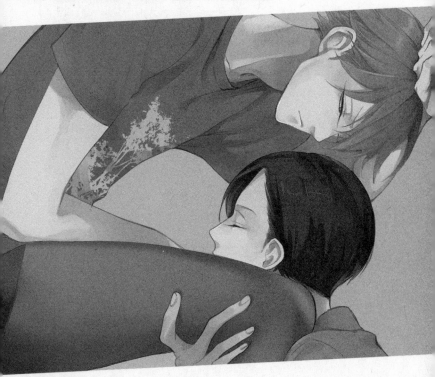

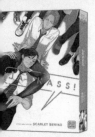

Practical Keisuke's incredibly handsome best friend Masayuki has always rubbed him just a little bit the wrong way. Maybe it's because Masayuki is rich, carefree, and so stunningly handsome that he can, and does, have any girl he wants? But one day, when Keisuke accidentally wears his older sister's panty hose to gym class, it's suddenly his hot friend who's doing the rubbing… on Keisuke's panty hose-clad legs! Has he unwittingly unleashed a secret fetish that will change their relationship forever?

MATURE

SuBLIME
SuBLimeManga.com